RAFFAELE CAPUTO has been a freelance writer on film for over fifteen years, contributing to various journals and newspapers. He has worked in other film-related capacities, including lecturing in film studies at Royal Melbourne Institute of Technology and La Trobe University. Between 1989 and 1993 he was assistant editor of *Cinema Papers*, as well as assistant editor and a contributor to two books edited by Scott Murray, *Australian Film: 1978–1992* (Oxford University Press, 1993) and *Australian Cinema* (Allen & Unwin, 1994). From 1994 to 1998 he worked as associate editor of *Metro*, a publication of film, video, television and multimedia, and took an editorial role on a number of publications produced by the Australian Teachers of Media.

GEOFF BURTON has been making films for thirty-six years. His first feature as director of photography was *Sunday Too Far Away*, the most recent as director was *Aftershocks*. His filmography includes forty feature films and more than 200 hours of television documentaries. He believes passionately in the need for a national film industry and sees its survival as the most effective protection against excessive foreign cultural influences. Burton regularly teaches cinematography and film direction. A proponent of new technologies and production methods, he encourages the exploration and challenging of the known boundaries of cinema storytelling. Currently he is editing an IMAX format dramatic film and shooting a documentary in mini-digital videotape.

For Sharon Bell and the *Carlito's Way* fan club, for whom it is better to live impossible dreams than to sleep with waking nightmares.

—Geoff

For Rebecca Maywald, whose faith is ambrosia and brought the warmth of the sun into my heart.

—Lino

second take

australian film-makers talk

edited by raffaele caputo
and geoff burton

ALLEN & UNWIN

**AUSTRALIAN
FILM
COMMISSION**

This book was assisted by the Australian Film Commission

First published in 1999 by
Allen & Unwin
9 Atchison Street, St Leonards NSW 1590, Australia
Phone: (61 2) 8425 0100
Fax: (61 2) 9906 2218
E-mail: frontdesk@allen-unwin.com.au
Web: http://www.allen-unwin.com.au

National Library of Australia
Cataloguing-in-Publication entry:

Second take: Australian film-makers talk.

  Includes index.
  ISBN 1 86448 765 8.

  1. Motion picture producers and directors—Australia—Interviews
  2. Motion pictures—Production and direction. I. Burton, Geoff.
  II. Caputo, Raffaele.

791.430230994

Set in 11/12.5 pt Bembo by DOCUPRO, Sydney
Printed by Australian Print Group, Maryborough, Victoria

foreword

as a film-maker myself, I didn't realise when I opened this fine book I would relive all my worst nightmares! Australian producers are compelled to visit fairly regularly two major markets to sell their wares, or hopefully raise monies for their future projects. The first is Cannes and its meat market of celluloid, the Marché du Film, and the second, Hollywood, the hellhole of promises we all grow to love and hate simultaneously.

A doyen of expatriate producers, Al Daff, a former head of Universal Pictures in the halcyon days of *Ma & Pa Kettle* and *Francis the Mule* movies, taught me a lot of the ropes the contributors to this book are about to unfold to you.

I had been in Hollywood for some weeks trying to raise money for a film to be shot in Sydney, set around the underworld, property developers and a missing heiress. I was told we had just the right ingredients, including a British star actress. Many meetings, late night calls, breakfasts, and several rides in the distributor's Rolls Royce later, I boarded my plane to Sydney convinced I had at last 'done the deal'. Opening *Variety* magazine on my return, there it was in print. The company I was dealing with had announced they were financing our picture. Then silence. I rang Al Daff and told him how perplexed I, my director and writer were, not to mention the British actress waiting to hear from me. 'Ah,' said Al, 'You've been kissed out the door.' In Hollywood they absolutely never say 'no' and rarely say 'yes', advised Al. Pauline Kael, the doyenne of film critics and critic for *The New Yorker*, once aptly summed up: 'Hollywood is the only place one can die of encouragement.' True. How many of us have been (and still are) 'kissed out the door'.

Bruce Beresford sums it up very nicely in his chapter, 'How I failed to make a greenlit movie'. Gillian Armstrong, on the other hand, possibly for the first time in a book, explains the importance and satisfaction of finding a producer who backs a director all the way. Her chapter clarifies for the uninitiated the relationship between producer and director, in such a way that I hope it will remove the mystique of our role as producer and the fact that producers can display aesthetic values, even in Hollywood! Gillian's views on 'Director's cut', coupled with Richard Franklin's harrowing tales of 'Director's cuts' and studio previews, will be a salutary lesson for any aspiring film-maker, and some professionals too.

Thankfully documentary is not forgotten and an interesting divergence of views are offered by Tom Zubrycki and Mike Rubbo. Michel Ciment and Thomas Bourguigon's probing and perceptive interviews with Jane Campion also make for absorbing reading.

As the outsider looking in, Martin Scorsese not only salutes the long-neglected pioneer, William Friese-Green, but sums up our craft eloquently: 'It's a movement in the mind's eye. But it's a collective as well as an individual mind, since the audience shares an experience, an emotion, a memory. Ultimately it's the communion, a moment of the spirit. I've always believed that film represents the answer to an ancient quest of humanity: the desire to share a common memory, a common heritage. That's why it's so universal.'

The great French director, Francois Truffaut, once said, 'Making a movie is like a stagecoach trip through the old west. At first you hope for a pleasant trip. Then you simply hope to reach your destination.' The journey Raffaele Caputo and Geoff Burton are about to take you on is altogether different. You will want it to go on and you will be sorry when it is over.

To paraphrase Dennis Potter, 'There are film books and there are film books. Am I right or am I right?' *Second Take* is unquestionably one of the best. Learn and enjoy!

Anthony Buckley, A.M.

contents

illustrations

acknowledgements

Our greatest thanks go to all the contributors and to three people who helped make them look good: Kari Hanet for her impeccable translation from the French of all five interviews with Jane Campion, Philippa Hawker for proofreading and commenting on portions of this book, and to Julia Ritson for her diligent transcription of interviews. Also to be singled out for thanks are Tom O'Regan, Rick Thompson, Ken Sallows and Sharon Bell for giving early support to the project.

A twinkle of sincere gratitude to a number of people who assisted along the way: Sharon Williams and Belinda Johns at Kennedy Miller, Kate Richter and Viccy Harper of Hilary Linstead & Associates, Chris Brophy at the Research and Information Centre of the Australian Film Institute, Helen Greenwood of the *Sydney Morning Herald*, Ian Collie and the Australian Screen Directors Association, and Daniella Esposito, Linda Fraser, Graham Shirley and Lyndon Sayer-Jones for their nuggets of assistance.

For reprint permission thanks are due to: *Cinema Papers* and MTV Publishing (for 'Pistols at Dawn: The "Art" of Film vs the "Science" of Previewing' from *Cinema Papers*, no. 95, October 1993); Scott Hicks (for 'From Sundance to Golden Globes: How *Shine* Seduced Hollwood' from the *Sydney Morning Herald*, 18 January 1996); Gerard Henderson and the Sydney Institute (for 'The Apocalypse and the Pig, or the Hazards of Storytelling', which first appeared in the *Sydney Papers*, vol. 8, no. 4, Spring 1996); a very special thanks to Michel Ciment and *Positif* (for permission to reprint in English all interviews with Jane Campion that have appeared in *Positif* so far); and to Martin Scorsese for allowing publication of his acceptance speech for the BAFTA Britannia Award, 1993. Finally, warm thanks to Kent Jones for being an invaluable guiding spirit.

what do film-makers dream about?

raffaele caputo and geoff burton

apart from specific interests the reader may have in one or more of the individual essays or conversations, it would be customary at the outset to inform the reader of the overall aim of this collection—and of the series. But let us first begin with a particular scenario.

RECULER POUR MIEUX SAUTER

Cast in mind a very familiar scene from many a B-grade western: a horse chase wherein a hero, or perhaps an outlaw, bounds away from a murderous pack in steady pursuit. He is gaining some distance when, suddenly, he is stopped dead in his tracks by a wide, seemingly insurmountable crevasse. With the pack behind pounding closer, our hero–outlaw can go neither to the right nor the left with any certainty of escape. He must take a chance on somehow getting directly across to the other side. He quickly draws back a few hundred yards, spurs his horse into a mighty gallop and then takes a mighty leap forward . . .

Unlike our hero, who is likely to just barely clear the gorge but still find firm ground and ride on to safety, *Second Take* is an experiment. For the time being there is no firm ground on the other side, no certainty; it's just a leap.

French film-maker Olivier Assayas was asked in an interview[1] to respond to the idea that the general impression of his film *Irma Vep* (1996) is of *reculer pour mieux sauter*. This common French expression roughly translates as 'taking a few steps back to make a running leap',[2] and refers to a general course of action undertaken when confronted by an impasse; of a necessary, temporary regression as a condition of escape. Assayas's response—'But then the question is: what kind of *sauter*? What will happen now?'—is curiously revelatory, and seems to suggest that there is already an end in sight, a guaranteed and desired outcome. But given that his reponse is also a question, it holds the end in suspension; there remains an open question. What counts most in Assayas's response-question is that it displaces the original question, not in a movement forward, but back. What 'danger' did Assayas avert? Or for our purposes: what is the condition to be escaped from?

Time for another scenario.

THE NOON-DAY SUN

In a charming, little-known film called *Macaroni* (1985) by Italian director Ettore Scola, Jack Lemmon plays Robert Traven, a top executive for an American aviations manufacturer who has returned to Naples for the first time in forty years since the end of World War II. He remembers very little of his time as a G.I. in Naples during the allied occupation. Nor can he recall his grand friendship with Antonio Jaseillo, played by Marcello Mastroianni, or his sweetheart Maria, Jaseillo's sister.

Traven is in his sixties, and although having climbed high on the corporate ladder, he can sum up his life and career in a few words. He is also in the middle of his third divorce, arid of feeling, and prone to hitting the bottle. When Jaseillo pays him a surprise visit at his hotel, Traven is Scrooge-like abrasive, believing the visit to be mercenary. Jaseillo is offended; he produces a weathered photograph of Traven with Maria, and reminds him that Maria received only two postcards from Traven since he left Naples in 1945. Traven is dismissive, the pair argue, sling curses at each other, and Jaseillo storms away, unaware that he has left the photograph behind. But the next day, with the photograph in his possession and with the Neapolitan surroundings beginning to take on a familiar air, the icy Traven slowly begins to thaw.

A recurring motif of *Macaroni* is the noon-day sun. In the courtyard of a church, Traven has a vision of a youthful Maria seated on a bench. The sun's rays mingle with his vision, are reflected off the bench and the light dances on his face. Then in a brief interlude, Traven is puzzled when he encounters an elderly man standing perfectly still in the middle of a street, eyes shut and face lifted to the sky, soaking up the sun's rays. When Traven finally discovers Jaseillo's address, ostensibly to return the photograph, he is not at home, but Traven is bewildered by the warm welcome he receives from Jaseillo's wife, Carmelina. As though Traven is a great and prestigious friend, Carmelina openly tells of her marriage to Jaseillo, and of what people said to one another on their wedding day: that the groom 'is as beautiful as the noon-day sun'.

Unlike Traven, Jaseillo has not been forgetful. After all, he works as a clerk in the archives of the Banco di Napoli, keeping records of financial transactions dating back to the fourteenth century. Thus he shares the historian's habitual disposition to facts; but he is also prone to invention. He reveals that in the forty years between Traven's departure and return to Naples, he has secretly written letters to his sister on Traven's behalf, delighting her with incredible tales of Traven's life as a globe-trotting journalist; of his adventures in exotic places and acts of heroism. Jaseillo is also possessed of writing plays for a local amateur theatre group, plays which are of the style of his letter writing—fantastical and wildly melodramatic. The title of the film, *Macaroni*, refers not necessarily to the pasta dish, which is served up only once throughout the entire film, but to macaronic verse—a type of verse that is an intermingling of forms, quackerish, and filled with mock heroics. Not only is Jaseillo not forgetful of the past, his taste for invention is the basis for renewal; indeed it is implanted in his very body, for on occasion he has been known to inexplicably die and re-awaken the next day at noon.

What is the noon-day sun in *Macaroni* but the metaphor of a crowning moment enclosed on either side by two half-states? It is a moment of complete illumination that is to be seen as either marching towards the night or towards another dawn. Hence, for most of the film, Traven is a figure of twilight at noon, seemingly glorious but whose light is about to be extinguished, while humble Jaseillo is of both the twilight and the dawn.[3]

THE MESSAGE IN THE BOTTLE

In his introduction to a special 1992 edition of the journal *Continuum*,[4] Adrian Martin describes his sense of alienation from an account of the film studies field as a predominantly professional and institutional one; an account provided by David Bordwell in his book *Making Meaning*,[5] where Martin should, but couldn't, find resonance of his own activities in the field. Martin offers an alternative story unfolding alongside, but also overlapping and engaging with, that of the university and the film theory journal. Martin's story is one of a fruitful network of publications and other media, film and non-film, professional and non-professional, often impassioned and sometimes short-lived, but a network that is for Martin and others paradoxically without or with very few 'visible connecting lines'.

Martin's introduction is in part a eulogy for what has been left behind—specifically a serious regard for film form—in the colonisation of film studies by 'powerful subject areas' like cultural or communications studies. Generally, it can be said to be a lament for the loss of a playful energy that has come with a dangerous shift from specialisation to over-specialisation in film thought—and, one should add, the same goes for de-specialisation. It is in part a warning—his introduction is aptly titled 'S.O.S.'—against stagnant and self-serving practices of critical inquiry that is the character of both over- and de-specialisation. Finally, the introduction was prophetic. If the hope of his *Continuum* piece was to be 'not so much a ship in the night as a message in a bottle', it was expressed under a noon-day sun that was already close to the dark of night before even having reached its height in the day.

Only a few years after Martin wrote his introduction two events occurred which seemed to strangely commemorate his words. The local film publication *Filmnews* was buried, long overdue in fact, while *Cinema Papers*, the other major national film publication, fully joined the ranks of the mainstream media, barely distinguishable from the generic lot of film promotion magazines lining the news-stands. The latter's move was astounding, but inevitable given the climate—it too could just as easily have been buried. None the less, the situation was not without a little amusement: for a good part of its history, *Cinema Papers* was often criticised unfavourably for being either too theoretical for the likes of a general readership, or not enough for the academy. Such a criticism (or virtue) could certainly not be levelled at the magazine today. In retrospect, it hardly seems like a criticism, for indeed there was something worthwhile in *Cinema Papers* having ill-defined contours: a small indication, if nothing more, that some form of dialogue was happening across the divide.

More so today than at any other time, the divide between two types of writing on film, that of mainstream film journalism (or what should be called, with some exceptions, film journalese) and that of the academy, is deeply felt. In words from the novel *Doña Flor and Her Two Husbands*, 'there is a place for everything and everything has its place'.[6] The ever-widening divide is the result of ecomonic rationalism across the whole social and cultural landscape. Privatisation, the down-sizing of human resources and funding cuts to public institutions are really the playing out of the notion of natural selection in another arena. The norm today is survival of the economically fit, and this scramble for survival has left quite a few cultural needs floundering.

It's little wonder editorial biases—whether for writing film journalism or film academia—allow little room for more playful, fluid, messy, speculative alternative voices. How can it be otherwise when both sides have been left with no other choice but to attempt to fortify their defences? But whether too broadly journalistic or too specifically academic, finally the orientation of each side largely underestimates and ignores the very thing that sustains their existence, the fertile ground that lies in-between—the voice of the film-maker.

This book—and the series—is not the vain flogging of a dead horse. On the contrary, the voice of the film-maker is the staple diet of film students, buffs, professional critics, scholars, and film-makers themselves. *Second Take* is fuelled by a timely and profound sense for *reculer pour mieux sauter*. We feel a tremendous need to take a few steps back, momentarily survey the landscape, and make a running leap.

HEREWEGOAGAIN[7]

The obvious reference point for *Second Take* is the UK-based *Projections* series, a valuable site, if for no other reason than as a sign of shifting values. But as another point of reference, readers should be reminded that the renaissance of Australian film in the early part of the 1970s was not simply a result of government support through direct or indirect financial investment; a priori of the renaissance was an investment in words. Through the likes of a Sylvia Lawson or a Colin Bennett, a Michael Thornhill or a Ken G. Hall, however divergent their views, the Australian film renaissance was talked and written into existence.

There is a long, if inconsistent, tradition of Australian film-makers contributing to the public written discussion of Australian cinema. Throughout the 1970s and into the mid-1980s, the now-defunct *Filmnews* served as an indispensable organ for the voice of the independent film-maker. For about the same period, within the pages of *Cinema Papers* film-makers could write or talk extensively about their craft, or issues affecting their craft. The same can be said for the short-lived film magazine *Lumiere*. And on occasion there was the publication of a book, like Tom O'Regan and Albert Moran's *An Australian Film Reader*,[8] which admirably tallied up and surveyed the field of writing by film-makers dating back to the late 1940s. Not only was there an open-door policy towards the contributions of film-makers, there was a greater sense of dialogue exchanged across the divide.

Since the early 1990s, perhaps even longer, the practice of engaging film-makers in dialogue has been corrupted and eroded. At best an engaging film-maker platform exists when it comes down to experimental film (*Cantrill's Filmnotes* remains a hardy journal in this regard), as always with little public profile and relegated further to the outer regions of film culture. At worst interviews with film-makers are locked into the release schedules of their respective works. So rather than an expansive engagement in a film-maker's forum, their voices are compromised by a powerful cycle of publicity and promotion—and, with each day, cinema seems less of a living art made by flesh and blood.

The idea for this series emerged from a consensual feeling among the Australian film-making community that a new form of film publication is in demand; a feeling symptomatic of a real dissatisfaction with current publishing practices. No publication of the nature of *Second Take* currently exists in Australia. Our general aim is to fill that void, pull out a space from beneath the twin spectres of publicity and promotion, and attempt to cast a (thin) corridor of light that could connect isolated tracts of thinking about Australian film. That is, like our Italian friend Antonio Jaseillo, to intermingle a little of the twilight and the dawn of Australian cinema.

The title of this introduction paraphrases the title of a 1975 article, 'What Do Critics Dream About?', by François Truffaut.[9] Truffaut wrote: 'Since I've been a director I have made it a point not to go too long without writing about films.' His article suggests that either side of the barricade is invisibly enfolded in one another. *Second Take* serves primarily as a platform for film-makers to write and talk about all aspects of their craft. There are always new things to learn, or old things to learn again, not only from the ideas and stories and experiences that film-makers may relate, but also from their biases, even their vanities and insecurities.

Second, it is to serve as a meeting place for dialogue. No one put it more pointedly than Michel Ciment on the occasion of the fortieth anniversary of *Positif*—'a circle of friends . . . would meet at one of their houses to talk about contemporary cinema (or perhaps just talk!)'.[10] At the very least the need for dialogue and the need to begin listening to film-makers again are uncertain leaps towards understanding how different parts of the Australian film community are enfolded.

We're not assuming there exists, nor are we demanding that there be, an angelic choir singing in unison. Our hope for *Second Take* is considerably less modest. Like we have been, we're hoping that the reader will be by turns sufficiently inspired, bored, empowered, or perhaps angered to want to engage in the dialogue.

[PART I]
TABLE TALK

he idea of the cinema as a sort of avatar of a spiritual reality has found expression in the work of a range of film-makers, stretching back to the early days of cinema. D.W. Griffith, Frank Borzage, Carl T. Dreyer, Roberto Rossellini, Henry Hathaway, Ingmar Bergman, Robert Bresson, Michelangelo Antonioni, Yasujiro Ozu, John Cassavetes are a handful of directors at different times who have exalted the spirit. We can also think of at least three much-favoured critics who have dealt with the subject at length. Paul Schrader, when he was a critic, and who joined the list of film-makers above with *Light Sleeper* (1992), had written the book *Transcendental Style in Film*.[1] André Bazin, particularly in his essays dealing with Italian neo-realism in the second volume of *What Is Cinema?*,[2] while avoiding the word 'spiritual', none the less makes unmistakable allusions to the spiritual dimension of neo-realism. Lastly, Raymond Durgnat, in his book *Eros in the Cinema*,[3] who, like Bazin, mostly keeps the word at bay, sees eroticism as inseparable from spiritual impulse as from animal instinct. In a nutshell, 'The path to truth leads through the turbulence of passions, not round it.' A quick glance over some of Durgnat's chapter headings indicates as much: 'Gods and the Gutter Arts', 'The Marriage of Heaven and Hell', 'Eternity in a Moment'.

As recently as 1995, in the British Film Institute's *Century of Cinema*, both Martin Scorsese and George Miller draw a parallel between the cinema theatre and church in their respective documentaries, as though, odd as it may sound, the film theatre is to this century what the cathedral was to another age. In a way, it is pertinent to ask how the cinema could *not* be seen as a divinity incarnate. For when watching a film one is watching something there and not-there at one and the same time, an experience fairly analogous to one praying before a religious icon, since the deity is also there and not-there.

Table Talk actually came together by chance as much as by design. The contributions by George Miller and John Duigan were expressly sought after. We wanted Miller to tell more of the influence of Joseph Campbell in his work, and Duigan to, in part, expand on the notion of pantheism as it figures in his still-to-be-completed trilogy begun with *The Year My Voice Broke*. We were a little aware, then, of the waters to flow our way; while we had chosen the players, the theme of the spirituality of cinema chose us. All the better, for this would seem to suggest that in these times the subject is neither publicly overworked nor a wholly private and unwieldy belief.

Yet we still felt some trepidation. As Schrader rightly points out, there is a 'critical queasiness' to the subject because the more unqualifiedly spiritual the art, the less one can talk about it. Our fear takes a related path: the more one talks about the subject, the more it becomes susceptible to stereotype and open to parody.

The following pieces enter the subject by calling attention to a higher purpose in cinema in different ways and with varying degrees of success. We are not sure sometimes if they talk of the same 'thing'. Nor can we decide whether talk of the spirituality of cinema at this moment in time is a sign of wisdom or a mere acknowledgement of its diminishing value. That indecision is left with the reader. What we can discern is a meeting place, of which the authors would be in accord in spite of any differences. At the risk of applying a platitude, when it comes to 'matters spiritual' there is a sticky ideological field of a mysterious relation between thing-ness and no-thing. For Duigan and Miller the cinema is to play a part in that field and its symbols can be made expressive of such a relation.

the ever-present serpent

john duigan

When I was a child, I remember one evening sitting for a long time watching the sun set over the low, bare hills that fringed the airfield I lived on in the north of England. It was late summer, but it had rained earlier in the afternoon, and the earth smelt rich and dank. A light breeze made patterns over the fields of crops, and once a stately owl flew low overhead, carrying a rat in its talons. I realised eventually that a long time had passed, unknowingly, as I sat in a companionable kinship with my surroundings. There had doubtless been many other such idylls, for six years of childhood was spent in the Lincolnshire 'wolds', as the hills there are known. But although I didn't even begin to analyse it, that was perhaps the first time it occurred to me that such an experience was something tangibly different to the normal humdrum of home, school and play. I had, in a very real sense, lost myself in the welter of tiny and vast interactions that surround us all the time but which, engrossed in our social preoccupations, we are seldom aware.

The word 'transcend' has been somewhat devalued by its adventures in the 1960s, but its use is, I think, appropriate here: for on such occasions we do transcend our usual state of consciousness and experience our interrelatedness of the physical world in a direct way. Such experiences are more common in childhood when we are not fully drawn into the world of society, the complexities of which come increasingly to dominate our thinking and to render certain parts of our brain largely dormant for the greater part of our adult life.

The term 'pantheism' means, literally, god in everything. My usage of the term has more to do with the fundamental interrelatedness of all things. On an obvious level, we have a great deal in common with the so-called inanimate objects around us: we all consist of atoms and molecules and so on, and very likely of other more subtle energies as yet unknown to science. I have never been convinced that the distinction between animate and inanimate objects is as cast iron as materialists would have us believe. To me, the worship of inanimate objects—the 'idols' of the Old Testament, for example—was certainly no less plausible than the worship of a disembodied and somewhat retiring God in heaven. The use of masculine and feminine categories for common-place objects in so many languages I always found stimulating, likewise the fact that most of us at some time or another come to value particular objects in a semi-superstitious sense, and frequently to invest them with certain powers. The legends of precarious stones that bring ill-luck to their owner are legion; the belief in the power of a blarney stone or the bone fragment of a saint to bring luck or good health is as powerful as ever. In more recent decades, the pyramid, the crystal and so on have won a whole new generation of believers. On a broader scale, so-called prim- itive religions hold particular places or geographical formations as sacred, or the whole landscape itself. Elements of all such beliefs hint at a pantheistic view of things.

Many writers from the romantic tradition express something of that wonder I first felt as a child, but the one whose work spoke most eloquently to me of the sense of oneness, of the interrelatedness or totality of things, was Dylan Thomas. I studied *Under Milk Wood* (1952) at school in Geelong, not long after my family moved to Australia, and the first few pages of narration plunged me back into the formless world of my English childhood. I *knew* what it was like to be in Llaragyb that night. To be touched by the wind drifting in the trees of Milk Wood, to watch it shuffling the dreams of Captain Catt down the cobbled village streets. I heard the water slapping the barnacled hulls of *Curlew*, the *Rhiannon* and the *Star of Wales* on the bible-black, fishing-boat-bobbing sea as absolutely as if I were there, a mermaid in the sea itself. By this time, as a teenager, I had come to treasure and actively to seek out experiences that gave me glimpses of this world-within-a-world. On holidays from my boarding school I would go out for walks in the countryside around Woodend, Mount Macedon and Hanging Rock, and call them forth by clearing my mind and almost willing myself to vault out of my body and melt into the world around me. It was always a solitary activity and I never mentioned it to anyone except, perhaps, Paul Dixon, my best friend.

It was hard to find any solitude at boarding school, but sometimes at night I would stand at the top of the small mound at the end of the rifle range, spread out my arms, and go racing down the slope full pelt, half convinced I could take off—or that my disembodied mind would take off and go soaring though the trees and into the night. In bed, other primal forces were at work, and I would dream of flying around the nearby girls' school, six feet above the pavements, hoping to peer into the dormitories, though with little idea exactly of what I would see.

The countryside around Geelong became very familiar to me. I particularly loved the two small ranges of hills I could see from the top of the rifle range, the Anachies, soft and rounded like waves, and the You Yangs, a jagged granite range rising sharply out of the plain. In those days, I wrote poems that groped towards some expression of these obscure sensations. Poems about landscapes and hills like the ones I could see, and about the sea. I also wrote fragments of short stories in which I gave some primitive voice to my awakening sexual feelings.

I didn't perceive the relationship between sexual feelings and those aroused by the sense of kinship with landscape until years later. But it is no accident that in *The Year My Voice Broke* (1987), *Sirens* (1994) and *The Journey of August King* (1996) the characters undergo complex personal odysseys within landscapes that are active elements in their immediate psychology. In experiencing a pantheistic sense of things, the blurring of the separation between us as individuals and the world at large, we become aware of the energy currents that stir through trees, hills, water and our bodies and minds. The ancients knew better than we do that the seasons of the material world stir equally in us; the moon tugs at our blood as it does the tides. As I said before, I suspect all manner of subtle energies pass through us in ways science hasn't yet begun to understand.

Looking back, another Dylan Thomas piece was probably a subtle formative influence in my perceiving that our sexual energies and awareness of the physical minutiae around us are complementary aspects of our most primal nature as living beings. In *A Prospect of the Sea* (1937)[1] a young boy's burgeoning sexuality is intertwined with, and inseparable from, his sense of being irresistibly a part of the hills, the cornfields and the windy sunshine around him. The breezes that stir the cornfields swirl the dress of the feral, bare-legged girl, brown as a berry, who is conjured to life in a daydream. It is this same nexus of sexuality and earthly surrounds I sought to express in *The Year My Voice Broke*, *Sirens* and *The Journey of August King*.

We first see Freya (Loene Carmen) idly caressing a rock as Danny (Noah Taylor) describes Willy Hill, the place that has been their playground and refuge since childhood. For her, he says, the rocks are living things, the hill a stately ship that sails through the night, lapped by clouds and mist. The energies of adolescence are gusting through him, and in his mind Freya's lithe body is as elemental as the beautiful rounded hills that curl around the town. In fact, the whole geography of the town has been etched out by the sexual currents running through it. On the flank of one of the hills is the ghost house—home still, perhaps, to the spirit of Freya's mother, used and abused by the town's menfolk years ago—haunting the town with a subterranean collective guilt. Danny's friend Jonah (Bruce Spence) suggests that every event, large or small, leaves its tiny imprint wherever it took place. Every part of the land is a kind of museum. Danny knows only too well that if this is true, his bedroom, full of his sexual dreamings and his secret collection of Freya memorabilia—photographs, poems, stolen pairs of knickers—is a museum of desire.

Danny's unwavering belief in the unreliable but eternally fascinating possibilities of hypnotism, telepathy, the transmigration of souls, and the possibilities of willing things to happen—or soliciting the help of a benign deity in, for example, preventing his beloved Freya from drawing the curtains when she is undressing—all these are parts of his instinctive, pantheistic sense of the world. Such feelings are not learned from books; they are felt as keenly as the sun shining on your face in the morning. When Freya and Danny walk through the sleeping town, the clatter of swarming insects on a lamp-post is mingled in the ether with the moans and clamour of dreaming inhabitants. When the two hear the dogs howl out in the far-flung valleys, they are certain the animals are mourning the departing soul of the old lady they visited a few days before. It is this sharpening of dormant senses that allows Danny, sleuth-like, to gradually intuit the truth of what happened seventeen years before, and the same fledgling senses that somehow, radar-like, divine Freya's distress when she is nearly dying up on Willy Hill.

In *Sirens*, the central theme is a playful exploration of sensuality and repression, in particular, the puritanical aspect of traditional doctrinaire Christianity. Simultaneously, I am continuing to try to express the pantheistic sense of the world begun in *The Year My Voice Broke*. The landscape around the Lindsay property, and the grounds themselves, are as ravishing and seductive as the characters who are living there—who themselves, in a number of scenes, merge with and emerge from the landscape as if they are part of it. In Estella's (Tara Fitzgerald) final reverie, she has joined her fellow Amazons on the crest of a mountain range.

Throughout the film I am playing around on a humorous level with a constant welter of imagery—for example, assorted metaphors on the Sirens themselves, the Garden of Eden and the *Titanic*. The latter two are part of a multi-layered metaphor suggesting, ironically, that the seduction of the English couple will lead to their doom. The ever-present

Danny (Noah Taylor) and Freya (Loene Carmen), *The Year My Voice Broke*

serpent, Sheela's (Elle Macpherson) apple, Estella's constant temptations and her husband's Adam-like resistance are all quite obvious. The *Titantic* allusions are a little more subtle. The ship the couple travel out to Australia on is, in fact, a model of the *Titanic* built for a long-forgotten 1950s version of the story I dug up from a library in Los Angeles. The Lindsay children have a model *Titanic* floating in their pond, another of the serpent's haunts. Implication—Adam and Estella will founder in the ocean of their unleashed libido, lured down by the Sirens, and, as in Genesis, it is Eve who is responsible for her spouse's—and for all humanity's—fall from grace. (The latter subject is taken up explicitly in the dialogue.) The fate of the English couple is emblematic of the fate of Western civilisation—witness the serpent coiling around Oswald Spengler's *Decline of the West* (1928), a copy of which Adam–Anthony (Hugh Grant) carries, Bible-like, everywhere, including to the lavatory.

The Sirens have, since time immemorial, together with their assorted sisters from various religions and cultures—Russelkas, Mermaids, Witches, Nymphs and Nymphomaniacs—brought untold disaster to fine, upstanding but frail males. (I am fascinated by the number of paintings of the subject done, inevitably, by male painters—for example, Symbolists like Félicien Rops and Gustave Moreau, in the late-nineteenth century—their classical pedigree giving such subjects legitimacy while allowing the painter to gloat over all manner of lewd possibilities.) Male terror and suppressed lust reach a crescendo every now and then, sometimes with far more horrific results—witness the various witch purges of the Middle

Ages. Norman Lindsay, on the other hand, celebrated an exuberant vision of female sexuality all his life, and while his subject matter was narrow to the point of obsession, and his techniques as a painter limited (his true talents lay in his drawings and etchings), I find his humour, his omnipotent appetite and his defiance of the wowsers who assailed him, a constant delight. In addition to his works, I based a few compositions in the film on other paintings—namely two of my favourite pre-Raphaelites, *Hylas and the Nymphs* and *Ophelia*.[2]

But for me the principal dimension of the film is the symbolic relationship between the little Lindsay community and the landscape around them. The sensuality of the women, and the 'blind' hired help, is a human expression of the disparate energies that literally hum in the air on a warm spring day in the Blue Mountains. One can readily believe, when the mortals retire to bed, that statues conduct their own elaborate orgies with the serpents and sirens of the river. The camera sometimes adopts oblique points of view that suggest other eyes are watching—a perspective Norman Lindsay would have enthusiastically endorsed with his abiding affection for the Olympian gods and goddesses that endlessly amused themselves with the human comedy.

In *The Journey of August King* Annalies (Thandie Newton) literally bursts from the landscape, from the waters of the stream beneath which she has ducked down to hide. August King (Jason Patric) is as stoical and granite-like as the mountains that have shaped him. Throughout the film, August and his beleaguered little entourage are cradled and nurtured by the vast mountain ranges that dwarf them. The Great Smoky Mountains, where we shot the film, often reminded me of the Great Dividing Range. Both are ancient chains of mountains, which seem at times to ache with the vastness of time and the accumulation of all they have witnessed. John Ehle, the writer, whose artistry I profoundly respect even though we had frequent disagreements about changes to the screenplay, had, I think, a similar sense of the interrelationship between characters and landscape. At one point August reflects how, if you cut open the mountains, blood flows out of them. Sometime later, you see this, literally, when August sacrifices his cow, and the waters of a rushing stream foam red.

August's and Annalies's journey leaves its imprint on the world as does Danny's, Trevor's and Freya's story in *Voice*—as literally as Danny's carving of their initials in the rocks of Willy Hill. We know now that man's physical activities have the most drastic environmental implications—the destruction of the ozone layer, global warming and so on. Like Danny's friend Jonah, I believe our actions leave other enduring legacies, that the land is a kind of spiritual repository of all that goes on, good and ill. The world has its own karma; you can feel it as a tangible presence in places of worship, or places of torment like Auschwitz. An incident of agony or joy accrues in the overall totality. A buried treasure, a radioactive waste dump, a copy of Shakespeare—all can have massive implications for future generations. That's obvious.

But I also believe that the act of barbarity carried out by Annalies's relentless pursuer, Olaf Singletary (Larry Drake), or the fleeting love and generosity of spirit shared by Annalies and August can, like the celebrated flutter of a butterfly's wing, conjure the human equivalent of a hurricane or a rainbow a thousand years hence. I sought to express something of that resonance in the endings of *Voice*, of *Flirting* (1991), of *Sirens* and of *August King*—in the latter as Annalies marches bravely forward on to the uncertain future she has fought for with such simple-mindedness and courage.

two out of three
the year my voice broke
trilogy: an interview
with john duigan

raffaele caputo

raffaele Caputo: *It's fairly well known that* The Year My Voice Broke *(1987) and* Flirting *(1991) belong to a proposed trilogy. First, was the idea of doing a trilogy conceived at the time of* The Year My Voice Broke? *Second, to what extent is the proposed trilogy autobiographical?*

John Duigan: There was always the idea of doing a trilogy if the first film worked but I didn't want to publicise the idea before *The Year My Voice Broke* was released. If *The Year My Voice Broke* had been a disaster then clearly it would have been very difficult to consider a trilogy.

Overall, the intention of the trilogy is to describe the evolution of a view or sensibility of the world. The films are not strictly autobiographical, for in many respects the character of Danny Embling (Noah Taylor) and his origins are very different to mine. For example, I was born in England and lived there until I was ten, and then moved to Malaya for almost two years before ending up in Australia. Danny, on the other hand, was born and bred in a small town in the southern tablelands of New South Wales. However, I drew a great deal from my years living in a country town in Victoria, and the two schools in *Flirting* are loosely based on Geelong College and its sister school, Morongo. We staged plays with Morongo, and in fact my initial interest in theatre was boosted by the opportunity it gave to meet girls.

In those days, schools like Geelong College were arguably even more brutal than the school depicted in the film. Caning was a day-to-day occurrence. There really was a teacher who put chalk on his cane so he could try to repeatedly strike the same mark. I got two lots of six-of-the-best in consecutive days shortly before I finished there—I was asked to leave after a series of assorted misdemeanours, although they let me sit my final exams. As in many schools, there was an on-going, merciless persecution of anybody who was remotely different, either in looks, temperament, disposition or personality—anyone who was an eccentric was a prime target.

What about the character of Danny?

I am very free in my evolution of Danny. He passes through experiences which are similar to mine, but many are different. For example, at that age I was never fortunate enough to encounter girls quite as magical as Freya (Loene Carmen) and Thandiwe (Thandie Newton). And of course Noah brings his own personality to the role as well. With any role that one writes, you have to leave space for the actor's contribution.

Why the specific shift in location from a small country town to a boarding school?

In terms of the filmic reality, it's a decision Danny's parents made to send him to a boarding school to try to stop him following in the footsteps of Trevor Leishman (Ben Mendelsohn). Being publicans in a thirsty town, his parents have the money to send him to a private school. Paradoxically, the restrictive atmosphere accelerates Danny's alienation.

   People can be terminally damaged by their school years. The kind of persecution Danny endures takes place in all schools everywhere. But not only in schools; *Flirting* is not specifically about life in boarding schools. There are very strong parallels with the society at large—similarly with the country town in *The Year My Voice Broke*. Schools and small towns are miniature societies, and share similar patterns of exploitation, manipulation and alienation with the larger societies of which they are a part.

There's something of an animist quality to Cirencester College, the sister school, when first viewed from Danny's dormitory window.

The two school buildings in *Flirting* do not actually face each other from across the lake. We created that. When we found the building that is used as the girls' school, which is on the outskirts of Sydney, I had the idea of putting the other school, which is in Bathurst, on the other side of a lake because I liked the idea of the two schools looking at each other and the romance of Danny rowing across. And of course there are all manner of classical allusions.

Is the Ugandan girl Thandiwe Adjewa an unlikely or uncommon figure to have come upon in a boarding school in Australia at that time?

I did think about the possibility of having an Aboriginal girl for the character of Thandiwe. I wanted this character to literally come from another planet. In a very real sense, an Aboriginal character would have come from a world unknown to Danny and could have brought with her a very rich, spiritual reality that would have expressed part of what the relationship between Danny and Thandiwe develops into. But it would have been highly unlikely because of the economic circumstances of Aboriginal people at that time and, more importantly, I wanted Danny to encounter someone from the world beyond Australia, who would broach all manner of other issues with him.

I wanted to bring a character who comes from a completely different world to any he would have even contemplated. He has come from quite a narrow environment in the country town, and in *Flirting* he's now in another very closed environment. First of all, I wanted someone whom Danny would find to be a fellow traveller. That's the kind of engine that drives the film: someone who has perceived himself as different—and has been told he's different in no uncertain terms by everyone around him—suddenly discovers he's not alone. He finds someone on his wavelength, who shares his view of the world and can appreciate him. Secondly, Thandiwe is a character who starts to give him an awareness of a whole lot of other issues: of politics, race, the concept of the Third World, and of Africa. He realises the primitive and clichéd view he has of the 'dark continent', as it used to be called. His awareness of that becomes a catalyst for him to begin to really expand his horizons. By the end of the story he is on the edge of the wider world, and I intend in the third part to take him into that.

Would you agree that The Year My Voice Broke *marks a significant departure from the preoccupations and style of your earlier films? One observation of both* The Year My Voice Broke *and* Flirting *is that they lack the political dimension of your earlier films. If one takes* Mouth to Mouth *(1978),* Far East *(1982) and* Romero *(1989), certainly politics is greatly evident, you can see it and point to it—it's institutional politics. Still, one could argue that in* The Year My Voice Broke *and* Flirting *the political dimension is there in a different kind of way. It's a politics about personal behaviour that extends to the social body.*

That's true. It is, in a more subtle sense, very much concerned with personal politics, sexual politics, and then the politics of how societies work. One can analyse miniature societies like the country town and the schools more easily than society at large, but the patterns of manipulation and alienation are similar.

On reflection, the characters of Morgan Keefe (Bryan Brown) in Far East *and Archbishop Oscar Romero (Raul Julia) in* Romero *paradoxically tend to look like precursors to Danny Embling. These are grim films in terms of outcome— both films end in death—whereas with* The Year My Voice Broke *and*

Danny (Noah Taylor) and Thandiwe (Thandie Newton), *Flirting*

Flirting *there's a sense of promise. Yet they're all alienated figures, they're outsiders.*

They are definitely outsiders, and all three men are striving to consolidate an identity in hostile environments. The miscellaneous bullies and authority figures in Danny's world, however, do not use guns, so he survives.

There are two angles from which to approach alienation in The Year My Voice Broke *and* Flirting. *On the one hand, the alienation experienced by Danny, Freya and Thandiwe is very tangible—it is connected to the familiar social or institutional codes of the school and the country town. On the other hand, there is also a kind of mystical element to the films which further alienates, and which is coded to some degree but one cannot quite put a finger on it. Do you see these two angles, or dimensions, or levels as contradictory or as two sides of the one coin, so to speak?*

I'm glad you asked me the question because it's that side of the films, the 'mystical element', that concerns me most. The sense of these characters—certainly Freya, Danny and Thandiwe—having some sort of oblique awareness of a larger reality beyond the merely social is probably the most important element in the films for me. I am attempting to express a pantheistic sense of the world.

That pantheistic sense is in part suggested by reference to a particular classical myth in both films—the Persephone myth. At the end of both films when Danny is up on the hill with the vast expanse of land before him, it suggests a little of the Aboriginal understanding of land as the source of all life.

And, for that matter, to myths of certain North American Indian peoples. Danny's first voice-over in *The Year My Voice Broke* is very explicit right at the start, and almost all the imagery in that film is connected to it. The Persephone/Demeter myth is about the founding of the seasons and about recurrence and rebirth, although I don't think any of the characters in *Flirting* are consciously aware of the place of that myth within their world.

Incidentally, those who look closely at the two films might pick up that the number of the room Danny and Thandiwe stay in at the motel in *Flirting* is the same number of the room Jonah (Bruce Spence) recalls in *Voice* when he describes his affair with a woman at the Lord Byron Hotel in Cootamundra. There are a lot of little things like that in the films, a lot of synchronicity. Towns like Cootamundra and Junee are mainly familiar to me from many overnight train journeys between Victoria and New South Wales, looking out through misted windows as the wide, empty streets and deserted platforms floated past.

Let's make this a little clearer. Two levels: one is the alienation with regard to tangible social codes, while the other is these characters' outsider status in a spiritual–mystical sense. Is the relationship between the two levels contradictory or complementary?

I think the two levels are two different facets of reality. My view is that when we are young we all experience reality as an undifferentiated whole. That is, we experience reality as a totality rather than an accumulation of specifics. As we learn language and become socialised, we start to distinguish ourselves as entities distinct from our environment. We start to separate objects, one from another, and ourselves from them. Now this sense of 'I' increases as we grow older and likewise the world around us becomes invested with all sorts of societal meanings. The philosophers Hegel amd Marx explored such matters from a rather different viewpoint, and subsequently moved to other conclusions. In *The Year My Voice Broke* the characters have preserved their childhood much longer than the people around them in part because they haven't been socialised to the same extent. In a sense, they retain a more primitive—in a non-perjorative sense—experience of the world around them.

I mean by this not merely the experience of the world as a totality but as a sense of flux; there is a continuous interaction between all aspects of the world, including what we think from a materialist point of view as inanimate objects. I don't think of inanimate in the same way as a materialist. At least one sense of pantheism perceives a kind uniformity of consciousness—consciousness, of course, in varying degrees, but which implies a causal interaction between all things. I was trying to express some of this through the characters of Danny and Freya in the first film. By *Flirting* Danny has already begun to analyse the world in a way Freya, a more earthy and intuitive character, maybe never will. I have, incidentally, done some early work on a novel about Freya's character set a few years after *Voice*. I don't know if I will ever finish it. She is working in a pub in a small town on the Suffolk Coast and becomes involved with an alcoholic school teacher still suffering from the hangover of a consolation bronze medal after a promising athletic career. She has left Australia to try to put the traumas of her life in Braidwood completely behind her. The bleak North Sea coast with its stretches of lonely beaches, sandbars, dunes and sudden storms has always been a very vivid place for me.

Are these phases what you meant by the 'evolution of a view or sensibility of the world'?

Yes, this kind of sensibility inhabits each of the films and, for that matter, *Sirens* (1994) and *The Journey of August King* (1996). All four films in an oblique way express or comment on it to different degrees. I would say this kind of sensibility can sometimes, paradoxically, endure as a result of alienation from society: the fact that Danny is both repelled by others and innately suspicious of society from his own personal experience. The Thandiwe character for wholly different reasons has a similar kind of alienation from her peers and the society she has come to, and probably from the one she has left. Maybe there is more chance of sustaining your awareness of your innate links with the undifferentiated world as an outsider from society because you are not so swallowed up by the minutiae of social immersion.

What of the category of the individual as proposed by thinkers like Friedrich Nietzsche and Jean-Paul Sartre? In one way Danny is the individual standing alone, responsible for his lot by his awareness of the self, and is by this experience free to reach beyond his lot. At one point in Flirting, *isn't Danny seen reading Sartre?*

In so far as he battles to sustain and develop his very own quite singular view of the world, the Danny character is certainly battling to live authentically in Sartre's sense. The books he would be reading at school are not the classic existential texts, like *Being and Nothingness*, but novels like the ones I read at school—Sartre's *Nausea* and *Iron in the Soul*,[1] and Albert Camus's *The Outsider* and *The Plague*.[2] Such choices were not altogether remarkable in those days; in my fifth form *The Plague* was one of our literature texts. Instinctively, Danny is constantly resisting the allure of society which would frequently involve him living in 'bad faith'. But Sartre never actually touched on the pantheistic aspect of reality we were discussing before. To Sartre talk of mysticism and the fundamental interrelatedness of all things would be so much mumbo-jumbo.

In other words, the works of Sartre and the political philosophy of Marx can be labelled, as in 'Existentialism' and 'Marxism', while what attempts to be expressed through Danny and Thandiwe is something that cannot be given a name?

Well, I would talk about it in pantheistic terms, and pantheism is not an area of enquiry much visited by the commonplace texts of contemporary Western philosophy.

To give an example: when Danny and Thandiwe say to one another, 'You're beautiful', they actually don't mean beautiful in the everyday sense of physical beauty, or even aesthetic beauty. There's an affinity to such notions of beauty, but is there something more to what they say or is meant by those words in that instance?

Yes. In moments of calm together, Danny and Thandiwe share a sort of tranquillity which, even though it might be invested with a certain melancholy, suggests they are in touch, perhaps imperfectly, with some fuller level of reality than can be experienced by those around them, who are more caught up in the babble and role-playing of the two schools. I think Danny and Thandiwe sense that in one another.

Now to go back to the subject of living authentically. In Danny's long voice-over that happens when Thandiwe is seen leaving the girls' school, he talks about not being a fatalist and seeing fate as the tide of events sweeping us along. He then goes on to say that you can actually make decisions through your own will which can inhibit the tide of events. You can swim against the current or stop the clock and steal a few precious moments. To do that you often have to defy conventional logic or the pressures to conform. If you don't at least try, as he puts it, you'll always be haunted by the very best dreams you might have had. If you don't make the effort the dreams will sort of taunt and tantalise you for the rest of your life. That is the kernel of a very important part of living life authentically. To a greater or lesser extent, it is resisting this sense we all really have of being swept along by things that are out of our control. With society having grown into a vast, multi-faceted creature, the pressures on the individual have magnified as the twentieth century has moved along. There are so many people one encounters who more or less accept that fate is irresistible, that it's an overriding principle. That for me is tantamount to saying 'no' to life—in fact it's almost a contradiction to life.

That said, the concept of the self and the battle for authenticity in personal action is a separate issue to the one I loosely call the pantheistic realm of ideas. In the earlier part of our conversation I was suggesting there is a relationship between the two, that the person who maintains a degree of distance from total immersion in society is both more likely to retain a primal sense of his or her interrelatedness with the world as a whole and is more able to strive effectively for authenticity of action. The pantheistic sense of the world as an interactive flux has, I believe, in past centuries been a primary source of spiritual contemplation and magic. It's that dimension I've tried to sustain as a fundamental dimension of these films.

It's difficult to talk about these areas with any kind of precision. For a while I wasn't entirely sure film was the best medium to explore them. Initially, I started to write *The Year My Voice Broke* as a novel because I didn't think I could broach these ideas successfully in a film. I changed my mind after writing about half of it.

Why did you change your mind?

As I was writing the prose I started to see images, scenes even. Then I started getting inside the characters, expressing their thoughts and writing their dialogue.

The characters Nicola Radcliffe (Nicole Kidman) and 'Backa' Bourke (Josh Picker) in Flirting *tend to mirror Danny and Thandiwe in a negative way; they seem to have lost something at some point in their lives, and yet they are finally, strangely affected by Danny and Thandiwe. Can you elaborate on that?*

One of the positive and paradoxical things that happens in the story is that you have these two characters who are perceived as eccentrics, as 'dags', ultimately influencing for the better the two leading 'hero' figures within the girls' group and the boys' group.

When Nicola catches Thandiwe coming back from her first love scene with Danny, she takes Thandiwe into her room and Thandiwe probably thinks she is going to be reported and maybe expelled, but when Nicola starts to open up and talk about her own secret world you feel this is probably the first time she has ever shared this with anybody. It is a similar kind of experience or sense of connection Danny had earlier in the film when he could suddenly share his point of view with Thandiwe, and vice versa. It's clearly a very positive and quite liberating experience for Nicola. There is real regret and yet also a sense of private resolution in Nicola's face when she gives Thandiwe a brief parting wave at the end. Up to this point in time, Nicola has always played the role of the 'Ice Princess', and expressed a very artificial sense of her sexuality; the privately treasured incident with the construction worker was a furtive, closed and very paranoid activity she could never mention to anyone. But she clearly recognises Thandiwe's freedom, and that the love she shares with Danny is something utterly different to anything she has herself experienced. By comparison, the approval Nicola gets from her peers as a result of her phoney role-playing is poor compensation. You feel by the end that her exposure to Danny and Thandiwe is an important step towards her blossoming as a character.

Likewise you see Bourke rising to Danny's defence and interacting with 'Gilby' Fryer (Bartholomew Rose) in a mutual concern for Danny and Thandiwe's fate at the motel. It would have been quite impossible at the beginning of the film for Bourke to have any kind of exchange with Gilby, who is to him even more of a ludicrous figure than Danny. Bourke has come a very long way too.

The Year My Voice Broke *has been described as a 'rite-of-passage' film. Going by what we're discussing it seems like the idea of a 'rite-of-passage', if it's there in the films, has to do with characters other than Danny, Freya, or Thandiwe.*

I think that's spot on. It's frustrating when people come to the film solely from the point of view of analysing it in the 'rite-of-passage' mode because that was not my preoccupation at all. People get a lot of different things out of *The Year My Voice Broke*, and those who only get 'rite-of-passage' messages are getting a very small part of the whole thing.

Yet one cannot discount the character of Jonah in The Year My Voice Broke. *His name is already highly suggestive, while at the same time being a character who exists on the fringe of the town and works as a signal man, a guide, for 'passing trains'—Danny and Freya.*

He is very much on Danny's and Freya's wavelength, and I guess he is a kind of gentle guide: he operates the signals literally and metaphorically. He is a resource who imparts his personal observations and gems of wisdom to his two young friends when they occasionally drop in to see him. He operates on an equal basis with them as well: he's interested in their ideas, and he tries out his own ideas on them. He appears to be totally self-sufficient, but also to have been wounded in love, and to have retreated from the wider world into which Danny and Freya are about to set forth.

Let's return to Far East *and* Romero, *and the question of fatalism to get a finer point on what we've been discussing. Morgan Keefe and the Archbishop are outsiders and so too is Danny. There's another connection in that these figures have actually cut out a little protective niche for themselves, but in* Far East *and* Romero *it's like the world is going to pull you out and down regardless, so one may just as well make the place for it. Thus, even though both* The Year My Voice Broke *and* Flirting *have a sense of promise, there's still a fatalistic aspect about them. In short, what I am suggesting is that perhaps the sense of dread in* Far East *and the promise of* The Year My Voice Broke *and* Flirting *may not be far apart at all.*

Morgan Keefe, Bryan Brown's character in *Far East*, as it were, digs a cave for himself. He has been through the Vietnam experience, and any kind of idealism he once held has been eroded by that. He is an embittered person who has created a cave for himself in the Koala Club, a place which, to some extent, prospers from the exploitation of the Filipino bar girls who dance there. But, as you say, the world finds him out eventually and the conscience he once had, which has been in cold storage, is re-awakened. Bryan's character in *Winter of Our Dreams* (1981) was a lapsed idealist of another kind. His cave is his bookshop where he plays chess, appropriately enough, with the ultimate in the impersonal, a computer. He has a reasonably stimulating intellectual life, but he is emotionally paralysed. These two films examine the implications of largely negative, pessimistic choices. The Danny Embling character, both Freya Olson and Thandiwe Adjewa, and for that matter Raul Julia's Archbishop Romero, choose to fight the good fight.

But initially, in *Flirting*, Danny could be going the same way as Morgan Keefe. In his second voice-over in *Flirting*, he talks about going into a cave inside one's head: that's the way to survive, by retreating, like a hurt animal, into a self-imposed isolation—as, in a way, Jonah has done in *Voice*. When we first see Danny in *Flirting*, that's where he is, skulking in his cave. The relationship with Thandiwe gives him the confidence to emerge from the cave, prowl around and start raising his flag and sketch out a little piece of the world for himself. Towards the end it looks as if events are going to extinguish this fledgling optimism. But in his obscure way Danny does his best to reach out across the ether to help Thandiwe. He writes to all sorts of people, including the Prime Minister, but most of all he concentrates. I'm not saying that through some kind of act of will or mysterious volition he literally saves Thandiwe. But in an allegorical sense, that is what he is trying to do, willing her to get through whatever is oppressing her. He believes intuitively he can make a difference. The individual can negotiate with fate. Just as he does earlier when he goes to the motel with Thandiwe. You live out the big dream. You say 'yes' to life. As he says, one can choose to battle with fate or to swim with the current. Such sentiments give these two films the optimism the two earlier films lacked.

The catalyst for change in the male protagonist is always connected to his engagement with a woman, or a 'feminine principle' if you like, which is both destructive and regenerative at the same time. The latter is a major underlying tenet of The Journey of August King.

In *August King* and in *Flirting* the regenerative aspect of the central relationship is mutual. Jason Patric's character is still dazed by the suicide death of his wife, and he is, when we meet him, like Danny in *Flirting*—recoiling from any human contact. He communicates far more with his animals, and the mountain landscape around him. Again, as in *Flirting*, Thandie Newton's marvellously spirited character ultimately jolts him out of his self-imposed isolation. But for her, too, the brief friendship is an enormous catalyst for growth. Her experiences with men—and particularly white men—have been exclusively negative and abusive. She sees others as impersonal or hostile elements she must manipulate as best as she can simply to survive. Both characters, however, find themselves unexpectedly touched and moved by the plight of the other. Their ability to empathise, which I think is at the heart of the ethical imperative, is renewed. By the end of the film, one feels both are once more open to the possibility of affirmative relationships with others.

*When thinking back to your films pre-*The Year My Voice Broke, *the 'potentiality' for regeneration has always been there, but never quite realised or realised too late by the male protagonists. In fact, one could argue that even in death, as with Bryan Brown's character in* Far East, *the male character realises a redemptive, if not wholly regenerative, principle in his life.*

An example would be *Mouth to Mouth*. The relationships between the two country boys, Serge and Tim (Serge Frazetto and Ian Gilmore) and the two delinquent girls, Jeanie and Carrie (Sonia Peat and Kim Crejus)—female precursors to Trevor Leishman—is redemptive for Jeanie, but Carrie's character relentlessly goes her own way on a path you feel will, inexorably, lead to her self-destruction.

In *The Leading Man* (1997), a more recent film, the regeneration of the wife, played by Italian actress Anna Galiena, comes from a wholly different direction. The dupe of a ghastly manipulation, paradoxically she ends up empowered by a revitalised sense of herself and her own talents. The unwitting victim of a dastardly plot becomes, ironically, the queen of her own destiny.

*Story time between each film has a three-year difference—*The Year My Voice Broke *is set in 1962,* Flirting *in 1965. Going by these dates, the third part would set Danny in 1968, which is a significant year for many, a period of social and political upheaval—race riots, war, student and worker protests. One cannot envisage events contained within the confines of a small town or a school. Can we get a picture of Danny's relationship to such events?*

I think the broad direction Danny is going is one way of gaining a perspective on the events that shape one's life. We must find a degree of detachment from the society and the social forces that shape us, both to understand and to evaluate them. Danny has always been expelled from his little societies, metaphorically and literally. He always ends up on his hill on the edge of town.

As I mentioned earlier, I wanted to take Danny's character out into the wider world, and I originally had the idea of doing the third part of the trilogy in Paris in 1968, set at the Sorbonne. Whether in fact I go in that direction I'm not entirely sure.

After The Year My Voice Broke *you could look towards* Flirting; *only one film intervened,* Romero. *Six films*—Wide Sargasso Sea *(1993),* Sirens, The Journey of August King, The Leading Man, Lawn Dogs *(1998) and now* Mollie—*have followed the release of* Flirting. *Can you still look towards the third part of the trilogy?*

I will do it at some stage, Noah Taylor permitting. I have half-written several versions, including the one in Paris and one in Kenya and Uganda. But I also have a backlog of other screenplays, two of which I would definitely like to make in the meantime.

the apocalypse and the pig, or the hazards of storytelling

george miller

This situation is not without its risks. You sitting there, attentive. Me with a chance to put some ideas forward in a much longer form than usual. So each table has been issued with a whistle. Gerard Henderson[1] suggested that if the going gets a little heavy, I could throw in one or two snappy anecdotes about Hollywood. So if you feel your eyes glazing over, you know what to do. Meanwhile, I'll take you through some of my adventures in storytelling in the hope that a few notions might be useful.

VISUAL MUSIC AND PUBLIC DREAMING

When I first took to film-making, my approach was very straightforward, I was interested in the pure plasticity of film. I was struck by Jimmy Stewart's lovely phrase when he described film as 'pieces of time' and each length of celluloid, cut to cut, running at twenty-four frames a second, is like that—a little piece of time you can hold in your hands. I was intensely curious about how you join these pieces together like notes on a piano. To me, films were visual music.

My first movie, *Mad Max* (1979), was purely and simply a piece of visual rock and roll. What I didn't know at the time was that there were larger impulses at work. As the *Mad Max* films made their way around the planet, they seemed to resonate somehow, culture to culture. For the French, these were postmodern, post-apocalyptic westerns and Max was a gunslinger. In Japan he was an outlaw Samurai. In Scandinavia, a lone Viking warrior. The movies had tapped into the universal hero myth and

Max (Mel Gibson), *Mad Max*

I was given a taste of what Carl Jung[2] was on about when he described the collective unconscious.

Here it was, first hand. And I, despite my creative vanities, was its unwitting servant. I was reminded that films, like storytelling, have deeper dimensions. And I learned to look beyond the obvious, to feel out *sub-text* where one is likely to find more elemental truths. Films are like dreams: when we congregate with strangers in the darkness of the cinema, it's a kind of public dreaming where we process, mostly unconsciously, the more insistent concerns of our lives.

FURTHER CONNECTIONS

Jung might have described the terrain, but Joseph Campbell[3] is the consummate guide. Until Campbell, I often wondered why I was mucking around in the film industry, indeed why any of us have this urge to communicate through narrative.

I learned from his dazzling scholarship, for instance, that the same stories arise spontaneously across time and space, and are told as a way of connecting ourselves to all that had gone before and all that will come after.

Because I'm a storyteller, I sometimes have a privileged view. In the mid-1980s, we wanted to shoot one of the *Mad Max* movies at Kata Tjuta (that place previously named after someone called Olga). Now, to the Aborigines of the Central Desert, this place is sacred and every bit as holy as a cathedral, a temple or a mosque. We were required to sit with the tribal elders of the Pitjantjatjara and present them with our story. We described the scenes and showed them our storyboards, and they responded with a short dance. They were excited; they had heard the *Mad Max* story before. Many of its motifs and archetypes corresponded to some of their own.

So here was this popcorn movie saga and here were the custodians of a culture 40 000 years old, and once again the connections were being made, but now across the expanse of time.

THE NARRATIVE IMPERATIVE

Somewhere in our neurophysiology we've been wired for story. There is a kind of narrative imperative: we can't be without stories and we find them where we can.

Out there in the calamitous give-and-take of life we look for coherence: patterns, beliefs and signals among the noise. It's one of the things humans do; we strive instinctively to distil meaning out of life. So all of us carry highly personalised narratives. They make up the mosaic of who we are and what we believe. Most of the time they are implicit or subliminal because we don't comprehend life by the intellect alone. Woody Allen was right—sometimes the cerebral cortex is a highly overrated organ. So we have this lovely mechanism to weave the ineffable, the mysterious and the diffuse into stories. We suck them out of the *zeitgeist* and carry them like a set of tools to help explain the world and to guide our way through it. When there is an interconnected set of stories, we call it a mythology. When it's shared by a group of people, it becomes culture.

Sometimes it's just a culture of two, shared with a friend, a lover, a mother. Sometimes it is corporate—an institution, a multinational, a football team, a city, a nation—and, at its most potent, it connects the entire expanse of space and time. That's one of the deepest functions of mythology: to give us context, to connect us, to help us embrace the numinous—that sense of dread and awe we feel when confronted with the immensity of time and space. Those kinds of mythologies are so potent, they become the great religious movements.

Storytelling is a force of nature. There should be one of those warnings stencilled on the container: 'Hazardous Material' or, at the very least, 'Handle with Care'.

the apocalypse and the pig

THE LOST TRIBE

You may remember that extraordinary event in the 1970s when a tiny clan of about thirty cave dwellers were discovered deep in the forests of the Philippine island of Mindanao. Their life was astonishingly simple; they hadn't yet learned to hunt, they just gathered. They had no rituals, no marriages, no funerals. And for a while we thought we had come across an authentic community from the middle Palaeolithic age, a tiny *cul-de-sac* of human evolution.

As it turned out, these stunted, naked people were the descendants of a coastal tribe who fled from pirates to the sanctuary of the forest 400 to 1000 years ago. The natural historians and the anthropologists were a little let down, but the mythologists discovered something thrilling. This small group of frightened humans had created a mythology *de novo*. Just a few simple stories that explained their universe to them. And their universe was tiny, just three limestone caves on a cliff, 120 metres above a creek and in the immediate surround of the forest.

Into their mythology they had woven stories of danger, instructing them how to forage safely and warning them never to leave the caves at night . . . it's probably the reason they survived hidden away for so long. And one of those stories even provided for a Messiah. When they were first discovered, they promptly deified the person who led the expedition, a gentle Filipino official called Manuel.

The gift we take from this huddled clan in Mindanao is this: you find your mythology where you can. If it's taken away from you, you'll work with what you've got to fill the narrative void. Think about where you get your narratives from. They come from your experience, from your affiliations and shared histories, and mostly they come without you having to think about them.

So what happens if you are suddenly without them?

THE DISPOSSESSED

Some parts of the world are experiencing a bewildering incidence of violent crime. The ghettoes of America, post-communist Russia, post-apartheid South Africa and Palestine are most often in the headlines. And it's not hard to see its pathogenesis.

In South Africa we have the appalling example of Sofiatown. Sofiatown was a cultural accident that happened on the outskirts of Johannesburg earlier this century. A developer couldn't shift his tracts of land because the council built its sewerage disposal next to it, so he sold it to the blacks and the coloureds. It was the only place in South Africa where blacks could own land and it developed into a close-knit community of extraordinary vitality. During the 1940s and early 1950s it was a cultural hothouse, giving rise to a remarkable generation of journalists, writers, musicians and politicians. It spawned the likes of Miriam Makeba and Hugh Masekela and even Desmond Tutu. It drew the Athol Fugards, the Alan Patons and the Trevor Huddlestons.[4] And there were also the prostitutes, the *shebeen* queens and the gangsters.

Its spectacular success as a community was a direct threat to apartheid and so, in 1953, the bulldozers moved in and Sofiatown was flattened. The rubble was cleared, the area fumigated and the 60 000 inhabitants were packed into government trucks and moved on.

In its place was put up a glutinous, Afrikaner suburb and, infamously, they named it Triumph. The crushing of Sofiatown was, one way or another, repeated all over South Africa for decades.

It doesn't take too many generations before you are completely dispossessed. It's one thing to revisit, or even recover, a piece of geography. But you can't retrieve your culture, not when it's been systemically destroyed.

If you're an African-American male, for example, only a few generations removed from slavery and trapped in the ghettoes, from where do you take your guiding narratives, your codes of conduct and your sense of honour? In South Central Los Angeles, they don't all troop off to Emma Thompson movies. They take it from what is nearest at hand, from the street, from television. You know the statistics—we've heard them so often now—the average child in the US has seen 8000 murders and 100 000 other violent acts on television before he or she leaves primary school.

THE DISAFFECTED

Let's look a little closer to home. You're a disaffected white male, seething with free-floating resentment, with not much in your life to give you cohesion or a sense of competence. You like to watch television, play video games, go to the movies. You lose yourself up in the world on the screen. A world which has little or no moral complexity, just the rudimentary notion that guns—big guns—are the answer to almost any problem. And this notion is reinforced, not once but by hundreds, if not thousands, of similar vicarious experiences. (Notice, by the way, how often in the last half-century movies have been touted by posters of men pointing guns.)

Then one day you're disinhibited by some mind-altering chemical, by alcohol, psychopathy or some other reality-perception problem. It is not too long a bow to draw to Port Arthur, Dunblane, and all those McDonald's stores and post offices in the US.

[34]

the apocalypse and the pig

MAD MAX AND BABE

How, then, do you approach censorship? I think we shouldn't even try. To withhold any information or idea from anyone goes against human intelligence and the curiosity that got us here in the first place. Some people argue it's easy to see the distinction, say, between *Platoon* (1986) and *Rambo: First Blood Part II* (1985), or even *Taxi Driver* (1976) and *Natural Born Killers* (1995). But, quite honestly, I can't even choose between *Mad Max* and *Babe* (1995).

The *Mad Max* trilogy is ultimately about the redemption of a lost soul. The first movie is pretty much a one-dimensional revenge fantasy, but in the second and third Max is the closet human being who, in the end, rekindles his compassion. Furthermore, by relinquishing his self-interest he becomes an agent of renewal.

The world Max must survive is dysfunctional and full of dread, but then that is exactly what it is in *Babe*. The very beginning of the film is set in a death camp, with Babe's mother being taken off to slaughter. For two-thirds of the story, the lead character has but one destiny—that is, to be eaten by a serial killer, the farmer's wife.

It's an old argument, but who makes the judgement call? And where do we start? At the more brutal passages of the Old Testament? Euripides? Shakespeare? Which fairy tale? *Hansel and Gretel*? Which nursery rhyme? *Three Blind Mice*? 'See how they run, they all run up to the farmer's wife, who'll cut off their tails with a carving knife.'

Censorship is ultimately impossible. As each day goes by, technology sees to that. It should be of no surprise that the fastest-growing use of the Internet is to be found in high-censorship states like Iran.

But there is a difference between the World Wide Web and broadcast television. For instance, on the Net the selecting intelligence is with the individual user. It's more like real life in the sense that it mirrors the normal distribution of concerns and allows us to join little ghettoes of like interests. The Net can take you to the Sistine Chapel to study the details of its refurbishment. You can share the latest joke with your cyber-neighbour in Poland. Or you can surf down into the nether world and sample some of the more profound evils.

Broadcast television is an entirely different matter. The selecting intelligence is localised with the broadcaster. When it comes to television, Marshall McLuhan was dead right: the medium is the message. Television is that ubiquitous and familiar window that allows us to watch the outside world from the safe haven of our living rooms. The received message is this: here is the larger world as it actually is, and here are the ways you might respond to it.

Broadcasters are very privileged and whatever they choose to show adds powerfully to the mosaic of our mythology. Censorship might not work, but prudence sometimes does.

CAUSALITY

The discourse on media violence is reminiscent of the debate on tobacco. It wasn't until the 1960s that we were alerted to its harmful effects, and we'd been smoking the stuff for centuries. Even then it took a decade or two to do something about it.

Cinema itself is just over one hundred years old; broadcast television not much more than fifty years; video and computer games even more recent. Culture, and the technology which facilitates it, is in rapid evolution. To say that there is no hard evidence of the harmful effects of media violence seems to me to be as disingenuous as the cigarette companies and their medical scientists, who for so long defended tobacco with the same cries.

It's tough for the behavioural scientists. There are no mathematical certainties. You try to establish a direct causality but the process is organic, it won't lend itself easily to reductionism. But as a practising storyteller, I could hardly fail to notice that movies and television impinge on behaviour. As a film-maker you receive some unusual feedback.

One day a man parked across from our office. Now not only was his costume identical to *Mad Max*'s, but so was his car. He didn't want to talk, or engage in any other way. He simply sat there staring ahead, each day, nine-to-five, for a whole week. Then he left.

A woman called from Ohio after she had seen *Babe*. She wanted the words of the song that the farmer sang to revive the spirits of the pig—she said her horse was depressed.

An Israeli physicist, diagnosed with a life-threatening illness, was planning the details of his suicide when he happened to see *Lorenzo's Oil* (1992). Inspired by the struggle of the Odone family, he changed doctors and became pro-active in the management of his disease. So far, it has gained him four more years of productive life.

I notice how I modify my own behaviour as a result of the movies. As a young doctor in the emergency ward, I was suddenly required to tell a woman that her husband had just died when I realised that nobody had ever given me advice on how to do it. So I resorted to all those behaviours I learned from the movies: I shook my head in that same slow, sad way and muttered all the clichés. But this was also her first time, and so she did the same.

How many of us, as kids during the 1950s, jarred our ankles badly when we jumped off the roof of the garage trailing a bedsheet, thinking we were Superman?

Watch children in the playground as an index of how much we take from American street culture via the movies and television. The caps worn backwards, the high-fives and the gesture 'yes!' from *Home Alone* (1990). Indeed, I was working with traditional women in an ancient Muslim village in the north of Kenya, their black *bui-buis* covering everything but their eyes, and when they finished an arduous day's shooting as extras, they, too, started to give each other high-fives.

If movies and television influence what we wear, the way we talk, the way we move, the way we play as children, how can we say with conviction that it doesn't influence our behaviour at a cognitive or moral level? The analogy with cigarette smoking, of course, we can't take too far. As a doctor, I had only one or two patients who tried to convince me that smoking actually improved their health. On the other hand, the narratives we experience through our media have the ability to cohere, amaze, inspire, and to heal.

THE PRIVILEGE OF THE STORYTELLER

If it's your privilege to be a storyteller, be aware that it's a force of nature. Don't treat it casually. Don't be afraid to address the darkness, or to shock or disturb. Like nightmares when we dream, these stories often have the greatest capacity to heal. They alert us to our pathologies and allow us catharsis.

Think of stories like food and try to provide nourishment. Don't serve up empty calories . . . the mindless can be toxic.

Apply all your wisdom to your work. If you're game to enter the debate, be broad and holistic in your approach, and avoid static, reductionist concepts. The latter is what I like to call 'noun' thinking. The process is dynamic, a verb. So try to see the dynamics of the whole for narrative practitioners are in a vigorous feedback loop with the cultures they are trying to explore. Look beyond the obvious. Challenge assumptions. Never foreclose on your understanding. Moreover, storytelling exists because often it deals with what is beyond the immediate reach of the intellect.

Stories are also experienced in the middle and early brain, so if you approach them with your intellect as your only tool of understanding, be careful. There will be great yawning gaps and conundrums, and the reptilian brain will be waiting, ready to bite you.

CULTURE RICH, CULTURE POOR

There are some societies, like Japan, that have a high tolerance for violence in their entertainment, but at the same time have almost no violence in the street or the home. But then the Japanese are *culture rich*. Their unifying narratives are prodigious and resilient, and surprisingly adaptive to the upheavals of the technological age. So the violence on their television screens and in their movie theatres is less likely to promote behaviour, rather it helps them let off steam.

For societies which are *culture poor*, it's a different matter. California is a place where you go to re-invent yourself. Post-war, it was a great locus of social experimentation. So whatever culture it has is constantly shifting. It doesn't have a chance to lay down deep roots. These culture-poor societies are susceptible to the quality of the media from which they replenish their myths.

So tentatively I offer this equation: if you're culture rich, violent media provides catharsis; if you're culture poor, it provides instruction.

MYTHOLOGY AND SPORT

I don't want to suggest that all our myth-making is confined to the media, the arts, or the church. There are two other arenas where high mythological content goes largely unrecognised. The first is sport.

Sport is the great secular ritual. It ritualises conflict and endeavour, and again provides catharsis. 'Make sport, not war' is its catchcry. Finally, it suggests how we may conduct our lives with honour and courage. This is what Campbell called the 'pedagogic' function of mythology.

The heroic figures in sport are not merely those who win, but those who win in circumstances where it is easier to give in to despair. Greg Louganis[5] came down to one final dive. Knowing that he is HIV positive, having cracked his head on the diving board early in the competition, he is required to execute a platform dive, rated to the highest degree in difficulty. It's known as the 'death dive'. One chance—and he pulls it off so exquisitely he becomes the first ever back-to-back Olympic diving champion.

These are sport's transcendent moments.

And then there's the pageantry. The ticker tape raining down on the parade of the returning champions, the trophy, a chalice or a shield, held high above the head of the victor, the laps of honour, the dancing maidens, the affiliation to tribal colours, the obsession with statistics— great deeds transformed into folklore.

This is why we find some of our best writing in the back of the newspaper.

the apocalypse and the pig

MYTHOLOGY AND SCIENCE

Now for science. There is a lovely interplay between mythology, with its impulse towards an all-encompassing metaphor on the one hand, and the slow small steps of objective elucidation that is science.

Let's take an ancient culture well before Copernicus,[6] for example. How did it explain the weather? Why did the wind generally blow in one direction? What causes the seasons? Why does the temperature change depending on whether we travel north or south? Compelled to explain their universe, they rely on mythology. Their stories are created from the known, so there is a god for each of the four seasons and a god for the prevailing winds.

Now time moves on. With the help of Copernicus, Johannes Kepler and Isaac Newton[7] we manage to take some representatives of this polytheistic culture to a vantage point deep in space. Suddenly it all becomes obvious because we see that the earth is tilted on its axis as it orbits around the sun. Because of this tilt the northern hemisphere receives less sunlight during one part of its orbit than during another. So we have a winter and a summer. And since the earth spins in only one direction—clockwise for someone sitting on the South Pole—it helps explain the prevailing winds.

So myths lose their power when they are no longer necessary. They evaporate to be replaced by metaphors more relevant to the time.

How amazing then is the resilience of Aboriginal Australian 'Dreaming' that it endures after 200 years of European settlement. This was the world's oldest living culture, reaching back at least forty millennia. After they were done in by disease, despair and outright genocide, there was a systematic attempt to de-tribalise them, to make them invisible. And yet fragments of the culture endure. Its resilience is a measure of its power.

Joseph Campbell had a wonderfully mischievous definition of mythology. Mythology is simply 'other people's religion' and religion he described as 'misunderstood mythology'. What he was getting at was the danger of concretising the metaphor. Taking the virgin birth, for example, as an anomaly, or the promised land as a tract of real estate in the Middle East. When you concretise the metaphor, you take all the juice out of it. It loses its poetry, becomes static and brittle, and then we get into all sorts of trouble.

It may even end in war. In the 1970s in Beirut, for example, the promoters of three differing inflections of the same idea of a single paternal God began unloading bombs on each other. As Campbell wrote, it all comes of misreading metaphors, mistaking denotation for connotation, the messenger for the message.

But back to science.

You may remember this from primary school. When we apply energy in the form of heat to a block of ice we watch it transform first into water and then into steam. These shifts are called phase transitions: a solid, a liquid and then a gas. Before this century, that's as far as the story could go, but continue to apply heat and the molecules are ripped apart into hydrogen and oxygen gas.

Go even further to 3000 degrees Kelvin until those atoms in turn are ripped apart and the electrons are pulled from the nucleus. At a billion degrees Kelvin, the nuclei break up into individual neutrons and protons like that in the interior of the neutron star. Now we need the physics of the middle to late twentieth century, because we go to ten-trillion degrees Kelvin and the sub-atomic particles become a gas of quarks and leptons.

Then we apply fabulous amounts of energy, 10^{32} degrees Kelvin, and all the forces known in the universe—the electromagnetic, the strong and weak nuclear force, and indeed gravity—will be united. That's when the symmetries of the *ten-dimensional super strings* appear.

We are now deep in the quantum realm, and this is the prodigious energy that was the state of the universe at the instant of the 'Big Bang', beyond which everything is unknown and the origin of the cosmos becomes the purview of mythology. Science has given us a simple story of the melting ice cube, but it sure takes us a long way.

Mythology accounts for that which is beyond the known, while science, cautiously, in its own good time, probes the borders and, with each success, claims a little more territory. I agree with those who say 'science is a slower but surer path to God'.

As we know, the growth of scientific knowledge is exponential. The more we know, the faster we can know more. We have acquired more knowledge since World War II than was previously amassed in the entire two-million-year history of our evolution. No wonder the world's great religions are fragmenting, retreating into fundamentalism, or being replaced by new fads that exploit our innate spiritual questing and compulsion to the ultimate in life.

For most of the time during the dialogue between the scientists and the theologians, they've tended to talk past each other. But now, more and more, their discourses intersect.

Even the earliest tribes have 'origin' myths that explain where they might have come from. And the scientists have got us as far as the Big Bang. They tell us now that we are children of the stars, that the atoms within our bodies were forged in the cauldron of nuclear synthesis in exploding stars long before the birth of the solar systems. We are literally made of star dust. And, what is extraordinary is, those atoms that make up you and me have, in turn, coalesced into intelligent beings capable of understanding the universal laws governing that very event.

That dance between science and myth is a gem to watch. Cosmology and theology. You are never quite sure which is leading the other. A final quote from Joseph Campbell:

> Indeed the first and most essential service of mythology is . . . [to] open the mind and the heart to the utter wonder of all being. And the second service, then, is cosmological: of representing the universe and the whole spectacle of nature . . . as an epiphany of such a kind that when lightning flashes, or the setting sun ignites the sky, or a deer is seen standing alerted, the exclamation 'Ah!' may be uttered as a recognition of divinity.[8]

If you think that this stuff is a little too intangible, I offer the fact that, as a storyteller, my tools are not as simple, unfortunately, as the word processor or the artist's pen. To tell my stories I use the great lumbering machine of film-making. So I'm big on praxis. To the extent that the road warrior and the pig may have impinged on the global culture, you might say I'm giving away my best industrial secrets.

[PART II]

JANE CAMPION AND *POSITIF*

the French film journal *Positif* has had a love affair with Jane Campion ever since her first outing at the Cannes Film Festival in 1986. When we first sat down to draw up our list of potential contributors for *Second Take*, we could not envisage it without the inclusion of Jane Campion. In that same moment, as Tristan is to Iseult, we realised that in wanting Campion we could not envisage *Second Take* without the contribution of *Positif*.

From our perspective in Australia the names Campion and *Positif* have sometimes appeared synonymous. In under a decade this small but highly influential journal has published five interviews with Campion, the first two appearing in the same issue. Like all great loves they have nourished one another in times of fortune. And like all great loves, the two have walked arm in arm weathering misfortune—the fifth interview included here is one of very few (though the only in-depth interview) Campion had granted amid the dense air of the box-office failure of *Portrait of a Lady*. Dare it be said, were it not for *Positif*, and particularly its editor-in-chief Michel Ciment, Campion's daring artistry would likely have been relegated to the dustbin.

Our words here and now run the risk of creating an impenetrably glorious monolith. Yet we do not wish to present here a single entry in the account book. To say that *Positif* discovered Campion or that Campion is a film-maker uniquely heralded with praise within its pages would be less than half-truths, faint shadows of the important cultural activity performed by *Positif* in its more than forty-year history. For the reader unfamiliar with *Positif* there is not the space to give a detailed account of its truly illustrious history. And yet we run the risk deliberately and necessarily out of the certainty that the readers would be hard up to find in this country a film magazine equalling the critical commitment exemplified by *Positif*.

We've chosen to honour Jane Campion via the English publication of her interviews with *Positif*. It should go without saying, then, that at the same time, via Campion, we hope to pay sufficient tribute to the stimulating and generous critical space maintained by *Positif*. Thus by publishing the complete set of five interviews with Jane Campion, we hold up *Positif* as a model. Not for imitation, but in recognition that theirs is a meeting place of a creative dialogue between film criticism and film-making, one untrammelled by the vacuity of fads or the publicity machine.

All five interviews were translated from the French by Kari Hanet.

two interviews with
jane campion

michel ciment

these two interviews with Jane Campion were conducted three years apart. The first took place in Paris a few months after the screening of her short films and telemovie, *2 Friends*, at the Cannes festival in 1986 in the section 'Un Certain Regard'. I had been struck by the audacity of their style, the extreme sensitivity and uniqueness of their vision. The second interview took place in Cannes [in 1989], following the screening of *Sweetie*, which confirmed her great talent.

Jane Campion is as impertinent, vivacious and charming as her films. She often punctuates what she says with an infectious laugh. This film-maker is certainly not squeamish; her view of the world is warm, yet humorous, and sometimes even has a cruel edge.

Whatever the very real merits (and we have written about these at length in the pages of *Positif*) of *sex, lies and videotape*, there is no doubt that *Sweetie* (which was completely ignored by the awards) deserved the Palme d'Or given the perspective chosen by Wim Wenders and his jury: to foreground a first feature that presented a personal vision and was made on a modest budget. No doubt the decision would have been controversial, but it would have shown real audacity. However, with or without an award, Campion will make her way and *Sweetie* already stands out for its originality and control. [Michel Ciment]

INTERVIEW 1: SHORTS AND MEDIUM-LENGTH FILMS

Positif: *You were born in New Zealand. In what sort of milieu did you grow up?*

Jane Campion: My parents worked in the theatre and their families had been in New Zealand for several generations. My mother was an actor,

[HILARY LINSTEAD & ASSOCIATES]

Jane Campion

my father a director, and both had trained in England. They formed a company in New Zealand, produced Shakespeare and toured the country. When I was born, they stopped and settled in Wellington, New Zealand's capital. That's where I grew up. Then they became farmers because they were tired of dealing with theatre problems and of not earning much money. From time to time, they would go back on stage. At home conversation would revolve around the classical plays they were producing and the actors' performances. I too had a passion for the theatre, which I explored while I was at high school. My brother, sister and I competed for our parents' attention, but we were also good friends. At sixteen, I went to university. As a child I enjoyed both the city and the country, because in New Zealand the city is never far from the country.

Why didn't you choose the theatre?

I gradually became very critical of the theatre. The actors I would meet seemed artificial and to lack spontaneity. I decided I would attack something more serious. I wanted to go to university in Australia. It's the kind of decision one makes at sixteen. I studied anthropology after trying psychology and education, which I didn't enjoy very much. My degree didn't really lead to anything, but we had a wonderful lecturer, a Dutchman who had studied with [Claude] Lévi-Strauss[1]—and he would talk about structural anthropology and linguistics. What interested me about anthropology was the opportunity to study 'officially' what I was already curious about: the nature of thought and its mythical content, which has nothing to do with logic, and human behaviour. I think actually that I have an anthropologist's eye. I have good observation skills. I used to enjoy the theory and poetry of anthropology.

Your short films, however, are different to many Australian films that acknowledge the Aboriginal presence and the role of myths. You seem to have more of a behaviourist approach to characters.

In fact, I don't think that the big myths of the Aborigines are really part of Australian culture. People talk about them, but only superficially. I am very interested in Aboriginal culture in the same way as I am fascinated by everything that relates to people, but it is not part of my world. On the other hand, I do think that humankind thinks itself a rational creature when in fact it isn't. Humans are governed by something quite different. That is what interests me. So I finished my studies and got my degree. But then I realised that if I continued down this track, I would have to express myself in such a way that I would only be understood by other anthropologists, whereas I wanted to communicate with people and find shared symbols. So I decided to go to Europe. That's where my heritage was, that was the history I had learned at school. I was curious to find out what it was really like. I also wanted to learn to paint, which is what I did in London, while working as an assistant on a film. But I didn't like London very much. I stayed a year, then went back to Australia because the enrolment fees at art school and the cost of living in London were too expensive. Everyone seemed a little lost when I was studying art, even the lecturers! On the other hand, my experience at the Sydney College of the Arts was wonderful. The teachers were young; they had a clear idea of what they wanted and were not encumbered by all the traditions that prevailed in England. I was particularly interested in the relationship between art and life, how one reacts visually to an experience.

What sort of painting did you do?

I wanted to paint what was important to me and I ended up telling a few little stories on canvas. My painting was figurative. Because I also enjoyed writing, I used to add captions to my paintings. I also produced theatre plays about love and disappointing experiences. They were filmed on video and I played some of the parts. I thought they were terrible and I didn't like myself as an actor. I then decided to make Super 8 mm films myself and direct actors in roles I would write for them. It was a very ambitious plan on my part since I knew nothing about film, everything came out of a manual. But I was very motivated, because I wanted to tell my stories. The result wasn't very satisfactory because Super 8 requires a lot of precision and I lacked experience. I made two films. One was called *Tissues* and ran for twenty minutes, the other *Eden*²—I didn't add sound, so it was never really finished. To some extent, *Tissues* heralded *A Girl's Own Story* (1983). People rather liked it, because I'd invested a lot of energy, but visually it was dreadful, because I didn't really understand what a shot was!

What sort of films did you like?

I wasn't really a *cinéphile*. I used to go to the cinema, but my choice of films was haphazard. But I do remember that I was completely engrossed by Luis Buñuel. I tried to see all his films. I also liked the work of film-makers such as Michelangelo Antonioni and Bernardo Bertolucci. Generally speaking, I was attracted to European cinema and to film-makers such as Akira Kurosawa, rather than to Hollywood.

What did you decide to do after art school?

I didn't know what the next step would be. I couldn't see how I could get in touch with people working in the film industry or with people at the Australian Film Commission. One day they seem to have faith in you, but then the next day they've changed their mind . . . So I decided to get into the Australian Film, Television and Radio School and decided I would try to make as many short films as I could during the three years I was there. I made *Peel* (1982) the first year, *Passionless Moments* (1984) during my second and third year, and *A Girl's Own Story* in third year.

What was the idea behind your first film Peel?

I knew a very strange family and I thought it would be interesting to film it. They were people who didn't really seem to control themselves. Being very honest people, they could recognise themselves in the scenes I would suggest. It was a very short film, approximately nine minutes long.

Passionless Moments *was a more elaborate film.*

It was the result of a collaboration with one of my friends, Gerard Lee. The starting point came from him and we wrote the script and made the film together. Once we had settled on the framework of the film—a series of little scenes—we tried to imagine as many stories as possible to be narrated in an ironic and distancing tone. In the end we wrote ten. Gerard and I wanted to show gentle and ordinary people, seldom shown on the screen, yet they have more charm than many well-known artists. They also possessed an appealing comic quality. The film was shot over five days, two episodes a day. I was also the cinematographer and I realised the benefits of film school, where in two hours I had learned to light and explore the possibilities of the camera.

All your short films have in common a sense of observation, moments that are so many epiphanies that reveal particular behaviours.

I have always been interested in people's behaviour. I can remember that at film school my friends wanted to deal with big subjects or spectacular scenes with car crashes. That was the last thing I wanted to do.

Do you like Katherine Mansfield,[3] your compatriot, who also enjoyed describing details?

Yes, I like her books. As a child in New Zealand, I used to play next to her memorial, which stood in a park close to home.

To what extent is A Girl's Own Story *inspired by your own childhood and adolescence?*

I wanted to pay homage to that period of our lives when we feel lost and alone. It is very characteristic of youth. It is a very curious stage in our evolution; we have adult emotions but no experience. With experience, it is easier to deal with one's emotions. The smallest things appear to be gigantic obstacles when one is young. I've lived through many experiences which I have never seen represented on screen. For instance, at school everyone used to kiss, but as soon as one got older, it stopped. Everyone behaved as if it had never happened. I wanted also to talk about The Beatles, whose music marked my generation—I was born in 1954. The episode about incest was not a personal experience, but I remember a very young neighbour who got pregnant by a school friend and the scandal that caused.

Did the actors bring elements or was everything already written beforehand?

Of course, the actors always contribute something. But in this particular case, the adolescents thought I was really strange and swore they had never done anything like it. In fact they basically read the text. I had a lot of trouble finding people to interpret the script. The first person I chose was not comfortable with the incest. She was too immature and I had to choose someone older, but who looked younger than her age.

Officially, the shoot lasted ten days but I managed to 'steal' extra time. The whole crew was a student crew and we didn't have much experience, but the film was well received in Australia and even won a few prizes. The response was good when it was screened, people laughed so much that at times it was difficult to hear the dialogue. I was very touched because my lecturers at film school had never supported my work. They were very conservative people, who thought that kind of film was too strange to help me find work.

You made After Hours *(1984) shortly after leaving film school.*

Yes. On the strength of my short films, the Women's Film Production Unit invited me to write and direct the film. I don't like *After Hours* very much because my motive for making it was compromised. There was a conflict between myself, the project and my artistic conscience. The film was commissioned and I had to be openly feminist, since it was about the sexual abuse of women at work. I was uneasy about it because I don't like films that tell you how you should or should not behave. I believe the world is more complex than that. I prefer to look at people and study their behaviour without blaming them. I would have preferred to put the film in a cupboard, instead it went around the world! I like to make the sort of films I would want to go to see myself, but that was not the case with *After Hours*. Nevertheless, it was important for me to make it.

Then you directed an episode of Dancing Daze *(1985) for ABC TV.*

That was a commission, light entertainment for television. I was writing a script for a television series about the New Zealand writer Janet Frame, and I wanted to know what it was like to work for television. It was an interesting experience, even if I don't like the film much, because I got to meet Jan Chapman, who later produced *2 Friends*. I had to work fast and shoot a fifty-minute film in seven days, including the song-and-dance numbers. It was the classic story of a group of young people who in 1986 wanted to form a dance company. I had to be visually creative. It was fun and I gained confidence about working in commercial cinema.

Shortly afterwards you made 2 Friends.

I had to be quick because the ABC had a crew available and a slot in its production schedule. Pre-production was short. And, as I said, the producer Jan Chapman offered me Helen Garner's script. We agreed on the objectives and we trusted one another. I also really liked the script even though I would not have chosen to tell the story backwards. What I liked was the freshness of the observation and the truth of the situations. I felt that I could do something with the script. Helen Garner had been inspired by the experiences of her daughter and one of her friends. I went to Melbourne to meet them. The school girl who played her daughter had fair hair and we thought she didn't look serious enough. We gave her hazelnut hair and cut it short like a boy's hair. Generally speaking, I don't think it is too difficult to work with adolescents even if there are days when they are emotionally very confused.

To what extent do objects, of which there are many in your films, help the actors in their work?

I like to first observe how actors behave normally in everyday life and then I remind them of it when we are shooting, so that their performance is natural and comes from their own life experience.

Do you have a lot to do with the camera?

I like to look through the view-finder because I am very particular about the framing I want. During the shoot of *2 Friends*, the camera crew resented me to some extent because they weren't used to directors caring about the framing. The director of photography did not really understand what I wanted and I had to be very obstinate to impose my views. In contrast, I had a very good relationship with Sally Bongers, a friend who had been at film school with me and who shot *Peel* and *A Girl's Own Story*. For *2 Friends* I had to work with the television crew. They were very competent but simply had very different shooting methods.

Do you do a lot of takes?

No. For *2 Friends* for instance, we had decided on a visual style. We knew that there wouldn't really be any close-ups, and that as soon as the actors had performed the scene and the tone was right, we would move on to the next shot. I didn't really 'cover' myself. As a whole, it was a very economical shoot.

Do you intend to continue telling such intimate stories?

I hope there will always be the same sense of observation in my films because I believe it's a strength, but I'm not sure whether my stories will always be as intimate. I would love to work on a larger scale with strong stories and different subjects. At the moment I'm working on a project which is close in spirit and atmosphere to a Grimm tale. It is a love story which takes place in New Zealand around 1850 in a rather gloomy climate.

Did you choose to paint youth in A Girl's Own Story *and* 2 Friends *because you felt safer making your first steps as a film-maker dealing with themes you were familiar with?*

For *A Girl's Own Story* I did want to talk about a world I knew well. I also like young people very much: I find them free and generous. But I'm not obsessed with youth! Of course, every time someone writes a story about young girls, they think of me to direct it. But I'm interested in every generation. At the moment, I am re-reading *Treasure Island* [Robert Louis Stevenson, 1883] and loving it. I like its strength and daring, but also the keen observation. In any case I always look at life rather ironically.

INTERVIEW 2: *SWEETIE*

Positif: *What have you been doing in the three years between your short films and* Sweetie?

Jane Campion: After the screening of my films at the Cannes festival, I thought carefully about what I should do, given the opportunities that Cannes had created. The first project I wanted to do was *Sweetie* because it seemed to represent the most modern and provocative point of view. Furthermore it was financially viable. I also thought that it might be difficult to make *Sweetie* after a more 'serious' film! I have a provocative streak in me and I was keen to attack such a subject. I started to develop the story with my co-writer Gerard Lee, the friend with whom I had already written *Passionless Moments* and who is very intelligent. He knew the subject well; it belonged to both of us and we were on the same wavelength. It took three years to make *Sweetie* because I was also developing other projects at the same time. One is *The Piano Lesson*, a very romantic subject in the Brontë sisters' style, which I would like to make later. Another is *Janet Frame*, which will be my next film and is the portrait of the New Zealand writer. She's published several volumes of her autobiography which deals with creativity and growing up. I love the style of her autobiographical trilogy: *To the Is-Land* (1982), which deals with her childhood, is very fresh and the most appealing of the three; *An Angel at My Table* (1984) and *An Envoy to Mirror City* (1985) in which many of the events occur in Europe. That's why I have been looking at locations on your continent recently. I will make it for television in three one-hour parts with the option of a version for theatrical release.

Did you have trouble financing Sweetie?

Finding the money to write those three projects wasn't difficult. As for the production of *Sweetie*, it was quite straightforward because the film was not expensive—it cost less than one million dollars. The script was written with just such a budget in mind. It was inspired by people and

[JOHN MAYNARD AND BRIDGET IKIN, HIBISCUS FILMS]

Sweetie (Genevieve Lemon) and Kay (Karen Colston), *Sweetie*

events I knew. I always work that way. I then have more authority over my writing and even if I later move away from these experiences, I still have a basis I can come back to. The character of *Sweetie* was inspired by a man but for family reasons we changed the gender. I was disappointed at first but I respected my co-writer's feelings. What I loved in *Sweetie* was all the potential she had and the way it crumbled. It happens to us all. One day we explore what we could be, but the day vanishes and it's too late. *Sweetie* is a poignant character, but for whom there's no hope.

In a way Kay (Karen Colston) is the central character. The others gradually join her story, first Louis (Tom Lycos), then Sweetie (Genevieve Lemon), then her parents.

We called the film *Sweetie* because it's a lovely title, not because she's the heroine of the story. Kay changes, she has more courage by the end of the film. I also think that one cannot love without a real foundation otherwise one only loves an illusion and it can't work. Most of us, though, create some kind of illusion about our lives. We create an idea of who our companion is and find it difficult to accept the fact that they are different to that idea.

Did you always plan to start with the voice-over and with what is going on in Kay's head?

No. At first I had thought of beginning with shots of trees. They were beautiful shots but I thought that they would disorient the audience by introducing too many elements to put together. At the same time, when I am filming, I think I can do everything, that I am completely free so long as it contributes to the story, that it has meaning. I like things to be fresh and surprising. With Kay's voice-over, we wanted to indicate right from the start that we were not only interested in what the characters do, but also in what they feel and think.

In what part of Australia does the action take place?

Most of the story takes place in Willoughby, a suburb of Sydney. The scenes in which they go to visit the mother were shot at Warren in north-western New South Wales, a wonderful town, and a centre for cotton growing and sheep farming. I loved filming there. We trampled the soil to give it the dry desert look of certain parts of Australia, which were locations we could not afford.

In Franz Kafka's Metamorphosis *(1916) everything is observed from the 'abnormal' son's point of view. Here instead it's the family's point of view as it deals with Sweetie's otherness.*

Yes, although I thought that from time to time it would be good to feel what Sweetie was feeling or thinking, for instance, when the family goes west and we understand by her reaction how much of a baby she is. Her father is a traitor and a bastard who gives her false hope. He knows that if he takes Sweetie, he will never be able to bring back his wife. I remember that the actor who played Gordon (Jon Darling) had the same reaction as his character: he was really in a fix at that point!

Did you study psychiatric cases or read books on the topic?

No, not really. We had living examples around us. And we talked a lot to people we knew who had gone mad. We also sent Genevieve Lemon to a re-education centre so that she could observe the patients. We wanted her to feel the threat. It was a trying experience for her: one patient in particular kept threatening her with a razor blade. We didn't do any in-depth research, but what we did do was borrow a lot from personal experience. It is a subject I thought about for approximately a year. I didn't want to deal with the usual narrative constraints, instead I wanted to describe states of mind and emotions. I wanted to talk about the difficulty of loving, as well as introduce more sombre subterranean currents. That's when I had the idea of using superstition. I also wanted to use metaphors because I believe people think in metaphors much more frequently than one assumes and we don't see such thought very often on the screen. That seemed to give the film an extra dimension.

Then I reflected on the kind of story we wanted to tell. So Gerard and I put a bit of money together and spent two weeks in a house on the beach where we discussed and performed each of the characters. We thought it was important to find the tone of each scene and the way people would talk. The development of the script was an organic process. I didn't know that Sweetie would eat the china horses before reaching that point in the story, when I wondered what she would do. We never knew what the next stage would be before actually reaching it. So much so that we had great difficulty re-organising the story. It was like a chain with links that can't be shuffled around.

Did you work on the dialogue with the actors?

Everything was already written but we rehearsed a lot, which is especially useful to get to know the actors and to allow them to trust me, so that we also know how to support each other. It is an opportunity to explore the possibilities of the characters. Each actor is different and I worked with those differences. Genevieve likes to be told everything she has to do. I had to trick her and put her in situations where she would have to discover for herself what was needed. Karen Colston, on the other hand, knows exactly at any one moment who she is and what is required. My method with her was to ask her what she thought Kay would do or think in 'such and such' a situation. It's strange though, because, in real life, Genevieve Lemon is such an intelligent and strong woman.

The subject could have made a sombre film. Instead you stylise ugliness and vulgarity.

The production designer purposely created dull and ugly sets. For the interiors we argued that people bring their own furniture into the apartments they rent, yet hold on to objects that belonged to the previous tenants, and this creates a mixture of styles. What is ugly can also be elegantly captured by the lighting and the framing. It's a sign of sympathy. I find it more moving than a 'pretty' set which offers much less opportunity for contrast.

Your framing is astonishing. Is it pre-planned or does it come about during the shoot?

I had nothing to lose, it was a low-budget film and we could afford to be daring and to take risks. We make films for our own pleasure. A lot of things had been pre-planned. Sally Bongers, my director of photography, thinks the same way as I do. We talk, drink tea, laugh, imagine shots, look around to steal ideas. We're both very visual and have a similar aesthetic sensibility. Sally also approaches scenes very practically: she frames for the drama of a situation in order to create a poignant emotion, but without drawing too much attention to the shot itself. We did make that type of mistake, though. In some scenes it didn't feel as if the characters weren't talking to each other, because they were too much on the edge of the frame! We had to re-shoot the scenes. Sally Bongers and I are friends, but it doesn't stop us from arguing, but it's always about who's going to be in control. She's very stubborn, very strong and sometimes wants certain things. And since I am like her and sometimes have the opposite idea, conflict is inevitable! These are not so much disagreements as the result of the pressure produced by a film shoot.

Sally was largely responsible for the lighting. She is very intuitive. But we had discussed the lighting beforehand and we wanted a soft light on the faces because that corresponded to what we felt for the characters. At first I was afraid that my framing would appear pretentious, but I no longer have that horrible feeling. I wanted to cross the line and go for framing that creates the poignant feel of a situation like you get in photography, which is a much more adventurous artform than cinema. There is a sensitivity and sophistication in photography that I don't often find in the cinema and I'd like to continue exploring this kind of visual expression while still developing the story.

Were the nature scenes, such as the day at the beach or the dance at night in the bush, filmed as planned?

I prepare a storyboard which helps me to see what I need, but we often change it depending on what happens. For instance, the shot in which the two cowboys teach each other to dance came from what I observed between two actors, one showing the other a dance step. I thought it was charming and decided to use it in the film. One needs to be on the lookout for such details; they give the feeling of things but, of course, the great obstacle is time. We had many more ideas but we didn't have the time to film them during the forty-day shoot. Eight weeks is a fairly standard schedule, but with our way of working it was quite restrictive.

The scene with a clairvoyant and her mentally retarded son heralds the appearance of Sweetie.

Except that the son is really stupid. I liked the idea that this elderly woman should so easily accept her son's condition. Clairvoyants are often like that: contrary to what one might think, they're very down-to-earth people. Sweetie's parents behave very differently.

The scene in the cemetery at the end, with the wind blowing through the tree, the tracking shot along the neat hedges, then the shot of the grave with the plant growing out of the hole, was it completely planned beforehand?

It was different in the script. But when I saw the cemetery, I liked the formal quality of the place and I wanted to underline it. I also noticed that the tree seemed to be breathing. But it was especially during the editing that the tree's living character appeared. I spend a lot of time in the cutting room, twelve hours a day, six days a week. I love editing, one can still bring a lot at this stage, even original ideas. The first assembly was two and a half hours long, but I always intended that the film should run not much more than ninety minutes.

Where does the music come from?

We used an Australian choir of thirty singers, called Cafe at the Gates of Salvation, but it's not a church choir. They sing original compositions inspired by the white gospel tradition. The singers are very giving and have a great sense of orchestration. They meet for the pleasure of being together and to listen to them sing is a very powerful experience. The last song is not one of theirs, it comes from a book of Jewish prayers. We were worried that the songs might appear religious, but once we had laid one of the songs over the sex scene in the carpark, we didn't worry! I am not systematically in favour of music in film, but there are moments when music really makes a difference. Such as in the sequence in the carpark between Kay and Louis, when the music allowed us to establish an ironic point of view on the two characters at that point in time.

The danger with this type of film is to be condescending.

I thought that because the characters were very vulnerable, very raw, they would eventually win the audience's sympathy. I wanted the audience to end up identifying with the characters. In real life I find people are both funny and tragic and I don't mind laughing when they're in a difficult situation. Sometimes people are grateful, because you have allowed them to see that there is another side to every coin. We take ourselves too seriously, but there should be a limit. Indeed, events are only tragic if seen in a certain light. I'm not necessarily moved by the tragedy in people's lives, yet I am very sensitive to it. Personally, I tend to complain a lot about what happens in my life, but others find it irresistibly funny!

Are you aware of a difference between your short and medium-length films and Sweetie?

Not really. Except that *Sweetie* is the best and most powerful film I have made. It's a film I've had less control over, which took me places I wasn't really aware of, and in that sense it was a great adventure. And because of that, I am satisfied.

Do you know of any films that have a similar approach to your own, that like to describe states of mind?

It's common in literature and I don't see why one shouldn't do it in the cinema. All that's required is to want to do it, like David Lynch. One doesn't find truth only by developing an intrigue, but by exploring several levels. I don't want to look only at people's behaviour, I also want to discover the way people think and feel, like in the novels by Marguerite Duras⁴ or Flannery O'Connor.⁵ I think the latter is at once an exquisite, ruthless and honest writer. *A Good Man is Hard to Find* (1955) is an extraordinary book, hilarious and horrible at the same time. I feel quite innocent before stories of that type! I liked very much the adaptation John Huston made of *Wise Blood* [in 1979]. In fact I like most of John Huston's films.

I think people understand the world in a very symbolic way. Things are rarely what they seem, they're metaphors of what is or might be. And that applies also to our inner turmoils. One day a friend came to stay with me because she was in a real quandary. She didn't know how to choose between two men. I remember that the whole world became a metaphor of her personal problem. When we went shopping together and she noticed extravagant shoes, it would mean that she wanted to live with the more adventurous man or, on the contrary, that her own adventurous spirit needed the more stable of the two men. When we were out driving and she saw a number plate beginning with J, it would mean that she should live with John. We all do this to some extent.

Do you know Emily Dickinson's poetry with its blend of the metaphysical and the concrete?

No, but I like the combination!

In your work you too create a metaphysical feel from small concrete details—the root of a tree, for instance, with which you suggest a relationship between the inner and outer worlds of the character.

That's how I feel things. I think my generation is drawn to spirituality and is less keen to participate in the hustle and bustle of the world. Personally I've been using meditation for five years. It helps me to control myself. I'm also more aware of my real feelings. Often one does things out of sheer excitement, when really it doesn't fit one's real self.

Your characters are very solitary beings.

Sweetie isn't. She's very communicative in her own way and is even sometimes dishonest! She befriends the neighbours straightaway and takes Louis to the beach. No one understands the threat that Sweetie represents except Kay, who's the most vulnerable one. It's difficult to know to what extent Sweetie is mentally retarded. For me she's normal or at least has been. Right from early childhood the gradual pressure from her family pushed her over the edge and eventually she lost her sense of balance and responsibility. In other circumstances she might have been different.

Was Sweetie's barking inspired by a patient you had observed?

No, I invented it. There were a lot of rehearsals for the scene. It took courage for Genevieve to manage to frighten everyone. It was a decisive moment in her interpretation of the part. She really became the character once she felt she had power over the others and that she could frighten them.

Why did you dedicate the film to your sister?

Because I was very touched by what she did. While we were filming, my mother became very ill, she was dying in fact, and I had to decide whether to stop filming, let another director finish the film or continue. My sister, who lived in England, returned to New Zealand to look after my mother, which allowed me to keep filming.

red wigs and
autobiography:
interview with
jane campion

michel ciment

Positif: *What did Janet Frame mean to you before you thought of adapting her book?*

Jane Campion: I remember when I was thirteen years old, reading her books lying on my bed and the impact they had on me. There were a lot of poetic passages in her novel *Owls Do Cry* (1957), such as 'Daphne in the Quiet Room', which had a special sadness and evoked the world of madness. There was a lot of tragedy in her family. In *Owls Do Cry*, the sister falls into a pile of burning rubbish and dies. In Janet Frame's autobiography, the sister drowns, but it still causes the same terror. At thirteen, one is very young and impressionable and especially moved by poetry that speaks of the inner life. I must have been deeply affected, because when I wrote novellas at school, I called one of the characters Daphne. I can also recall what I read about Janet Frame, in particular that the way she wrote was linked to her schizophrenia. There were a lot of rumours, a whole mythology surrounding her, and when I would walk past a psychiatric clinic, I would ask myself questions about Janet Frame, just as she did of the people she described in her books. That's why, when I heard that she had written her own version of the story of her life, I very much wanted to read it. And that's how I discovered the first volume of her autobiography, *To the Is-Land*, when I was about twenty-eight years old and at film school. At first I was curious about what had really happened in her life, then I started to enjoy discovering the freshness of her narration and the richness of the details. It conjured up my own childhood memories and I really felt her book was an essay on childhood in New Zealand. I loved it, it was very emotional, and I wanted to share my experience with a lot of people.

The task of condensing the whole of her autobiography (three volumes of two hundred and fifty pages each) must have been enormous.

It certainly was. I think I initiated the project and spoke about it to Bridget Ikin, who at the time was head of production for John Maynard. I was visiting the set where they were filming and told Bridget about the autobiography, which she said she had loved too. I suggested we do the project together. It was a rather cheeky and ambitious thing to say, since I hadn't made very much by then, maybe *Peel*, my first short film.

Did you conceive of it first for the cinema or for television?

I always thought of it as a film for the small screen. I couldn't imagine anyone would want to see this story on the big screen. My idea of what was suitable for the cinema was clichéd, the sort of story that had lots of action or panoramic landscapes, whereas this was a very intimate story. I thought it would be very difficult to convince producers that the story would be of interest to a lot of people. In fact, we did have problems, because many of the people we spoke to didn't think Janet Frame was a very likeable character, at least as she appeared in the book! It is difficult to believe it now, when she seems so intensely likeable in the film! At any rate, that is how Laura Jones, the scriptwriter, and Jan Chapman and I, who collaborated on the script, saw her. Everything that related to her was seen in a delicate and soft light. The filming was harmonious, unlike that of *Sweetie,* which at times was quite fraught with difficulty, and the whole of the production seemed to be bathed in the relaxed atmosphere that Janet Frame was able to create.

I didn't censure myself because I was working for television. The subject didn't lend itself to an experimental style the way *Sweetie* did. Quite the opposite. For me, the way Janet Frame tells her story calls for the square frame of the television screen. Sometimes, the substance of a film can be lost when it's shown on television, but not in this case. There are a lot of close-ups, for instance, but they are right for this kind of intimate story.

The problem with films made for television is that often they are not made with enough care, because the production schedule is too short. For *An Angel at My Table* (1990), the conditions were similar to those of a feature film production: twelve weeks of filming, including two weeks in Europe. It was tough—the conditions were not quite as good as for film, but it was all right. The real problem was the number of new actors we had to meet each day because there were so many characters!—it was like a series of interviews! Everyone arrived feeling anxious and eager to do their best, yet knowing that in most cases they would only have one day on set. The only character that really holds the screen is Janet Frame, but she had a lasting relationship with very few people. So my main task was to get the actors ready as quickly as possible.

Your mother plays a part in the film.

Yes, she's the teacher who reads [Lord Alfred] Tennyson's poem, 'Morte d'Arthur' (1842).[1] My mother was a very good actor and one can see the special intensity with which she interprets the scene. She's like that in real life too. She seldom performs now, but her perfectionism verges on the neurotic. When I'd tell her that she was very good, she would shrug her shoulders, because she thought she was dreadful. I'm like her: when I receive compliments, I tend to reject them. I would tell my mother that she should be pleased with her work. But she'd reply that was impossible, because she knew she could have done so much better. In her mind, to be satisfied with her performance would mean she was becoming lazy!

This is the second film, apart from 2 Friends, *for which you haven't written the script. Does this make it very different on set?*

Not really, in so far as I nevertheless closely collaborated in the writing of *An Angel at My Table*. It makes the filming easier later on because one is intimately acquainted with the material. I would talk to Laura Jones a lot in order to reach a truly shared vision, then she would write, and I would suggest one or two changes. In any case we could always go back to the book for mediation, which really helped us share the same vision. I've never tackled an adaptation on my own and I don't think I'm tempted to either. Quite frankly, I got more pleasure out of sharing. It was a simple story and we thought anyone could understand it. In that sense it was a good topic for television and there was no reason to obscure the story unnecessarily. What we did was read the book a great many times, then we'd put it aside after each read and write down everything we liked most. We would then compare our lists, which were pretty close anyway. Afterwards we discussed how to combine what we liked most about the book and Laura strung these elements together. When I'm working on a script I don't think about the images, that comes later. In the same way when I'm filming, I have to be totally impregnated by the text so that I'm free to think only of the visuals, and that is why I collaborate so closely with the writing process although I don't actually write the script. In any case, I was making *Sweetie* when Laura was writing *An Angel at My Table*. The film was not an experimental or intellectual challenge for me. I needed to have a truly simple and honest approach to the story.

In fact, my approach to *Sweetie* and *An Angel at My Table* is quite different. I really like *Sweetie*, it's a beautiful tragedy. I think it's a film with a lot of depth, with obscure and difficult layers, in which the emotions are more complicated, less accessible. It's a film that stays with you longer. Whereas *An Angel at My Table* establishes a fantastic relationship with the audience by speaking straight from the heart. As a person, that's all I want, but as a film-maker, the film is less exciting than *Sweetie*. But get ready for a shock with my next film—I won't be as well behaved as with *An Angel at My Table*!

Sweetie and An Angel at My Table *share the same elliptical sense. You get the story to really flow and yet you also interrupt it abruptly.*

That has a lot to do with the way the script was written. And also because I invent a lot of things during the rehearsals. I had an enormous amount of material by the end of the shoot. I would imagine different beginnings and endings for scenes and during the editing I would cut in the middle of sequences. Hence the abrupt and condensed feel of certain passages.

One of the most remarkable aspects of the film is the continuity you establish between the three actors playing Janet at different stages of her life: Alexia Keogh, Karen Fergusson and Kerry Fox.

The red hair helped us a lot to establish the likeness! The third time young Alexia Keogh put her wig on, she began to cry. She was so mortified to have hair that colour! It was funny to see all three of them in their wigs at lunchtime. There's no doubt it was one of the most complex problems we had to solve. I remember that, after watching Bertolucci's *The Last Emperor* (1987), we discussed at length the transition from one age to the next. I preferred the actor who played the emperor in the middle period. He was good at expressing the feeling of being privileged. I was very attached to him and found it difficult moving on to the next actor because I had established such a strong relationship with that character. I was afraid the same thing might happen with young Janet in *An Angel at My Table* and that the audience would regret leaving her behind. We kept thinking about these transitions during the scriptwriting stage as well as during casting and the filming itself. In the end, during post-production, Veronika Haussler [editor] showed me that I needed to film extra shots to build greater fluidity. I could see she was right, so I filmed the shot of the second Janet sitting on the slope of the hill, reading poems from her journal, which gave the audience a moment alone with her. In fact, each of the three Janets is given such a moment: the youngest when she comes towards us on the road and

Back: Janet Frame. Front (left to right): Karen Fergusson, Alexia
Keogh and Kerry Fox, *An Angel at My Table*

the third one when she reads a poem beside the railway line. The
transition from the second Janet, Karen Fergusson, to the third Janet,
Kerry Fox, was difficult because children and adolescents are so honest
and innocent that it's difficult for an actor to measure up to the absolute
charm of the very young. We had to work very hard with Kerry in
order to choose carefully the right moment for her to first appear on
screen and not seem sullen. The audience had to like her straightaway,
there couldn't be any problems.

Karen Fergusson, who precedes Kerry Fox on the screen, is dread-
fully shy and very intelligent. We chose her from a classroom in which
she and the other students were reading John Keats' 'Ode to a Nightingale' (1819).[2] She was the only one able to recite the poem by heart
after only two readings and she had an amazing capacity for weeping.

I have never met an adolescent capable of such empathy. I adored her. She was fourteen years old when we made the film, the same age as Melina Bernbecker, who played her friend, Myrtle. Melina was like her character, very sexy and keen on boys. Karen was the opposite, just like Janet Frame. She was very reserved and wore a little cardigan and a very ordinary skirt. It was fascinating to watch these three Janets, sitting together, all three interpreting the same character. The youngest would love being cuddled by the two older Janets.

Did Janet Frame get in touch with you during the production of the film?

She read the script and loved it and came to visit us on the set. We were very anxious to know how she would react to the adaptation. But she is a very mature woman, who knows that the story of her life is also a fiction. She was even generous enough to tell Laura Jones that the script was better than her own book. It was a big deal for Janet Frame to visit the set because she hardly ever travels. She came by train with my godmother, who's also one of her best friends. They formed a strange couple. Janet is very curious and gave my godmother no peace during the trip, drawing her attention to everything happening around them. At first Janet was very shy, but by the end of the week she became quite close to us. Sometimes, she would comment on what her father was saying in the film and would suggest changes.

The film is faithful to Janet Frame's autobiography, but there are themes and preoccupations that we also find in your other films, even elements from your own life, such as your discovery of Europe when you were young.

Everyone in New Zealand goes to the old country one day! But it's true that I'm usually drawn to characters who are neglected and abandoned and in whom no one is interested. That's why I liked Janet. I am not aware of my choices. I suppose it is like falling in love. One doesn't ask questions, one just dives in! And one is grateful for the opportunity to love something or someone. When I started out I wanted the film to serve Janet Frame and her vision. But there is certainly more of me in the final result than I had been aware of when I began. My aim was to put on the screen what I'd felt when I had read the book. I don't know to what extent *An Angel at My Table* is about me. I'm a bit like an actor who chooses her projects and likes to do different things. You're probably better placed than me to comment on what I do!

Did you choose a palette of colours? Did Janet's red hair determine the chromatic range of the film?

I had always thought of red and green for *An Angel at My Table*. Green is the colour of New Zealand and red is the colour of Janet's hair. They were primary colours. By starting with the red hair I could either play with a set of soft, muffled tones or on the contrary, give more radiance to the film by having the red clash with bright colours like green, which is what I decided to do. If you go to New Zealand, you notice how different the light is. The first European painters, Dutch and British, who returned with paintings of their journeys faced incredulity back home. Everyone thought the colours were exaggerated and unbelievable, because the light in Europe is softer and more diffuse. There's also a lot of wind in New Zealand and it sweeps everything away. The air is transparent and from Wellington one can see mountains 400 kilometres away. That's why the shadows are so dark; one can't distinguish anything. I'm enthralled by the intensity. The contrasts are so strong that it's difficult to film. We used filters in order to obtain yellow and bronze colours for some of the childhood sequences.

In what part of New Zealand did you film?

We weren't truthful to the autobiography because we filmed around Auckland, whereas Janet Frame grew up in a very different area, near Oamaru. Nevertheless, I was able to find a similar landscape. It isn't the same type of nature, but it has the same feel.

How did you approach the scenes in Europe? Were you not afraid of being exotic by filming in Ibiza, London and Paris?

I was aware of the risk of presenting touristy clichés because I don't know Europe well, the way I do my own country or Australia, although I had lived in London for a while. Paris was a problem because we only stayed half a day and therefore I filmed it like a tourist. Paris is completely exotic for me. As for Ibiza, we didn't go there, because the place looks nothing like it used to in the 1950s. We found the equivalent at Cadaques and on the Costa Brava. With my director of photography, we tried to find different and bizarre places, with a mixture of the old and the new to avoid clichés. Of the European sequences, I prefer the scene in which Janet is seen walking while reading a poem by Shelley.

You didn't adopt a naturalistic style for the hospital scenes, instead you opted for a kind of stylisation, which still revealed the cruelty of the psychiatric treatment.

I think it's quite traumatic enough as it is! To add to it wouldn't have made the scenes more convincing. I wanted to show Janet's progressive decline, as she went from being normal at the beginning to sort of mad at the end. In her autobiography she doesn't talk at all about her time in a mental institution. But she does talk about it in one of her novels, *Faces in the Water* (1962), which we used for inspiration. The book contained fascinating material which Janet Frame was not keen to let us use at first. In the end though, she agreed.

You never use dialogue to explain Janet's gradual descent into depression, which was linked to her sister's death, her brother's epileptic fits, etc. There are suggestions, hints, rather than the statement of a doctor, for instance, which is what you would find in many films to help the audience understand the evolution of the patient's condition.

I don't like to explain. I wanted to create an intimate feeling for Janet's state of mind rather than reasons for it. I find that explanations destroy the dramatic essence of a story, but of course the danger is that the audience may not quite understand what's happening! As a viewer, I don't like being given a sermon. I expect the film-maker to find a more subtle solution to lead me to discover the key to a character's behaviour.

One of the problems of making films about artists is how to show the creative process. It's practically impossible to film.

Towards the end of the shoot, I was very embarrassed to realise I had made a film about a writer who's never shown writing! I then filmed a few typewriter shots. I was worried by such an omission, though. On the other hand, how does one film the act of writing? Of course, there are physical details: Janet Frame is almost neurotically afraid of noise when she's writing. Apparently, Kipling needed the blackest ink possible and liked the smell of orange peel. Others drink very strong coffee. Everyone needs some sort of ritual to allow the subconscious to take charge. I have read a lot of literary autobiographies recently, but I still find it as difficult as ever to express visually the process of writing.

You also have a strong feel for the loneliness of the artist. Whether she be at school, among her family or with friends, Janet Frame is still fundamentally alone.

Janet was afraid when she read the script that people would feel sorry for her. She would tell me that she didn't feel lonely. In her eyes, the sky and nature are living presences, to which she felt very close. I tried to show that Janet was not unhappy. On the other hand, I don't think that Janet was capable of having a sustained relationship with anyone. It is too complicated for her. But I don't think it's all that serious since it's too complicated for most of us as well!

jane campion:
more 'barbarian'
than aesthete!

thomas bourguigon and michel ciment

talent, chance and circumstances have put Jane Campion's first three films on the cover of *Positif*—the only film-maker apart from Andrzej Wajda to whom this has happened. *The Piano* (1993) is her best film yet, and is the work of a mature artist. It is the result of a long gestation and development that saw her gradually move away from the references, the history and genres she used as source material to achieve a unique and profound vision of Humanity and Nature, which gives the film an independent existence, a life of flesh and blood.

The Piano is unique with its violent, romantic and carnal music. Instead of the art of digression seen in *Sweetie* and the elliptical narrative of her biography of Janet Frame, *An Angel at My Table*, here is a script that seems clear and simple, yet is as deep as the seas and forests of the South Sea Islands.

Positif: The Piano *is your oldest project, since you started it even before making* Sweetie. *What was the starting point for the film?*

Jane Campion: After finishing film school, I thought the next stage naturally should be a feature film. I had two ideas: *The Piano* and another, *Ebb*, which was more fantastic and more in keeping with my style at the time. *The Piano* seemed more commercial because it was a love story, but the story also required greater maturity. I wrote almost half of it, but I felt that with a small budget I wouldn't do justice to the landscape. In any case, I didn't have enough experience as a director and couldn't really understand all the themes I wanted to deal with: an archetypal story, the relationships between primitivism and civilisation, a whole construction based on opposites. Therefore, I decided to put aside the project. In the meantime, I had met Pierre Rissient,[1] who screened my short films in Cannes. That was an important experience for me as I realised something I hadn't realised in Australia, and that is that there was an audience for my voice and that I didn't have to compromise. So I came back to Australia to make *Sweetie*, which was in the same vein as my film-school work and seemed to fit my state of mind at the time. I wanted to make something more provocative and more rebellious in terms of cinema.

What was Ebb *about?*

It was an imaginary story about a country from which one day the sea withdraws never to come back, and about the way people have to find a spiritual solution to the problem. The natural world had become artificial and unpredictable, and the film was about faith and doubt. The inhabitants of that country began to develop a particular form of spirituality and to hear voices and have visions. At the end, the father of one of the key families of the story, a man least likely to have a spiritual adventure, was having the most extraordinary experiences. He was the one who made the sea come back and his tongue began to taste of salt! He became a sacrificial victim.

How much has The Piano *changed since you first thought of the idea?*

At the start, there were quite simply the piano lessons. But the ending was very traditional, the drama being resolved through a very violent deed. After *Sweetie* and *An Angel at My Table*, I came back to the project and thought that the central idea was much too good to have such a predictable ending. Through discussion with my producer Jan Chapman, and Billy MacKinnon,[2] who helped me write the script, I started to ask why we were being so reticent, especially me! Stewart was killed by Baines, more fingers were severed, and it was much more violent. We then decided to go much deeper into the psychology of the story. The second version of the script had Ada (Holly Hunter) go back to Baines (Harvey Keitel); Stewart (Sam Neill) would see them together, fall in love and become more vulnerable. The changes were mostly made in the last fifty pages. We introduced the characters of the aunts, made the protagonists less rigid because they seemed too much like the characters of a fairytale.

The film does have a fairytale, the shadow theatre performance of the story of Bluebeard.

That sequence corresponded to a certain type of experience for the audience, but I wanted the central story to be as strong and emotional as possible. The drama sequence was always in the script. I had been struck by the photograph of a woman during the colonial period whose head appeared between sheets. These amateur theatre groups have always impressed me with their inventiveness. For me the scene represents all the power of storytelling; although we know the story is invented we still believe it. It's about the very nature of performance. People love being duped. When the little girl tells her aunt her father's story, she believes it despite knowing it's a lie. The desire to believe is stronger than anything else.

In the story told by Flora (Anna Paquin) there is a shot in which you use animation techniques to show the father burning in the flames.

We found a wonderful illustrated children's book from the period and decided that in the story, the book would belong to Flora. This was where it was possible to introduce such surprising graphic work. A member of the technical team even believed Flora's story. There was also a practical reason for the animation: it allowed us to link two shots in which Anna Paquin had given her very best.

What was your approach to the period film?

I did a lot of research. I have a good ear for dialogue and I'm good at imitating people, and my husband's even better at it. But of course, I didn't have any models for these characters, I couldn't use people I knew as a starting point. My problem was how to make them human and use my observation skills. I read diaries written by nineteenth-century women as well as the accounts of witnesses to the European landing in New Zealand. I tried to capture their voices and their way of thinking. I also read period novels until, in the end, I decided I had to solve the issues in my head. I suppose I needed to feel protected because this classical story presented obstacles which I couldn't solve using my usual narrative technique of creating a diversion; that really leads nowhere. I wanted to work within the classical tragic mode, yet at the same time I wasn't equipped for it and I had to develop new skills. Each scene had its own problems and I couldn't set off in all directions as I had done with *Sweetie*. I had to find a through-line.

Did you do research on the relationships between the Maori and the Anglo-Saxon colonials?

I couldn't study these first contacts because no one really knows what happened. But the consequences are with us now. I'm not really an expert in the field and there were things I wanted to say in the film, but my Maori advisers convinced me that that was rubbish! Of course,

I spoke to specialists, especially since there is a Maori culture renaissance. Some Maori tend to have a heroic view of their past, which I didn't want to show. Moreover, there are often conflicting points of view. I preferred to look around and observe how people behaved. For instance, the homosexual Maori character in the film greatly upset the community. They said that if someone had been homosexual at the time, he would have been killed! But Maori are quite open about sexuality, they're always talking about their genitals, it's just part of how they see others. Maori culture is not prudish like Protestant culture.

The Maori background is like an objective mirror to what the heroine feels: their culture encompasses spirituality and sexuality, as well as the purely material.

Yes. They highlight the puritanical side of the colonials. The Maori have a much more harmonious relationship with nature; it's stronger too. Anglo-Saxons haven't solved the relationship between their animal and sexual part and their rational part. Baines is between the two—he doesn't belong to the whites or the Maori. He was probably a whaler who settled there, and his unfinished tattoo shows that his desire to assimilate is not quite complete. He also has made the effort to learn the Maori language and acts as interpreter between the Maori and the Europeans. In fact, Harvey Keitel learned to speak Maori and he knew more than most of the extras! He was a very good student, whereas most of the indigenous people couldn't speak their own language very well.

What led you to quote the poet Thomas Hood?[3]

In fact, I asked my mother, who reads far more poetry than I do, to find a quotation about the sea. At first, I had intended to use it for *Ebb*, because originally *The Piano* did not end with the sequence it does now. So I put the quotation at the end of *The Piano*. The film used to end with the concert. Baines would arrive, pick Ada up at the theatre and leave with her and her daughter. Stewart would notice their absence and set off in pursuit. A postscript was to say he had disappeared in the bush, never to be found. There were no love scenes. Stewart was more of a one-dimensional character; jealous and angry. In the final version he is a much more rounded and vulnerable character.

You use slow-motion several times.

There's even one place I use slow-motion and one doesn't notice it. It's a way of observing the characters more sharply. Some sequences were even shot in slow-motion *in* the camera. I could do this because it was a romantic story told in a more dramatic and lyrical style. Slow-motion can sometimes appear facile and in poor taste. At other times, it's all right. When she comes out of the water, the shots were ordinary without slow-motion and I wanted to show the shock this represented for her. I think it works.

There are several angels in your films: An Angel at My Table, *Flora dressed up as an angel, and the comment Stewart makes to Ada when he tells her he's clipped her wings.*

I don't believe in angels, but I do believe in the hope of being an angel, every human being's desire to be saved and to be able to fly away. It comes down to talking about artists. The artist expresses a dissatisfaction, the will to escape oppression, a form of hope. I don't suggest a solution but I do express a state of the soul. To me important people are those who give meaning to life, artists and poets, who try to understand and who ask questions that help us better understand. I cannot imagine life without such a quest. At the same time, I am not an aesthete or a *cinéphile*. I quickly lose patience with films that demand too much concentration. There's a barbarian side to me! Ada is an artist but I don't think she needs an audience. She plays for herself. We modelled her a little on the Brontë sisters and the imaginary worlds they had created for themselves. I am attracted to romantic literature and I wanted to contribute to the genre. In literature I especially think of *Wuthering Heights* (1847), and in poetry of Blake, Tennyson and Byron. I went to the village where Emily Brontë grew up, I walked around the moor and tried to remember the atmosphere. Of course I was not trying to adapt *Wuthering Heights*, in fact I don't think that story can be told now. It's a saga that stretches over two generations and, of course, I am not English. I belong to a colonial culture and I had to invent my own fiction. I wanted to deal with relationships between men and women, with the complexity of love and eroticism, as well as the repression of sexuality. I am indebted not only to Emily Brontë, but to many women artists. There are some specifically feminine qualities in the film. Ada is an extremely feminine character with her sense of secrecy and her relationship with her daughter. I also read a lot of Emily Dickinson's poetry while I was writing the script.

You didn't use any romantic music or composers, such as Schubert or Schumann.[4]

That was never our intention! I wanted to give the film a musical identity, not make it a pastiche of nineteenth-century composers. I needed a personal voice, musical compositions which Ada might have written. Michael Nyman decided to use Scottish tunes, pieces that Ada might have heard at home and which would suit her personality. I don't know much about music and I asked advice for the choice of the composer. Several friends recommended Michael Nyman. Of course, I was familiar with his work on Peter Greenaway's films, especially *Death* in a French Garden [*The Draughtsman's Contract*, 1982], for which Nyman had found the tone of the period as well as his own very personal style. Michael Nyman is not only a film composer, he is also a musician in his own right. I wanted a similar integrity for this film and not someone who'd simply use tricks. I am pleased with Nyman's work, of the violence of the music especially.

You also use Maori songs for the sequence at sea.

I don't know Maori culture very well, but I can tell you this is authentic. We could have inserted more Maori elements but they wouldn't have been integrated into the story. There were some forbidding stories and exciting aspects we just had to leave out in the end. We only kept what could be fully integrated into the story.

The romantic dimension of the film is enhanced of course by the use of the environment. How did you choose the landscapes?

I knew about the atmosphere and power of the landscape, having grown up with it. I would go bushwalking and camping, which is common in New Zealand. I used to love going on long bushwalks with my father. There is such intensity in some parts of the bush that it feels as if one's under water. The landscape is at once foreboding, claustrophobic and mythical, and the feeling was made stronger by the complicated itineraries we used to take. We wanted to give an underwater feel to the bush scenes in order to link them to the final sequence. Europeans were very disconcerted by the landscape when they first arrived and, because they didn't appreciate it, they cleared a lot to make the landscape look European. I thought such wild landscape suited the story because romanticism is misunderstood today, especially in the cinema. Romanticism has become 'pretty' and pleasant. One has forgotten how harsh and dark it was. I wanted the audience to feel afraid of the power of the natural elements. That is, I believe the essence of romanticism: that respect for nature seen as greater than you, your spirit or humanity even.

How did you choose the two American actors for the roles of Ada and Baines?

It was quite a mystery actually. I hadn't thought of using American actors in the film. Or New Zealand actors in fact, since the story is about a time that almost precedes the creation of New Zealand. At first, it might have been more logical to use English actors. I even thought of French actors, but it's strange how your compatriots—at least those I spoke to—are reticent about their own actors. I was more enthusiastic than they were. But I suppose it's the same everywhere: one never appreciates as much one's own culture. I met many wonderful French actors but there was the language issue. In England, too, I met a great number of people. But we never carried out a systematic and methodical search. It was more like a world-wide flirtation! We were lucky in the end to make the right choices because our method was rather vague. In London, for instance, I didn't find anyone with the same presence as Harvey Keitel. That I thought of him seemed strange to some. Harvey was associated with very strong filmic memories from my youth: *Mean Streets* (1973), *Bad Timing*[5] (1980) or *The Duellists* (1977). I thought he would be interested in something different and in experimentation. I was told his age might be a problem. So I looked at one of his recent films, *The Two Jakes* (1990), and thought he was very good, and that he looked young. I sent him the script, which he loved and because of what was happening in his life at that moment, he wanted to work on a film about relationships between men and women rather than another cops and crims story. He hasn't often been given the opportunity to express the tenderness he possesses. I think that at first I was intimidated, but the more we got to know each other and the more we talked, the more we developed a natural and easy friendship. Harvey is a shy and attentive man, very different from the brutal and macho image of his films! He thought I was funny and I respected him, so all was well! I liked Holly Hunter very much as an actor, but I didn't think of her straightaway, maybe because, like everyone else, I had a stereotypical view of the romantic heroine, tall with exquisite manners. Then I thought the film might have a stronger impact by working against the stereotype. And I was lucky enough to get Holly Hunter, because even she has her own beauty; it is not what she puts forward, she has very strong feelings, relationships with others and not only an appearance. She is also capable of great concentration and is very vulnerable. She's a small woman who exudes a lot of power.

Does Holly Hunter actually play the piano?

She could play very well before the film. She has a grand piano in her home. Of course that was an asset. I think a lot of people were sceptical about my choice without daring to say so. I think Holly is wonderful in the film, acting with great restraint. In addition, we communicated very easily, we really were on the same wavelength. She's very practical like me, and neither of us has any great theories. I was lucky to have such a passionate collaborator because she really did have her work cut out: she had to learn sign language and play the piano, all that's not easy.

You chose Sam Neill for the third main character.

I chose him very early on. He's a very handsome man and he liked the idea of the 'bad guy' looking like a 'mummy's boy', that he didn't have the ruddy face and physical ugliness usually given to such characters.

Ada (Holly Hunter) and Baines (Harvey Keitel), *The Piano*

This meant that the audience was able to discover the character's real qualities and to see him as a human being. Stewart is a man who transforms himself and that's difficult to express. Sam Neill has succeeded in showing this even though he doesn't have the same experience of the acting milieu as Harvey Keitel, who went to the Method Actors Studio, or Holly Hunter. Sam works at home and comes back with the choices he's made. I like to protect my actors, I respect their personal approach to performance. I also think they were very seduced by the natural environment. After the filming, Holly explored the bush with her sister for two weeks. I think Holly and Harvey are the sort of people who can work anywhere in the world without missing Hollywood. They don't behave like stars. Anyway, it would be impossible in New Zealand where people would immediately have tended to put them down. They're not used to dealing with stars.

Did the editing take a long time?

The usual amount of time for that type of film. I didn't film many takes even if I used more stock than for my previous two films. We didn't really have that much money: the budget was US$6.5 million. The film looks as if it cost more than it did, that's because the US dollar is worth three times the New Zealand dollar.

The original title is The Piano.

I wanted *The Piano Lesson*, but it was already the title of an American play and we weren't able to obtain the rights. With Ciby 2000 we agreed on *The Piano*, but in Europe—where the same copyright issue doesn't apply—the film will be called *The Piano Lesson*. I'd also thought of *The Sleep of Reason*, but it wasn't very commercial!

What you've said about the Stewart character could be said about the film as a whole: unpredictable in its unfolding and with ever-changing perspectives on the various people and their actions. For instance, when Ada caresses Stewart.

She is thinking of Baines while she is doing so, but more particularly of her own eroticism. She has become eroticised by the whole process of the piano lessons. It reveals her sexuality even if she thinks she's resisting it. It is the surest way to seduce someone when that person is not conscious of a deeper motivation. Ada of course has a sexuality, but it has been repressed at some stage. She doesn't realise she has feelings for him; he is a sexual object in her eyes. She doesn't quite realise what she is doing, she almost behaves like a sleepwalker. That scene is very ambiguous and I discussed it with Holly and Sam. I had written it, but I still needed to completely understand it with them! When Ada caresses Stewart, she is looking for herself. Usually it is the reverse: women often feel they are being treated as objects by men. Maybe it's a cliché, but often men want a sexual experience without being emotionally involved. The film wants to show that men too are vulnerable, sexually vulnerable as well. They need to be loved and to feel protected.

Ada's past is quite mysterious.

My attitude in this regard is very simple. My characters meet at a certain time of their lives, just as we don't know the past of other people and it's part of the mystery of being with people. We talk to people and their past is within them, before us, even if we don't know about it. I have a past, but I am not sure I understand it to be able to say why it has made me who I am. We do know certain things about Ada: she stopped speaking when she was ten years old and doesn't know why. I remember reading that Emily Brontë didn't like being with people, that she rather despised society and didn't like speaking in public. Charlotte used to take her out with her friends and she wouldn't say a word. Ada's problem is that she's too obstinate, she's so romantic that she's capable of dying for her ideals. In order to live, one has to compromise one's ideals. Young people often have very strong convictions. Strangely, to grow up is to adapt and I don't think that's a bad thing. Pure ideas don't take into account the complexity of life. Ada, in the end, can live her ideals in her imagination, she can fantasise about herself and be happy in real life. She's able to separate art from life. Up until then she had a poetic idea of herself—she was in love with her romantic ideals, which in the end dominated her, so much so she couldn't live.

Do you discover much of yourself in your films: Kay, Sweetie's sister, Janet Frame and Ada who correspond to different stages of life?

I don't think that I project my fantasies on my characters, and in any case I don't know who I am. We are everything we do. On the other hand, I am very fond of these women even if none represents me, although Kay is closer to how I used to be. What is part of me is a certain sense of the absolute and the desire to control things. I've always had trouble under-standing the separation between myself and the world; the mystery of sexuality, of hatred, of passions, has always been a problem.

Sweetie *was dedicated to your sister,* The Piano *to Edith.*

That's my mother. That makes sense, doesn't it?

At the end of the film, you inscribed the words 'kia ora' *on the screen.*

That means thank you in Maori. It is meant for the actors and the crew. It is also a way of taking leave.

You used the same cinematographer, Stuart Dryburgh, as for An Angel at My Table.

In the previous film, we were committed to a certain restraint in the cinematography because it was not a 'big' story. We didn't want to stifle Janet Frame's autobiographical story. For *The Piano*, it was great to have a more flamboyant and cinematic style.

Some of the shots have a fairytale feel, a strangeness, such as when Flora runs in the hills.

I liked those hills and I thought of having the little girl's silhouette in them. I suppose it was a way of controlling the landscape because sometimes it dominated me so that I wasn't sure how to interpret it in a personal way. But these hills were so beautiful that I wanted them in the film. Anna Paquin on the crest of the hills looked so tiny that she almost disappeared. We had to replace her with someone bigger so that she could be seen. Anna was furious and felt humiliated!

In your films, death is linked to nature. Sweetie dies jumping from the tree. In An Angel at My Table, *two sisters die drowning. Here, Ada nearly perishes at sea.*

I have never thought about it, but I'll try to answer! Maybe it is always the same story: we think we can control nature, yet it's stronger than us. To survive, we must make peace with nature, be humble and accept that part of nature in each of us. Human will can become disproportionate in its relationship to the world. As a child, one believes one can command the universe, and one must learn this is not so, otherwise a difficult journey lies ahead.

Ada and Flora's relationship is more a friendship than a mother-and-daughter relationship.

Their situation is very specific: neither has a husband nor a father. There's suggestion that Flora's an illegitimate child. Ada doesn't speak and Flora speaks for her, which makes her important for her age. She relates to the world for both of them. They're almost inseparable. They plot together, have a specifically feminine intimacy. When Stewart sees them together, he feels they hold a power which he doesn't really understand in the same way as Ada's relationship to her piano is a mystery to him.

The Piano *in a way is a synthesis of your first two films. It has the strength of* Sweetie *and the narrative flow of* An Angel at My Table.

There's even more story in *The Piano*, not only a story but also an intrigue. I hope one also finds the sense of surprise and poetry that *Sweetie* has. In *An Angel at My Table*, I was faithful to a book I respected. *The Piano*, like *Sweetie*, is more faithful to me or certain aspects of my personality. But *An Angel at My Table* was important not because it corresponded to my idea of cinema, for I knew I was filming for the small screen, but because it gave me confidence on set. I was relaxed and felt able to improvise. I learned to better understand the actors, to leave them more room. I think there are things that I wouldn't have been able to do in *The Piano* had I not had the experience of *An Angel at My Table*.

Do you have other projects?

Two, in fact. The first is the child I shall give birth to in two months' time; that's a big project and I want to enjoy it. Then I have two adaptations in mind: the first is *My Guru and His Disciple* (1980) by Christopher Isherwood for Ciby 2000, and the second, *Portrait of a Lady* (1881) by Henry James for the American company Propaganda.

a voyage of
self-discovery:
interview with
jane campion

michel ciment

*ositif: Two of your films are original scripts whereas the other two, which
were written with Laura Jones, are literary adaptations. Was adapting
Henry James's* Portrait of a Lady *different to adapting Janet Frame's* An Angel
at My Table?

Jane Campion: James's novel is a great work of fiction and a story with
a very complex structure. It also presents a lot of strong characters
whereas Janet Frame's stories really only have one character. *An Angel
at My Table* follows the course of one life; *Portrait of a Lady* carries
philosophical implications, it is the journey of a young woman into
darkness and subterranean regions. There's also a mythical dimension
with an awakening at the end. Adapting James's novel for the screen
was difficult, and at times scary, given the scope of the work.

When did you discover it?

I don't remember exactly when it happened, but it must have been
when I was about twenty and used to devour that type of fiction. I've
wanted to turn it into a film for a long time. I remember mentioning
it to a friend at a time when I used to fantasise about starting a production
company to adapt to the screen classical novels such as James's, or those
of Jane Austen, whose complex stories were a welcome change to the
boring films we used to see then. Evidently, in the past few years, a lot
of people have had the same idea!

*You were dealing with a book over six hundred pages long—how did you decide
what to cut out, such as the first chapters in New England, for instance?*

Of course it was difficult to choose, and at first we even wondered whether it was possible to adapt such a novel. Then I realised upon re-reading it that we were not going to film *Portrait of a Lady*, but only my interpretation of the story of *Portrait of a Lady* together with part of the dialogue. I love James's subtle psychological analyses, his way of weaving his web around his characters, but, obviously, that's not what you can do on film. My weapons were to make the situations physical, to develop sexual elements that were only suggested, to give Isabel Archer (Nicole Kidman) fantasies. Also Laura Jones and I didn't have too much trouble sacrificing the first third of the novel, which is a kind of lengthy prologue with conversations about a possible marriage. We began by dissecting the novel but it got us nowhere. On the other hand, very early on, we thought of the symmetry between the nourishing tree at the beginning under which Robert Goodwood (Viggo Mortensen) asks for Isabel's hand, and the bare tree at the end, in the middle of winter, when everything seems vulnerable and denuded like Isabel herself. So much has happened between the characters and within each one that many people don't realise it's the same tree.

Your last sequence differs from the end of the book; it is more 'open'. James's Henrietta tells Goodwood that she has left to join Osmond, although James doesn't exclude another future for Isabel.

I also believe James doesn't want his reader to actually know which road the heroine will take. I think there are contradictory tensions in the book, which explain the suspenseful ending. On the one hand, there's the fairytale/melodrama quality to the story and, on the other, the weight of reality he brings to bear on the story, since James is a realist, with characters described in a strong, intimate and truthful manner. He tries to fuse these two tendencies in the epilogue of the novel. Personally, I didn't want to conclude and preferred the symmetry of the two trees and Isabel running in slow-motion.

Isn't there also a conflict in you between a taste for romantic stories and a desire to tell stories 'realistically'?

I like to enter into a story like a member of the public. I like to experience without restraint the reality of the drama I am retelling, as that's one of the great pleasures of fiction. And all my efforts go into sharing this impression of reality with my actors, then with the audience. At the same time, I love 'romance'—it's part of my nature as I am very romantic in the way I lead my life. I don't mean that from a sentimental point of view, but in a wider sense: I'm fundamentally an optimist.

Isabel is close to your other heroines. She goes on a journey to discover life.

She has courage and is in search of truth; that's what pushes her forward. Personally, I feel within me, among other things, two main forces guiding me: the excitement of discovering the truth about things and people, whatever that might be, and the desire to be loved. Two such companions are difficult to accommodate. If, for example, one of my films becomes very popular, I start to ask questions about the amount of truth it contains, and wonder whether that truth wasn't too easy to accept!

In Portrait of a Lady, *you didn't take the easy path. For instance, you have avoided the decorative aspects of period reconstruction so often associated with this sort of adaptation. Instead you concentrate on passions.*

It was a very conscious decision. We knew that a period background was necessary because it was in such a milieu that the story unfolded, but the real subject was the intimacy of the relationships between the characters. It's a very demanding narrative and that's what I was more interested in rather than the splendour of Italy. We also needed to show the darkness, and that was only possible in winter: the sombre face of beautiful Italy, which is like the faces of Madame Merle (Barbara Hershey) and Osmond (John Malkovich), whose sunny side Isabel only sees at first. I too have experienced that side of Italy; when I was twenty-one I went to study art in Venice. I spent the winter there, deeply depressed by the cold, the humidity, the confinement. I was also terribly lonely because I didn't know anyone. That was my first real experience of isolation. It helped a lot to understand how Isabel feels, especially as the summer before my time in Venice, I had spent a wonderful summer in Perugia where everyone loved me and the weather was great and I thought I was in Paradise. A few months later, I really felt the fragility of my happiness!

Three times in the film, you avoid a 'realist' approach to the narrative. Right at the beginning, for instance, during the title sequence, with the conversations of young girls in voice off.

I thought I needed to suggest to the audience what might be the romantic aspirations of young girls. I decided very early on that I'd have that introduction, which is also a link to our period, and is like a poem before a young woman's journey. She begins that voyage with a mythical vision of life, and the process of disenchantment will be a very difficult experience. That's when I thought of assembling all those intelligent and vivacious young girls I'd met in Australia during the preparation of the film and to ask them to ad lib about their hopes and experiences in love. Friends joined them, for instance Genevieve Lemon, who played

Sweetie. They turned out to be fascinating conversations—you only hear fragments in the film—but they'd make an astonishing radio program, even if you only used the stories about kissing they exchanged!

There is also a dream sequence in which Isabel makes love to three men. Did you think of introducing other similar dream sequences?

No, not really. The development of the story is so dramatic that I couldn't see how I could interrupt it. I did film another such sequence, but I discarded it during the editing. At that point in the story, I wanted to show that Isabel was a woman with very strong sexual desires, who really does want to be loved and feels frustrated. Although she speaks of very different things, of a career, and so on, deep down, she's looking for passion. A critic of James's novel has written—quite accurately I think—that Isabel is split in two. On the one hand, not having known her father, she's looking for a substitute. On the other, she's fascinated by images of domination and submission. I think her attraction to Osmond took her by surprise and that she trusted him because what she was experiencing seemed so strong. In fact, she likes the idea of not being in charge of her destiny and being able to entrust it to this dominating 'genius'.

In a way, Osmond is a negative mirror of Isabel's spiritual aspirations. She refuses Warburton (Richard E. Grant), who offers her material security, and Goodwood with his physical seductiveness, for Osmond whom she idealises.

She believes she's looking for light whereas she's attracted by the shadows, by a sombre adventure that will engulf her. When Osmond declares his love, it's in a dark place with shafts of light. The decor seems haunted.

The third imaginary sequence is the journey to the Orient, filmed in black and white like an early silent film.

We saw it as a personal mental diary in the form of a home movie. It is very playful, a bit like *Sweetie*. The shots with moving mouths are risky, but I think that it's the type of thing that either works or doesn't, and that one has to take the risk without agonising too much about its meaning afterwards. The sequence also helps us to understand why she falls in love with Osmond, because the audience tends to see him as a bad choice. The problem is that Isabel is an easy victim because she so wants to fall in love. During that journey she convinces herself to make the fatal decision.

When you chose John Malkovich, you knew that, given his sly screen persona, the audience would discover the real nature of the character before Isabel.

But James himself, in his introduction to the character of Osmond, tells us there's no revelation to expect and describes him as he is. I like the idea, because it allows the reader to be in on the secret of the ploy devised by Madame Merle and Osmond to conquer Isabel. Similarly, I wanted the audience to know that Osmond was an evil character. The reader or the viewer feels that the author is revealing all in advance. Hence the total surprise when they learned that Pansy (Valentina Cervi) is Madame Merle and Osmond's daughter.

Did you think initially of casting William Hurt in the role of Osmond?

Yes, but Hurt would have projected a more subtle image of the 'baddy'. He refused my offer because it disturbed him to play an evil character with no redeeming feature. One cannot convince an actor to play a part he doesn't want to assume, and his refusal was my good luck as Malkovich was quite happy to explore the darkest areas of a human being. Also, we can easily identify with Madame Merle and Osmond when, for instance, they criticise people they know. What's also curious about Osmond is that he always tells the truth even if it's in a devious manner.

Madam Merle shows more compassion than in the novel.

For me, she's a great character. And I agree with James when he says that great literary characters are great because they understand their own tragedy. Madame Merle, deep down, loves Isabel and she's repulsed at some point by what she has embarked on to protect her daughter.

Nicole Kidman, with her red hair, reminds one of Kerry Fox who plays the adult Janet Frame in An Angel at My Table.

It was Nicole's idea to have frizzy hair, as her hair was like that when she was young and she didn't like it. She certainly didn't want her character to be a 'beauty', although in real life, that's what she is. Nicole is a very intelligent woman, but she doesn't like to show it, in fact she's very reserved. When Laura Jones, my scriptwriter, Janet Patterson, my costume designer, and I spoke about the character of Isabel, we wondered how we would dress her were she our contemporary. For us, she was the type of young woman who'd wear black tights and men's shoes, who wouldn't dress in a very feminine way and would want to have her ideas taken seriously. There are very beautiful women who don't want to be elegant. Isabel doesn't know who she is and when she goes on a journey in search of truth she has embarked on a voyage of self-discovery. At the end, when she admits to herself that she loves Ralph Touchett (Martin Donovan), she is completely naked, simple, sure

[MONTY MONTGOMERY, PROPAGANDA FILMS]

Isabel (Nicole Kidman), *Portrait of a Lady*

of her emotions and determined to show him her feelings for him. She has found her real self.

You already knew Nicole Kidman before working with her.

We had met several times in Australia, without really being friends. I had thought of her in 1983 for one of my short films, *A Girl's Own Story*, which I made while I was at the Australian Film, Television and Radio School, but she had to sit an exam and wasn't available. Later, I dreamed of bringing her back from Hollywood to play Isabel in a theatrical production of *Portrait of a Lady* that I wanted to produce in Sydney. At the time, I didn't think one could make a popular film out of the novel and I wasn't confident enough to tackle the complexity of the novel and translate it into images. The stage seemed more appropriate. When finally I decided to make the film, I thought of her because she's a woman who feels she can aspire to anything, that she has a right to things, and enjoys a superior intellect. At the same time, she's also humble and can spend her time apologising. In a word, she's quite brilliant. She can be very frank, then regret having offended. I needed such a personality—strong, courageous and intelligent—to interpret

Isabel. She's also able to switch between emotions very quickly. She really is one of the princesses of our generation. Moreover, she supported the project right to the end, she was a 'fan'!

I have the feeling that New Zealanders and Australians are like Americans were at the beginning of the century, less blasé, less superior than they are today, and who set out to discover Europe to gain experience.

Yes, we do have a certain innocence. Our countries are younger than the United States. The States are now very powerful and the relationship is reversed. It's now Europeans who cross the Atlantic to discover the power that exists there. We don't have that power, we lack experience, and our heritage comes from Europe. That also brought me closer to James. I remember that when I first saw Paris and Rome, I really felt I was in 'another place'; I was overwhelmed.

You've foregrounded the melodramatic side of James's art, linking him to [Honoré de] Balzac, whereas one tends to see James as the forerunner of Marcel Proust. Your film offers a magnified, 'theatrical' reality just as do James's novels.

We use that kind of dramatisation to talk about life and people. It's very useful! James understood the public's taste for drama and used these well-known forms to explore the human being. That's what made me think that it could work in the cinema, because it's essentially a beautiful story. I tried to discover the power of intimate relationships, to render them dynamic, cinematic, by filming the confrontations between the characters. I could have been more restrained, and told the whole story in a shot/reverse-shot style with the characters seated in chairs and talking. It might have been interesting for a handful of people, but no doubt not for the majority and maybe not even for me. I really wanted to involve myself violently in this story so that the audience in turn would share my emotions.

You use a lot architecture and the background to express these emotions, such as in the scene with Henrietta (Shelley Duvall) and Isabel in front of the reclining figures at the Victoria and Albert Museum in London, or the scene with Madame Merle and Isabel in front of the statues on the Capitol in Rome, places that were not in the novel.

I like the romantic morbidity of the reclining couples and I thought the setting of that museum, which I love, was appropriate to the conversation between two friends touring London. For the second scene, I chose the Capitol statues because they have always moved me. I don't know why they make such an impression on me. Maybe it's because of their size and because they're broken. There's an echo of Isabel's emotional state. In James's novel, she went to the ruins in the countryside.

Why do you tilt the frame to show the Duomo in Florence and the Colosseum?

In the first case, in order to show the top of the cathedral. In the second, to avoid showing what must not be seen: the cars and other modern details. I don't mind tilting the camera from time to time!

How did you decide on the chromatic texture of the film with your cinematographer, Stuart Dryburgh?

We made two major decisions: to make the interiors in Italy as dark as possible and to have almost over-exposed exteriors in order to obtain those incredible contrasts. It corresponded to the emotional reality of the story, with the opposition between light and shade. We also wanted to avoid the glamour of those intimate scenes, to be as close as possible to the bodies.

You had never worked before with the musician Wojciech Kilar.[1]

At first Michael Nyman was to have written the music. In the end he turned it down, and I think that was for the better because he had a number of reservations about the novel, which he didn't really like. But it did create problems as we had to find another composer rather late in the piece. I knew a student in Sydney who'd been recommended to me and was totally obsessed by film music. He's very intelligent and very sensitive, works in a CD shop and owns an incredible collection of film-tracks. He made me listen to an enormous amount of music for films written by Americans and Europeans until he came to Kilar's composition for [Francis Ford] Coppola's *Bram Stoker's Dracula* (1992), which immediately seduced me. I liked its romanticism without sentimentality, the sense of mystery and depth. We knew nothing about him, but we phoned him in Poland. He didn't want to write music for film any more, but was prepared to reconsider his decision. He came to Australia, liked the film, in which he found a romanticism close to his own, but he still refused to work for us. He felt blocked and, since he was a real artist, there was no way of making him change his mind. A week later, he sent a fax saying that he thought he'd found solutions to various problems we'd discussed together. I went to Poland and I was dazzled by his work and the way he had understood the film.

It's a film in which one really feels the passage of time and how much the central character changes between the first and last image.

Evidently, there is no satisfactory solution for Isabel. The man to whom she is closest, Ralph, is going to die. Her marriage to Osmond is not viable either. For me *Portrait of a Lady* is about the choices one must make in life and that one can give a meaning to one's destiny—however disastrous it may be, as in Isabel's case—with love, honesty and self-discovery. That, for me is the meaning of the voyage Isabel has embarked on. She thought the voyage would be about battling with the elements, an external adventure; in the end, she realises that she has made an inner journey in search of her self.

[PART III]

WHAT PRICE HOLLYWOOD?

from its very beginnings the Australian film industry has had, inevitably, to turn its face towards the mecca of movie-making, Hollywood—and this is true even when facing in the opposite direction. Hollywood, or the American market, is so ingrained in the development of the local industry that the steady flow of Australian film-makers and actors to Los Angeles since the early 1980s at times appears to look like an antipodean pantomime of a Horatio Alger tale.

The film-makers who hitched a wagon train early on are many: Peter Weir, Philip Noyce, Bruce Beresford, Fred Schepisi, Gillian Armstrong, John Duigan, Richard Franklin, Phillippe Mora, Simon Wincer, George Miller. The cinematographers: Don McAlpine, Dean Semler, John Seale, Russell Boyd. Then there are actors: Judy Davis, Bryan Brown, Mel Gibson, Paul Hogan. In the 1990s Hollywood has all the more served as a distant and powerful magnet: Nicole Kidman, Nadia Tass and David Parker, Jocelyn Moorhouse and Paul J. Hogan, Bill Bennett, Russell Crowe, Guy Pearce, Baz Luhrmann, Scott Hicks, and lesser-known directors like Stephen Hopkins and Alex Proyas. The roll-call is selective. Even so, it seems Hollywood has had its arms outstretched, ready to embrace much of our local talent. For in recent years Oscar ceremonies have tended to reflect the romance, having bestowed honours (in nominations if not actual awards) on a string of Australian film-makers, with a few feature films thrown in—*The Piano* in 1993, *The Adventures of Priscilla, Queen of the Desert* in 1994, *Babe* in 1995, *Shine* in 1997.

It's a rosy picture from afar, though an insincere one as well. For one thing pilgrimages to Hollywood, for whatever reason, are nothing new—Hollywood, after all, was established by foreigners. More to the point, success in Hollywood, even for many of its own, is always hard won and always fragile.

We have engaged here three of the early pilgrims: Bruce Beresford, Gillian Armstrong and Richard Franklin. The experiences they relate, often with good humour, are mixed, though they are in accord on at least one point: neither commercial success nor creative integrity is a guarantee of anything in Hollywood. Their writings amply bear witness to a rocky wagon ride, marked by detours, with each step to be taken gingerly and on different terms.

how I failed to make a
green-lit movie

bruce beresford

i t was a rather dispiriting weekend in my Los Angeles apartment. I
had determined to read, or at least read as much as I could bear, the
various scripts that had accumulated over the past few months. This was
a bizarre collection, varying from the merely incompetent and derivative
or plagiarised to the truly dreadful, derivative and plagiarised. The ones
from independent producers were, almost invariably, the best, but equally
invariably had only partial or no finance at all. The studio ones were
fully financed, often with some quite inappropriate star attached, but
were so formulaic that only a director desperate for money, such as
myself, would even contemplate undertaking their production.

Halfway through a totally chaotic feature film version of the old
Have Gun Will Travel television series (1957–63), written by someone
without even an elementary grasp of plot or characterisation, but who
would certainly have been paid a fee of some hundreds of thousands of
dollars, a phone call came from Richard Zanuck to say he was sending
a script over and wanted an immediate answer as the film was 'green-lit',
meaning that the studio (Fox) had accepted the budget (a modest $14
million), and was ready to go ahead.

Zanuck had produced *Driving Miss Daisy* (1989), which won the
1990 Academy Award for Best Picture, although my directing contribution had not warranted even a nomination. Despite the fact that we had
spent almost two years scraping up the very modest $7 million budget,
potential investors declined, on the grounds that 'no one could direct a
film about two old people chatting in a kitchen entertainingly enough
to hold an audience's attention'. I'm not *really* patting myself on the

back—I suppose I did do something right—Alfred Uhry's wonderful screenplay and an amazing cast were major factors in the film's success.

Zanuck, son of the famous Darryl F. Zanuck and probably the only son of any Hollywood legend not to end up alcoholic or as a petrol pump attendant, or both, is a small man, absurdly fit physically due to a daily eleven-kilometre early morning run and workouts on the top floor of his house. He is a tennis player of such legendary competitiveness that I've refused all invitations to play, on the (unstated) basis that what little credibility I have as a typically athletic Australian will collapse. Zanuck is mercifully free of intellectual pretension. He's not much of a reader and has no interest in music or theatre, but will discuss baseball (not with me) for hours. On the other hand, he is a shrewd, perhaps uncanny judge of film scripts, and has something else very rare in Hollywood—excellent taste. He took over Fox studios at the age of twenty-three and produced a string of hits, beginning with *Compulsion* (1959) and including *The Sting* (1973) and *Jaws* (1975). He headed the studio for some years, then set up as an independent producer and made a distinguished series of films in collaboration with David Brown. After that, his new co-producer was a new wife, Lili Fini Zanuck. She and Richard provide endless entertainment for Los Angeles diners with their pastime of having abusive screaming matches in fashionable restaurants.

The script—*Goodbye Saigon*—was, as I expected, wonderful. Adapted from an excellent novel by Nina Vida, it is the story of a Vietnamese family in Los Angeles, attempting to cope with a new lifestyle. The roles were all for Asian actors, except for one excellent part—an American law clerk (a woman) who forms an alliance with a Vietnamese—a charismatic, opportunistic woman in her late thirties in some dubious business ventures. As well as being very moving, the script was unexpectedly amusing, full of fascinating characters and packed with incident. So good, in fact, that I told Zanuck I found it hard to believe any Hollywood studio could possibly be interested. Fox, he assured me once again, loved the script and, subject to my coming on board, had already given the fabled green light.

Everything seemed too good to be true at first. My agent quickly made a deal with the studio, a 'pay or play', meaning that if the film didn't go ahead I was still to receive my full director's fee. I'd had a number of these deals in the past, had films cancelled for various reasons, and never received a single penny. This would not happen, I was assured, with a studio as reputable as Fox.

Unease entered the scene at my first meeting with Laura Ziskin, the Fox executive in charge of the division which was to produce the film. She wore dark glasses, an overcoat (a rare sight in Los Angeles) and stared fixedly at the floor as we discussed the film. Her manner was that

[BRUCE BERESFORD]

Richard Zanuck and Bruce Beresford

of someone who'd recently returned from a coffin fitting. As we walked to the car my first remark to Zanuck was 'they're never going to make this film'. He vigorously countered by insisting that Ziskin may be somewhat dour but had kept repeating 'we're gonna make this movie'. I had become unnecessarily cynical, he said. I countered by telling him that for a man brought up in Hollywood he was unexpectedly and refreshingly naive, with a delightful tendency to assume he was always being told the truth.

I returned to Australia for a few months to finish off my film *Paradise Road* (1997), based on a true story about (mostly) European women prisoners of the Japanese during World War II. This was also partially financed by Fox (a different division from that headed by Laura Ziskin), who were now drowning me in unhelpful and usually contradictory advice, now that editing was in the final stages. One fax arrived, almost as long as the script of the film, with a mountain of suggested cuts. Although I didn't agree with more than one or two of them, the editor and I went ahead and did them all, just out of curiosity about the final result. The film now ran forty-one minutes, two of the major characters (Cate Blanchett's and Frances McDormand's) no longer appeared, and the Japanese appeared to be running a Club Med rather than a tough POW camp.

Back in Los Angeles for previews of *Paradise Road* (one of a respectable length), word filtered through to me that Frances McDormand, who was to play the one European part in *Goodbye Saigon*, had 'no following in Europe' and had to be recast. I countered by pointing out that not only had Fran been offered the role officially, but was a wonderful actress, and was almost certain to win the Academy Award for her role in *Fargo* (1996). This, I was told (filtered method) was highly unlikely and, while I was at it, why didn't I remove her entirely from *Paradise Road*? Further, why hadn't I extended all the close-ups of Glenn Close as requested and removed those of the other actresses in the film?

Who was to replace Fran? After quite a bit of discussion and the proposal of all sorts of unsuitable people, I was told that Andie Mac-Dowell would be acceptable to the studio. The drawback, I could see, was that they were willing to pay her only around one-quarter of her usual fee. I called Andie's agent and arranged a meeting. Andie was charming and straightforward and even more beautiful than she is on film. The fee was absurd, she said, but she'd taken risks before (*Four Weddings and a Funeral*, 1994), and, as she liked the script so much, would accept the derisory offer. I quickly relayed this information to Fox and had a celebratory dinner with Zanuck. Now we could quickly get into pre-production . . .

A week or so later, Andie's agent called to say she'd not yet heard from Fox. A week after that Andie called to ask me what was going on. I called Fox and was told that Andie's agent had asked for 'unacceptable' items in the contract. Once again, the agent assured me that far from asking for the unacceptable she'd yet to have any conversation at all. Somebody was lying. Andie MacDowell slowly faded from the scene.

Meanwhile, with a casting director, I interviewed almost every Asian actor within reach of Los Angeles. Many of them were superb and I proudly took a videotape of some of the scene readings to Fox, convinced that this would sway anyone who was wavering over spending money on a film about Asians. Who could resist the scene where the mother talks about having to abandon her child as there was no more room on the overcrowded fishing boat leaving Saigon harbour? Laura Ziskin and her associates, for a start. 'Not very good,' they commented and asked if we'd seen the Chinese girl who was a star of kung-fu movies and had just been in a film with Richard Gere.

Complaining on the phone to someone in Ziskin's department about the lack of movement (other than the reverse) on the film, I was assured that once the 'partner' was in place all our problems would be solved. I hung up the phone, thought for a moment, then asked Zanuck about the 'partner'. He laughed. There's no 'partner' he said, Fox is financing the film. Why would they need a partner with a budget of only $14 million? I asked him to look at the contract. No partner was mentioned. Unsatisfied, I asked him to call Laura Ziskin, just for reassurance.

Reluctantly, he did so, and was airily told that he must have known Fox wanted a partner. The project, after all, was out of the run of the usual Hollywood movie so it was a good idea to split the risk, and with *Titantic* (1998) running so far over budget they had to be careful and so on.

Even the normally optimistic Zanuck was momentarily depressed by this news. It was different, he said, when he ran the studio. In those days, a green light was a green light; they didn't keep moving the goal posts. Following another morbid meeting in Ziskin's office, Zanuck paused and stared towards the skyscrapers of Century City. That was the old 'back lot', he told me, where they used to shoot all the westerns in the old days. As a boy, when his father ran the studio, he used to go down there selling newspapers for his pocket money. 'That's a long way,' I said, impressed. 'Did you walk?' 'Actually,' he replied, 'I used to go in my Dad's Rolls Royce.' How much, I asked him, did they want this 'partner' to kick in? Six million dollars. Shouldn't be a problem.

Usually, in pre-production on a movie, dozens of people are employed, rushing around making all the arrangements—locations, transport, accommodation, and so on—that will make the actual shoot as smooth as possible. On *Goodbye Saigon*, however, we were not given permission. Without the 'partner' being signed we were told not to employ anyone except a production manager. This man, Gary Daigler (who had worked on *Driving Miss Daisy*), had recently emerged from a spell in hospital after managing a film with an eccentric actress, Ellen Barkin, whose demands had resulted in a mental breakdown (Gary's, not hers). Now recovered, and given to lying in a darkened room with a large blue stone on his chest, Gary was under instructions to cut the budget even further, though he was well aware it was already at a minimum. Under huge pressure from Fox, I could see the hospital room beckoning him once more—$14 million sounds like the GNP of Paraguay, but it goes a surprisingly short distance these days on a movie. On most films, it wouldn't even cover the fee of the lead actor.

Paradise Road opened in Los Angeles. I was hoping that a success with this film would give the dormant *Goodbye Saigon* a boost. Some hope. *Paradise Road* proved to be the critical disaster of my career—so far. Box-office results were correspondingly dismal. I told Zanuck that our chances were now further diminished. Optimistic to the end, he assured me that *Paradise Road* would have no bearing on the new film. He pointed out that Francis Ford Coppola hadn't made a film that returned its investment in twenty years; that Luchino Visconti had bankrupted every company he'd worked with; and that they'd all remember the huge returns on *Driving Miss Daisy* with only a tiny production cost.

Could any of this be true? I know that many directors go from one huge-budget film to another despite a series of financial disasters, but equally, and inexplicably, others find their star waning with one failure. I suspected I was a member of group two.

The search for the 'partners' continued. I had a series of lunches with serious men in expensive suits. They expressed enthusiasm for *Goodbye Saigon*, but nothing seemed to happen. One group told me that Fox had asked for $7 million instead of their initial figure of $6 million. When this was agreed to, they made it $8 million instead of the $7 million. At this point, the partners decided to invest elsewhere.

As I predicted, Fran McDormand won the Academy Award for *Fargo*. Word now came from Fox that it would be a good idea to call her and re-offer her the role in *Goodbye Saigon*. I told them this call would not come from me and that someone of Fran's character would not reconsider the role after being treated so peremptorily and shabbily. Zanuck made the call. Fran refused the role.

In London for a few days for some reason or other, I had an urgent fax from Fox telling me they thought Téa Leoni would be ideal for the part. I'd never heard of her and thought it odd they would not do a deal with Fran McDormand or Andie MacDowell but were prepared to go with a television star. I saw a movie with Téa Leoni and thought she was okay, but considerably too young for *Goodbye Saigon*. When I returned to Los Angeles a few days later and relayed this opinion, everyone seemed to have forgotten about her entirely and I was asked why I kept bringing up her name.

Six months had gone by. We had no 'partners', no leading lady, no Asian actors and no crew. My cameraman, Peter James, after waiting all year for an offer that never materialised reluctantly went off and shot *The Newton Boys* (1997) in Texas. The ship wasn't really sinking as it had never floated.

'Why,' Zanuck asked me, 'would they keep insisting they want to make the film if this isn't the case?' 'Because,' I told him, 'if they actually *say* they don't intend to go ahead they are obliged to pay me my full director's fee and they will do virtually anything to avoid this step.'

Zanuck, bless him, said they couldn't possibly be so unethical. I asked my agent, an old Hollywood hand who once represented Elvis Presley, Claude Rains and Edward G. Robinson, about the pay or play clause. 'If Fox do actually *officially* call off the film,' I asked (not that I regarded this as likely), 'what are my chances of collecting the fee they will then owe me?' 'That depends,' he told me, 'on how much they value the "relationship".' If the 'relationship' is one that they would like to maintain then they would honour the pay or play. If this 'relationship' is of no real importance to them then the payment is highly problematic.

They would always, for example, honour a deal with a big star or a director of undoubted commercial hits, but, as for me, with the disaster of *Paradise Road* in everyone's mind . . . The fact that they legally owe the money is neither here nor there. I could, of course, sue, and would undoubtedly win, but this would take years and would cost more than the fee I was pursuing.

The last gasp on the film was a phone call from Diane Keaton, with whom I'd worked on *Crimes of the Heart* (1986). She loved the script and was willing to do the film for almost nothing. I called Fox and excitedly relayed this information. 'Washed up,' I was told. 'No one wants to go and see Diane Keaton. Finished.' 'What about *First Wives Club* (1997)?' I countered. 'She seems to be pretty popular in that!' 'She had co-stars. They were carrying her,' was the reply. We weren't going to get anywhere with Diane Keaton.

I resigned shortly after that and took another film with a different studio. Fox were quick to point out that my 'pay or play' didn't apply if I quit and that if only I hung on a bit longer *Goodbye Saigon* was bound to begin production.

Why didn't I believe this?

little women:
little by little

gillian armstrong

even though *Little Women* had quite a big budget by Australian
standards, in a lot of ways the pressure on shooting the film was
pretty similar to shooting an Australian feature. It's part of the reality of
film-making in the US: budgets might be larger but the above-the-line
money is what goes to the stars and producers, and studio overheads are
also much higher. Of course I had more back-up money for costumes
and special effects, but it still wasn't luxurious and so our day-to-day
shooting felt pretty much like we were shooting a film in Australia.

Part of my deal for *Little Women* was that I could bring Australian
cinematographer Geoffrey Simpson, editor Nicholas Beauman, and my
first assistant director Mark Turnbull on to the set with me. It's thanks
to these three Australians that the film managed to get as much screen
value as possible. I think the Americans were lucky to have had a key
group of Australians who have been trained in an industry where we
have little but we aim for a lot.

THE STUDIO AND THE PRODUCER

I was offered *Little Women* by the studio Columbia. It was a project
developed by a woman executive, Amy Pascal—Amy Beth Pascal—
named for two of the 'little women'. It was a very personal book for
Amy and her mother, and she developed the film in conjunction with
the producer Denise DiNovi.

There are so many components at the very early stages of a film that
affect the final result. I think the relationship with the producer is one

of those key components. When I was first offered *Little Women* I turned it down, but they chased me for about five months. I was working on another project which then fell through, and still hoping to re-finance *Oscar and Lucinda* (1998). Part of the reason I first turned down *Little Women* was because of its similarities to *My Brilliant Career* (1979); I thought I had already dealt with similar themes. It was Denise DiNovi who managed to talk me into it. She pointed out that *My Brilliant Career* was made fifteen years ago and that there's a whole other generation who has never seen it; even if I was telling a similar story I would be telling it to a new generation. More importantly, though, she pointed out that *Little Women* was much more a story about family, about belonging and about home, whereas *My Brilliant Career* is really about a solo journey or an individual quest, about a young woman finding herself and who is ahead of her time.

I had a very unhappy experience in the US on *Fires Within* (1991). Part of the reason was because you need a sympathetic producer, someone who shares your vision, when doing any big production with an American studio. It's a risk for any director going to work in the US because, really, only a handful of directors have final cut, and only if they have had box-office successes of a couple of hundred million dollars. It's a big risk knowing that in the end your film could be taken away from you, re-cut and totally changed, as had happened on *Fires Within*. Few directors actually have right of final cut and, unless you make a film with a budget of under $7 million, much negotiation goes on with studios to actually get final cut. Younger directors may laugh at this, but one day they too might experience their films being re-shot and totally re-cut, or happy endings added on. This happens all the time.

The director's cut is always a complicated situation and it can depend finally on how much the studio likes you, whether you have a name, and if they want you to hang around to do publicity at the end of it all. Generally the first thing the studio does is bring in another, fresh editor. Sometimes it's give-and-take and a director will actually stay on and agree to re-cut the film as long as the studio editor doesn't touch a particular sequence. Sometimes re-editing can go on for months, especially when scenes are to be re-shot. Sometimes directors hang in there and sometimes they walk. Mostly they hang in because it's so hard to get a break, to get a feature film in America. It's so competitive that many directors feel it's worth having their name on it.

I didn't contractually have final cut on *Little Women*. I had a contract which stipulated that if the studio didn't like my cut I could have two preview-audience marketing tests and if I didn't get good results, or high marks, they could take over the film and re-cut it. Luckily, we didn't have any problems because the studio liked my cut of the film. I think that was due in large part to the producer, and, of course, a good preview-audience test.

When I went across to the US to meet with Columbia, the most important thing was that Denise answered certain criteria. Above all, that we share the same taste and vision. We did, and Denise was a fantastic producer in that she allowed me great freedom and support. If she felt strongly about a decision at all, she suggested her view in a way that was very sympathetic and in the manner of a producer who didn't need to prove she was in a position of power. She would say things like 'This is what I think, but you can decide', which is almost the cleverest way of suggesting something because you never forget what was said. In that way, Denise became the kind of producer a director actually turns to for advice. I was eager to have her opinion on matters, even though ultimately the decisions would be mine. (Someday I would like to run a course for producers from a director's point of view because I think it's the most important training skill needed!)

That she had power and prestige was another reason I thought the film would be worth the risk. Denise had been Tim Burton's associate producer and had produced a number of commercially successful films. Commercial success is what obviously gives you power and prestige, and it was due to the success of *Edward Scissorhands* (1990) and *Batman Returns* (1992) that she had some clout. I decided to make the film because I felt I was in good hands with the producer, who managed to weave the production of *Little Women* through the studio system. There are so many battles during the course of making a film with studios, who are constantly and obviously worried about their investment. If you were running a studio you would probably operate in the same way, making sure a film will be accessible, commercial, and will not offend. Studio films can become a daily battle about the budget, so obviously there's a lot of pressure and it takes a lot to keep your integrity. With *Little Women* we did manage to keep our integrity and to make the film the way we felt it should be made.

I was also happy when I met Amy Pascal because she said the studio didn't want another *The Color Purple* (1985): they wanted *Little Women* to have an edge of reality. That's another important thing when dealing with a studio: a director has to make sure the studio doesn't want to turn the film into something that's not the style of the film you want to make.

WINONA RYDER

Winona Ryder was already part of the package when this film was offered to me. The film had been green-lit, which meant it had its money,

Winona Ryder wanted to star in it, and it had to be out by Christmas 1995. Basically, Amy Pascal quite cleverly talked the studio into investing in *Little Women* by saying she knew Columbia didn't have a Christmas movie and that here was the perfect film. She also knew that Denise DiNovi, who had produced *Edward Scissorhands* and *Heathers* (1989), had a working relationship with Winona. When Denise became involved she knew how much Winona liked the book, so that's how Winona came on board. Then they all got together and discussed directors because Winona has the power to say whom she'd like as director. Winona chose me to direct—I think it shows she has extremely good taste!

After I decided that the producer was okay and that the studio was okay, the final piece in my decision to do the film was whether I thought Winona was right for the part of Jo. In the past I've actually turned down films that have had huge stars attached to them because I hadn't felt they were right for the part. It's finally your movie and if in your heart you feel they are not right you should never do it, no matter how much money is offered. The producers knew when I was meeting with Winona that I was ready to walk away if I didn't feel she was right for the part. Because of Winona's dark, haunting beauty she has often played introverts, yet when I met her I discovered a whole other side that we haven't seen on screen—that she is very bright and alive, passionate, quite funny and intelligent. I thought it would be fun to bring out that side of her. That was what finally inspired me and made me feel I wanted to do the film.

However, it has often been remarked that Winona Ryder's obvious beauty and vivacity worked against the role of the plain sister. I've been asked this all around the world, and I lost it and actually poked my tongue out at the last journalist who queried me about this in England. Winona isn't in the film only for her beauty—in fact, you'll notice in the film that Jo is surrounded by sisters who are more like conventional Victorian beauties. If this were Victorian times and I stood Winona, Trini Alvarado, who plays Meg, Kirsten Dunst and Claire Danes on a stage, Winona would be the last person picked as a traditional Victorian beauty. In real life Louisa Alcott was not plain, she was actually quite a striking woman, yet she was not a conventional beauty for her time, and so one brief to the casting director was to find actors with regard to playing traditional Victorian beauties in order that Jo looked scrawny, different, and altogether unconventional next to her sisters.

I have quite a strong political feel for this issue. Years ago, one reason I agreed to direct *My Brilliant Career* was when I overheard a man say that we would have to cast a woman who was very plain looking. I thought, 'My God, that's a man's point of view about a woman who wants a career.' That was why I decided to do *My Brilliant*

Career and why I poke my tongue out at people about this very issue. For a woman to realise that her exterior appearance is something like her ticket in life, that she is going to be judged by her appearance for the rest of her life, is such an important part of adolescence. Every young adolescent girl stands in front of a mirror and generally criticises her own appearance, and I believe nearly all are forever always insecure about their appearance. I was too when I was young, and the way women are so often portrayed throughout the history of cinema is by putting them into very simple boxes, often by men. So to equate a woman who wants a career as being a plain tomboy is a terrible cliché. It's dreadful to think that just because Jo is a tomboy she doesn't care about how she looks, and because she is a woman not interested in the conventional mores of society does not necessarily mean she has to be ugly.

STORY AND SCRIPT: ADAPTING *LITTLE WOMEN*

Once I committed to *Little Women*, I basically started casting and working on the script with the writer Robin Swicord. Robin had actually worked on the script on-and-off for ten years, but no one was interested in making *Little Women* during that time. She was an old friend of Amy Pascal and both of their careers had started to rise. Robin had that same year sold to Steven Spielberg a screenplay, an adaptation of an F. Scott Fitzgerald story, 'The Curious Case of Benjamin Button' (1922),[1] and she had also done a big deal developing *Matilda*, the Roald Dahl story,[2] for Danny DeVito. Robin was becoming a name and Amy was quite powerful at Columbia.

I had a very short time-span to make the film; in fact it was the shortest time, from start to finish, I've ever had because of the Christmas release in the US. I came on board around the end of October 1994, so I really started work in November and had to cast, find locations, decide which country to shoot in, and work on the screenplay. And because Robin had been attached to this for a very long time and had developed it with Amy, I found it quite hard to get her to change things. It was a very long screenplay and to have a writer who was as good a debater as Robin was, and to try to get changes was of course the last thing I wanted when I had so little time.

Robin had done so much research on the period and on Louisa Alcott that it all seemed to have been included in the screenplay. Generally I felt the script needed to have more humour and more of the book. Jo needed to 'fail' a little to give the story a greater dramatic line; that is, for an audience to care about, and share in, her journey. I think the other film versions had become a burden for our writer. Beth getting the piano, for example, wasn't in the original screenplay. Robin said it was because it was in the other films. But if something is good and it still works, then one would have to forget about the other films, especially if it's a scene in a book that is known and loved by many generations of women.

I had a greater freedom as I hadn't seen the other two or three versions of *Little Women* at all. I felt the best thing would be to go back to the book. Basically we were bringing a classic alive and to me it was almost irrelevant that other films had been made; it would be better to have the story in my head totally free from the other films. That would be the only way I could do my own version. I actually wouldn't have done *Little Women* if the other versions had been fresh in my mind. I was offered *The Secret Garden*—the 1993 version—years ago but I still remembered the wonderful BBC version and said no because I didn't feel I could do another. With *Little Women* we had a certain responsibility to the book and felt that only so much could be changed. We had taken on a book that is loved and treasured and has been passed down from generation to generation. We weren't there to try to be different, but to capture the spirit of the book, particularly in the US, where it is still read and studied in schools.

We were re-writing the script right up to the early part of shooting, all the time going back to the book. I think Robin did a wonderful job, but it would have been nicer if we had four months together to work on the screenplay. Our time together was mixed in with me flying back and forth to New England and Vancouver scouting for locations, and with casting in Los Angeles and New York. I started working with Robin in November, came home for Christmas, then went back and moved to Vancouver to start pre-pre-production at the end of January. She came up on location and did some polishing and re-writes once the actors had started rehearsing. In all we were only together for eight weeks.

An additional pressure on the script was the very tight budget we had for shooting a period film that had two major stars. We literally had eleven weeks and two days on the shooting schedule, so we had to be strict and cut a lot of stuff. We cut a couple of transitional scenes and a couple of exteriors, which were a real pity because I think the first half of the film is a bit claustrophobic.

When I read the book again as an adult I felt a lot of admiration for Louisa Alcott for having written something that was ahead of its time, and also because her observation of her sisters was so honest and real. I did some of my own research, read all I could about Alcott's life, and it was interesting to discover that one of the reasons the book was such a 'hit' when it came out was due to her honesty in writing about adolescence. There wasn't even a term for adolescence at the time—you were either a child or a woman. It's interesting that over the years there's evolved an attitude, probably because of the 1940s film version, that the book is very sentimental. But it's actually fresh and honest and the sisters are portrayed warts and all, with fights and jealousies. I wanted Robin to keep that aspect of the book. In adapting a book like *Little Women* one has to ask why is it still being read. I think it's the fact that so much of *Little Women* was based on Alcott's life—she did have three sisters and one sister did have scarlet fever and then die. It was written very truthfully and I think it was our duty to capture that truth in order for the film to be very real for a contemporary audience.

The most tricky thing for Robin in adapting *Little Women* is that it was actually modelled on John Bunyan's *The Pilgrim's Progress* (1684). Alcott's father suggested she should write a book for girls that is like *Pilgrim's Progress*, so every chapter is a moral journey and has a message, and the narrative line is not very straightforward. The book is very stop–start: there is a little story and then another little story and then another little story. Its episodic quality was one of the trickiest things to deal with, which is why we set up the early scenes detailing Jo's hopes and dreams, to get some sort of through-line for the film.

Another tricky thing had to do with the old, grizzled German professor. Quite a number of articles commented on the casting of Gabriel Byrne as being too young and too sexy. That was one of the major changes in the adaptation and it was done on purpose as a modern feminist statement. It's difficult adapting a story from a particular period for a contemporary audience: there is a lot that is true and a lot that is fantasy, yet you have to create a world the audience is going to believe in. Gabriel is certainly older than Winona, but certainly not as old as our stereotypical image of a professor. The Professor is written in the book as buffoonish and sort of portly, yet at the same time Alcott wrote that once Jo was away from him she pines for him. By the time he appears at the end and proposes to her, she is deeply emotional and in love with him. But my memory of reading the book as a little girl—and most women I talked to felt this way as well—is of feeling disappointed that Jo ends up with the Professor and not Laurie. We felt that perhaps Jo's acceptance of marriage was due to the censorship of the time, because Louisa did not really want to marry Jo off.

I should explain that the novel was originally published as two books. *Little Women*, which appeared in 1868, ends with Beth getting better from scarlet fever for the first time, and the second book is called *Good Wives*—it came out in 1869—in which the girls grow up. For the second book, Alcott must have had huge pressure from her publishers or from, say, her marketing people to have Jo marry when she obviously didn't want to. I've always felt that Alcott did a half-hearted character in the Professor, so we thought that if this man is going to appear at the end, whom Jo is meant to be in love with and the audience is not meant to feel cheated about Laurie, then he should not be portrayed as in the book.

Maybe Alcott couldn't write a real romance, especially in Victorian times, because these books were meant for girls and young women. At the same time one also feels that she did create the modern man, the feminist dream man in some respect, because the Professor is a man who loves Jo for herself; he appreciates and encourages her talents, and he is great with children—in the film you see him around the boarding house playing with Kitty and Minnie. By the end of the film I think the audience feels that they are going to be equals, that their relationship is a partnership: they are going to open the school together and he has no problem with the fact that she even offered him a job. So one of our questions when adapting the story was how we could have all that happening and not also have some feeling of a sexual relationship between the two. Some people have said we put a lot of feminist words in his mouth, but I say the only really conscious changes were to cast an attractive man as the Professor and to give him and Jo some real sexual feelings. We felt Alcott wouldn't mind because she probably couldn't do it at the time. To adapt a book written long ago, one has to try to keep the spirit of the original, but not make an old-fashioned and stuffy film.

CASTING

In the US if you have actors of some status, or who are stars, it's customary—and it would only be political—to actually have them involved in the auditioning process to help them feel secure about the people they are to perform with. To cast somebody whom your star is not happy with can lead to terrible problems on set. At the same time, if you really want a person with whom your star is uncertain you would do everything possible to seduce one into liking the other. But with Winona there were no contractual or creative rights over who was cast, and in no way was I ordered to see particular actors or to have them in the film.

Winona actually has great taste and judgement in casting. She put me on to Christian Bale, whom I had never heard of. She also told me about Claire Danes and about how fantastic Claire was in a television pilot. We got to see the pilot even though we didn't know which sister Claire could play. She also suggested Trini, whom I had worked with on *Mrs Soffel* (1984)—I hadn't even thought about her for the role of

Meg. There were other people we talked about who didn't work out, but even though I might have tested fifty people for each part, it's interesting that the three people Winona recommended were the best and ended up in the film.

The key cast, however, did have to be approved by the studio and they were very worried about Claire as Beth. The studio people came to a reading at the beginning of rehearsals and freaked out when they saw how tall Claire is because Winona is very tiny. Every time Claire was near someone in a shot I had to tell her to bend her knees or to sit down so as not to look too tall. She also has a round and healthy-looking face, which was a worry because we had to make her look believably sick later on.

The one reason I like to talk about the casting of *Little Women* is because people have asked why Beth's death scene feels so truthful. Well, part of the reason is on account of finding someone as wonderful as Claire Danes. I had said to the casting director that what I was looking for in Beth was someone with a sort of shyness or reserve about her. But when Claire read there was an extra quality, and I knew that we really needed her for Beth. She has a unique, other-worldly quality, a slightly mystical feel, like an old soul, and that is what absolutely hit home. I never actually realised that the other-worldly quality was the key to her character until she read.

For the character of Amy we had to decide at what age to cast the actress. The other versions had cast a much older actress, but Robin felt very strongly that young Amy had to be played by a real twelve-year-old. We actually looked at twelve-year-olds and we also looked at young women, say, seventeen-year-olds who were baby-faced and smaller than usual to see if they could play both the younger and older Amy. It was Amy's behaviour in the first half of the film that made us finally decide to split the ages and cast two different people. It was very important that Amy burning her sister's journal be seen as the behaviour of someone young and impulsive. That decision was quite risky: an audience always gets to know a character in the first half of the film and to suddenly have somebody else play her in the second half was something we had to seriously consider. A number of people had said that maybe we would lose half the audience, that it would be a disruptive thing in the middle of the film.

We cast young Amy very, very late. We had heard that an extraordinary little girl, Kirsten Dunst, was shooting in London with Brad Pitt and Tom Cruise on *Interview with the Vampire* (1996), and that they were really thrilled with her. She did a videotape audition for me in London and sent it over. I had another actress whom I quite liked, who could possibly have played Amy, but we decided to wait for Kirsten to finish shooting in London, come up to Vancouver and do a live audition. Kirsten was great and she was the last person cast, and she matched Samantha Mathis, the older Amy, the best.

The hardest part to cast was actually that of Laurie because so many young American actors have absolutely no skill with period dialogue, and physically they are so wrong because it's so fashionable for actors to work out, build muscles and have a suntan. Robin had written dialogue that kept the feel of the period without being totally into the period, but I found that the minute many American actors come across that sort of dialogue they become terribly formal, too British and artificial. It's dialogue that's impossible for anyone to improvise, except in very small ways. Period dialogue just doesn't come naturally, and people are much more likely to slip into words that were not even thought about, so we ended up casting Christian Bale, who is English and brilliant, and we had a dialogue coach who worked with him on his American accent.

For the role of Marmee, we thought it was either going to be Meryl Streep or Susan Sarandon. Actors of their status are generally booked up for years, so out of practicality we knew we'd better cast Marmee pretty quickly. We sent the script to Susan first because we found out that Meryl really wanted a break, and you cannot send it to both of them at once. We heard back from Susan quite quickly, that she was interested and that she loved the book. Actually, her agents did not want her to do the film because she wasn't the star and they didn't want her to play Winona's mother. But I was thrilled when she accepted because it shows she does what she wants to do. She did an interview saying she did *Little Women* for her daughters, that it was lovely they could finally go to see her in something.

The other tricky part was that because Susan has three small children, she wanted to limit her time on set. She had to come across and shoot some of the exterior scenes at Orchard House first, then go back to New York where she lives, and then come back to Vancouver when we were shooting in the studio. Most of her scenes at the studio were often rehearsed on the day and I think that's one reason some of her dialogue is still a bit overwritten, or a bit too long. If we had time in the preparation period to rehearse and then get on to the writer to edit some of it down—rather than doing it on the day—some of Susan's dialogue would have been more successful. Robin was actually re-writing some of Susan's stuff right up to the last minute. Susan saved it because she's such a fantastic actress, but I think a couple of her speeches are more like monologues.

For auditions I generally choose two pieces, something emotional and something funny, so that there's a contrast, two different sides of the same character. I found that I had to be really careful not to kill scenes from the script, especially if you're seeing lots and lots of people read the same scene: when it comes to finally directing the scene it can often go dead for the actors and the director. I did actually get Robin to write a few scenes for auditions, especially for Beth, because she didn't have much to say in the early scenes of the film. I bought a book on casting a couple of years ago and read about Steven Spielberg's attitudes to casting; he has scenes specially written for auditions. What I often do now is use a scene from an early draft, one which is longer so actors have more time to get stuck into it and I can watch them for longer, particularly in this case because it was important to find out if actors could deal with period dialogue.

It's very hard explaining how one actually casts a film, what criteria one has. For me it's often a gut feeling when hearing the words come alive. There are actors of a particular status who won't read—they hate reading because it's not the finished performance and they haven't really found the character yet. I really like to watch actors read, but I have a huge battle with this in the US because so many well-known actors not only do not want to read, they do not want to be put on tape. I think it's extremely important to get an idea of how people come up on screen; it always helps me to gather an impression of the way to go. For all the years I have been in this business, I still feel one cannot judge how an actor is going to work on camera from watching him or her live. Quite often I will meet and have discussions with actors and then beg them to please come for a screen test. Then once I have a small group of four or five that I think are the most likely contenders, I will bring them in to read with each other. This was especially important for *Little Women* because we had to have the feeling of the actors being sisters.

REHEARSALS

The crucial part of rehearsals were the two weeks in Vancouver when we had Winona, Christian Bale, Gabriel Byrne, Kirsten, Florence Paterson, a Canadian actress who plays Hannah, and pretty much everybody else. There are actually three key things you are doing in rehearsals: you are trying to help the actors find their characters, you have a chance to do some blocking of scenes, which allows a director time to go away and think about how to shoot them in advance rather than on the day, and you are also building up a working atmosphere of trust and respect so the actors can then take risks.

The beginning of the rehearsal period is always a terrible time. We all really wish we knew each other and were more relaxed. So, part of the rehearsal process involves getting through that anxiety with the hope of everyone coming together by the time you start shooting. Two weeks isn't really a very long period and so I've found that it's great when actors have to learn a skill together. It gives them extra time to get to know each other without the pressure of working on the film. For *Little Women* I was very lucky because both Christian and Winona had to learn how to skate. They started two months before they came up to Canada which meant they were already old pals by the time we started rehearsals.

In the actual physical rehearsals I try to find some way to break the ice. It could be a theatre game, even just getting a group of actors in a room, giving them a ball and have them toss it at each other while shouting out character names. Many will freeze up and refuse to do it, so it's better if there is something they have to do for the role but has the same effect as a ball game.

I'm going to tell you one of my biggest tips in film-making: dancing is the most fantastic way of bringing actors together. I discovered this on *Starstruck* (1982). Before we started shooting there were a number of actors and extras who learned dances twice a week for two months. In that instance, the group of people in the bar in *Starstruck* were so relaxed they felt they had known each other for a long time. It was fantastic and I really think it helped the film. So on the first morning of rehearsals for *Little Women*, Mark Turnbull (my assistant director) and I, along with our choreographer, set up dance classes with a number of the actors. Winona and Trini had to dance in the film, and we felt it was important for Kirsten's character to know what period dances were like because she's the one who wants to go to the ball. That's how we got the ball rolling on building a group feeling. They also took singing classes together because they had to learn the Christmas carols. It was a great way to start because they really did click together, enjoy each other's company and care about each other, and I think it shows on the screen.

Otherwise, I usually start rehearsals in a casual way with people talking about the characters, the story and what it's about. I think acting is so much about doing. There is a point where people have to get up and actually start working out where they would come into a room and how they would react to another character in the room, and through the actual physical aspect of rehearsing they can begin to behave like the characters. From this point I would then work them through in a more traditional manner, just as if one were rehearsing a play: who the character is and what the character would feel or do in a particular situation.

Part of the rehearsal process is also to gradually introduce the crew so that on the first day of the shoot actors are not suddenly surrounded by strangers. It's one of the reasons I always insist on hair and make-up tests. It's a great way for them to start to meet. Because the first few days are very precious in having the cast and crew get to know each other, I generally invite the focus-puller and the sound recordist to the make-up test. Then once rehearsals start I ask Geoffrey to pop in. He will watch rehearsals from the side and quite often when the actors break for lunch, he and I will talk about what we had seen and what might be the best angles for shooting the scene.

SOME ASPECTS TO SHOOTING *LITTLE WOMEN*

Opening sequence

The opening sequence of *Little Women* isn't the original scripted opening of the film. The film was originally to open with the scene of the girls all dressed up and acting out scenes from Charles Dickens's *The Pickwick Papers* (1836). We were to begin with a big crane shot which revealed Laurie's house and then, still from outside, to see Laurie framed by the window looking up at Orchard House. Cut to Orchard House from Laurie's point of view, watching Jo at the window walking back and forth, and then go inside Orchard House and find all the girls in top hats and costumes, play-acting and talking about Laurie. The writer's idea was to open in a way that was different from the other movies, which I believe opened with Marmee's reading of the letter from father who is away fighting in the Civil War.

At the end of the *Pickwick* scene we were to cut back outside and see Marmee arrive home through the snow, and have the scenes of the family gathered together reading father's letter, singing the Christmas carols and then trotting off to bed. The interesting thing is that I storyboarded and shot the *Pickwick* scene with a lot of coverage to help establish the characters. Even so, we felt there was too much for an audience to take in at that early stage. The girls were a bit disguised in those top hats and there was so much dialogue in the original opening that the audience wasn't going to know who the characters are, and not going to be listening to what they were saying and getting the jokes which passed between one sister and another.

In retrospect, I feel there's perhaps still too much dialogue in the *Pickwick* scene. We decided to transpose that scene and open instead by establishing the family and then showing each of the characters one by one as they go off to bed. I think the beginning of the film is a little clumsy and a bit slow; by having the letter reading followed by the girls singing Christmas carols, the film tends to have too many openings. But the studio insisted that they sing—it was after all their Christmas movie!

And, of course, we could never get rid of it after Geoffrey lit and shot the scene so beautifully with each of the girls kissing Marmee goodnight.

I also felt the film took a long while to get into Jo's character and so we added a voice-over in post-production. The script was not written with a voice-over but it was very important to hear Jo's inner thoughts and then to see Laurie standing at his window looking up. By actually opening in this way, when the *Pickwick* scene finally comes around the audience listens and understands what's going on, and they get the jokes. It was something we picked up on only after we had the first cut of the film.

Scenes in the snow

I was very lucky to get Jan Roelfs as production designer. He designed *The Cook, the Thief, His Wife and Her Lover* (1989) and *Orlando* (1993) with his partner of eight years, Ben Van Os. Jan had recently started working in Los Angeles and, soon after I met with him for *Little Women*, he went to Canada to investigate the possibility of shooting there. Because the story is told over four seasons, we had to decide whether to start the shoot in a cold climate like Toronto, where snow already existed, or to shoot somewhere like Vancouver where the snow had melted and we would have to create it.

Toronto had a dreadful winter that year and Jan had come across another film crew—painters and carpenters—who were trying to build the set of a small town and apparently had to go inside every thirty-five minutes because it was so cold. They realised it was virtually impossible to paint a set in freezing weather. I was thrilled when Jan came back and recommended we not go to Toronto, because I had shot *Mrs Soffel* in real snow and I never wanted to do that again! We decided it was easier to go to a place where we could shoot over the spring and autumn seasons and create our own snow for the film's winter. Of course the difficulty with having to create snow is that camera angles become limited. For example, I could not do 180-degree camera moves, and I had to define exactly in the storyboards the camera angles and the area to shoot so that the art department knew how much ground and trees to cover with pretend snow.

The first time we see Orchard House in the daytime I start with a wide shot of the girls coming out of the house from Laurie's point of view. The audience doesn't realise it's from his point of view until we cut to him watching from over the horse and carriage. He then gets in and starts to ride off. The next shot was planned particularly to capture the joyous spirit of this lovely, warm family of girls and lonely Laurie wishing he was with them. For the first time in the film you see the

Gillian Armstrong with Mark Turnbull (first AD) on set of *Little Women*

whole situation, including where Laurie's house is located. It's obviously also the first moment when Jo and Laurie connect.

That said, all the snow you see when the girls come out of the house was all manufactured and it was the biggest area to cover. I had to shoot sideways to get Laurie's point of view and then the girls' point of view back at him. But I couldn't shoot too much in the direction of Laurie's house, or cover too far or too high otherwise you would have noticed in the background mountains without snow. I had to compose a lot of shots so as to avoid any distant greenery showing up in shots. In the far distance of shots we had snow blankets down, in the middle distance we had foam, which you would never have anybody walk through because foam sticks and would be a dead give-away, and in the foreground, or anywhere our cast had to walk, we put down packed ice. All the snow exteriors around the two houses were shot over a four or five-day period. We did all the spring and autumn scenes first, because once we put down the packed ice, it would eventually melt and turn the place into a total quagmire. Meanwhile our biggest worry was rain because it would have washed away the snow and there'd have been a real mess. We were very lucky with the weather, but it was still four or five days of incredible trepidation.

We made our fake snowballs out of fine biodegradable paper that had only just been used in Europe at the time. That was one of the handy things about having a newly arrived Dutch designer—he was up on the making of snow. Jan also very cleverly created fruit trees with detachable branches, which were all placed in the front garden. These little trees could be moved around in the event of having to achieve particular camera movements, and Jan could put up branches with leaves on them or have the trees with bare branches. For example, when we were shooting that part of the story set during autumn, we sometimes hung orange and brown leaves in the foreground.

Ice-skating sequence

The second biggest area we had to create snow and ice for was the ice-skating sequence. The scene in which Amy burns Jo's book ends with Marmee's fingers combing through Jo's hair, and then the film goes into a few shots the next morning when Jo stomps off and goes skating with Laurie. I regret that at the start of the ice-skating sequence we had to drop a little transition scene in the kitchen the next morning, with Jo angry and Amy asking her to forgive her. Because I couldn't have the transition scene, I was going to cut straight to the ice-skating sequence. But it was too abrupt and we were worried about whether the audience would understand that Jo is still angry when Amy turns up at the pond. I think people needed an emotional bridge at that point, and it was one of those situations where I really do believe this film needed an extra \$300 000. We saved it in the cutting room—luckily there were a few extra landscape shots I did while on our real winter location to add to the sequence.

We had a day and a half to shoot the whole ice-skating sequence, which is very tight, and on the second day we also had to shoot the scene of Beth with the baby at the Hummel's. This was a very tricky sequence because it was the one thing we really didn't quite know how to achieve; indeed, we had made the decision to shoot in Vancouver without ever really knowing how we were going to create ice! We originally hoped to freeze a small valley, but that was too expensive. We did a number of tests and what we finally used was teflon, as in a teflon bread board. But we realised that if we were to have it in big sheets, the teflon would warp with the heat from the lights. What you actually see on screen is a whole series of teflon tiles joined together. Then, as it turned out, the tiles were of different shades of white, and so we were concerned about seeing the joins and had to find a surface to put onto the tiles, but something a person could still skate on. It couldn't be anything like paint because that would take away from the skate-ability. In fact, teflon is not an easy surface to skate on anyway—it blunted the blades and we had to keep sharpening them. The substance we came up with was cornflour rubbed all over the teflon ice and, again, we were very freaked that it might rain and turn the cornflour into glue.

In fact, only very restricted members of the crew were allowed on, and we all had to wear socks that were like surgical booties made out of Chuck's Wipes over our shoes, because if our pretend snow was dirtied or wet in any way we'd be in big trouble.

We basically had to build a whole dance-like floor in a valley and put a hot tub underneath for where Amy falls through the ice. We had a wax plug built over the top which blended in with the teflon ice. I only had two wax plugs, which cost $2000 each, and which meant I could only get two takes of Amy falling in. Also for this sequence we had to put a whole row of pine trees down one side and cover them in snow. Because it was near a national park and they didn't want us to do any damage, we had to bring in and take out our own trees. It caused a huge fuss with the studio; they wanted me to cut the whole sequence because they felt it was costing too much money. They suggested that Amy should just fall into a river, or something like that. But I begged them to agree to the ice-skating sequence because it's a very well-known part of the story and something that could not be changed. It was a concept thing as well: I said that if they wanted to make those sorts of changes then *Little Women* was going to end up looking like a tele-movie rather than a real movie. In the end we came to a compromise and made the skating distance shorter than I originally wanted. We had to do some major cheating with the distance—pad things out—because the actual area we finally created for the pond was not huge.

I did shoot the two takes of Amy falling through the ice, but in the end it was more dramatic not to see her fall in. That is, to hear the scream and the splash and to play the event on Jo's face. I think Nick Beauman, the editor, may have come up with that idea. It is more chilling to cut around and see Amy has disappeared than to actually see her fall in. In the final shot when Amy is pulled out, she couldn't have her skates on because the hot tub was lined in plastic and the skates would have cut the plastic and the water would have leaked out underneath. Instead, I had extra takes of Jo and Laurie lifting her out and carrying her away, and then we cut before her feet were revealed at the end.

I think of shot sizes all the time and try to vary them according to the emotional power a scene is meant to have. The central idea for the ice-skating sequence was to have the camera give a feeling of a graceful, dance-like movement. The first shot was planned with the camera moving slowly and gently out, to then come down to see Jo and Laurie in medium shot and, from their point of view, to see little Amy coming down over the hill. Then the idea was to see Amy putting on her skates, but that she's left behind, that the audience momentarily forget about

Amy and get caught up in the close-ups of Jo and Laurie having fun, spinning and swirling on the ice.

For the most part the camera gives the feeling of a gentle dance, but not that the audience would consciously think that Jo and Laurie are dancing. It moves with them while they are playing and dancing, keeping the camera quite close on Jo and Laurie and only come out wide to set up the distance between them and Amy. And then to actually keep decreasing the distance as Jo and Laurie are coming closer to where Amy falls in. Once they get into the rescue, I keep the camera very close and only came out wide and high at the end as a way of diffusing the drama, as a way of saying that Amy's okay and the scene has ended. That was the theory.

On the music side, originally we started with sound effects, morning sounds, like birds chirping, to give the sense of a new day. Then we thought it would be nice to have the sound of skates cutting through ice and then we went into a great debate about whether we should have music when Jo and Laurie are skating down to rescue Amy. And if so, what type of music? To suddenly have 'adventure' or 'action' type music would have been really inappropriate with the style. When I started working with the composer, Thomas Newman, I explained to him the problem of the time jump—from the burning of the book to the ice-skating scene—which the audience could have found a bit emotionally confusing. The composer actually had a piece which is like a dance, but also sort of abstract, slightly eerie or ethereal. He suggested bringing this piece of music in at the beginning, which continues to play behind Jo and Laurie as they play on the ice. There is a real sense of foreboding, that something terrible is about to happen from the very start of the ice-skating scene—the music creates that. Then because there was so much music in the film we agreed that it would be better not to have any when Amy falls through the ice. All we have at that point is a bass rumble and sound effects: she falls in, we cut to a wide shot where you see nothing and all music stops. It was a very good idea of the composer's.

Beth's death scene

Beth's death is the most powerful scene in this story. *Little Women* is probably the first book one reads as an adolescent that deals with death, and it's something everyone remembers. Even cartoons have referred to it, where characters in a low voice say, 'Shhh, she's reading *Little Women* . . . It's the Beth scene!' We felt it was extremely important to bring it off truthfully and, hopefully, not mawkishly.

I decided that to get the best performance I had to shoot the scene very simply and quickly, not only because the scene is so much about performance but also for the sake of the young performers. A director has to respect actors doing emotional scenes. They can be very hard on actors, and knowing that one can only do two or three takes of a really emotional scene I planned the shots not wanting to tire them out. Claire was only fifteen and I felt it was very important that once the scene got going we should be able to move from Claire's close-up to Winona's as quickly as possible. I did not rehearse this scene. Claire read it once when she did her audition, but never with Winona. It would have been killed off if they had rehearsed it too many times. I also felt we should shoot all the lead-ups to the death scene in order, so that by the time we came to do it, Claire and Winona would know exactly who their characters are and how much the sisters cared about each other. I think this was the best way of bringing the scene alive—the words had to be fresh and spontaneous and honest.

I had given them very simple directions, such as not to worry, not to feel like they had to act, to just listen and react. Both were obviously quite worried about whether the emotion would come out, whether they would be able to cry. Claire had talked to a death counsellor about children dying and, as had Winona, read some books on death. Winona had also talked to some of the cast and crew members who had been present at the death of someone close. She came to me and said their instinct was to get up on the bed with the dead person. That actually wasn't written in the script, but I thought it sounded like a great idea. After we had done a couple of takes it suddenly hit me that she should also just hold or hug the dead Beth, and at that point I wanted the camera to float away.

Now we had a very happy shoot, but if one had to talk about things that can go wrong, the death scene is a good one. Nothing major had gone wrong until then. We had a fantastic lab in Vancouver, but the negative report the next morning said there were dark spots all over it. Nick had already seen the rushes that morning and found the spots, and the producer had to go and check as well because I couldn't believe it and didn't want to listen until absolutely certain. We were lucky the lighting is quite dark in that scene—we managed to save Winona's close-up, but had to re-shoot Claire's, and we couldn't save the wide shots at the end when Winona gets up on the bed and the camera tracks back. It was the most dramatic moment of Winona's performance, coming back from the window, finding her sister is dead and then getting on the bed. We had to re-shoot that part because we could see dark spots all over the bed-spread when the camera goes high and wide. It was the worst thing possible you can imagine happening; it was hard enough doing the scene in the first place. They got it right and it was a great relief the first time, everyone was very happy about it, but then to come back and tell them they had do the scene again was hideous! I literally had two actors who were so devastated that they didn't sleep the night before and hardly talked to me on set the next day.

I played music on the second day to help Winona cry—music from *Schindler's List* (1993), which can make me cry at the drop of a hat—and only turned the music down as she walked towards her sister. At one point Winona wanted to have false tears in her eyes because she was worried she wouldn't be able to cry. I actually don't care if someone puts false tears in, but for her sake I just pulled her aside and said no because I knew she could do it and I didn't want her to give up that soon. I think half the battle is won by believing in people. I gave the same sort of directions to Claire and then we did two more takes and they were both fantastic.

The only positive thing about having to re-shoot was that overnight I thought it would be appropriate if Beth made a gesture and said something to Jo. It's a scene about dying and saying, 'I'm all right but you're the one who is being left behind.' Here is Jo crying and it was always known that Beth was the one who always cared for and listened to Jo. So on the second go I had Beth touch Jo's hair and say, 'My Jo'. It just hit me that it was wrong not to have Beth say something of comfort to her sister who was distraught. That was the one good thing about having the chance to shoot the scene again.

From the camera floating gently away there is quite a savage cut to the close-up of red rose petals being ripped from their stem and falling onto a polished wooden surface. The audience is meant to think that this surface is a coffin, until it's suddenly revealed to be Beth's piano. I wanted a sense of agony to fill the screen, that's why the camera is so close to the rose petals. Then I wanted to go straight into scattering rose petals on the bed and on the dolls, but on the day Florence Paterson— who plays Hannah—did the scene, her face was so intense and emotional that I decided to do a shot going up to her face to insert right after seeing petals being ripped. Now this sequence was always going to end with one take of the camera moving in on the dolls, but on the day I suggested that Florence touch one of the dolls as a parting gesture. On the first take she just stroked the side of a doll's face, which didn't work, it seemed artificial. I then suggested she touch the doll some-where else, and in a moment of inspiration she squeezed the doll's hand. The timing worked out perfectly: as the camera moved in on the doll, her hand caught Geoffrey's side light and it's an absolutely beautiful improvised moment of Hannah's old wrinkled hand against the little doll's hand—and her hand trembles a little as she releases the doll. It was magic.

gillian armstrong

AND LIFE GOES ON

In conclusion I have to say that *Little Women* is a film I was personally affected by when watching it, but I don't think my approach to the film was in any way consciously different to that of my other films. With every film one hopes to learn and improve as a director, and I feel I am still doing that. The composer, Thomas Newman, composed the main theme for the character of Jo to reflect her journey. It's a piece with a 'And life goes on' feel to it. Whatever the price, I think that's what really pays off in the long run.

pistols at dawn: the 'art' of film vs the 'science' of previewing

richard franklin

my reaction to the news that the marketing 'experts' have moved in on our industry may appear to be one taken wearing only my director's cap. But I wish to say at the outset that my comments about 'power politics' relate entirely to my experiences with the Hollywood infrastructure. Having also worked as a producer, my concern, on behalf of all who are creatively involved in our industry (dare I say 'artform'), is that it shouldn't happen here.

There is a saying in Hollywood that 'Every dog has to piss on the tree to make it its own'. In 1986, I was there watching my picture *Link* get 'whittled down' by a succession of owner–distributors[1]—each new one chipping a little more away, until my wife was moved to liken the plight of my monkey movie to that of the horse in *Black Beauty*.

I then had a call from the Academy of Motion Picture Arts and Sciences asking if I would assist in the cataloguing of the private film collection of my one-time mentor, Sir Alfred Hitchcock. I agreed, with an ulterior motive. I had been searching for some years for the only missing Hitchcock set piece of which I'm aware—the original ending to *Topaz* (1969)—in which the hero and villain duel with pistols at dawn in a Paris soccer stadium.

Topaz is generally dismissed as a failed work, but had particular interest for me as it was the picture on which I watched Hitchcock at work. I was aware of his exhaustive research, which had established that clandestine duels still took place in Paris. He had gone to enormous trouble to show the exact protocol of the ancient ritual (they don't take ten paces then fire) and spent more time on this sequence than any other

[RICHARD FRANKLIN]

Richard Franklin with Terence Stamp on set of *Link*

in the picture, re-shooting portions of it on three separate occasions. Imagine, therefore, my disappointment when the film arrived in Australia minus the scene which should have been (and is) the best thing in the movie.

I made enquiries and discovered that although Hitchcock hated previews and normally took the view the audience could accept the picture (or not) the way he wanted it, he agreed to preview *Topaz* in San Francisco. In spite of all his efforts, there was apparently some scattered laughter during the duel scene and a few people commented they thought duelling in the present day 'silly'. In this case, truth was stranger than fiction, but, as is always the case with previews, the negative voice of a few spoiled things for the many.

It might have been possible, for example, to stem laughter by preparing the audience through advance publicity. Even if Hitchcock had not done his usual pre-release monologue, he was already at work on a print ad which featured the duel as the centrepiece. And an audience going to a Hitchcock picture expecting to see a pistol duel would almost certainly have behaved differently from the unprepared San Francisco audience.

But back at the studio, when Hitchcock was asked what to do about the laughter, he simply ordered the entire scene removed. Such pique might sound extraordinary, but presenting one's 'baby' to the world can be a touchy thing. (John Ford once removed the entire fight from the end of *The Quiet Man* (1952) because Herbert Yates said it was 'a little long'.) At seventy, Hitchcock had gone through the frustration of two unrealised personal projects ('Maryrose' and the original *Frenzy*), had accepted *Topaz* as an assignment and laboured to elevate it with his own original climactic set piece (I believe that duel was his *raison d'être* for doing the picture).

There was laughter at a single screening (someone may have farted) and the man who had once tricked his producer into letting him make the first European talkie found himself without the energy to defend his work. A freeze frame was inserted to suggest the villain had suicided, and the rest is history. But it might not have been . . .

After the television version was prepared in 1972, Universal's editorial department ordered all additional material (trims and out-takes) destroyed, and even the negative of the duel scene was 'junked'. The scene was gone forever, until a can of Technicolor IB release print, which Hitchcock had secreted in his garage, was opened at the Academy in 1986. And both endings are now available on the MCA laser disc of the picture.

I was moved by Peter Bogdanovich's book *This is Orson Welles*[2] to buy the Voyager Criterion CAV laser disc of *The Magnificent Ambersons* (1942), which, with Robert Carringer's audio essay, an entire side of Welles's uncut screenplay, the complete storyboards and the original Mercury Radio version of *Ambersons* is film scholarship of the highest order.

For those who don't know, one of the greatest tragedies in the brief history of our art occurred in Pomona, California, on 17 March 1942, when Orson Welles's second film, *The Magnificent Ambersons*, was previewed. His first, *Citizen Kane* (1941), is widely regarded as the greatest ever made, but Welles himself believed *Ambersons* was a better picture.

Before leaving for South America,[3] Welles had finished a director's cut of 132 minutes. Although he described the picture as 'epic', he planned further cuts (*Kane*'s length is 119 minutes) and left on the understanding that his editor, Robert Wise, would follow with a print of the film. But in his absence, the studio immediately screened his cut, removed two scenes and set up a preview.

It went poorly. There were walkouts and derisive laughter and, of 125 comment cards collected, seventy-two were negative. The fact that fifty-three positive cards included comments like 'masterpiece', 'best picture I have ever seen' (while the negatives included gems like 'people like to laff', and 'as bad if not worse than *Citizen Kane*') did not deter the studio from cutting a further seventeen minutes before organising a second preview two nights later. At this second screening, only eighteen of eighty-five cards collected were negative, but the executives were in panic, and so ordered the picture completely re-cut 'with a lawn mover' (to quote Welles). A further thirty or so minutes were removed and Robert Wise made his directing debut in Welles's absence,[4] shooting, among other things, a new (happy) ending.

Rival studio head David O. Selznick suggested to RKO that Welles's version should be copied and deposited at the Museum of Modern Art but, far from heeding the suggestion, the new head of RKO, presumably eager to 'sweep clean' (and cover his tracks), ordered some fifty minutes of Welles's footage immediately 'junked'. *Ambersons* was released at its present eighty-eight minutes on the second half of a double bill with a Lupe Velez comedy entitled *Mexican Spitfire Sees a Ghost* (Leslie Goodwins, 1942), and by the time Welles returned from South America, his reputation for profligacy was well and truly entrenched (the RKO publicity departments having been ordered to spread anti-Welles propaganda in his absence). He was unable to get a directing job again for four years.

What remains of *Ambersons* certainly suggests that it (alone among Welles's films) was technically equal to *Kane*. I personally prefer the understatement evident from the first shot to *Kane*'s showy deconstructionism. The literally 'magnificent' three-storey set for the Amberson mansion makes the second-hand Xanadu sets pale in comparison,[5] and Stanley Cortez's rich imagery makes Greg Toland's much-lauded deep-focus work look stark and almost functional by comparison.

I'll admit it's hard to believe that the soap opera-like story of the 'comeuppance' of the highly unlikeable George Amberson Minafer (Tim Holt) could ever have had the complexity of *Kane*'s examination of America and its failed dream. But the novel was a Pulitzer Prize winner and Welles argued that what remains is only the prologue to a dark study of the decline of middle America, with the coming of the machine age (particularly the automobile).

Welles had said he had paralleled the fall of the house of Amberson with a series of documentary sequences showing the changes in the town and it's possible these alone might have had an enormous effect. Consider, for example, how *Kane*'s sociological perspective would be diminished with the simple excision of the 'News on the March' sequence.

All but a fragment of one of these scenes and fifty minutes of what may well have at least been in 'the top ten of all time'[6] are gone—seen by a handful of executives, a few technicians, and condemned forever by eighty-nine out of 210 members of the preview process on two nights in 1942.

One can hope a stash of negatives or decayed workprint may one day emerge from a vault or garage as with *Topaz*, but since Welles himself tried for many years to find the missing material, it seems unlikely *Ambersons* will ever be restored to magnificence or otherwise. And the tragedy of a loss which might have changed the history of the cinema, and of the director who got his 'comeuppance' by being run down by a model train,[7] can never be righted.

This brings me to my own experiences of the preview process and market research as I have experienced them in Hollywood.

Previews are of two basic types: paid and unpaid. Unpaid previews are either by invitation, or the picture is run along with another (two for the price of one). In the latter case, an audience who has paid to see one movie is then asked to view and assess another, which is unfinished and may suffer by comparison[8]—especially since few people are now used to sitting through double bills.

But if the audience is invited, then one must question who is invited, and for what purpose? I am not against previews *per se*. I personally had considerable success in my pre-preview days in Australia, running my own. As a part-time lecturer, I had access to students of film and related disciplines who were of the movie-going age, but considerably more articulate (and educated in the process) than the 'person on the street'. In addition to being able to ask them to fill out forms of greater length than those used by market researchers, I was able to get up in front of the group and field questions and criticisms, using the old teacher's trick of throwing questions back on the class, so I could instantly see what others thought, and assess the breadth (or otherwise) of the problem.[9]

Another method I have used (I daresay most film-makers have) is to show the unfinished picture to friends, acquaintances, business colleagues and, most importantly, a broad demarcation of friends of all of the above. In this way, the feedback has a degree of objectivity, but is also able to be followed up with a fair knowledge of the personality and tastes of the person making the comment.

In spite of his dislike of formal previews, Hitchcock always used this method and had a trusted band of constructive critics he took from film to film. Buffs will be amazed to know that he screened *Vertigo* (1958) to this group MINUS the contentious letter–writing scene[10] which let the cat out of the bag prior to the twist ending.

Professional preview organisers, on the other hand, usually try to get a so-called 'representative cross-section' of total strangers, in order to avoid pre-judging the type of audience they think the picture will appeal to. Combing the shopping malls, multiplexes and their previous audiences, they assemble the most disparate group imaginable. Not only are some people who would never have come in the first place (and may even actively dislike the type of picture they're being shown) asked to participate, but the response of ALL the minorities[11] is judged by a sample which should never be committed to statistics (for example, 'all the one-legged jockeys felt . . .').

Advertised 'sneak' previews, for which admission is charged, are thought to be better as they at least eliminate the influence of those who would never have come in the first place. However, they are considerably more costly as they require advertising. This necessitates the evolution of at least a facsimile of the advertising campaign, which opens another whole can of worms, since inevitably one is told that no one-legged jockeys turned up. Then an argument ensues about whether the problem was the picture or the ad.[12]

I'm no statistician but, with previews, I believe it is necessary to try to minimise the advertising variable. However, from experience, movie advertising is a law unto itself and one finds oneself debating the even bigger question of whether advertising should reflect the form and content of the 'product', or whether all that matters is whether or not it 'works'. This would be fine except that the effect of 'dishonest' preview advertising is that you can get an *entire audience* of the people you wanted to avoid—those who would never have come to the picture in the first place.[13]

Further, no one can provoke hostility by asking an audience to pay for something which may genuinely still be unfinished AND for the privilege of filling out forms. And those who are motivated by temporary advertising to join the élite group who will be the first to see a movie may not be in any way representative of the picture's eventual audience.[14]

But whether the preview is invited, advertised, paid or unpaid, it is obvious that people respond differently when invited to be critical of a work which is represented as being 'in progress'—especially when it is so new they do not have the benefit of advance criticism or word of mouth.[15]

'Everyone is a critic' (or, if you prefer, 'everyone knows his/her job AND how to make movies'). But the idea of inviting people who do not understand the movie-making process to give their opinion of how a picture might be changed is like asking them off the street to try a little amateur brain surgery.

This is the first major problem I see in the preview process as practised by the 'experts'—BEGGING THE QUESTION.

In the type of preview I used to run, there were two types of audience member: the good ones came with an open mind, the bad ones with a clipboard, flashlight and supply of pens. (On one occasion I removed same from an associate, asking if, on his first exposure to the picture, he wouldn't mind watching the screen.)

But at organised previews, audiences are told ahead of time that we want input. On one occasion, I had to threaten to leave[16] if a pre-title disclaimer was not removed from the head of the picture which said something like:

> We are not sure whether or not the picture is finished, and we want YOUR suggestions for ways in which it could be improved.

This half-assed approach is my second complaint: it pre-supposes (a) the creative process is entirely one of bumbling trial and error; (b) the only possible outcome of the preview is to change the picture; and (c) that the only worthwhile *feedback* is NEGATIVE.

People are already insecure enough about their opinions. While derision may be cause for concern, nervous laughter seems to me a pretty natural reaction to the process; at the other extreme, the first preview of the Marx brothers' *Night at the Opera* (Sam Wood, 1935) got none.[17] It is a source of continued wonderment to me that even friends trying to offer a compliment still feel compelled to the obligatory, 'The only thing I didn't like was . . .', as if I'll think they haven't thought about it otherwise.

In the 'experts' lexicon of accentuating the negative, the ultimate is the 'walkout'. When Joseph Tura (Jack Benny) ponders wishfully that the man who walked out of his soliloquy in *To Be Or Not To Be* (1942) may have been dying, I cannot help but think that Ernst Lubitsch was referring to previews. 'Walkouts' are the worst and, since the process deals only in negatives, I have found that I must personally count the 'walkbacks' in order to diminish this most damning of statistics. Most executives are still of the pre-television generation and thus unaware of the movement in modern theatres, where people behave as if they're in their own living rooms.

Worst of all are those who wait till the movie starts to decide to buy popcorn, need a drink to counteract the salt, then cannot make it through to the finale because of poor bladder control. I've followed them into the lobby and even made conversation at adjacent urinals in order to counter the fact that their anonymous silent action is given more credence than Pauline Kael (indeed, real critics are actively despised by executives and distributors), but this sort of thoughtless behaviour is allowed to have real impact on the creative process.

Next come the statistics. Audience members are asked to identify their gender, age group, and so on, then to rate the picture and the various performances by checking boxes ranging from EXCELLENT to POOR. Number values are assigned to each, converted to percentages and compared (arbitrarily) to every other movie ever tested.

To be ready to respond to the 'statisticians', who sit in the lobby whipping through the cards like tellers counting money, then holding a finger aloft to reduce a year's work to a 'fifty-three', or decimate an actor's entire career with a 'twenty-two', you flip feverishly through the discards and work out that a high percentage rated your picture 'good to very good'. But for some inexplicable reason, the 'experts' say, 'We don't count good—and only X per cent rated it excellent'. So why do they bother to put 'good' on the form if it's considered meaningless in a world of advertising hype? Might an audience asked to rate a film about Mary McKillop or Mother Teresa not use the word 'good' out of preference to the adjective in the title of *Bill & Ted's Excellent Adventure* (Stephen Herek, 1989)?

This is as far as it goes on the night, but as you head for your car or Lear jet,[18] you watch the paranoia set in among the 'suits'—the distributors and executives who have their money and/or jobs on the line—and act as if you don't.

A day or so later, the 'experts' have produced a bound document, and everyone is on tenterhooks waiting for their crystal-ball predictions. All the statistics have been analysed and they start talking about the 'skew' away from one-legged jockeys, or the fact that the one octogenarian in the audience had his pencil break and the butterfly effect this may have in Poughkeepsie.

Most of the card is multiple choice, easily converted to statistical though it should be observed that objective answers are only as good as the alternatives given. On *F/X 2* (1991), despite my protests, they were given the choice of two alternatives: 'TOO VIOLENT' or 'GOOD AND VIOLENT'—a comment on the American psyche perhaps—yet no reference was made to what I felt was the picture's major strength, its humour.

But the card ends with a half-page that cannot be interpreted statistically as the audience is asked to list the scenes they like and dislike, usually prefaced with leading questions about 'pace' and 'boredom'. Using phone follow-ups—whereby people who answer ads for part-time marketing work (and have generally not even seen the picture) call the more outspoken audience members and discuss ways in which the picture might be changed (the blind leading the blind)—the problem areas are supposedly identified. But as with the walkouts, one 'don't like' outweighs three 'likes', so virtually *every scene which stands out is under threat*.

Last, there are four or five lines headed 'comments'. Although film-makers say they take no notice of critics, I have personally read every card from every preview I've ever had. But I've never known distributors or executives to go beyond the 'expert' analysis and the comments appear to be merely the token that such things become on multiple-choice forms—there to fill out the last page, read only by the director, editor and occasionally the producer. The 'suits' do no more than glance at them, before giving the cards as a parting gift to the director. Which is how the positive ones (such as the *Ambersons*) get overlooked, because, like the 'squeaky wheel', the negative expletives are the only ones that get noticed.

I have deliberately started using the term 'suit' (as used in Hollywood) to point up my third major gripe: the preview has become the battle-front in the power politics of *disenfranchising 'creatives'*.

From time to time, 'superstar' directors are given the right to 'FINAL CUT' because they have the clout (and lawyers) to ask for it. In Hollywood, this has nothing to do with creative ability, but a peculiar fusion of Keynesian economics and the American dream, whereby those who have a picture in last summer's top two or three, or are perceived to be 'hot', are imbued with the box-office equivalent of Midas's touch. (And like all dreams, someone eventually wakes up.)

Orson Welles must be one of a very few who had it on his first picture (on the strength of his radio version of *War of the Worlds*) but lost it (with a vengeance) on his second. Beyond this, my information is largely anecdotal, simply because NO director is willing to discuss it. Directors' salaries—their 'market value' (which like a house at auction is a function of what people are prepared to pay)—can be known by anyone who wants to hire them. But 'FINAL CUT' is something no one admits to not having (the double negative is deliberately obtuse).

In spite of *The Bridge on the River Kwai* (1957), David Lean couldn't have had it on *Lawrence of Arabia* (1962) or they wouldn't have got all that mileage out of restoring it. In spite of *Alien* (1979), Ridley Scott couldn't have had it on *Blade Runner* (1982). And in spite of *Platoon* (1986), if Oliver Stone had it on *JFK* (1991), there wouldn't be a laser-disc version of his 'Director's Cut'.[19] I would guess Steven Spielberg had it after *Jaws* (1975), lost it after *1941* (1979), regained it with *Raiders of the Lost Ark* (1981), lost it with *The Color Purple* (1985) and almost certainly had it on *Schindler's List* (1993).

But even if a director had it, I wonder who would be willing to assert it, especially in the face of the preview process? Terry Gilliam did, when Universal wanted to change *Brazil* (1985) for the US and ended up making his next picture in Rome.[20] Hitchcock was probably the most consistently successful director in history, not only producing his own pictures, but, by the 1950s, all rights in *Vertigo* and his Paramount pictures reverted to him personally. By the time he made *Topaz*, he was the third-largest stockholder in MCA, Universal's parent company. So if he didn't have clout, I don't know who did.

For most directors, however, the Director's Guild contract allows supervision of a cut then, according to status, to one or more previews.[21] You would assume this would be comparative: that is, if there is the 'director's cut' and (an)other version(s), there would be a number of 'play offs', scores would be compared and the best version would win. But since editing on film is, as already observed, like whittling,[22] and since by definition the director hands over the picture at the preview, the attitude seems to be 'let the director have his screenings, then we'll do what we want'. It is a rare executive who, like Darryl Zanuck, in the face of bad cards and laughter at the first preview of *The Grapes of Wrath* (1940), says: 'Ship it. Don't change a frame'.[23]

There's a Hollywood story (probably apocryphal) of a director who persuades the studio to give him an extra preview away from Hollywood. He's so protective of his version that he carries it to the airport and books an extra seat so he doesn't have to let it out of his sight. They take off and he's momentarily relieved, until the in-flight movie starts and it's his picture—the studio's version.

Making a film is an excruciatingly drawn-out process of day-to-day, shot-to-shot, frame-to-frame minutiae. When I visit someone else's set, I generally can't see the difference between the first and last take. And even on my own set, when the camera's not rolling, I often have to ask my assistant which of the army of technicians we're waiting for. So I can't blame people for likening the process to watching grass grow. And I don't blame the 'suits' for staying away.

But the irony of post-production in Hollywood is that having allowed the director to choose every shading of every line, costume, set dressing, camera angle and move, suddenly, at the previews, the director loses his or her voice—in the name of 'objectivity'. 'You're too close to it,' they say, while studying second-hand accounts of the barely coherent scrawlings of total strangers.

I believe that the fact that the director and the editor have been in the trenches with the picture for so long gives them a better idea of its strengths *and weaknesses*. And far from being too close, the extreme *subjectivity* of 'creatives' should be harnessed.

Billy Wilder cut the opening of *Sunset Boulevard* (1950)[24] and Frank Capra talks at length in his book about cutting the entire first reel of

Lost Horizon (1937) as a consequence of the agony he went through at a preview.[25] He argues that those directly involved in the creative process are acutely sensitive to every ripple and movement in the audience and that previews have to be endured and analysed from one's intimate knowledge of the material.[26] Following his model, I make a point of never screening even rough-cuts alone, since I've found that when I'm anxious to get to the next scene, there's something wrong with the one we're watching. For when a scene's playing well, I want it to go on forever.

I submit the notion of 'objectivity' is a furphy, a weapon used in power politics. Objectivity as opposed to what—passion, sensitivity, knowledge of the material? It could be argued that executives, who also sign on at script level (often *before* the director), are not objective either. But since it is they who pay the market researchers, it's not surprising the objectivity argument is endorsed by 'experts', who are the very soul of it—being about as far away from the making of the picture as you can get.

David Niven once described critics as 'eunuchs in a brothel'—they watch all the time but couldn't for the life of them do it. As noted, critics are reviled by movie executives and distributors, yet market researchers, who are far more destructive (since they deal with the picture before it is finished, and cannot justify their existence by saying that it should be left alone), are treated as if they know the whereabouts of the Holy Grail. Directors are treated like they lost it.

The 'experts' earn their money by demystifying the whole process, turning a complex collaborative artform into a set of numbers (which are then *re-mystified* by them into a secret formula with which they alone know to turn dross into gold). They're objective because they've been standing at the back, going in and out of the screening, readying forms, sharpening pencils, counting walkouts or not even that. And if distance from the creative process is regarded as a good thing, then in the competitive world of market research it's almost an advantage to ignore the picture, since it's then easier to act omniscient (or at least blasé). Distributors and executives do it by taking phone calls all through screenings. Market researchers do it by acting like they've seen it all; like they do this every night of the week; like they were the ones who did the market research on *E.T.: The Extra-Terrestrial* (Steven Spielberg, 1982) and know the secret of what made *Star Wars* (George Lucas, 1977) work.

Well, market research may be okay for pet food and soap powder, but not with something as complex as a motion picture. Here are a few stories the 'experts' don't tell.

In early 1977, Twentieth Century Fox acquired an independent 'pick up' made in England. After research, they asked the producer–director to change its title, because market research held there were two words which were absolute poison at the box office: 'war' and 'star'.

After market research on 'Night Skies', the script for the sequel to Columbia's top-grossing picture of that year, *Close Encounters of the Third Kind* (Steven Spielberg, 1977), the experts recommended the project be put into 'turnaround'.[27] Spielberg took it to Universal and made *E.T.*

Coincidentally, in the same year, Columbia held one of the only successful previews ever, for *The Wiz* (1978). To my knowledge, its scores have only been bettered by one picture since, Richard Brooks's *Wrong Is Right* (1982). In both cases, they were wrong.

Which brings me to my fourth final beef with the process: the assumption that to any perceived problem there's only one solution (always negative)—CUT.

If there really IS a problem, there are several POSITIVE options. Re-writing, re-casting and re-shooting are all expensive (especially on Australian films, where the producer has been encouraged to auction every prop and costume that's not nailed down before post-production even starts). But from my experience, even the possibility of the relatively inexpensive option of post-syncing is generally overlooked as distributors start making proclamations like 'the CORRECT length for this type of picture is . . .' and the executives round on the director and editor with scissors in their eyes.[28]

Imagine arguing that an abridged novel was always better than the 'unabridged', or that a 'condensation' was so superior to the original that the manuscript and all copies should be destroyed. As crazy as it sounds, this is the modern Hollywood credo.

After the preview, the term 'less is more' takes on new and horrifying proportions and P.T. Barnum's maxim 'no one ever went broke by underestimating the American public' rules. The 'experts' start talking about Saturday-morning television and how audiences are either 'smarter' or 'dumber' (according to their argument) than when any relevant picture, of which you quote the running time, was made.

Any suggestion that adding material that has already been removed may solve a problem is seen as further evidence of creative 'indulgence'. And 'cutting' in the hands of a committee is a one-way process—'down'.

As the whittling begins, 'doesn't further the plot' is the catch-cry, and the shadings, nuances and graceful notes start to disappear. And since any writer worth his or her salt usually furthers the plot with at least one plot point per scene, the plot too starts to unravel as the threads of 'indulgence' are pulled at. By now the committee knows the picture so well that phrases like 'we don't need that' and 'the audience can make that jump' start to creep in; pretty soon the horse is becoming a very small camel. To quote Welles on *Ambersons*: 'Using the argument of not central to the plot, what they took out was the plot.'

With the process at its worst, the committee can only finally pull out of its downward spiral when the running time has reached some notional minimum (a running time of under ninety minutes might suggest to the rest of the industry there were problems). Usually by then, even directors who have stayed aboard have totally lost their voice. Many abandon ship, some are seduced to stay with arguments like 'You can either help us, or we'll do it without you',[29] or the lock on the editing room door is changed.[30]

The final absurdity of the process is that once the picture has been 'fixed', even the market researchers (who would otherwise tell you the more times you paid them the better) do not ever suggest trying the end result on an audience.

To sum up, let me illustrate the 'science' of the preview with an analogy: if motion pictures were dishes in a restaurant and 'experts' were sent among the diners with the mandate that any ingredient that anyone was even slightly dubious about would be removed from the kitchen, the only thing left on the menu would be two all-beef patties, special sauce, lettuce, cheese, pickles, onions—on a sesame seed bun.

And I've yet to meet an Australian who liked the pickles.

In the hands of those who are creatively involved in the film-making process, previews (formal or informal) are an extremely useful tool. But market research as a pawn (rook, bishop, knight, queen or king) in a game of power politics can be extraordinarily destructive.

'Creatives' should be given at least an equal voice in the process as their interpretation of the data is uniquely informed.

If the process breaks down, play off the different versions, let mutually acceptable 'audiences' decide. But in case history proves them wrong, keep the elements of the other cut/s for posterity.

[PART IV]

THE EMPIRE STRIKES: THE BRITISH IN AUSTRALIA

for many the lean years of the Australian feature film industry, roughly between the start of World War II and the late 1960s, were not so much a complete wasteland as a culture and industry out on loan, held buoyant to a large extent by documentary and foreign productions. No less important here was British film production, particularly that of the Ealing Studios and then much later, in more reserved manner, films by Alexander Korda, the Rank Organisation, Michael Powell, Tony Richardson and Nicolas Roeg. With the British enjoying a solid film industry in the immediate post-war years, one that began to rival the might of Hollywood, the Ealing films effectively opened Australian gates to an uneven assortment of many other foreign productions and co-productions for well close to three decades.

Well aware of his high regard for British films, and sensitive to blurred memories of just how significant British cinema has been, internationally as well as locally, we invited Martin Scorsese to provide a small introduction to this part of *Second Take*. What better voice than Scorsese's? Not only does he speak with authority on British cinema, as a film-maker actively involved in film preservation his voice is crucial to empowering others to the rediscovery of particular cinemas, as well as to maintaining a dialogue between the past and the present.

In an endeavour to provide a bit of an archeological expedition into the sites of British and Australian hopes—and predicaments—we have also lured to these pages, from film historian Philip Kemp, a revealing micro-history of Ealing's attempt to set up an Australian production base and an interview about the making of *Walkabout* with Nicolas Roeg conducted by Richard Combs. Looking back from today's vantage point, it seems the British spirited forth a development in film production that could only have turned against itself. Yet at a time when the Australian feature film industry was virtually stagnant, British cinema can be seen as the umbilical cord to its revival by the early 1970s.

british movies:
an introduction

martin scorsese

i'd just like to say a few words about British movies and what they've meant to me. British cinema has been very special to me; it certainly has influenced my formative years as well as my work. The first time I can remember British cinema was when my father bought a television set back in 1948. During the late 1940s and early 1950s British movies used to be on television a lot—I watched them repeatedly. And in fact my entire movie experience was formed by British films and, of course, American films, and a few Italian films, neo-realist films that were also shown on television in the late 1940s. But somehow the British films were distinctive to me. From elements as basic as the light—that overcast British sky which made their colour films so unique, and the black-and-white pictures, too—or the calligraphy used in their titles and credits, especially brilliant in the Powell–Pressburger pictures, like *The Red Shoes* (1948)—these, along with the major elements like the writing, the acting and the directing, gave me a whole other view, a whole other way of looking at the world. And later in film school, from Carol Reed to David Lean, and then in the early 1960s and late 1970s, when the British Film Institute started restoring so many of the great films of Michael Powell and Emeric Pressburger. And these films found their way into the films I would later make.

Just a few examples: the use of the voice-over narration—the humour, the understatement expressed through it—found its way into a short film I did at New York University called *It's Not Just You Murray* in 1965, which, in turn, showed up twenty-five years later in *GoodFellas*, which, in turn, showed up again in *The Age of Innocence* (1993) and again in *Casino* (1995). Looking back, I realise that the humour and the understatement are directly inspired by the wonderful voice-over in a beautiful film called *Kind Hearts and Coronets*, made back in the late 1950s by Dennis Price and Robert Hamer. There's a great sequence in *The Life and Death of Colonel Blimp* (1943) by Powell–Pressburger, in which Roger Livesey and Anton Walbrook prepare for a duel. And the whole thing is in the preparation: when they start to fence, the camera backs away, just backs through the skylight and leaves, because it wasn't the duel that was important but the preparation. It was the basis for the entire film, because Roger Livesey and Anton Walbrook become friends after this. And that inspired the scene in *Raging Bull* (1980) when Jake La Motta enters the arena, in a long steadicam shot going into his championship bout.

Later in 1960, in *Saturday Night and Sunday Morning*, when Albert Finney is staring at himself in the mirror he says, 'What am I?'—this directly inspired the pre-credit sequence in *Mean Streets* (1973) where Harvey Keitel wakes up from a nightmare and looks at *himself* in the mirror and wonders the same damned thing. Then there's the anti-hero of *This Sporting Life* (1963) by Lindsay Anderson, who is directly in line with *Raging Bull*. In a broader sense, the film techniques used in *Tom Jones* (1962) were very liberating, and together with the French New Wave, it freed us—the film students of the early 1960s—from traditional narrative structure. This was quite extraordinary at the time. But perhaps the most dramatic impact from British cinema, and one of my primal film experiences, goes back to a film called *The Magic Box* (1951).

The Magic Box was directed by John Boulting and produced by Ronald Neame, whom I had the pleasure of meeting, and who is also a great director of films like *The Horse's Mouth* (1958), *Tunes of Glory* (1960) and so many others. As far as I know, it was the only film ever made about the invention of cinema. It was also the contribution of the British film industry to the 1951 Festival of Britain, which coincided with the fiftieth anniversary of British cinema. And what a time for me to have seen that film! I was ten years old. My father took me to see it at the Academy of Music in New York in 1953. The film told the story of the British inventor, William Friese-Greene, one of the unsung pioneers of the invention of cinema. And it was quite a revelation.

There's a scene in which Friese-Greene, played by Robert Donat, explains the concept of persistence of vision, which is really the concept of motion pictures itself. He explains it to his girlfriend by flipping a series of drawings he's made on the margins of a book: these are all separate, static images, but when they're flipped, they miraculously *move*. So for the first time I understood what motion pictures were. As a ten-year-old, movies had captivated me from my earliest memories: I suddenly realised how you could make them. And I haven't been the same since. But the film also showed the life of Friese-Greene, and watching this man suffer to create an incredible machine that would open the horizons of the human mind and soul left an incredible mark on me.

It's interesting that my father took me to see this film, for in many ways it represented the very beginnings of my vocation. My father wasn't what you would call an educated man: there were no books in the house, and he was a working-class guy, a presser in the garment district. But he loved movies.

I still wonder why he took me to see *The Magic Box*. I had asthma, and my parents would take me to the movies all the time. I liked westerns, and usually he would take me to see a western that was on the bottom half of a double bill: on the top half you had these great movies like *Sunset Boulevard* (1950), *The Bad and the Beautiful* (1952), adult films, so I'd get to see other pictures. But *The Magic Box* . . . we did some research some time ago, and when it played at the Academy of Music it was playing with a film called *Secret Flight* (1946), directed by Peter Ustinov, a British film. So I found it particularly moving that this guy, this garment-district worker, just wanted to see a movie about the beginning of movies. And it makes a point to me about the universality of cinema, that its power can cross boundaries of all kinds and speak to anyone in the world. There was no way, of course, that he could realise the impact the film would have on me.

I think about the film constantly. Ultimately, what did I find so astonishing about it? Was it the beautiful colour? Was it the style? Was it the struggle for the technology to make movies? Was it the human story of Friese-Greene, his family's struggle? Or was it the great actor Robert Donat, whom I had grown to love in repeated viewing on television of this other great British picture, *The Ghost Goes West* (1935)? Maybe it was all of these elements, because all put together, they form the elements of Friese-Greene's obsession. It's an obsession I carry with me to this day. The same wonder I experienced watching the persistence of vision sequence in *The Magic Box* when he flips the pictures, the same wonder I had then—I'm glad to say I still experience it today in the editing room with Thelma [Schoonmaker]—the two of us watch these pictures go by.

It's quite extraordinary. I mean, you take two pieces of film: one piece moves and the other piece moves, and when you cut them together, something else happens. The cut itself creates another kind of movement. It's a movement in the mind's eye. But it's a collective as well as an individual mind, since the audience shares an experience, an emotion, a memory. Ultimately, it's the communion, a moment of the spirit. I've always believed that film represents the answer to an ancient quest of humanity: the desire to share a common memory, a common heritage. That's why it's so universal. The power of what Friese-Greene helped to create is so overwhelming, it's no wonder why he was so driven. He was in awe of his own creation. He had found the key to a different reality, to another level of human experience.

As we enter the second century of motion pictures, British cinema remains a major point of reference for me, from Filippo Del Giudice's Two Cities Films to Alexander Korda's London Films, from Rank to Ealing Studios, from Gainsborough to Hammer to Woodfall to Goldcrest to Handmade, not to mention the Archers, Powell and Pressburger. Such a tradition as the British cinema keeps on recreating itself because that tradition is a foundation on which you can build and rebuild continually. It's a great honour for me to have my acceptance speech for the 1993 BAFTA Britannia Award open this particular section on British films in Australia, and to have the opportunity to pay tribute to British movies once again, because, as I said on the Awards evening, I *really* do love British cinema. It has meant a great deal to me; it has taught me a lot.

on the slide: harry watt and ealing's australia venture

philip kemp

In late 1944, the Ealing director Harry Watt arrived in Australia to make a movie. The wartime journey from Britain was difficult, and expensive, and Ealing, under its financially canny studio head Michael Balcon, wasn't known for wanton expenditure. Yet Watt landed in Sydney without a budget, a script or even a subject for his proposed film—and spent the next five months trekking 25 000 miles around Australia looking for one.

The original impulse for this back-to-front approach to film-making had come from the Australian Government, concerned that Australia's contributions to the war effort were unappreciated abroad, especially in Britain. The Australians complained to the British Ministry of Information (MoI), who passed the gripe on to Balcon. Ealing, its reputation for quirky comedies still some years in the future, had a solid track record for gritty, down-to-earth war propaganda features like *Next of Kin* (1942), *Went the Day Well?* (1942) and *San Demetrio London* (1943). To Jack Beddington, head of MoI's Films Division, it seemed the ideal studio for the task.

Balcon, a staunch patriot—and further encouraged by the promise of Federal Government support for virtually any film on an Australian subject he chose to make—readily accepted the assignment. As it happened, he had already been involved in an Anglo-Australian venture a decade earlier as production head of Gaumont-British. Gaumont, then under the erratic sway of the Ostrer brothers, harboured dreams of a world market, and as part of this ambition entered into partnership with the newly formed Australian company National Productions. With

Gaumont's assistance, new studios—the first in Australia since 1912—were constructed at Pagewood outside Sydney, and it was announced that the great documentarist Robert Flaherty would be coming to shoot a film. Flaherty never showed up; instead, the actor and occasional director Miles Mander arrived to make *The Flying Doctor* (1936).

Mander was a fair actor (he starred in Alfred Hitchcock's debut feature, *The Pleasure Garden* (1926)) but no great shakes as a director. According to Watt, who on his arrival was regaled with stories of this previous Anglo-Australian misfire, 'he had been badgering the Gaumont management to direct, and they got rid of this embarrassment by assigning him to Australia, a traditional British gesture. Apparently he was more interested in the graces of Australian living than in the enormous possibilities of [his film].'[1] *The Flying Doctor* proved poor stuff, and soon after its release Gaumont-British, under-funded and mismanaged, suffered a major financial collapse and reneged on its distribution deal with National. Pagewood studios closed down not long afterwards.

Possibly Michael Balcon saw the MoI's request as a chance to redeem the earlier debacle, though it had scarcely been his fault. But as it happened Australia once again offered a neat solution to a personnel problem. Harry Watt was a vastly more talented director than Mander, no question of it, but finding the right slot for him at Ealing was proving difficult. The Australian excursion might have been tailor-made.

Watt, 'thick-set, genially-explosive, adventure-minded',[2] was born in Edinburgh, the son of a colourful local politician. After a suitably picaresque youth—deckhand on a transatlantic cargo schooner, balloon-seller in a fairground, café waiter, manufacturer of cut-price beach-balls, and the like—he fell by chance into the fledgling British documentary movement, working with John Grierson in the GPO Film Unit. For this outfit—or, after the outbreak of war, for its successor, the Crown Film Unit—Watt directed some of the finest films of the genre: *North Sea* (1938), *Night Mail* (1936), *Britain Can Take It* (1940), *Target For Tonight* (1941).

An early exponent of dirty realism, Watt deplored the tendency of certain documentarists to ascend into high-flown poetics. The people in Flaherty's films, he observed, 'remained exquisite objects, and hardly ever living, sweating, smelling human beings. No one in Flaherty's films . . . ever spat, or retched, or even seemed to want to copulate, lovely though they were'.[3] For his part Watt prided himself on his common touch, ascribing his knack for putting his subjects at their ease to 'an innocuous Scots accent, a knowledge of football, boxing, cricket and horse racing, plus a few dirty stories . . . and a capacity to swear, without repeating myself, for about two minutes'.[4] He treasured his colleague Alberto

Cavalcanti's comment that 'Harry Watt put the sweaty sock back into documentary'.[5]

In 1942 Watt followed Cavalcanti to Ealing, which soon became the most documentary-influenced of British studios. His first film there, *Nine Men* (1942), was a tough, pared-down war movie set in the North African desert (though filmed in Wales). It enthused the critics, and was hailed by *Documentary Newsletter* as 'the purest of the pure imaginative documentaries'.[6] But Watt hankered after more frivolous matters. As he put it, 'I was fed up with sweaty heroes on the skyline, and the sexual excitement of a film studio, after the rigours and Calvinism of the GPO and Crown, made me want to surround myself with lovely dames'.[7] He talked Balcon into letting him direct a vapid comedy, *Fiddlers Three* (1944), in which a pair of servicemen played by Tommy Trinder and Sonnie Hale find themselves transported back to Ancient Rome. Direly unfunny, it proved that Watt couldn't handle comedy. It also suggested that he was at his best out on location, as far as possible from studio control, and that directing actors was perhaps not his forte.

With the war drawing to a close, the extrovert, restless Watt seemed the ideal director to pioneer Ealing's first overseas venture. He arrived in Australia to find the local film industry at a low ebb, and morale even lower. Only one film was in production, Charles Chauvel's *Rats of Tobruk* (1944), and 'one frank Australian reckoned I must be on the slide to have come over at all'.[8] Watt viewed some native productions, which 'convinced me of one thing—that studio facilities and equipment were so poor that indoor films were useless to attempt in Australia, and that that had been the basic mistake of Australian film-makers. Their huge, exciting, hard country had never been used by them at all. So I set out to find an almost 100% exterior subject.'[9]

Not wanting to clash with Chauvel's film, Watt ruled out a straight war movie; yet his brief was to celebrate the Australian war effort. Following Grierson's dictum—don't impose your story, look for it—he set off round the country. At the end of his 25 000-mile trek 'I'd had five ideas and scrapped the lot'.[10] Unexpectedly, he found his subject in a government office in Canberra. Summoned there to advise on making documentaries, he heard about a true wartime incident when, in the face of imminent Japanese invasion, 100 000 head of cattle were driven 2000 miles across the outback from the Northern Territory. His imagination gripped, Watt saw his opportunity to make the first Australian western.

Watt's account of the making of *The Overlanders* (1946) goes to town on the problems, privations and disasters of the shoot. 'Much of it,' he asserts, 'was such a nightmare that it is best forgotten.'[11] In fact he remembered it in considerable detail, and it's clear he was having the time of his life. Since Chauvel was using most of the experienced Australian technicians, Watt 'decided to look for young enthusiastic amateurs or semi-amateurs'.[12] He was allowed three production personnel from Britain: the cameraman Osmond Borradaile, the editor Inman Hunter, and Jack Rix as production manager and technical supervisor. He also had the help of the Anglo-Australian Ralph Smart as associate producer and co-scriptwriter:

> The rest we assembled from eager 16 mm enthusiasts, from internment camps for German refugees, from sound recording studios, or just from the street. They turned out to be one of the most enthusiastic and co-operative units I have ever had.[13]

His cast was an equally eclectic bunch, mainly recruited from local amateur dramatic societies. These, rather than seasoned professional actors, were just the kind of players Watt was used to working with from his years in documentary.

Having combed the entire country for equipment ('We . . . found two Mitchell cameras, one tucked away in a businessman's safe, where it was held against a bad debt'),[14] Watt and his company—some twenty-five in all, cast included—took off for the Northern Territory. Once there:

> every road, every track, every cattle-yard and most of the close bush in which the cattle appeared on the screen was built by the unit . . . by the technicians, the actors, the drivers, the cooks and the secretaries . . . We lived in army camps, usually about 200 miles from anywhere. We saw our rushes about once a fortnight on a portable projector with a screen like a postage stamp.[15]

Even this was more than anybody at Ealing got to see. Balcon had approved the subject via a terse exchange of telegrams ('Are you interested in film of trekking 100 000 head of cattle across Australia?' 'Yes—go ahead.')[16] and logistical problems ruled out any idea of sending rushes back to Britain. Watt, isolated in the outback, was left free to shoot his film just as he saw fit, and eventually got back to Ealing ahead of the finished product:

> For safety, we shipped the whole negative back to Britain in a warship, which unfortunately got diverted to Hong Kong. So I arrived home empty-handed. As Ealing had not seen a foot of film during the whole eighteen months I'd been away, I imagine they wondered if I'd made a film at all.[17]

Any misgivings Balcon may have had were soon assuaged. Skilfully edited by Leslie Norman (who shot some additional footage in Kew

The Overlanders

Gardens) and provided with a masterly score, his first and only film music, by the composer John Ireland, *The Overlanders* scored a huge critical success. It was premiered at the Lyceum Theatre in Sydney on 27 September 1946, a few days later at the Leicester Square Odeon in London, and was hailed in both countries for its freshness and gutsy energy, its vivid sense of place and the sweep of its narrative drive. A minority of reviewers noted weaknesses: the often stilted script and the wooden acting of many of the cast, especially the pair of simperingly tennis-club young lovers.[18] But the public loved it. Although Watt had easily exceeded his initial budget of £30 000, the film recouped its cost several times over, and turned Chips Rafferty into the first international Australian film star (unless you count Errol Flynn). It also did well in the US, where it was given a photo spread in *Life* magazine, and became the first Ealing film to gain wide-scale distribution in Europe.

In later years Watt liked to refer to *The Overlanders* as 'a sleeper . . . a cheap little picture that becomes a world success. I tell you frankly, it was as big a surprise to me as to the business.'[19] But months before the film was released both he and Balcon seem to have sensed they had a hit on their hands. In May 1946, plainly elated, Watt wrote in *Picture Post*:

> I'm planning and hoping to get out to Australia again and make some more films. In the Dominions is the chance for the British film industry, already with its tail up, to consolidate its success against Hollywood. The outdoor action picture, shot in real exteriors, has always been an American monopoly. We can challenge this monopoly in our Dominion films . . . By creating a solid foundation for a film industry in a young country like Australia we can establish the cultural roots that transform a country into a nation . . . I hope this empire film idea comes off, because I'm willing to stake my career and future on it.[20]

Michael Balcon was equally bullish. In April 1946 he wrote to John Davis of the Rank Organisation, with whom Ealing had a distribution tie-up, enclosing a detailed proposal for an ambitious £250 000 Australian production program. The scheme proposed six films to be made by Ealing in Australia over two years, financed and distributed by Rank. *The Overlanders*, said the unsigned report, had:

> every promise of a successful film. This is because it has taken advantage of the unique pictorial and story opportunities in existence in Australia. It is this quality the Australians have heretofore failed to grasp and this failure has kept their films as pale imitations of Hollywood or Denham. But it is this quality that makes Australia an ideal centre for British film production. Given the proper equipment and qualified technicians, Australian films can compete with the world.[21]

Watt's remarks and those in the report both share, along with a faintly patronising air, a fatal confusion of purpose: was Ealing planning to make Australian films, or British films in Australia? In the long run this ambiguity would help undermine Ealing's Australian program. For the anonymous cynic who had greeted Watt on his arrival in Australia wasn't so far wrong, merely a little premature. With *The Overlanders*

Ealing's antipodean venture, and Watt's career, hit a high point. From now on it would be all downhill. Both Ealing-in-Australia and Watt, though they didn't yet know it, were indeed 'on the slide'.

But for the moment all was optimism and expansion. The report Balcon sent to Rank recommended the leasing and re-equipping of Pagewood Studios, possibly in partnership with distributor–exhibitors Greater Union Theatres. A full team of British technicians would be sent out to staff the new set-up. In effect, what was being proposed was an Ealing of the southern hemisphere, comparable in size and output to its northern counterpart. The studio's geographical remit would be broad: 'It should be emphasised that Australia can be used as a springboard for production both in New Zealand and the Pacific Islands.'[22] Fourteen possible subjects were outlined, splitting evenly between contemporary stories and episodes from Australian history:

> [They] should be primarily outdoor stories. They should . . . be on a large enough canvas to appeal to world-wide audiences. And they should compensate with action what they will lose through lack of polish in the actors.[23]

Prompt action was needed, the report stressed, since already in the wake of *The Overlanders* other production companies were sniffing around Australian properties: Hitchcock had bought *Under Capricorn*, and various classic Australian novels were being optioned by Hollywood. Luckily Ealing's proposal caught the Rank Organisation in a receptive mood. J. Arthur Rank, a naive and well-meaning plutocrat almost wholly ignorant of film-making, had found himself, at the beginning of the 1940s, rather to his surprise, heading the largest film combine in Britain, dominating every facet of the industry from production to exhibition. After the war he set out to expand his empire, offering unstinted funds and freedom to some of Britain's finest film-makers (David Lean, Carol Reed, Michael Powell and Emeric Pressburger), launching a crusading March-of-Time-style news magazine, *This Modern Age*, and setting up an animation department planned to rival Disney. Like Gaumont-British before him, but from a far more solid base, he aspired to crack the American market and rival Hollywood at box-offices worldwide. Ealing's antipodean scheme meshed perfectly with Rank's ambitious thinking.

While negotiations for Pagewood got under way, Watt began planning his second Australian feature. Two subjects in particular attracted him, both period dramas: *Robbery Under Arms*, Rolf Boldrewood's classic 1888 bushranger novel; and the famous clash between British troops and immigrant goldminers at the Eureka Stockade in 1854. Since there were problems over the rights to Boldrewood's novel, Watt plumped for the historical drama, attracted by the idea of dealing with 'one of the most important moments in Australian history'.[24] In 1947, he returned to Australia to start work on the production. Ralph Smart had by now turned director and made a well-received children's film, *Bush Christmas* (1947), for Rank, using many of the *The Overlanders* team. His place as Watt's associate producer was taken by Leslie Norman, supervising editor on *The Overlanders*. Watt also had the help of Eric 'Bungy' Williams, an ultra-reliable Ealing veteran who had served successively as Head of Sound, Chief Engineer and Studio Manager. He was sent to take over the management of the newly equipped Pagewood studio and act as Ealing's representative in Australia.

Watt embarked on *Eureka Stockade* (1949) with his habitual energy and enthusiasm, welcoming its historical basis as a challenge:

> We documentary people had never tackled history, and here was an important historical moment that fell so perfectly into film shape that there was no need to distort events or create false situations. It could be treated completely realistically . . . It needed, of course, much more of the 'feature' approach than *The Overlanders*.[25]

He also conceived it 'as the first of a series of films to be made around the Commonwealth showing the birth of democracy',[26] a project that appealed to his socialist views.

With a script written in collaboration with Ralph Smart and the left-wing English novelist Walter Greenwood (*Love on the Dole*, 1933), Watt began assembling his team and scouting locations. Since Ballarat, site of the original stockade, had changed somewhat since the 1850s, it was decided to reconstruct the town as an outdoor set. Watt wrote:

> We took over a virgin valley called Blind Creek, 160 miles from Sydney. We built a main street with pubs, a court-house, chapel, theatre, bowling-alley, and the like, and tore up with bulldozers two square miles of country to simulate the diggings. We erected 700 tents of all descriptions, with winches, mine-shafts and mullock heaps in front of them. On a neighbour-ing hill we built the police camp . . . We dammed the creek and built a bridge across strong enough to carry stagecoaches.[27]

The Australian government, initially highly supportive of the whole Ealing venture, lent 200 troops to act as extras.

It was planned to shoot the film in the latter part of 1947. But with production about to start, the British government dropped a bombshell. In August 1947, the Chancellor of the Exchequer, Hugh Dalton, struggling with a huge balance-of-payments deficit and noting that Hollywood movies were taking $70 million a year out of the country, slapped a 75 per cent *ad valorem* customs duty on all imported films. In the long run, this back-handed move would precipitate a major crisis in the British film industry. But one immediate effect was to halt all work on *Eureka Stockade* while Ealing argued with the Board of Trade whether this new duty should apply to Watt's film. Finally a compromise was reached: it would count as a British production on location if extra actors and technicians were drafted in from Britain. But meanwhile ten crucial weeks had been lost. 'That initial knock,' wrote Watt, 'started a run of bad luck from which we never quite recovered.'[28]

Even before production started Balcon had misgivings about the script, consulting his script editor Angus MacPhail ('Do please advise me whether you think Harry, in attempting to meet my point of view, has flattened certain scenes, also whether some scenes have now become repetitive')[29] and passing the script to Henry Cornelius, director of *Passport to Pimlico* (1949), for his comments. Cornelius responded with criticisms that, although tactfully worded, betray an overall unease:

> I am firmly convinced that the present script is *considerably over-length* . . . Never having worked with Harry I can only guess that he does not bother to write atmosphere into the shooting script . . . Some of the characters 'read' a little 'obvious' and unsubtle . . . There were moments in the script . . . where my moral support for the diggers was strained to an uncomfortable degree.[30]

Wary of upsetting the volatile Watt, Balcon wrote anxiously to Leslie Norman with a copy of Cornelius's report:

> I am writing to you because I deliberately don't want to disturb Harry . . . I know how he gears up to make a picture and what he takes out of himself and therefore any detailed comments on the script at this stage are likely to infuriate him . . . However . . . I do feel with Cornelius that there might be a tendency towards over-length. I also agree with him that the points he raised . . . can quite easily be dealt with whilst the film is in production and this is where you come in. It seems to me we must keep Harry quite clear for the job of work in hand, but if with others you can find time to consider the points and attend to them if they are worthwhile, I don't think your time will be wasted.[31]

With production at last under way, a harassed Norman replied in mid-December:

> After careful consideration I have decided not to show Harry your letter or Corny's comments—it would worry him unduly at a time when I wish to keep him as untroubled as is possible during the period when the world or the weather seem so dead set against us. You have been told of all the incidents that we are coming up against, such as *Smith Weekly*'s attack on the Government, using our employment of the Army as a weapon, and also the latest moves by Actors' Equity to make us pay the Army the award

rates, etc, etc. Well to top it the weather is the worst . . . that has ever been experienced since they took Met. recordings. We have not shot a foot of film this week so far.[32]

Having been forced to sit idle during ten weeks of dry, temperate weather, Watt had scarcely begun shooting before the production was hit by weeks of wind and torrential rain. When this at length gave way to sunshine, temperatures regularly topped 100°F (38°C). During the first five weeks of production, Watt recalled ruefully:

we had only five shooting days . . . Our complete unit town was blown down twice! We had to transport the complete unit sixteen miles each way in buses every day, and our roads became so bad that we had to walk the last two miles . . . Our dreams of easy film-making had gone with the tax. As the order for our fine new equipment had been cancelled, we improvised again, and shot most of the film on a camera made by [cinematographer George] Heath himself![33]

This time Watt found little fun in roughing it. The sense of pioneering had gone, and with it the easy camaraderie and mucking-in together of the tiny *Overlanders* unit. He wrote to Balcon:

We are all getting very physically and mentally exhausted, and this makes it a problem to keep up the enthusiasm which is so necessary to impart to the Army who are now quite completely 'browned off' . . . The Minister and the General have assured us that they will stand by us in our trouble, but they cannot guarantee that the rank and file will not finally make such a fuss that co-operation will be almost impossible . . . The discipline of the Australian Army is very different to the British Army, and the officers have little control. They themselves are a poor type generally.[34]

Altogether, Watt found himself increasingly disillusioned with Australia in general:

I do admit that the initial enthusiasm with regard to Australia as a production centre was mine, but you will remember that, after my short visit at the end of 1946, when Actors' Equity attacked us and I found that the general attitude was that we were an English capitalistic concern trying to put something over on Australia, my attitude began to change . . . I was carried on by enthusiasm for this subject but my interest in the Australian scene and the Australian character has progressively waned . . . Rather than have you feel that I am letting you down, it would be better to let me go altogether. Actually and practically I don't think I could cope with this continual strain.[35]

Not only were the troops acting up, but Watt was having problems with his cast. Too late, he realised that most of his local players lacked the range and experience to take on complex period roles. Apart from anything else, they looked sadly out of place: 'Natural actors look wonderful . . . when they're playing themselves, or in their own environment and class, but when I took the amateurs of Australia and put them in beards and knee-breeches, they looked the hams they really were.'[36] In particular his lead actor, Chips Rafferty, who had exuded such relaxed authority in *The Overlanders*, was hopelessly overparted as Peter Lalor, the leader of the miner's insurrection:

> Three weeks after we had started production this was becoming obvious, and Leslie Norman . . . proposed we sack Rafferty and promote a young Australian actor, Peter Finch, who was playing a small supporting role, into the lead. I refused through conceit and sentimentality towards Chips. It was an enormous mistake on my part.[37]

Nor were all the imported players proving ideal. As the shoot dragged on, Watt's tone turned steadily more sour:

> Being idealistic, I believe film a creative medium, even perhaps an art. And I find the fact that one has to interpret this art through the lowest form of casual labour, the actor, more and more frustrating. Straightforward picture film-making, with artists, is a monumental bore. Taking a bunch of indiscriminates and making them into actors is interesting and exciting. But one must never see or associate with them again. Give them a chance to become decent citizens again. The story documentary is obviously my meat. The trick of dramatising reality is what I should stick to.[38]

By farming out much of the shooting to a second unit headed by Leslie Norman and the assistant director Julian Spiro, Watt finally completed exterior shooting in May, and moved into Pagewood to shoot interiors and post-sync dialogue. Even then, his problems were far from over. The studio was only partially re-equipped—'We should have started working on Pagewood two months ago,' he noted gloomily[39]—and the Modulite sound system, installed by the Sydney-based Commonwealth Film Laboratories, proved woefully inadequate. 'We have recorded and post-synched some scenes five times,' reported Eric Williams, 'and each has been rejected for mechanical, electrical, process-ing or recording faults, in turn. The acting personnel become irritated and more difficult to handle.'[40] While this was going on, a much superior GB-Kalee sound system, supplied and shipped over by Rank, was sitting in crates on the studio floor. Williams, uncertain whether Ealing's plans to take over Pagewood were definite, had been reluctant to incur the expense of installing it. Ironically, its cost was charged to the *Eureka* budget anyway.

Production of *Eureka Stockade* was at last wrapped in mid-August. It had taken nine months, and cost some £200 000—nearly as much as Ealing's initial estimate for the whole of a six-film, two-year production program. Watt, preparing to return to Britain, wrote to Balcon, 'The actors have now all left, thank God. They have been a fearful nuisance with their conceits and egocentricities and I have no doubt they will land on you with numerous complaints.' He excepted Gordon Jackson, who 'as usual was the best trouper of the lot,' but reserved particular venom for Jane Barrett, who had played Lalor's love interest:

> I understand that Jane Barrett . . . has a long list of complaints of her treatment and I hope you will give her even less change than the others because quite frankly we all think her a selfish little bitch. She has done nothing but moan of her treatment since she came here and has antagonised everyone.[41]

His jaundiced attitude extended to the local industry:

> There is little film gossip from here. The usual crooks are wasting film, goodwill and sponsor's money by making 'stinkers'. A man called Collins has just made a film costing £35 000 called *Strong is the Seed* [aka *The Farrer Story* (1949)]. I think it is the all-time low in horrible amateurism . . . Business in general has fallen off and only comedies show much success.

More optimistically, he added that, 'The country as a whole is very interested in *Eureka* and [we] have had good publicity here. We have excellent goodwill from the press who look upon us as efficient and knowing our job.'[42]

Meanwhile, the future of Pagewood was still under discussion. Midway through *Eureka*'s troubled shoot Balcon's partner Reg Baker, financial director of Ealing, had arrived in Australia to conduct negotiations. He soon realised that Norman Rydge, head of Greater Union Theatres, had no intention of coming in on the production side, despite his encouraging comments at the time of *The Overlanders*' success. Even though Greater Union controlled Pagewood and Cinesound Studios, Rydge—an accountant by training—far preferred to make money out of distributing imported features. As Baker recalled it:

> I said, 'Why don't we work out a deal here, Norman? We'll make films here in Australia . . . three, four a year, whatever you like. I suggest that we put up three-quarters of the negative costs, and you put up one-quarter . . . You take the whole of the Australasian territory . . . and we will take the rest of the world . . .' He wouldn't have it all. Wouldn't listen to it . . . He didn't want to take a plunge, and have any money in a film.[43]

At Rank, too, attitudes were changing. The *ad valorem* duty had been withdrawn as abruptly as it had been imposed, and Rank, who had plunged into overproduction to make up for the Hollywood films withheld from British screens, faced financial ruin. J. Arthur Rank himself began to withdraw from day-to-day running of his unwieldy organisation, leaving control in the hands of his lieutenant John Davis, another accountant with a strong mistrust of the production side. The Australian director Ken G. Hall, visiting Britain around this time, picked up a hint of how the wind was blowing when he met Balcon:

> Mick Balcon . . . was as keen as mustard about a joint-production operation in Australia and said Arthur Rank was too. But, in his polite English way, Balcon left a distinct query hanging over John Davis' attitude. 'Accountants,' he said, 'have plenty of faith in bricks and mortar. Like theatres. They seem to forget that somebody has to make the pictures to play on those theatres. They very much like to have somebody else take the admitted risks of production.'[44]

Baker soon came to realise that if Ealing wanted to press ahead with their Australian venture, they could rely on little support from Rank and still less from Greater Union. None the less, reluctant to write off the time and money already invested, he bought the Pagewood lease from Rydge (the freehold was owned by the Australian government) and returned home 'rather disappointed'.[45] It seems likely his decision was influenced by a sanguine view of *Eureka*'s chances at the box office. According to Balcon he was 'very excited about the picture',[46] and hoped for a smash hit to equal the success of *The Overlanders*.

If so, he was due for another disappointment. *Eureka Stockade* opened in January 1949 and received tepid notices from British and Australian reviewers alike. Most of them, inevitably, compared the new film with *The Overlanders* and found it a sad let-down, with inept acting, a confused story-line and, worst of all, a feeble anticlimax of an ending that quite failed to live up to Watt's ringing prologue. ('The story of the world is the story of man's fight for freedom.') Richard Winnington, one of the most perceptive of the London critics and usually sympathetic to Ealing, observed that '*Eureka Stockade* does not seem to have any clue to the business of narrating a story by means of the movie camera', and summed it up as 'an honest boyish sort of film from a gifted documentary director who somehow shies from putting a developed human being squarely on the screen or telling a grown-up story.'[47]

Matters weren't helped by what Ealing saw as hostile sniping by the Australian press. The Sydney-based *Sunday Telegraph* ran a story from their London correspondent Dick Kisch alleging that Rank's bid to give *Eureka* a grand premiere on Australia Day had misfired badly: 'The film outfit chose Australia Day so late that the Commonwealth's representative, and most of the officials at Australia House, were already engaged [elsewhere].'[48] He also hinted that Australians were being shabbily treated in having to wait months for the film's release; and the rival *Sunday Herald* ran lukewarm preview comments on *Eureka* from the London trade press. Eric Williams attempted damage limitation tactics, but the harm was done.

Even worse, another Sydney paper, the *Sun*, quoted Harry Watt as criticising the Rank Organisation for skimping on *Eureka*'s publicity budget, and followed up with an article by the paper's editor, Tom Gurr, complaining that the film should in any case have been made by an Australian.[49] Balcon, contacted by Rank's publicity chief Sydney Wynne, shot back a hasty denial of the Watt story:

> Harry Watt has known [Tom Gurr] for some time and . . . there seems to be considerable ill-feeling between them. Harry denied he made any such statement and in the circumstances all I can do is accept his explanation . . . I cannot imagine he would be stupid enough to say anything to the detriment of the picture.[50]

Rank, though, with Davis now firmly in the saddle, were indeed cutting back on publicity along with a good deal else, and the remarks don't sound out of character for the combative and outspoken director.

By this time Watt was in South Africa, looking for his next film subject, rather to the alarm of Michael Balcon, recently returned from a visit there. When Watt first broached the idea, Balcon said:

> The difficulty about sending you out there would be that I should have to extract a solemn promise from you to keep silent from the moment you land. I am quite sure you would want to fight everybody all the time, and if you did, you would most certainly get knocked off . . . Politics are dynamite out there and you would get yourself into very serious trouble if you came out with things you really thought.[51]

Watt's reply can hardly have reassured Balcon much:

> It really would depend on how silent you meant . . . Socialism is a religion with me and I refuse to deny it anywhere. I do know that in this business . . . one has to associate with reactionaries and capitalists and I could very easily undertake not to involve myself in political arguments with them. You have no idea how circumspect I have been with the dreadful horrors who represent the film industry in Australia.[52]

Much to Balcon's relief, Watt soon decided that South Africa had little to offer him, and moved north to British East Africa to make his highly successful game-warden movie, *Where No Vultures Fly* (1951), and its sequel, *West of Zanzibar* (1954). It would be ten years before he returned to Australia.

In the meantime, Ealing's Australian program limped on to its third production, *Bitter Springs* (1950), directed by Ralph Smart. This was another period film, a turn-of-the-century fictional story about settlers in the South Australian outback coming into conflict with an Aboriginal tribe. A promising subject, taking a far more sympathetic attitude to Aboriginal land rights than was common at the time, it was ruined by a combination of factors: bad weather (again); the imposition from London of the egregious comedian Tommy Trinder in a leading role; and, as with *Eureka*, the fatal Ealing weakness for resolving all conflicts with a fudged, compromise ending. This too, it would seem, was imposed from London: Smart's original script ended, far more plausibly and dramatically, with a full-scale massacre of the Aboriginals at the hands of the whites.

The failure of *Bitter Springs*, following so closely on that of *Eureka*, put the whole Pagewood venture in doubt. The studio was rented to a couple of outside productions—*Wherever She Goes* (1951), directed by black-list victim Michael Gordon, and Lewis Milestone's *Kangaroo* (1952)—while Ealing considered its options. Eventually it was decided to proceed with the long-delayed production of *Robbery Under Arms*, in partnership with the veteran Ken G. Hall as director and producer. At which point Robert Menzies's conservative Liberal–Country Party government, which had replaced Ben Chifley's Labor administration in 1949, announced that the proposed partnership fell foul of recent legislation. Government support was withdrawn, and Ealing was warned that its lease on Pagewood would not be renewed. In January 1952 Eric Williams despondently announced the closure of the studio, and a year later Pagewood was sold to Associated Television. The rights to Boldrewood's novel were ceded to Charles Chauvel, and passed through several hands before the film was made—rather badly—by Jack Lee in 1957, with Peter Finch in the lead.

A few months earlier, Finch had at last secured the lead in an Australian Ealing film, ten years after narrowingly missing one in *Eureka*. In *The Shiralee* (1957), directed by Leslie Norman, he played a roving swagman who, when his marriage breaks up, is obliged to tote along his five-year-old daughter (his 'shiralee' or burden). At first resentful, he's gradually civilised and softened by her presence. In the end he settles into a new family unit with his daughter and his patient girlfriend. *The Shiralee*, with its largely English cast, feels less of an Australian film than a British production made on location. Amiable, predictable and under-characterised, it conforms to the late-Ealing pattern whereby a sense of adventure is tamed into safe domesticity.

By now Ealing had become a shrunken shadow of its former self. The link with Rank, increasingly strained by the mutual antipathy between Balcon and John Davis, was finally severed in 1955, and without Rank's financial backing the company was forced to quit its premises. Ealing Studios were sold to the BBC, a new distribution deal was negotiated with MGM, and the depleted outfit, renamed Ealing Films, moved into a corner of the Metro lot at Borehamwood. Six films—one of· them *The Shiralee*—were produced under the agreement. But there was little rapport between Ealing and the MGM management, and in 1958 Balcon and his team moved again, this time to the Associated British Picture Corporation (ABPC) Studios at Elstree.

Even before the closure of Ealing Studios was first announced quite a few of its personnel, sensing the end was in sight, had moved on. Harry Watt was one of them. Early in 1955 he quit Ealing for Granada Television. Balcon was hurt by his departure; he always hated to let people go, and had long been on bad terms with the head of Granada, Sidney Bernstein. He wrote to Watt:

> I do think it is a bad thing when anybody like you, who has been so closely identified with Ealing, is obviously working somewhere else without any explanation having been made . . . It would, I think, have been nice had Sidney made at least some formal approach to me . . . but I have not heard a word from him. I would have acted differently had the situation been reversed.[53]

But Watt was unhappy at Granada, and after 'two frustrating years'[54] (less than eighteen months, in fact) asked for his old job back. Balcon agreed, but the relationship was still strained, and when Watt voiced his discontent with the material he was working on—the thriller *Nowhere To Go* (1958), eventually directed by Seth Holt—Balcon was driven to uncharacteristic exasperation: 'I now blame myself for giving you the privilege of returning to Ealing, bearing in mind the circumstances under which you left us.'[55] At length matters were patched up between them, but both men seem to have concluded they got on better at a distance, and when Watt came up with an Australian subject Balcon took little persuading to let him direct it.

The Siege of Pinchgut (1959) was adapted from a story idea by the director Lee Robinson (Chips Rafferty's partner in the production company Southern International) and the British editor Inman Hunter, who had worked with Watt on *The Overlanders*. Robinson and Hunter originally conceived it as a wartime story, in which escaped German POWs hold Sydney to ransom by threatening to fire a big gun sited on the islet of Fort Denison (locally known as 'Pinchgut') into a munition ship moored in the harbour. Watt, working with the novelist Jon Cleary, updated the idea, with the threat now coming from an escaped convict who claims he's been unjustly convicted.

If *The Overlanders* was an Australian western, *Pinchgut* was an Australian gangster movie. It was also the only one of Watt's three Australian films with no factual basis. Unusually for him, he went into the production (or so he later claimed) with a frankly commercial motive:

> I determined on my return to film to make a box-office success. This was the first time I had thought like this because before that I had just made pictures, and if they were a success, so much the better.[56]

Even so, he told Balcon at the time that: 'As always, I'd be willing to make it without stars and, in point of fact, prefer it.' He had hopes that MGM, under whose auspices the project was started, might agree to let him 'make this film really cheaply with almost unknowns'.[57] But ABPC, to whom Ealing switched while the script was being finalised, insisted on a big name, American for preference. A wide range of stars was canvassed—so wide, indeed, as to suggest that the lead character, escaped con Matt Kirk, lacked definition as written: Stewart Granger, Trevor Howard, Errol Flynn, Van Heflin, Arthur Kennedy. Finally the choice fell on Aldo Ray, known for his roles in tough war films like *Men in War* (1957) and *The Naked and the Dead* (1958). 'He turned out to be an amiable, rather second-class actor,'[58] noted Watt laconically.

Altogether, *Pinchgut* was the least Australian in personnel of Watt's Australian films. Most of the lead actors were British, and 'the whole unit, over sixty in number,' as Watt recalled it, 'had to be brought from Britain, so the picture was very expensive'.[59] Among them was Eric Williams, now acting as Watt's associate producer. By ironic coincidence, it was while *Pinchgut* was in production that Williams's former headquarters, Pagewood Studios, once planned as the antipodean Ealing and the hope of the Australian film industry, finally closed down and were sold off to the motor manufacturer Holden.

Bringing in Jon Cleary as co-writer was Watt's idea. Balcon had misgivings:

> Despite Cleary's international reputation, he is an Australian which will mean that the picture may be too Australian in its outlook, whereas I was relying on the fact that you have a fair knowledge of Australia and its background, and the international aspects might be better protected by our working with a British writer.[60]

It was a far cry from the day when Watt had waxed bullish about Ealing's plans 'to put Australian films on the screens of the world'.[61] Evidently worried that things might be getting 'too Australian', Balcon repeatedly asked Watt to come back to Britain and talk over the script. Watt kept putting off the trip, but finally came over for a few weeks shortly before shooting started in November 1958.

Various mishaps dogged the production of *Pinchgut*. Bad weather struck yet again—not rain this time but high wind. Local authorities, despite lavish promises of cooperation, proved obstructive. L.C. Rudkin, the production manager, reported to Hal Mason, Balcon's right-hand man:

> The police have been stupid, petty and as Harry says 'provincial'. Even when permission was approved we had difficulties getting uniforms. Bungy [Williams] says he has had to have a by-law introduced to allow actors to portray police in uniform!![62]

Early on in the shoot Aldo Ray tore a leg muscle while jumping into a boat, and a specialist was called in to treat him. Watt himself sustained an injured foot and had to limp around with a stick 'which makes me look ten years older than God'. He found Ray, despite his injury, 'a very willing worker'. He told Balcon:

> The stuff we have been mostly doing with him is action. I have played him pretty broad because he is a broad type. I did want to get much more quietude and depth in the interior playing scenes but, quite frankly, to do subtle stuff in the boiling sun and a howling gale, with a very tight schedule, is not easy.[63]

Still, setbacks of this kind beset most film shoots, especially when much of the action is on location. If the overriding mood of *Pinchgut*, as Bruce Molloy suggests,[64] is one of bleak pessimism, events back in Britain were probably most to blame. Soon after shooting had started, ABPC announced to Balcon that they no longer wished to support Ealing's production program. Since, under the deal as signed, ABPC had acquired all of Ealing's assets, including their entire back catalogue of films, this was a sentence of death. Towards the end of November Hal Mason was obliged to write to all members of *Pinchgut*'s crew, Eric Williams included, and tell them that once the production wrapped they would be out of a job.

With a partially disabled lead actor and an understandably demoralised crew, the film not surprisingly began to fall behind schedule. ABPC, concerned only to be rid of their unwanted obligation, became impatient, and Balcon, protective as ever of his directors, found himself having to field complaints from ABPC's managing director, Robert Clark. 'We very much regret the position,' he wrote soothingly, 'and everything is being done to prevent a deterioration . . . but the film will suffer if any further pressure is brought to bear on the director.'[65] Additional irritation came from the Government-funded National Film Finance Corporation, from which Ealing had secured a long-term loan. It was headed by John Terry, a nit-picking and literal-minded lawyer, and Balcon was forced to waste his time documenting exactly how long Watt had worked on the screenplay of *Pinchgut*, or explaining the difference between associate producer and a production manager.

These distractions, and the guilt Balcon felt at having to fire colleagues who had worked with him for twenty years, may explain why he treated Watt's growing dissatisfaction with *Pinchgut* with atypical impatience. In late February, with principal shooting complete, Watt cabled:

> Earnestly suggest massive cutting to create filmic speed often fallacy many films have lost dramatic shape this stage because cutting destroyed tempo which in any film is integral element and does not need to be fast to be suspenseful *stop* what we need is suspense in last part night sequence therefore shooting time inserts first consideration *stop*.[66]

Balcon retorted:

> Telegram suggests you and temperature again normal and although delighted please spare us your over dramatised theories which we know as much about as you do *stop* . . . there is obvious overlength due in some respects to original over writing and later over shooting and we are determined to present this magnificent film in its best form.[67]

Watt's argument, in its telegraphese form, may have been garbled, but the end result suggests that he was right. As a thriller, *Pinchgut* is badly off in its pacing, which Jon Cleary was one of the first to sense. Having seen the finished film in Sydney, he wrote to Balcon:

> I don't know why, but the tension was higher at the beginning of the picture . . . than at the end. The evacuation scenes had nothing, I thought—one man . . . commented aloud that it looked like nothing more than the usual Sydney on a Sunday morning: empty, but with no feeling of foreboding or impending doom.[68]

In a later letter he added, 'Harry Watt and I had talked about another *Wages of Fear* [1952] . . . I thought we had the opportunity to make a classic suspense film, and I just don't think we have.'[69] Watt himself, having presented the film at the 1959 Berlin Film Festival, told Balcon: 'I don't think we'll win a prize. They look on our film as about the best *commercial* proposition seen but not as a *festival* award. How are the mighty fallen.'[70]

As it turned out, *Pinchgut* was no great shakes commercially either. In later years Watt blamed ABPC: 'They thumbed down on it immediately, didn't try to publicise it and gave it a very poor distribution, so that . . . it was a resounding flop.'[71] No doubt ABPC's indifference contributed, but the film's evident faults seem quite enough to explain its failure. Not only is the pacing slipshod and Ray badly miscast, but the ending is even worse fudged than those of *Eureka Stockade* and *Bitter Springs*. Matt Kirk's motivation isn't the desire to escape, but to draw attention to what he maintains—with reason, it seems—is an unfair conviction. Yet by the end this issue is simply dropped; Matt is killed, as though deserving nothing else for his threat of violence. No matter that this stance has been largely forced on him by the authorities' intransigence and duplicity; by switching our sympathy to his more conciliatory young brother, the film implies that violence against the powers that be, whatever the provocation, can only be wrong.

Such a conservative, even reactionary, attitude was a sad end for a studio of Ealing's former liberalism, to say nothing of Watt's proudly proclaimed socialism. And an end, regrettably, was what it was. *The Siege of Pinchgut* was not just the last of Ealing's Australian films, but the last film to carry the Ealing name. It was also Harry Watt's last adult feature film. After this he directed a few television episodes, and a children's film for a Danish company, *The Boy Who Loved Horses* (1961), before retiring from film-making at the age of fifty-five.

Ealing's Australian venture, and Harry Watt's involvement in it, can well be seen as a decline in both creative and ideological terms, revealing (in Bruce Molloy's view) how the film-makers 'became progressively disenchanted with aspects of Australian society and of the Australian character'.[72] Equally, it could be read as a reaction to the often fraught circumstances of production, and to the lack of support and vision shown by the studio's backers in Britain, potential partners (notably Greater Union) in Australia, and the British and Australian governments.

Even so, it would be a mistake to write off the whole operation as a tale of failure. Ealing's investment in Australia came at a time when the native film industry was at its lowest ebb. Between 1946 and 1959 only thirty-three Australian feature films were made, visiting productions included. Ealing's five features therefore represent some 15 per cent of Australian output of the period—not bad for a tiny, undercapitalised British studio—and, whatever their flaws, rank high within it for quality of acting and production values, with Watt's trio easily the strongest of the five. The success of *The Overlanders*, in particular, attracted overseas attention and investment in the form of such films as *Kangaroo*, *On the Beach* (1959), *Summer of the Seventeenth Doll* (1959) and *The Sundowners* (1960). These productions, along with Ealing's, helped sustain the industry and provided vital continuity through the fallow years. When the great Australian revival finally came at the end of the 1960s Ealing had been dead and gone ten years; but Balcon's studio had done much towards making that renaissance possible.

not god's sunflowers:
nicolas roeg on *walkabout*

richard combs

richard Combs: Walkabout *(1971) existed as a project before* Performance *(1970), and was intended to be your first film as a director.*

Nicolas Roeg: Yes, I was going to do it for an American company called National General with the producer Jack Schwartzman. It was just after I'd shot *Petulia* (1968) for Richard Lester in San Francisco in 1967, and Schwartzman said, 'Hey, someone sent this book, take a look at it.' The book was called *The Children* (1959), by the American writer James Vance Marshall.[1] But it wasn't so much the book; I just liked the idea of people lost somewhere. It's very easy for a child to be lost, emotionally or physically. And I liked the idea of a great landscape, like the Australian outback, which had hardly been surveyed and would be like a backcloth, a big, empty backcloth but visually very beautiful.

A book stirs you to all kinds of things. People say, 'Oh, it isn't like the book.' A film can never be like the book. Van Gogh's sunflowers are not God's sunflowers either. The children in the film are English. But that's all right; there are English people in Australia. And I like that, not being able to place people immediately. It's probably very irritating, but I like it when you can't instantly come to an opinion or a decision about something. Which we all try to do—you look at someone, see how they're dressed, where they live, what they've got, and then you have a picture of the person.

That's why I like Thornton Wilder's *Our Town* (1938) on stage.[2] You just have these people on a set of steps, a staircase, and you don't know who's the mayor or who's what. There's something very attractive about that, and difficult to do, unless you're doing a quite stylised thing.

Perhaps that's why I like the work of Edward Bond, the playwright.[3] I wrote to him and described the thing, described what I wanted to do, the story of two children. I don't think I sent him the book. I was told that he was doing a new play and wouldn't have time to write a script. But he wrote back a very simple thing, which also drew me to him tremendously. He said, 'Yes, I've been thinking about writing a play about a journey.'

He was living in Cambridge at the time and I went to see him. I asked if he wanted to go to Australia, and he said, 'No, I don't think so'. He did no research about Aborigines or anything. It was about a journey, the journey of life, and discovery, and growing up, all kinds of things. He went off and came back with a fourteen-page screenplay. There was no description, which was fair enough; he wasn't writing a book. He was writing it like a play. It was perfect—just typed, rather crappily typed, in fact.

It was lovely to be able to do the sense of a journey in an hour and a half: caught in a moment of a journey. But then, of course, there were meetings. I was pulled in, and there was a story editor, and I was told this doesn't work. The story editor knew everything about it, all the jargon, and I was told about structure and so on. Finally, one of the heads of the company from the London office asked me to write a letter excusing him, saying it wasn't his fault that we'd come up with a fourteen-page script. He said, 'Just cover me, Nic. I've got to send this to the coast.' I'm laughing now, but I wasn't laughing then.

I said, 'We'll try to pad it out a bit.' I think we got it up to forty-six, fifty pages, but there's only so much you can do. But it was beautiful, when you think about some of the things said. There was a line from the boy when they come to the top of the hill. He looks out over the landscape, and in the distance there's the shimmering of a mirage. As he turns to his sister who's older—she's in charge, holding his hand like his mother, doesn't want to frighten him—he says, 'There's the sea! It's the sea.' Then, 'It is the sea, isn't it?' And she says, 'Maybe.'

That's the scene. That's film, that's terrific. But it's very difficult for an executive to read that. They say, 'Hey, what's happening?' So they didn't like it.

I saw Edward Bond for the last time at an agent's office in London, where we wrote the last couple of pages. The last line was, 'Come on, Sidney'—that was the first time we actually hear the boy's name. Unusual name, I thought. The girl calls out, 'Come on, Sidney. We've got to go now.' Bond was looking out the window. I said, 'Bye, Edward.' And without turning around, he said, 'I think that's the best thing I've ever done.' Which was very flattering. I was flattered that he agreed to do it and that we'd had some kind of communication. He felt that his work was safe in my hands, and I felt mine was safe in his.

That was it. There was no need for more. And I kept the screenplay, offered it to a few other people. But then the producer Si Litvinoff[4] was over in England. We were friends, and we talked about it, and he said, 'I know what you can do'. He had a backer, Max Raab,[5] who had made a great deal of money from his own business but who preferred film. I had just one copy of the script left, and Si said, 'You've got to get it to Max at the Dorchester, he's leaving tomorrow morning'. I said, 'Yeah, sure, I'll put it in a cab.' And I didn't. But the next morning Max was on the phone asking where it was, and offering to send someone round for it. I was trapped! So I put an envelope in with it and asked him please to send it back, it was my only copy. He said, 'Sure, I'll read it on the plane', which was what everybody said then. But bugger me, he did read it on the plane. And he phoned from New York and said, 'I'll do it. I want to do the film.'

Many of the ideas in Walkabout *to do with identity, and people being lost, seem to find their way into* Performance.

Well, I did this thing before *Performance*. Donald Cammell[6] read the script for *Walkabout* and liked it. Max Raab came into it after *Performance*; in fact *Performance* was in limbo for two years, nearly three, because Warner Brothers was so worried. Once there's someone like Max who can sign cheques and say yes, then it's on. But it's very rare to find someone who can do that without going through all the usual hierarchy and studio decision-making. François Truffaut had that kind of person. I like that.

It cost about $750 000. That's like a $5 million movie now. Max was a very rich man, and quite extraordinary. He liked to make films with people he liked, about the things he thought and felt about. Then he sold it to Fox, who used it in their promotional campaign. There was a big takeover bid at Fox at the time, and they sent the film to Cannes.

Did you always have the idea of using your own son Luc as the boy?

No, I did a lot of tests with kids. It was Si Litvinoff's idea, actually, to use Luc. He said, for one thing, 'We won't have to bother with the chaperone thing'. Luc was very young, six-and-a-half, and Jenny Agutter, who plays the fourteen-year-old girl, was actually about sixteen, and David Gulpilil [Gumpilil], the Aboriginal boy they meet, was young too. It was like a family outing. David didn't know much about filming, obviously. I found him, with the help of an Australian production manager, Grahame Jennings, on a mission station in the Northern

Territory. He had never acted—he was not stained by anything, except by life.

He went to Cannes as the first full-blooded Aborigine to be given a passport. Before we arrived, they were worried: [in French accent] 'Will he behave? . . . Does he have clothes? . . . We have something for him for the Grand Palais . . .' It was marvellous to watch because David had a natural elegance. All manners became real with him. Jenny and Luc and David came down the steps of the Palais, and Jenny had a long dress on. David, who had never been anywhere like this before, thought, 'She could fall down, I'll give her a hand'. And he led her down and led her out.

And when we went to this huge dinner they'd laid on, he didn't glance sideways to see which knife and fork to use. He just assumed 'They wouldn't expect me to take the third one in from the right or the second one from the left'. He just started from the outside. And he never put a foot wrong. It was the other guests at this great banquet who were looking around, trying not to make a *faux pas*. And he didn't make one. He put his hand on the glass when he didn't want any wine. It was superb.

Was shooting really like a family picnic? How far out did you go?

We covered many thousands of miles. I didn't want the film to have just one look. Australia's rather like the US in that way. It's a huge land area, of which there are many hundreds of miles of red desert, and that's it. Then there's a hugely lush area two thousand miles to the north. If you look at the landscape the children cross, they could never have walked that. They were going from the dead centre, around Alice Springs, up to Darwin and then down, just north of Adelaide.

We lost fourteen vehicles that blew up or burst. We'd travel on dirt roads, off the bitumen—the 'bit', as they called it. [In Australian accent] 'The bit'll be coming up in a couple of hundred miles.' We were a small crew travelling around, just stopping, not always knowing where we'd be next. And people like call sheets and things like that, knowing where they are. We were out for fourteen weeks. A lot of people dropped out; they'd just steal away in the night. We had somebody go crazy—space fever.

We even had a mini revolt: If you think what it would be like to go camping for a long time, especially with hairdressers and people, and not a lot of water, not a lot of showers, and no bars for the crew to go to after work. They wrecked the camp one evening. I flew Luc and Jenny out one day to go into Alice Springs for some injections, and the crew were on their own for two nights without command! They got smashed and ran a bit amok, wrecking tents.

[POTENTIAL FILMS]

David Gulpilil, Jenny Agutter and Luc Roeg, *Walkabout*

So you didn't scout locations at all in advance?

No, it would have cost a fortune if we'd done that. I'd have spent fourteen weeks looking for the places. But we had a marvellous tracker, whom Grahame Jennings found, who was also our mechanic. I'd talk to him in the evenings, and he'd say, 'I know a place that has a waterfall and where there's a little hidden valley'. In the film, they're the same place although in fact they are miles apart. We didn't completely wander out into the centre of Australia; we had some idea of where we were going.

Max Raab was very good, he put it all in my hands. I was also director of photography, which reassured people. They knew that the technical thing was taken care of. Nobody really knew what they were doing, but at least I knew when it was f-11.[7] I knew it would come out.

Were you still working from Edward Bond's minimal script?

I added things along the way that couldn't have been imagined. We came across some people with weather balloons and added that scene with actors playing the meteorologists, a little sexual *frisson*. And that weird little outback statue factory, we eased that in. That was the beauty of the script—it was about what do you find? You've got to find something on your journey too. That gives it its heart. When that happens, it opens your eyes more, especially in a landscape that is bare and serene, that hasn't been tampered with. You suddenly see the way a ridge twists—it's extraordinary, like a painting. And foreigners to a place see more than the locals. People go past things and don't see what's in front of their eyes. When Roman Polanski came from Poland and made his films in England, people's behaviour seemed extraordinary to him. I like doing things in foreign places.

You can see that it's a journey. And at the end, when David gave his dance, and Jenny wasn't sure what was happening, it was quite wonderful. It was his wedding dance. We were like a small family travelling a long, long way from home. I had two of my boys with me, and it stayed in their minds. It stayed in Luc's mind. Altogether I think we were away about six months. It was part of his development, as a child, a person.

I said to Edward that I'd love the three of them to have a family story. Many families have a family story. I know we have—funny things that my father said to me and I repeat to the kids. And you have to tell it exactly the same way every time, every word. 'No, it's *then* he went to, not *and* he went to . . .' I told Edward, 'I've got one, totally original, that my father made up, a fairy story, but I would like another one, someone else's family story'. He said, 'I've got one, but I don't know if I want to give it to you . . .'

Anyway, he told me that story, which Luc tells during the film, about the blind woman, the mother, and it ends, 'He fell off and broke his neck!' It's a fantastic story. I tried to make it like a family story because the girl corrects him at one point, when he gets a word wrong. Of course, the Aboriginal boy had no idea what he was talking about. It had a reality and a truth to it, which was very difficult to find because Luc was only six-and-a-half.

When the father takes his children out for a picnic at the beginning, just before he commits suicide, he is reading something called Structural Geology, *which sounds like the book* The Fragile Geometry of Space *John Baxter (Donald Sutherland) wrote in* Don't Look Now *(1973). They both seem to be caught in some fatal, elemental design.*

The father was exhausted by things, by life. I like the beginning, when he goes back to his apartment, and obviously something is going wrong with his job. They have got everything: the boy and girl are at their nice schools, with their uniforms, and they are polite and nicely brought up kids. But suddenly there is an emptiness in his life. He's some sort of salesman, or a mining engineer, a mining proprietor or a surveyor of some kind. His hopes were semi-fulfilled. He did it very well, I thought, John Meillon.

His home is very neat. When they go for the picnic, it's all very natty, with a tablecloth; the mother is preparing something, a delicate dish, in a clean kitchen. He goes out and looks from a balcony at the children swimming in a pale blue chlorinated pool next to the ocean. I noticed that a lot in wealthy suburbs in the US, in Malibu. People who live on the beach have pools. I saw it in Sydney too.

At the end, when she's grown up, the girl seems to occupy the same apartment, or a similar apartment, with her husband.

It's funny, but I've always thought that it was the boy she was with, that they're brother and sister living together. But I suppose it has to be her husband. He was played by our young grip [John Illingsworth] on the film.

I like the cutting of the liver in that scene. Her hands are on the flesh, and she remembers a time when . . . It had sunk in, in her journey in life, and I'm sure her values as a young woman will be different than they would otherwise have been.

I think these primal things are very exciting. We have lost touch with our primitiveness. When you make a movie, it's easy to lose sight of your original intentions in making it. And it's very difficult to hang on to your primitiveness. The child's first question—I heard it on the radio again the other day, and I've known it for years, having had six sons, that sooner or later, maybe around three or four years, in some way, a child asks, 'Why am I here?' Parents try to be reassuring—'Mummy and Daddy love you, now don't you worry your head about that'—and then close the bedroom door. 'You're going to be a very good marketing research person, that's why you're here.' Somewhere in our sense of things, it's our journey to find out.

There's a negative connotation when people talk about primitive attitudes, which I can't accept. Sophisticated civilisation may be more comfortable, and consumer things nice to have, but I don't think it's better. I was shooting in Morocco last year [1997], and one of the crew was disparaging about how people lived. I said, 'Well, what haven't they got?' All he could think of was television. They had the wind and the sea and the stars and the children were happy. Dates fell off the palms. What haven't they got? A water mattress or something.

We've lost touch with food, with what food *is*, the meaning of hunting. You see it in all these food scares. In fact, we had another mini revolt with the crew over this, on *Walkabout*. Odd people were joining us on our journey. They'd come across the camp and join our caravan for a while, trooping through the desert. A rabbit hunter stuck with us for two or three days. At this stage, we were eating out of cans and shooting a few things. And some of the crew said, 'We must have fresh vegetables or we'll all get scurvy'. We'd only been out about three weeks and they were talking as if it was two years before the mast and we were eating salt pork or something.

Then this drover turned up to give us a hand for a couple of days, and he lived on meat pies. [In Australian accent] 'I'll have a meat pie and a beer.' And he was so hard and lean and fit. You could go to eighteen personal trainers in Beverly Hills and they'd never make you as fit and healthy and resilient as that drover. He didn't have spring-heeled trainers at 150 bucks a throw.

Why did you use Stockhausen's 'Hymnen' on the soundtrack?

I like Stockhausen,[8] not that I like to listen to him all the time. It has to do with order and chaos, and there's something extra-planetary about it, the music of the stars. It's like the moment when the children's radio suddenly starts to work again, and there's a burst of music and chatter from the outer world. Or a plane passes over . . . when you fly over somewhere, you look down and you wonder. We fly over a lot of stuff, and here two children were lost. When you used to travel by train, you could look at people's back gardens and things. You'd see life. But in a plane you're more detached. What's down there?

Did you always have that kind of structure, with the elaborate intercutting, in mind?

No, that's the journey. I like shooting a lot of stuff. After all, we're taking in a lot of information all the time. And I like to be able to get that in the film. You can move it all around, first of all because you have a moveable audience. It's why a film has nothing to do with literature or theatre. I like shooting a lot of stuff because when you see the scene cut together, you might think, 'What is going on in their heads? What's happening here?'

But it stayed spare, *Walkabout*. It was set against a beautiful and not a vicious landscape. It's not a vicious place. It has dangers, but life has dangers. But it's not 'Beneath every bower there are lions and tigers'. That's another area of life. It'd be another journey, a journey through the Hindu Kush or somewhere.

Walkabout is one of your films that still comes up a lot; it seems to have stayed in people's minds.

It might be because it has a kind of universal appeal. You don't have to be of any particular culture to get it. That was the beauty of Edward

Bond's writing, of those snatches of words. You can understand the film without knowing what they're saying. 'There's the sea! It's the sea. It is the sea, isn't it?' If that were said in Swahili, you could see that he goes through excitement, doubt, questioning, disappointment. All those emotions are expressed.

The film was re-released in Australia in 1998. It is out on video and it will be released on laser disc. But I've never had a penny out of it. It's one of those things you can't trace. I haven't had one residual cheque. It might buy me a packet of fags, it certainly won't buy a carton.

[PART V]

IN THE MARGINS: DOCUMENTARY

e rnst Lubitsch was quoted as saying, 'Make documentaries and first of all film mountains, then you will be ready to film people'.[1] It's now common understanding that the documentary has been, through and through, the keel and rudder of the film and television industry. Quite a large number of the feature film-makers of the 1970s renaissance emerged out of a long, hefty tour-of-duty in documentary. And some still dabble in the form between features—Gillian Armstrong being one prime example.

This section presents a rather selective assessment of where documentary is at and where it might be heading. In recent years it seems the documentary has been enjoying greater critical attention, as well as appreciative audiences at film festivals, on television, most notably on the ABC, and in film theatres.

Tom Zubrycki provides a personal view, although he takes a more reserved and discretionary look at the state of documentary by reflecting back on his own career, detailing the general principles which informed it and the specific pre-occupations with subject matter that changed it. By article's end, with the advent of lightweight, digital technology and television's penchant for 'reality' programs, he offers his misgivings and a few hopeful possibilities for the future of documentary.

Zubrycki's words find echoes in Mike Rubbo's. In the last few years Mike Rubbo has been active at the ABC's documentary division, where, among other things, he has been responsible for bringing observational films to the frontline of attention, always a prickly area of aesthetic and ethical debates.

documentary:
a personal view

tom zubrycki

What I love about documentary is that it conveys the textures of everyday life like no other form can. It captures spontaneity and immediacy. It involves a process of discovery with often very unexpected twists and turns. There is never the opportunity to do a second take. I find this exciting on the one hand, but exhausting on the other.

Unlike scripted drama, you can't plan a documentary. The best ones unfold of their own accord. It's in watching the unexpected coalesce or unravel which is the thrilling part of the process. From my experience it all depends on good planning, some intuition and a bit of luck.

The Internet is revolutionising the communication industry making the definition of what constitutes a documentary very slippery these days. There exists an American web-cam site called *Jenni-cam*. A student in an American university dorm leaves a camera sitting on the top of her computer broadcasting images of herself every two to three minutes into cyberspace. It won't be long before we'll all be eavesdropping into public or private situations around the globe, while non-professionals will broadcast their own home-movies down the Net!

The nexus between technological changes and film aesthetics has always been a close one: witness the French new wave of the 1960s when film-makers like Jean-Luc Godard took to the streets with light hand-held cameras, and the grassroots film movement that sprang up around Super 8. Documentary is no exception. The lightweight 16 mm cameras in the early 1960s produced the 'direct cinema' and *cinéma verité* movements which resulted in film-makers engaging in intimate ways with their subjects. The cost of camera and sound equipment, however, combined with 16 mm filmstock and processing, limited film-making to a professional elite able to secure the necessary finance.

It has taken thirty years for this situation to change. In 1996 digital video cameras appeared on the domestic market which returned broadcast-quality images, but were also at an affordable price. The time is now fast approaching when everyone will be able to afford desk-top non-linear editing. The question is, how's this going to change the documentary? Will it survive in its present form or will it re-surface in different shapes and styles? I believe it's possible to observe some of these changes already taking place.

I started making my first films in the early 1970s—the early dawn of this technological 'revolution'. It was soon after video was first invented and the first primitive reel-to-reel, portable, black-and-white videotape recorders made their appearance. These were cameras attached to large bulky recorders that you were meant to carry on your shoulder. These dinosaurs were the equivalent of the modern digi-cam. In fact, so primitive was this technology that I abandoned it after a couple of years in favour of 16 mm!

What initially made black-and-white video popular was the claims it made for enabling social change. 'This new technology would assist the empowerment of disadvantaged communities,' asserted the Canadian Film Board in the late 1960s. Australia followed, and the Whitlam government established video-access centres across the country, attracting idealistic sociology graduates like myself who wanted to change the world!

The first video program I ever made was in 1974, about an area in Sydney I lived in—Balmain—still then mostly working-class. It was on the subject of how people felt about container traffic plying the narrow residential streets making life hell for the residents. I shot the video in three days and then screened the roughly edited tape a week later to a big crowd at the local town hall, who sat with rapt attention watching themselves and their friends debate the issue. A few weeks later a delegation of residents walked into a meeting with the minister responsible, set up the video play-back and forced him to watch the program. The container terminal closed within a year and the trucks disappeared!

I was part of a group numbering less than twenty. We called ourselves 'guerilla video-makers', as we placed ourselves at the disposal of resident groups across the inner-city making 'agit-prop' videos. The causes ranged from stopping expressway development to clamouring against people being uprooted for re-development. We turned each program around in less than a week, screening it to crowds in halls, pubs, or simply in the street.[1]

My first film, *Waterloo*, grew out of this video work and the connections I'd made with people protesting against the break-up of inner-city communities. Waterloo is a suburb in Sydney where a group of people in 1977 were prepared to sit in front of bulldozers to prevent the state Housing Department from demolishing their terraces to build thirty-storey towers. I had conceived the film as a 'blow-by-blow' account, anticipating that the shooting would take place over a twelve-month period. I was wrong. The issue was actually resolved very rapidly in the first few weeks of filming. What could I do? I had to find another angle or another story. It was a situation I had to confront time and time again in subsequent documentaries.

It soon became obvious that the back story had to become the film. The struggle to save a few blocks of houses in Waterloo needed to become a larger story of this working-class suburb and its history. The idea was partly triggered by Margaret Barry, a woman who led these 'battlers'. Marg had lived all her life in a small terrace house, and had become increasingly isolated by the devastation around her. She had a great sense of history, she knew every planning scheme, every govern-ment minister responsible for this urban 'blight'. It seemed to me sensible that this person who had 'been through it all' tell this story of fifty years of misguided urban planning and the dislocation it caused.

Making our films was one thing, but showing them to audiences was another. It was the late 1970s and early 1980s, yet it was still unheard of for the ABC to buy in independently made documentaries. Apart from film festivals and the educational market, the little cinema in St Peter's Lane, Darlinghurst, was our only window to the world. People flocked to this 100-seat screen in the same way as they now flock to see Flickerfest or Tropfest. I remember making repeated representations to the documentary department of the ABC and being told that, in spite of the prizes it received, my film was only of limited general appeal. It was not only me, but David Bradbury had the same problem with his acclaimed film *Frontline* (1979). Meetings were called, petitions gathered and letters written. Finally, by the mid-1980s, independent documentary moved on to occupy its rightful place in the mainstream of public television.

In 1977, I went to the now-famous ethnographic film conference in Canberra, where I met the who's who of documentary. It affected me profoundly. I was suddenly introduced to the films of D.A. Pennebaker, Richard Leacock, the Maysles brothers, and Judith and David MacDougall. The *cinéma vérité* style personified through films like *Primary* (1960), *Salesman* (1969) and *Takeover* (1980) influenced me greatly and opened the door to whole new ways of making films. I responded to the spontaneous moments the roving camera captured, and how they mirrored the textures of everyday life.

For a while I rather fancied the idea of the camera being simply an objective recording device. My next two films borrowed heavily the purity of that style, but unlike my mentors of the 1970s I was not content to be just a 'fly on the wall'. Besides observation, I wanted to use a whole range of other devices: re-enactment, reflexive camera, acted voice-over. I also quickly came to the realisation that the camera was far from neutral.

Kemira—Diary of a Strike started spontaneously. Sixteen miners from a BHP colliery were suddenly presented with retrenchment notices. They barricaded themselves underground in a mine near Wollongong on the New South Wales south coast. It was an event that perfectly captured the spirit of the times. It was the early 1980s and the comfortable days of near-to-full employment were over: unemployment rates were sky-rocketing and traditional industries like coal and steel were shedding labour. But this time I didn't want to make a film in retrospect, I wanted to capture all the drama that was there in the heat of the moment.

Looking back it seemed a crazy thing to do. I had around $4000 saved, enough to buy and process just a few rolls of 16 mm film. I decided to take the plunge, shoot as much as I could with a crew working on deferred wages, and then present it to a funding body for post-production. The gamble worked. To have gone through the funding agencies would have necessitated the usual three-month wait. (These days having a digital video camera (DV-cam) and being able to shoot high-ratio makes such gambles less risky.)[2]

Kemira marked the devices I was to explore in my later films. They would have one or two strong main characters and a series of minor ones, plot turning points and sub-stories—all classic narrative fiction devices. I would also learn the discipline of editing in the camera as I went along, based on what might happen the next minute, the next hour, the next day or the next month. With a low-ratio film camera one had to be very careful when to roll-over, so you always had to keep one step ahead of the action. Of course predicting the future was speculative at best! This did not become any easier if the heat of the moment threw up a totally unexpected incident. (I am constantly amazed at how people in an undiscplined way now often shoot 120 hours of video for a one-hour program.)

In *Kemira* events are presented chronologically in the form of a diary. The surface of the mine is the stage where the drama unfolds, told through our main character Ngaire Wiltshire, the wife of one of the striking miners. What she thinks and feels at any given time gives the film emotional layering. We follow what happens to Ngaire over the ensuing months, chart her growing self-confidence following the break-up of her marriage against the growing demoralisation of the retrenched workers.

I decided to construct the story using all this compelling raw footage without a conventional narrator. Instead I used radio reports to provide my voice-over links and explanation. I also wanted to complicate the story by adding other voices and other points of view. Why not intersperse the pit-top drama with another drama happening in another location—the Coal Tribunal where BHP was doing battle with the union officials? So I got hold of the Tribunal transcripts and then reduced the essential arguments down to a few lines. Actors playing the key protagonists read these lines, which were complemented by a written text being typed onto the screen. Several months later I also reconstructed the occupation of the mine with the original underground strikers, and found archival footage which gave the film the necessary historical context.

Critical success with *Kemira* enabled me to obtain a Documentary Fellowship. This was a rare scheme initiated by the Australian Film Commission allowing a film-maker to make a film of his or her choice. So I decided to exploit my impeccable contacts with the union movement to do a film about another conflict. But this time I wanted to be much more 'on the inside'. I had the perfect opportunity. In Queensland 800 electricity workers had walked off the job to protest the government's intention of privatising the South East Queensland Electricity Board. The state was close to chaos with electricity blackouts every other night. Joh Bjelke-Petersen, in the twilight years of his premiership, engineered the show-down with the unions that he'd long planned.

I wanted to present both sides of the 'battle', but in different ways. I managed to get access to the minister given the job of resolving the dispute, Vince Lester. Vince was a farmer from central Queensland whose claim to fame included walking backwards for charity and inventing a novel way of locking toilet doors. He provided me access to meetings in the bush, to debutante balls, country shows and garden parties—everything that was quintessentially Queensland.

I approached the film chameleon-like, with a dinner jacket in my suitcase. Sometimes I would change clothes twice a day, flitting between a National Party barbecue and the union office. I felt I was capturing the extremes of Queensland political life: the arrogance of a government that knew it could win versus an embattled union tearing itself to pieces in trying to find a way to seize the initiative and win the strike.

There are no heroes in *Friends & Enemies*; I constructed them all as ambivalent characters. Vince was a clownish minister of state, but Bernie didn't fit comfortably into the stereotype of a working-class hero either. He was an angry, bitter man who dominated the strike committee through sheer force of personality. He was the one who organised the pickets. But when strikers—except for a core group of activists—stopped turning up, Bernie ran out of ideas. He then turned his aggressive anger against the union officials, blasting them about the way they ran the strike. As the strike dragged its way into the eighth month he grew more and more vociferous. He banged the table, harangued people who were his former allies, but ran out of puff when his wife started to turn against him. It was the women—the mothers and partners of the striking workers—who finally took over the organising role. Their warmth and dignity came to represent the moral conscience of the strike.

Unlike most of my films where I give my subjects the right of final approval, in *Friends & Enemies*, because of the bitterness and extreme divisions, no one person could ever possibly fit that role. As it stood, the film had no narration, just a few intertitles to signal where you were in the story. I tried to present the different political currents and sub-plots that unfolded over the eight months as fairly as I could, but a person could read different things into the film depending on which part of the political spectrum he or she stood.

The film premiered at the Sydney Film Festival where it received a very strong response, but what happened at its Brisbane launch took me completely by surprise. A packed audience at the Schonnel cinema witnessed that historic screening. A section of the crowd clapped but then Bernie suddenly leapt to the stage and denounced me for allegedly misrepresenting him and leaving out crucial parts of the story. The audience erupted. For the next two solid hours the stage turned into a soap-box where the film was debated and argued by protagonists on both sides. It was an experience that left me wounded and dazed.

Between 1987 and 1990, I made several films in quick succession. *Strangers in Paradise* (co-directed with Gil Scrine) was about a group of American tourists confronting indigenous Australians during the Bicentennial celebrations; *Bran Nue Dae* about Jimmy Chi's musical of the same name; and *Amongst Equals*, a feature-length documentary about the history of the Australian trade union movement.

Amongst Equals is a *cause célèbre* in trade union circles, and got me into big trouble with the Australian Council of Trade Unions (ACTU) when I released the film illegally after a protracted battle over the fine-cut. The film was my idea originally, but became a bicentenary project funded with taxpayers' money, 'sponsored' by the ACTU and produced through the government film arm Film Australia, who held the copyright. I knew that having a final film that would please everybody, including myself, would be an enormous task. Nevertheless, I pressed on and travelled the length and breadth of the country speaking to all the relevant historians, and looked for suitable interviewees. I then wrote the script which, to my amazement, met with total ACTU endorsement. Later I discovered they hadn't actually read it!

The peak union body's concerns didn't materialise until I had shot and cut the film. It emerged that what they'd really wanted was a hagiography which downplayed the history of industrial struggle and highlighted the government-union Accord and the arbitration system. Naturally, I objected on the grounds of censorship and the abuse of intellectual property. I had no intention of making a 'commercial' simply to suit the ACTU's political agenda at the time.

Several months of meetings proved futile and I simply contacted the best journalist I knew on the *Sydney Morning Herald* and told him the story. It featured on page three, displaced from page one only by the Gulf War. The reaction caught me completely by surprise; usually film-makers break their back trying to get the attention of the press. This time, however, I couldn't keep them away! Finally we decided to have a one-off screening of the film at the Chauvel cinema in Sydney. A few discreet posters and flyers went up around town. Well, the crowd stretched around the building—it was a night I won't forget in a long time!

In retrospect I was naive to think a film for a sponsor like the ACTU could ever be historically accurate. It was a bitter lesson in institutional politics, rife with moral questions for a documentary film-maker. I decided it was time for me to change course—at least in terms of subject matter.

I'd read in a newspaper about an Englishman, Alistair McAlpine, who apparently owned large tracts of Broome, a town in the remote north of Western Australia. The report implied McAlpine had major designs on the development of the whole region and Broome was quite divided over his presence. The tourist operators salivated at the prospects of rapid growth; the large Aboriginal population was concerned about the impact of development on land and indigenous culture.

McAlpine spanned a number of contradictions. He was a true blue Tory, who held important offices inside Thatcher's Conservative Party, but he was also a small 'c' conservationist—having lovingly restored many of Broome's classic pearler villas plus the town's ancient open-air movie theatre. I obtained a letter of interest from the ABC, cashed in my Bankcard and headed north, having arranged to meet McAlpine in his private zoo. To my surprise he readily agreed to be involved. Soon, I found myself filming the Redex rally and its motley crew (including McAlpine) arriving in Broome, to the astonished stares of the mainly Aboriginal bystanders.

What fascinated me was the complexity of McAlpine's relationship with the Aboriginal community. He really polarised opinion. Many thought change was coming too fast. Others, including an elder Paddy Roe, were convinced that sacred sites would only be protected with a conservation-minded developer, and McAlpine represented that ethos. The eventual film covered a year in the life of the community portraying how McAlpine cleverly endeared himself to both sides by bankrolling various projects, including Jimmy Chi's spectacular musical *Bran Nue Dae*.

My filming, however, was beset by frustration, especially the fact that McAlpine never gave me the permission to film at his home or at meetings. I resolved this problem to an extent by setting up situations where McAlpine would interact with other characters in the film and then stand back to film what would happen. Access is a problem that continually bugs documentary-makers. This hasn't been made any easier by people's growing distrust of the media and the unethical tactics that many journalists employ.

By the time I started my next film I was convinced that the best documentaries were the ones in which the action came directly from individual characters. Naturally one always has to start from an original idea, but the next step is to cast aside that idea and concentrate on finding a suitable character-driven story. This was the spirit in which I approached *Homelands*—probably my most satisfying film—although also probably the toughest.

My initial idea was to make a film about trauma and torture survivors, people who had survived a civil war and made their home in Australia. I had in mind to look at the social and psychological problems caused by the process of living the pain day by day, and how these were reflected in the tensions between the generations of a family. I decided to base myself in the Salvadorian community. Salvadorians had been arriving in Australia since the late 1970s under the government refugee program. A civil war had raged in the country for eleven years, claiming 80 000 lives and forcing 20 per cent of the population to leave the country as refugees. Human rights abuses were widespread.

However, as my research progressed and I started to 'audition' possible subjects, my ideas about the film began to change because the situation in the old homeland was also changing. In El Salvador peace talks were in progress and a permanent settlement was in sight. Many families I met were torn by a practical need to stay and an emotional desire to return. The idea of homeland meant different things to different families, and to different individuals within those families.

Maria and Carlos perfectly epitomised these tensions. I stumbled on to them by accident. They'd been going through a stormy and difficult period. Carlos had never really wanted to leave El Salvador and the struggle, where he had trained people as urban guerillas. One of the

[TOM ZUBRYCKI]

Maria and Carlos, *Homelands*

guerillas was his wife, Maria, who had suffered a lot—she was kidnapped for three days and tortured. The brutality of what both of them had been through was reflected in stresses within their marriage. These tensions were heightened as a result of their different experiences in Australia. Carlos worked as a cleaner in a hospital, while Maria had a professionally fulfilling job as a teacher. Their children were well settled into Australian schools. Yet it was no surprise to me that Carlos wanted to return as soon as the situation allowed. He actually left not long after filming started for an undisclosed period, perhaps around six months.

The price one pays for having a subject-driven film is that you break the traditional film-maker's role of being an uninvolved observer. You try to win over your subjects so they cooperate in the film. A degree of seduction is involved, to put it rather bluntly.

I was frankly unsure of my relationship with Maria. There was certainly trust on her side, but she also set up an emotional dependence. For me the roles of film-maker, friend and counsellor overlapped and merged, and as the filming continued (it took place over a twelve-month period) Maria, Carlos and I became involved in a complex three-way relationship. It all suddenly came to a head when Maria decided to leave Australia to track down Carlos. When we arrived in El Salvador Carlos turned a cold shoulder—in retrospect, not at all surprising. I realised later in the editing that something needed to be acknowledged: my presence was obviously affecting the dynamics of the situation. I decided to embark on a voice-over narration. I had never written one before because I always pretended to be invisible, but after four months of editing I came to the conclusion my own voice as the film-maker had to be clearly heard and identified. A writer friend helped me to inject the necessary 'nuance'. I believe it added an important layer of meaning to the film.

There always remained the possibility that at any time Maria and Carlos would simply withdraw their cooperation, which made for extremely anxious moments. When you make a film like *Homelands* you enter a form of 'social' contract, a mutual understanding. The film's subjects want something from you and you want something from them in return. I wanted the best possible film, and they wanted one which would educate the wider community about the real issues confronting refugees such as themselves.

Naturally I needed to show the film to the family at fine-cut. I sat there terrified, knowing that they had the ultimate power of veto. (Formal releases don't mean a thing in this kind of documentary.) Maria even brought in her own audience of work colleagues and twenty of us crowded around the Steenbeck (a 16 mm edit machine). In the end a few tears were shed but there was nothing to fear.

So did the film turn Maria into a martyr? Or did it really empower her to take her life into her own hands? (Her marriage with Carlos broke up a year after the film was completed.) Did the film act as a psycho-drama and have a therapeutic dimension? Five years on and these questions still go through my mind.

In my next film, *Billal*, my desire was to take an approach of a participant/witness, and I made that very clear from the start. It was a technique of getting around the ethical dilemmas that loom as soon as a film-maker wants to make somebody else's trauma the subject of a film.

Billal fell into my lap more by chance than design. My original intention was to focus on a group of teenagers who were about to leave high school in the outer west of Sydney where racial tensions controlled life. I planned to follow their lives over the ensuing twelve months, but then a dramatic U-turn suddenly occurred.

It was the Easter weekend of 1994. I hadn't started filming and was still in the process of 'auditioning' the film when I was called by one of the kids, who told me that their friend Billal, a Lebanese-Australian, was a sudden victim of a 'hit-and-run'. The sixteen-year-old teenager was lying in a hospital bed in a coma with serious brain damage. I immediately changed tack to follow the new story—of how Billal's family were to sort out their shattered lives over the ensuing fifteen months. The ABC, which had pre-purchased the original film, was easily persuaded to this new idea.

The family needed me as much as I needed them. They felt isolated. They felt they couldn't trust anyone, even social workers from their own community. I was the closest at hand. My role as film-maker quickly became complicated as I became their counsellor and advocate. Our interpreter, Alissar, ended up as an intermediary between the family and the bureaucratic outside world, and as the film progressed she herself became an important on-screen character. Through a process of reciprocity we forged a relationship that went beyond the film itself. As the film-maker I felt myself to be part-creator, part-facilitator. This notion of advocacy is, I believe, one way of confronting the ethical problem of documentary.

Billal turned out to be a waiting game. My original plan was to film key scenes that marked various stages of the boy's recovery. This was to be the film's main narrative line. Simultaneously I concentrated on fleshing out the other characters, especially the two brothers. However, unexpected events were to intervene. The family's aborted attempts at finding a new house suddenly created a separate dramatic line. The film then became not one story but several stories knitted together. To create some sense of all these story-lines and the various twists and turns, I adopted a technique I'd used in past films, which was to begin the editing process from a very early stage. Rather than wait fifteen months to start putting together the story, we began the edit just after the first scenes had been shot. We did this on-and-off over six months of the following eighteen, as we accumulated more material.

The art of making a film like *Billal* is to predict exactly just how things will turn out, and therefore just how long the shooting is going to take. The idea is not to be too intrusive, but also to not miss any vital moments. All we had going for us was the opinion of a few specialists who warned us of various stages of emotional and psychological adjustments Billal's parents were expected to go through. As the months went by, we were told they would eventually become reconciled to their son's disabilities. Up to a point this happened, but nothing prepared us for the shock when Billal's behaviour started to radically deteriorate after an operation which was supposed to actually make him better. It came as a stark surprise, not only to us, but to the family as well.

What difference, I wonder now, would it have made to *Billal* if we had digi-cams? Not much at all, I would suggest. We shot on a 20:1 ratio on 16 mm to make a ninety-minute film, and I would not have shot on a much higher ratio with tape. We had the family's privacy to consider, and to have over-shot would have alienated their trust.

As we near the end of the twentieth century, I see three main genres of documentary emerging, prompted in part by the new advances in digital technology, and also by a much more competitive broadcast environment.

FACTUAL SOAPS

These blur the distinction between documentary and entertainment. There is a strong appetite for them on television as reflected by the prime-time slots they occupy. A good example is the British series *Driving School*, which first appeared on the ABC late in 1997. *Driving School* follows first-time drivers and their instructors, and much of the action is shot from the back seat of a car with concealed cameras. The series is made up of a number of half-hour episodes, each shot over a period of about five days with two weeks to edit. Each episode comes with a fair dollop of humour usually at the expense of the poor complicit subject, and is cut in such a way that it ends with a cliff-hanger. The idea is naturally to lure the audience and entice them to keep watching the following week.

I imagine these docu-soaps taking over many of the prime-time slots, forcing higher quality documentaries to later evening spots. This has certainly been the British experience, and it presents a worrying pattern.

VIDEO DIARIES AND GUERILLA FILM-MAKING

Gaining access to difficult and exotic locations with a digital camera has led to a new genre of personal documentary or, more accurately, 'first-person reportage'. This initiative has been mainly broadcaster-driven—witness *Race Around the World*, which also aired on the ABC in 1997. The weekly half-hour programs made up of a number of four-minute documentary 'sonnets' shot by different individuals definitely captured the public imagination. But what accounted for their success?

The 'game show' package certainly helped. Other reasons included viewers' vicarious fascination with unfamiliar and exotic locations, plus the strong presence and stamp of the selected film-makers.

The British have taken this one step further. The 'local' has also become the 'exotic': *United Kingdom* is a twenty-six-part series of varying lengths, shot solely by one-person crews using digi-cams, and was commissioned by the BBC in 1996 (aired in the UK in 1997). Forty low-skilled crews—usually first-time film-makers—took to the roads and gathered an enormous amount of footage covering the dreams, struggles and ordinary situations in the lives of their fellow citizens all over the country.

MAINSTREAM DOCUMENTARY PRODUCTION

I fear for this sector which I earn my living from, especially the feature documentary. There is always going to be a high demand for nature, animal and adventure documentaries, but who is going to make those long, carefully crafted, observational films which capture the spontaneous drama of everyday life? Who is going to make the long archival-driven films demanding meticulous research?

I personally believe there will always be a place for the feature documentary. It will survive because people respect and enjoy strong compelling narrative, and some stories, like good fiction drama, demand ninety minutes or more to unravel. The availability of low-cost, high-quality camera technology will inevitably influence the kinds of stories that are told and the style in which these films are made. My feeling is that documentaries will become increasingly linked to a director's singular vision. *Exile in Sarajevo*, which I produced between 1995 and 1997, is a good case in point. This ninety-minute film is set in Sarajevo in the final year of the siege of the city. Having a Hi-8 camera allowed the directors Tahir Cambis and Alma Sahbaz to take over the shooting when the original cinematographer was forced to leave. They remained in the besieged city to witness the final 'act', the liberation and re-unification of parts of the city under Bosnian-Serb control.

I'm currently evaluating the impact of digital video (DV) and where this work will take me. I still want to make documentaries of quality, to which I am emotionally and intellectually committed to the subject matter, and which allow me to research, shoot and edit over a relatively long period of time (between one-and-a-half and three years). However, to be given this opportunity is becoming an increasingly rare privilege. One reason is that the independent documentary sector in Australia between 1994 and 1997 has shrunk by 40 per cent. Another reason is the segmentation of the industry.

documentary: a personal view

Making a viable living from documentary is becoming harder rather than easier. For many years I managed to get by with making one film and then another, but now my personal income is drawn from a variety of sources—directing, producing, teaching, consulting, script assessing. In 1997, a group of documentary-makers spent more time organising campaigns and representations to government than working on our projects!

Advances in digital technology, and the renewed interest in documentary, have caused need to be coupled with continuing growth in government support. Fortunately there are presently many avenues through which support is provided—Film Australia, through its National Interest Program, the Australian Film Commission, the Film Finance Corporation, plus the ABC and SBS through broadcast pre-sales. Nevertheless, the total funding envelope has remained static for several years despite repeated arguments for the documentary's crucial cultural relevance.

Making something without a broadcaster requires enormous enterprise on the part of the film-maker, yet risk-taking is increasingly becoming the essence of the business and more and more people eager to make their first films are going down this track. You first must buy a digi-cam. You invest all your time and your spare cash into the film, shoot it yourself or deploy a small crew to work on deferred wages. You then present the film at rushes or rough-cut stage to a broadcaster. If you are very lucky you secure a licence for broadcast which allows you to hire a qualified editor for a few weeks to do a proper on-line and sound mix. It seems a desperate way to prise open a broadcaster's door. A colleague of mine recently tried to go down this road. For someone like her, in mid-career, it caused much physical strain and enormous mental anguish.

Will DV affect the way I make films? Having a broadcast-quality camera on permanent stand-by will certainly allow me to do a lot more spontaneous shooting both in the research and production stages. However, in the overall budget DV should only bring down costs marginally. It will not make a huge impact on the key production roles—the editor, for example, whom I consider to be the most important creative collaborator in any documentary. Good intuitive editors are hard to find and to my good fortune I have worked with editor Ray Thomas on the last five films. Ray and I have a very close working relationship and I get him involved in the film as early as practicably possible. Because the story inevitably takes shape as I shoot, Ray's constructive feedback from the very first set of rushes is absolutely crucial in determining what I do next.

In choosing ideas I will look for situations that are as much character-driven as event-driven. Instead of focusing on a crisis or flashpoint like the strike in *Kemira* or *Friends & Enemies*, I'm more interested in situations that will yield multi-layered characters . . . a bit like Jose Ramos-Horta, the exiled Timorese leader, in my current film *The Diplomat*. With a mix of good characters and the right elements of conflict and irony it's not hard to find a narrative structure. I'm also more inclined to rely on hunches and intuition based broadly on the experience I've gathered over the years.

In theory there is no place where a digital camera can't go, yet I predict that films dealing with society's core institutions are going to be harder to make. The problem will be getting around the spin doctors who manage access to these corridors of power. (How often do we see anything like *The House* (1996), a four-part, *verité*-driven exposé that eavesdropped on crisis management in London's troubled Covent Garden?) Paradoxically it will be easier to turn the cameras onto the victims of society. In the American show *Cops* (1989–) the camera follows a group of police to nail down an alleged criminal. The spectator is reduced to an uninvolved voyeur of another person's suffering. The powerless have the status of oddly anonymous beings and become the subject of the camera's fascinated gaze. Intimacy at a serious ethical cost.

As documentaries are being appropriated by the needs of television, and as docu-soap is eating into the definition of what used to be called documentary, I believe new challenges will confront the documentary film-maker. What will become important are the struggle over access, the re-definition of ethical boundaries, and experimentation with new ways of telling stories. The democratisation that DV has introduced also means that the very act of documentary production has to be viewed differently. More and more, pressure will fall on the film-maker—who continues to have ultimate power—to use the form responsibly.

the man behind the picture: an interview with mike rubbo

geoff burton

g_eoff Burton: The_ Lumiere _interview details how you went off on travels from a young age, making pilgrimages to different places and people, recording events and stories with a tape recorder, painting, taking still photographs. One could say here is the seed for_ Race Around the World _(1997–)._[1]

Mike Rubbo: I think that's true. Of course in those days, which were the early 1960s, I never conceived that I could ever release travellers' tales to a large market, as we do with our *Race* stories. When I came back and told tales of my travels, the biggest venues would have been at universities, but mostly it was to friends. It was a thrill to be captivating people with my combination of slides and tape recordings, but I never ever conceived that this sort of material would come anywhere close to a mass audience. Too low-tech, too personal.

I think what has happened now—which is wonderful for this new generation of young people, a generation which is of the age I was back then—is that there has been a tremendous breakthrough in terms of access to national audiences for their work, work not that much different from what I was doing. Then and now, it's very personal stuff. When I say breakthrough, I'm thinking of all the places you can now get wide exposure for short experimental works, the Tropicana Film Festival[2] here in Sydney, for example, and lots of other short film festivals around the country. Also, we have had this month of television called *LOUD*[3] on recently, which was a whole month of young television. What a showcase!

Then there's *Race Around the World*, which has become a sort of flagship example of young people being given tremendous freedom to go out and explore the world as I did—and to then see it actually go to air. That's the thing that the racers have trouble getting their heads around—not only do they do the work, but with virtually no delay the deftly edited result is showcased on television, week after week. No one gets such rapid exposure in real life. It's magical. Magical, too, how quickly they become well-known identities and well-formed film-makers.

One of the racers in Canada who had been on the Canadian version of the show—by the way this show originated in Quebec, and was in French[4]—said it was like a whole film career condensed into twenty weeks, a whole lifetime of film-making, of producing, getting feedback, improving, all at cyber speed. Looking back on my modest days, I suppose I'm a bit jealous. But then again, I can now say to myself that I was practising for something like *Race*. I was just like many other Australians, a good traveller, very open and empathetic with people. Documenting my travels with whatever technology I had at hand was just a logical add-on to the rich emotional process of interacting with people. After all, documentary is all about getting access to people's lives and having those people willing to give you good stories under certain circumstances. It is an exchange of valuables, meaning they get something and you get something. *Race Around the World*, the process of travelling with tiny unobtrusive cameras, is perfect for that negotiation to happen.

So it's probably a two-handed change in a way. Not only is it access to television and access to a large audience, which we didn't enjoy in the 1960s and early 1970s, but also access to more user-friendly and cheaper technology. There's a technological strand as well as a distribution strand.

Yes, the technology has made a huge difference. On my trip to India back in the 1960s I had a little Philips reel-to-reel tape recorder—no pictures on that trip. I came back with twenty tapes which I absolutely loved to play to people, especially the interviews with Satyajit Ray that I made in Calcutta, but my caught reality was very limited. Ray's deep sonorous voice blended in with the mournful cawing of crows in the background as he talked of films like *Pather Panchali* (1955), and how he'd moved from law to feature film-making. It was good stuff in its day, but now it would have very limited impact. Now, with these little cameras the racers use, you can bring back such incredibly intimate and vivid reports of your travels. It's quite a different impact.

We had a lucky break with *Race Around the World*. It so happened that just a month or two before the racers were about to start travelling, Sony came out with a tiny digital camera with a side-opening viewer. Now, not only is the camera palm-sized, easily carried in a pocket and looking like tourist gear, but the side-opening viewer makes for a

[AUSTRALIAN BROADCASTING CORPORATION]

Racers, 1997, *Race Around the World*

tremendous breakthrough, a leap the Canadian show had yet to take. This side viewer meant that the eye did not have to be locked to an eyepiece; the racer did not have to be separate but could be actually in the shot as just another informant.

Gone was the need to put the camera on a tripod and do a piece-to-camera as journalists have normally done. Racers found that they could simply park the camera at the end of their arm, turn the lens and viewer back on themselves and get on with the fun of being a traveller. In fact, it looks like the racers are in the films because there is a full crew behind the camera, but there's really nobody but themselves.

In a way, this flexibility of the camera has also made the personal vision in documentary more acceptable. When I was travelling as a documentary-maker in my National Film Board (NFB) days, there was a certain resistance on the part of most people to the film-maker being as personal as I tried to be. I was a bit of a leader in this, and it was a lonely and thankless role. It was considered self-indulgent, or you were considered a bit full of yourself, as if being personal was just a means of self-promotion. It had been all right with those audio tapes from India in the the context of talking to friends or to fairly small groups of people but, on television, they didn't like personal, anecdotal travellers' tales such as I often delivered.

In fact, my early films for the NFB in Canada suffered a great deal because they had the word 'I' in them. I was told you could not use the word 'I': you were not supposed to have opinions or feelings, you were supposed to be neutral and just a filter that collected stuff. But we are now in a much more personal era, when people's personal visions very often are valued even more than objective visions.

Times have really changed. Nobody has minded our racers filtering their material so personally, and in such a biased way. The king racer last year, the favourite, was John Safran, who just went around the world doing jokey stories about his own angst and his own religious feelings and sending the world up, using the world as a straight man for his humour. I don't think that would have been possible in the days I was working. It would have been considered really frivolous and a waste of resources and a waste of time.

But from very early in your career you were personalising your films.

Yes, as I said, I was something of a leader, but it was not something which was approved of, or written about as an interesting development. Even Dave Jones, who wrote the *Lumiere* article, gave me a hard time as if this tendency to personalise was a weakness that he was struggling to forgive.

Was it a problem for the producers?

Yes. The film I made in Vietnam, *Sad Song of Yellow Skin* (1970), had difficulty getting to air because my personal experiences in the war zone were perhaps thought to be trivialising the situation. I remember getting a stern lecture from an old hand just after I arrived, an American journalist who covered all the hot stuff. It was something to do with the need to be steered by concept and story, not personal encounters as I planned to be. Years later, I ran into him again and he confessed sheepishly that the film I had made in my whimsical way was one he wished he'd made.

It got worse for me with *Waiting for Fidel* (1974), which was never on television in Canada in spite of the fact that, among other things, it's a wonderful portrait of a much-loved Canadian folk hero, a former politician called Joey Smallwood. Can you imagine that?

I had a certain revenge. It was never on television and yet it became a sort of cult movie on the documentary festival circuit, and all because it's so personal and off the point in the usual sense. It is a film about a non-event, about waiting to meet a famous man, Fidel Castro, who never shows. As we wait, me and oddball companions fight over what we are seeing of the Cuban revolution.

Can you point to a change that has made the device of personal involvement in documentary more acceptable?

Print journalism became personal in flashes. There was Hunter S. Thompson with his so-called 'new journalism' or Gonzo journalism. I don't know how it might have happened with television—it just seeped into television. I think it probably happened earlier at film festivals with films like *Sherman's March* (1986),[5] Ross McElwee's film on going home to the South of the United States. He has made three of them now, a personal trilogy: *Sherman's March*, *Time Indefinite* (1993), and the first one, whose title I can't remember.[6] *Sherman's March* is a wonderfully, unabashedly personal film and a milestone in a way. You hardly ever see Ross, but you hear his voice—a worried, neurotic voice, a sort of waspish Woody Allen—wondering what his life adds up to as he wanders the South, meeting up with old flames, many of whom would like to flame again. The women of the South are very explicit, at least Ross's women are. He becomes this funny put-upon character.

The film uncovers a dark side, too. Nasty, extremist One Nation-types enter the frame. The film was a breakthrough. I'm trying to think of others. Shirley MacLaine made a film about China[7] for which she took a bunch of American women from very diverse backgrounds to China. It is quite personal. Perhaps the personal had crept in through other legitimising factors—the status of MacLaine, for example. In other words, the personal is excused because the person being personal is famous enough to require us to pay attention.

But you have caught me unawares here. I do not know what the change would have been, though I do think it probably happened through the longer documentaries at the film festivals; I've had good luck at film festivals, I've won prizes there and have had some recognition. But, as I said, I never got on television very much.

But at the same time as you were making films it seems there was also a very strong school of purely observational film-makers, especially among the Americans. Films that stood outside of what was going on and took a fly-on-the-wall approach to filming, religiously it would appear, and they took on a veracity as well. These films were especially effective in exploring institutions.

Yes, like Frederick Wiseman and the Maysles brothers, Albert and David, and Donn [D.A.] Pennebaker, and there were some big names in Canada too. I think that's true. The fly-on-the-wall approach was easier to take. Robert Drew, the daddy of this genre with his series for *Time-Life*, had got the observation idea from the photo-essays that *Life* made famous.[8]

It was more legitimate because it was about what it was about. It didn't have this other agenda of being personal. It is true that the personal can get in the way. It often drags the process into the story, and who really wants to know about the process?

I argue for the personal in another way. Very often, I think, the documentary film has to be personal in order for the audience to understand how the thing got made, not because that is interesting in itself but because one wants to know what the deal was, and if it was a fair deal. Remember that almost all documentary-making is an invasion of privacy. If you, an audience member, do not know on what terms the invasion has taken place, you may be made uncomfortable. Of course, you can be watching it in a purely voyeuristic way and quite enjoy seeing people's terrible pain and being privy to moments of death and so on. Enjoy in the sense that you are glad it is not happening to you. But if you don't know the terms of the agreement, you may be quite upset, or it can leave a very bad taste in your mouth. You may fear that hidden cameras have been used, or that people have been tricked into being seen in such vulnerable situations.

For example, take a film like *Grey Gardens* (1977) that the Maysles brothers made. It's a very famous film about a mad mother and daughter, the Beales, relatives of the Kennedys—Jackie Onassis actually—who live as recluses in a mansion in Long Island. That film was really problematic with some viewers but the Maysles got away with it because at the very beginning of the film you see them on camera talking to the younger Beale. She is very pleased to see them and seems to flirt with them. This glimpse allows you to conclude that a personal relationship has been established, that they've come into these women's lives because the women are lonely and they like the attention Albert and David are bringing them. Once you understand that, then you understand why you are seeing naked flesh flopping around, screaming fights and moments of tears. The material was obtained not through trickery, but through an exchange of valuables. The key question: what is the trade-off that happens in the documentary-making process? The audience sometimes has to be let in on this or those watching will feel uncomfortable.

I think one of the reasons Dennis O'Rourke got into such trouble with his *Good Woman of Bangkok* (1992) is because people didn't quite know what the deal was. We meet this beautiful prostitute in a hotel room in Bangkok. The man behind the camera is her lover, O'Rourke. She is so vulnerable and the situation is so strange. He is looking after her, he apparently loves her, and yet she is often revolted. He is making gifts to her, but imposing conditions, and the film-maker, handsome or ugly, thin or fat, remains unseen. You feel more sorry for her as the relentless questioning from behind the camera continues. More and more you ask why she is letting this happen. Does she love this man? Is she in his thrall? Does she hope to rip him off? Is it payback for the gifts? You don't know, and you get progressively more upset.

It would have been different if O'Rourke had come from behind the camera, if he had shown his fat flabby self, and let us judge him as much we judge her, for all this is body-trade stuff. Was it a fatal error? Would his visible inclusion have saved him from the wrath of audiences? Probably never has a film been so attacked, yet O'Rourke has said that he was quite conscious of what he was doing and that in fact he was sacrificing himself to make a point about how we white males exploit Asian women. And even about how all documentary film-makers exploit their subjects ruthlessly to their ends. It is no accident we speak of shooting a documentary. O'Rourke claims that to have been a more likeable person doing a fairer deal would have hidden the truth he wanted to show. No other documentary film-maker I know has laid himself out to blows like this. There has been a very interesting book[9] written about this actually, well worth a read. Conscious or not, the film offends mostly because the exchange of valuables is both unclear and very suspect.

I was shooting something else on two occasions in Bangkok when O'Rourke was making that film and from what I understand an early brief to himself was to appear on camera and that it would be a much more personal self-condemnation of being in an exploitative role, and through that to explore the other issue of sexuality. In the process of making the film that idea completely changed, and as a result perhaps made a more controversial film. From what you are saying, not necessarily a satisfactory film.

Well, for his critics it's not satisfactory. But I think that in a funny, back-handed way it's a wonderful film because it has provoked so much debate, and in that way the film has served a great purpose. Also, an excellent text, the book I referred to, has been written, and so it's a very interesting film to teach and from which to ask these sorts of questions. So thanks to O'Rourke for doing that, thanks for not making it more politically correct or more sensitive.

Nick Bloomfield does this. He puts himself in his films to the point of being offensive and you know to a degree where he is coming from; you know how he got access to the touchy situations he enjoys. It's partly because he is very handsome and very charming and ingratiating. He gives people's lives and situations deep and reverential thought, and this is flattering. But he also has a profound understanding of the dynamic of the situation into which he enters, whether it be an army barracks or a brothel. And he is relentless! You see his relentless pursuit of people, and so the process is itself a little part of the product.

More and more I feel that something of the process must be there. I think with *Race* we've very much made the process the product. We've shown the whole country how we chose the racers, the whole country knows how we trained them, knows their backgrounds, and when they go out on the road and have troubles, they or we tell the audience that too. The exchange of valuables is clear.

And what their reward is for success.

That's right. In a way *Race* is somehow a culmination of a lot of things, and it is being delivered in four-minute bites, which seems to be the perfect mouthful for the attention spans of today.

Is it culmination of a lot of things for you?

I think so. Although I'm not actually making it, I'm behind the scenes. I'm not the series producer, I'm not in charge of the daily business. I hope I'm the guru behind the scenes. I must confess that when *Race* got going I had no idea it would work out like it did. I didn't realise there was this huge potential on the part of a younger audience to be so interested in the documentary. I had not imagined that the twenty-to-thirty age group was that interested in documentary. If you are living life to the hilt, do you also want to sit and watch it? I was not sure.

We knew that the new element of the show, Richard Fidler's total command of the scene and racy humour, would appeal. But the *Race* documentaries are not that much different from what one sees normally these days. They're just the shorter versions of what we have been talking about, of this personal aspect of documentary that has been growing over the years, so we were worried. Will a nomadic family in Kurdistan really hold this audience when they won't watch the same thing on *National Geographic*? Yes, and the reasons are because of the personal, the authorship and the packaging. By packaging I mean the host, the judging, the scoring, the winning and the losing—all of that enriches those four-minute slices of life from around the globe.

The judging process seems to be important because, once you have them formally judged in the studio situation, this gives everyone else permission to judge as well. So people sit at home arguing about whether a particular judgement was fair or not. Perhaps judging is satisfactory for another reason. If making the documentary film is always problematic, the business of collecting bits of people, of perhaps ripping people off, then having judgements passed may make it seem all right. The contest is changed. This brings me to the documentary we censored, the one we didn't run, for instance.

The confessional one?

Yes, John Safran's piece on the Catholic Church in Brazil. I was behind that decision and I must say there were many people at the ABC who were very much against me for censoring it. They agreed it was unethical documentary-making, but they felt the judgement on the piece could be passed in the show by the judges. Bob Connolly, for example, said to me: 'Let it go on and we'll just rubbish it as judges.' But I thought no, that just lets us off the hook. To use an extreme example, we would not run a snuff movie and then let the judges abhor it. This is not a snuff movie but it does betray a fundamental principle of documentary-making in my book, and that is you don't use hidden cameras without a very good reason, if at all. I was caught in a dilemma. The piece was funny—Safran at his best or worst—but because the show is premised on the whole idea of how one ethically gets access to people's lives—the exchange of valuables—how could we run something in which the film-maker flagrantly ripped off people who had no idea he was making them the butt of his flabby jokes?

Here was a case where the film-maker had hidden the camera in his crotch, sitting in confessionals, shooting priests without their knowledge. If he had gone to them later and said, 'Look I've videoed you,' then that would have been fair enough. Or if the people had been evil in some way, torturers or corrupt officials, really reprehensible people, then that would have been all right too in my book. Bottom line is, I thought that in this particular case, the hidden camera was really wrong. It was also against the written rules in as much as a release had to be obtained from all who are filmed. Normally we don't check. The visibility of the camera to the subject can be taken as an agreement, as Wiseman argues, but none of this was true here.

If you don't mind me pursuing the issue further, do you have a particular religious bent or responsibility which required that response? Because, as you say, concealed cameras have been used in all sorts of situations, sexual or assault situations, especially when involving confrontations.

But isn't that usually to do with exposing some wrong-doing?

I guess it is, which makes it more legitimate. Whereas this was an intrusion against peaceable, innocent people who assume that what is being said is going to be confidential, and so it was wrong to violate that confidentiality.

If it had been some hard-hitting piece on the hypocrisy of the church which, say, grants absolution on sins but then we learn that the priests turn around and sin themselves, abuse small boys or something, then to me it would have seemed quite okay.

As proof of the fact that my decision wasn't based on my religious sensibilities, we happily ran Safran's story before that, where he had made fun of African Baptists. I love it because Safran made himself as vulnerable and as silly as the locals. He had himself baptised in a filthy river, a dangerous thing to do. Then, he played with the idea that he wasn't a Jew any more and that his parents would freak. And he included in his documentary the expectations of the Baptists, namely that he go back to Australia and spread the word.

In a way, this documentary is a perfect example of what I've been talking about, namely that there was an exchange of valuables in the sense that, even as they gave themselves to Safran's camera, the local Baptists thought they were getting something in return. Not only did he exchange valuables but he also exchanged vulnerabilities by being dunked in a very dirty river, probably full of guinea worm and other nasty parasites. They were exposed on film, he was exposed in another way—a fair exchange. Safran paid his dues to get his story, and the camera was never hidden—it was very open, even though it was equally mocking of religion. The same can be said of his story on Jerusalem where he streaked through the old city and, as a Jew—he was back to being a Jew again—seriously mocked his own sacred site. I thought these two documentaries were fine.

To have these debates on television or at a film festival or in the seminar is part of the fun of documentaries. They are always problematic and must be constantly debated. Sometimes you may be reducing people's safety by exposing them to a corrupt regime that will shoot them, or to others who may disparage and mock them in some way. All these very problematic issues will never be eliminated. This moral risk is even a part of the excitement, the *frisson*, as the French say, we find around the documentary.

Sometimes the exchange might seem 'suss' for other reasons. Underneath an observational guise, is the film-maker actually in cahoots with the subject to promote some cause or creed? I was executive producer of a film in 1997 by Graham Chase, one of our great documentary film-makers, who unfortunately died of cancer in 1997. Not long before he died, he made an observational film about Graeme Campbell, a Western Australian politician of the Pauline Hanson ilk. The film followed Campbell through an election. It was not judgemental, neither approving nor disapproving. Or was it? The audience at the Sydney Film Festival hated the film; they hated the screen time given to this man. They also hated what they took to be a false veneer of objectivity— objectivity masking approval.

A very interesting debate followed about whether the film enhanced Campbell's prestige or whether it just showed him candidly and openly. There seems to be something particularly insidious about using the noble cloak of the documentary to drape over hidden agenda work. I don't think Graham Chase did this. I know he did not. Graeme Campbell was a strange creature, a phenomenon to be observed, almost like a gorilla in the wild. Anyway, that kind of debate will never stop.

It's a debate one rarely has around fiction film. I can't think of many fiction films that fire such ethical debates, apart from films dramatising the life of Jesus, and perhaps *Schindler's List* (1993); films which have people very upset because of a connection to a reality they cherish. But in documentary it happens much more frequently—all the time, in fact.

And of course this raises a profound question about the responsibility of the documentary film-maker. For example, in all the work I've done with Curtis Levy on Indonesia, you realise you are speaking to people who know anti-government leaks and are speaking to you because you represent another country in another continent, but they are putting their lives in some jeopardy by being outspoken against the regime.

That's right. And what do you do about it? That's the constant questioning. Do you say they should be aware of that situation, or do you take on a custodial relationship regarding their safety?

I think you take on a custodial role, don't you?

Yes, I do.

And ultimately what we have to decide is whether what they are saying is worth the personal risk to them by using it.

Absolutely, that's an important question.

Let's just swing this a little more personally if you don't mind. You worked at the National Film Board in Canada and you're a film-maker; you were not a television animal. What was the experience like of heading the documentary division at the ABC?

Awful! No, it was both exciting and awful. It was exciting in the sense that Penny Chapman, who had recruited me, gave me a lot of freedom. Secondly, I would say my collegues at the ABC in upper-management were quite helpful because it was soon understood that I didn't know anything about television management. It was assumed that I would make some mistakes—and I indeed proceeded to make lots of mistakes. What was really daunting about it was that for more than a year I'd go to meetings and at these meetings they were talking television jargon, about windows of opportunity, markets and market share, and I understood nothing. I was a very slow learner. Ratings I understood, of course, but most of it just went over the top of my head, and I became known as somebody who wrote in notebooks. I filled some thirty notebooks, furiously scribbling all that was said in the hope that by writing it down it would become clear to me sooner or later. But I have never read those notes, thousands of pages of notes—they are all just sitting there.

But, in the meantime, I did have a clear idea of what I wanted to do. I wanted to bring observational films to the ABC and I wanted to get things like *Race Around the World* going. The new digi-cams had just arrived and I wanted to explore making films in a much more free and flexible way. But I ran into fierce opposition from some local film-makers who were accustomed to making a lot of essay type films and had no interest in the observational genre. They saw me as a real threat, because admittedly I was touted as someone who would not commission anything that was scripted or of the essay type. As a result, I quickly made some very powerful enemies who proceeded to effectively white-ant me. My problem was compounded by the fact that I am not a good networker. I went home to my family, and not out with those who held the purse strings. It did not seem to matter that I wasn't against the essay-type of film particularly, and in fact commissioned quite a few, even acted as executive producer on some. Don Pahram did a film for me called *Love Tragedies* (1998), an essay on adultery, very much a talking-heads film almost in a David Goldie way, and I was David Goldie's executive producer on *Burden of Proof* (1998), and I worked with Judy Darling on *Dead Letters* (1997),[10] a touching essay on the dead letter office.

I loved all of that, but at the same time I also had a vision and direction. I felt that observational films at the ABC had been languishing. There had been some glories of the style, films by people like Dennis O'Rourke, Tom Zubrycki, Graham Chase, and there was Bob Connolly and Robin Anderson, a wonderful team doing observational films. But they weren't being done on a regular basis at the ABC, and didn't have the status that I thought they should have. The style was considered rather flaky and eccentric and accidental, whereas I wanted it to have a philosophical position in society.

So I call these films the background briefing papers on the way we are. We have news and current affairs which tell us about daily events and then we have these 'backgrounders', if you like, which delve into the actuality of the moment and archive society as it's going along. For instance, I often ranted about the fact that Australia has gone through fascinating eras of politics, the Whitlam era and the Keating era, now the Hanson era, and there is nothing on film that was anything like what Pennebaker had done with Kennedy in the States. We have to have recourse to fiction, with shows like *The Dismissal* (1983), to tell us what happened. All those politicians of those times have been recorded on talk shows, *Meet the Press* style, in door-stop situations, but never just observed candidly, quietly.

So soon after taking over, the documentary division tried to get into the political parties, but without success. Everyone turned us down. But it has been done and it must be done. We did have some success with softer targets.

I also brought in a guy called Simon Target who did a marvellous four-part documentary on Sydney University,[11] and it's very much of the inner-sanctum type I was after. Simon actually took the observational film a little step further towards the personal as he became a voice behind the camera, empathising with the students and their lives. It is very charming and very right. In fact, this style follows in the tradition of Molly Dineen, the great English documentary-maker with her zoo film, *The Ark* (1992), and *Home From the Hill* (1986). Simon was actually a student with Molly, which impressed me since I admired her work so much. Simon is now doing some more documentaries in the same vein on a private school, of which I am the executive producer. So there's that project in the observational mode, plus a series we did with Film Australia on real-estate auctions, *Under the Hammer* (1997),[12] and many others. We got a lot of observational stuff going with people who had done little of it, like Tim Clarke, here within the ABC, who went out and did observational films. He and others then started to use the camera themselves, which was tremendously exciting.

But at the time I felt the situation was rather fragmentary. I was having all these little bitty successes. Nonetheless, it all began to come together towards the end of my tenure, and then *Race* came and that really became the pinnacle of the process.

So despite claims of an awful process, you've managed to achieve a very substantial body of work.

Yes, it's worked out extremely well. I think there are thirty documentaries on which I've had an intimate hand, and of which I'm very proud. Although I was very pissed off at the time, it has worked out well that I am not in the job any more, otherwise I couldn't be intimately involved with *Race*. Nor could I go back to observational documentary film-making myself.

It is a pretty scary thing to do because I actually haven't made a documentary for fifteen years, let alone shoot and do everything else myself as I am now doing. I'll tell you there were moments of real trepidation when I almost decided not to go ahead. I had every excuse to lie low. I was executive-producing several programs and I could have just sat here at the ABC until the end of my contract. But I thought, 'No, this is my chance to practise what I've been preaching.'

Tell us briefly about the project you are working on now.

It was actually suggested to me by my wife Katerina, who is Russian and has connections, through her family, to the world of violins. She kept saying that the violin is a fascinating instrument, and it's very strange that this little piece of technology, which was perfected 350 years ago, is still just the same today. There is no other 350-year-old machine in the world; the violin is a machine for making noise vibrations that we use by preference over a modern model. I got hooked. It's really weird—everything else has changed and not the little fiddle. I agreed that fact was really interesting, and it's very romantic, too, with the possibility of having lovely music in such a film. So, we started meeting violin-makers here in Australia and found them to be interesting characters. Then we thought we must go to the cradle of all this, to where violins were born, which is the town of Cremona in Northern Italy. This is where Antonio Stradivari and Niccolo Amati and Giuseppe Guarneri[13] worked, the three great names in the violin world, from around 1550 through to about 1750, the golden period of violin-making.

We've made it as a very personal journey in a *Race Around the World* kind of way. We filmed in Cremona for ten days and worked as a team: my wife in front of the camera to some extent and me the voice behind the camera as we recorded the process of discovery.

Perhaps the film, which is titled *The Little Box That Sings* (still to be released), will start with a phone call from Rebecca Anderson, a young Australian who is the only Australian at the Stradivari international violin school in Cremona. Rebecca had become a key contact and possible subject. I was going to follow her and discover what happens at the school.

We arrive and suddenly Rebecca tells me that she has decided to leave the school the next day. My talent is gone! So of course I rush to the house where she is staying, in the middle of the night because she is leaving at 7 a.m. the next day, and get it all on tape. While I'm shocked, I'm also excited at the twists life takes, as documentary film-makers should be. With Rebecca I find three other young violin-makers, also students, drinking by the light of a single bulb while Rebecca tells me why the school is no good for her any more. The next morning I'm telling Katerina about what's happened, and about a strange young German who was one of those at the table. He has a faun-like face, a very sensitive young guy who looks sort of like a human violin. I had found my camera drifting onto him, Rebecca forgotten. All this I tell to Katerina, also on tape, and so the show begins. Whether it will come out like this, I do not know. I have just been knocked back on the two hours I would need to follow this structure.

Anyway, if it happens as I saw it, it will be a very personal journey through Cremona and the world of violin-makers. We'll hear about Antonio Stradivari from the last surviving member of the Stradivari family, an actress in her forties who does *Commedia Dell'arte* theatre and doesn't want to talk about her famous relative, but about the castle she owns. Documentary-making is all about encounters, sensing their meaning and their value to the project in hand, while at the same time being a feeling human being who likes people and wants to spend time with them for other reasons.

And despite your trepidation you seem to have stepped back into that process very easily.

Absolutely, and I think I've gone further. I now don't have the same worries about being personal, perhaps because I might have a back-handed position in this film. Katerina may be in front and me just a voice. Katerina has a very calm persona; she is a sort of mystical creature, which seems to fascinate some of those who've seen the material. Our child, Ellen, is also with us, a charming little five-year-old who may briefly appear.

For me to be an off-camera presence feels very nice right now. It feels right because the project is due to my wife's interest in the subject. And her almost simple appreciation of the craftsmen we meet seems to be a good mediation with the subject.

Without being too profound about it, has there taken place a transference of involvement? In your early films you were there on camera, especially in Waiting For Fidel, *to take one example, but now you are actually representing yourself through your wife and child.*

Yes, it is a transference. It's interesting, too, because Katerina is twenty years younger than I am, and at my age, nearly sixty, to have a child who is five years old, is also like a transference of a life force. It seems very appropriate that they seem to be carrying the life of the movie, or taking the movie forward. The film might actually end with little Ellen in the back of the car saying, 'Stradivari! Stradivari!', rolling the 'r' as we leave town in pouring rain. She's fed up but she's been very good. But now I've struck a block, and will cut the Australian material first, in which Katerina is less present, so who knows what will happen.

But whatever happens with this project, whether it goes up or down, I think I would like to do more with Katerina. I think she's almost like a spiritual medium, and she plays the go-between not in a sort of cerebral way but in a feeling way. I have usually had go-betweens in my documentaries, westerners who filtered the exotic experience. Now I have Katerina. She has a strange effect on people. There are sequences, for instance, of a violin-maker called Alceste who, with his wife, Louisa, is custodian of a fourteenth-century monastery near Cremona. He's also a violin-maker but a real recluse. He sits monk-like at a little table, in front of a window in a huge room full of religious icons and strange echoes of the past. He is absolutely silent, scraping the wood, making no more noise than a mouse, scraping on the white-bodied little corpse of the violin. Then you notice that Katerina is standing there communing with this whole process. Then it turns out that he is letting us tape only because he is fascinated by her, although he doesn't talk to her, not till later at least, and I watch it all, even more silent than he. It's quite magical.

What you just said reminded me of the end of your interview with Dave Jones back in 1973 where you talk about pursuing magic.

I didn't mean magic in a literal sense back then. I think I was telling him that sometimes places are pregnant with strange feeling and meanings, as the Island of Peace was in my film *Sad Song of Yellow Skin*. This was a tiny island inhabited by the followers of a strange little monk, a Gandhi-like figure who was nicknamed 'the Coconut Monk' because he had once sat on top of a coconut tree for seven years without coming down, praying for peace in his war-torn country. With such a leader no wonder the place was magical. Devotees in rich orange-red robes flitted around, coming together for services which were part-religion and part-magic, services in which the monk would manipulate vegetable mortars and cannons to silence the real thing while often actual bullets flew overhead. It was the magic realism of [Gabriel] García Márquez, come to think of it. So you are right, and in fact the violin film is rather like that too. There are lots of these magical moments in places, especially with Alceste, the violin-maker in his monastic environment, with Katerina watching him work. Yes, that's what I am doing.

Let me just raise another point here about painting because painterly notions are rarely discussed in relation to documentary, yet you have, on occasion, made allusions to painting and its relationship to documentary.

I suppose I am a painter, but I'm also very much a documentary painter. I don't have much imagination, I don't really trust my imagination because it seems to me like a vague miasmic thing that I don't know quite how to capture. I fear to paint from my imagination.

So painting is for you another recording device, to put it very basically. Although the style of your paintings is very impressionistic.

Well, you can see them on the walls of my office here. They have a documentary style, don't you think? Most of these are of Quebec, where we lived recently, and then there are Van Gogh copies which I did for a kid's feature film. The paintings are very realistic.

But not in a photographic sense.

I don't know. I think by today's standards my impressionist style, if you like, is extremely realistic. I could show you photographs of the places seen in my painting and they look very much like the scenes I've painted.

I think what is more important is that I've always been interested in the business of archiving the times of one's own life, and the things and people around me. I have huge quantities of personal VHSs about Katerina and Ellen, which I may do something with some day—huge amounts of personal recordings and thousands of still photographs. I suppose I really like the idea of archiving.

But then to whom is it interesting besides me and my family? Ironically, all that material, in whatever medium, mainly becomes interesting if you are a famous person, because then your vision is treated as important. If you are not particularly notable then none of that material is really of much interest to anyone. Not that I particularly want to be famous. That would be a terrible burden, a burden to perform all the time, and even now there is a burden to perform, to come up to the mark all the time, which is exhausting. One needs to be well enough known to be allowed to do what one wants to do. And more than that, fame works in reverse too, stops you doing things. There is a teeter-totter point of ideal recognition, difficult to get to, and almost impossible to keep up without falling to one side or the other. Still, all that stuff is there and something will happen to it one day, if it survives.

One can speculate on documentaries of the future because of the extraordinary resources available to documentarians from people's home videos, if you like. For example, I did a feature film a couple of years ago at Sorrento,[14] down on the Mornington Peninsula, and we were keen to get some 8 mm footage to use in the title sequence, of people on the beach at Sorrento in the 1950s. We advertised in the local paper and had radio messages asking if anybody had any old footage. Thousands of feet of this material came in, and not only on Super 8 but on Standard 8. We went through hours of this stuff and built a beautiful little sequence out of it. Compared to that there must be so much more stuff that has been put away in people's cupboards or in cardboard boxes that will be available to someone in the future.

Absolutely. With little Ellen, for instance, I have so much video of her that if her life becomes notable in some way, you could almost live her childhood in real time. This girl will be able to see herself being born and relive every stage of her childhood—and so will other people if they are interested.

I think documentary seems to be going in three ways. One is towards the more formulaic essay-type films that are done for the Discovery

Channel, the big subject things. They tend to be very international in feel and not culturally anchored to any particular place.

There is the observational, fly-on-the-wall approach, and then there is a much more exploratory, personal, archival type of film, such as the one I'm doing at the moment, where my wife's interest and presence is as important to the story as the violins themselves. It's a hybrid film actually, because the topic of the violin is a perfect subject for the Discovery Channel too; the difference is that I'm actually doing it in a very personal way, or hope to.

I do think that the future of documentary, because of lightweight equipment, may go very much in the direction of people doing personal films. I notice at festivals that whenever these personal films pop up, they're popular and much loved, which means more outlets must appear. Maybe we'll have a special channel or outlet for these very personal films, these almost home movies. They are a bit like reading people's letters, and I think they're infinitely satisfying, infinitely interesting and very fruitful, because they reference right back into our own lives. For example, a couple of years ago, I proposed to my sister—she's in her fifties and sometimes lonely—that I would make a film where I would help to find a partner for her. We would record the process where I would audition people to see who would be worth her meeting. I'd save her embarrassment and I'd get myself a movie. A pretty good exchange.

She responded to that?

She was flattered that I cared. I would do all the auditioning and she could look at the tapes and I'd film her watching the tapes. I might actually do it, partly for my sister, as a sort of personal, playful thing, partly for myself.

That's an interesting idea. My assistant for many years, Lani Hannah, who has now become my cinematographer, is a girl from Western Australia who was adopted at birth. She recently went through the process of tracing her birth parents, whom she found after a lot of very difficult negotiations and quite traumatic meetings. Her first thought after having experienced all of that was to make a film about it. In fact, I've been encouraging her to, and she probably will. I think her story relates to what you are saying about people recognising in themselves something not only worth recording, but allowing other people to be a part of—that is, the joy she experienced in finding her real parents and all the personal anguish about what they will be like before actually meeting them.

The beauty is that no television executive can say, 'Well, we don't want that story because we already have it covered.' Nobody has your life covered, it's unique. Whereas if you have a subject on nuclear waste or

Tantric sex or even violins, there's always already a series of films existing on the subject. They tell you that the market has been covered on those subjects. But these personal stories are endlessly possible, as long as there are people and stories. Nor do I think people get sick of watching them if they are made tenderly and intimately. They also overcome the whole access problem because it's your life you're getting access to. You have every right to access the information of your life, and to negotiate with the people who are close to you to join you.

It certainly removes the sense of exploitation if the story is primarily about yourself—you are really the one who is baring your soul in the most honest way that you can.

Yes, of course. But, while I have been promoting the observational film and the personal journey, I have become a bit more hard-nosed about what works and what doesn't when it comes to documentary subjects. I am probably going to become very contradictory now, but I can be very hard-nosed at times. Too hard-nosed, sometimes. When I was head of documentaries at the ABC, I turned down a film proposed by a friend, which he got made anyway, which proved I was very wrong.

I'm harder than I was when I was at the NFB, which was a place where you were just allowed to paddle around and find things. You could go out with a camera and shoot endless amounts of material not quite knowing what you wanted. Sometimes masterpieces came out of it because you would intuitively latch on to something, or you just had good senses.

But when sitting in that top job at the ABC, having to pass judgement on the hundreds of ideas that came through, I found that you had to develop some sort of objective criteria. Otherwise, you got completely lost and completely intuitive in your judgements, and you could never explain to anybody how you were judging their proposals. People were continually ringing up and asking, 'Why didn't you like my idea?' And I would be saying, 'Well, I can't quite tell you.' It just was not enough. So, in desperation more than anything else, I came up with six principles which I found quite useful. The first one was to ask the potential film-maker: what is at stake in the situation? Is there something at stake or is there something out of balance? There is something at stake, for example, in the case of a film about my sister, which is that I feel she needs to be with someone but isn't.

The second principle was: does the exploration of the situation at stake reveal interesting characters? Everybody is interesting to a certain degree, but some people are more interesting than others, or prepared to let themselves go in a way which is more interesting. So, if there is going to be a principal character in the story, is this character inherently interesting in some way?

My third principle was: is there a story-line here? Documentaries love stories as much as the fiction film. There is an insatiable need documentarians have for stories. Is there a beginning, middle and an end? There certainly would be in the case of a film about my sister.

Then the most important, which I think is often ignored in documentary, was principle number four: is the story touching or does it touch our emotions? That's often ignored because documentaries have always been thought of as teaching tools. Documentary has always been confused about its identity, thinking its primary job is to be educational in the Griersonian tradition. But, in fact, documentaries have greater value when we ask whether we are going to care about the person or the subject of the film. If we do, then all the rest can go out the window. For example, we took a punt last year on Belinda Mason, Dick Mason's daughter, who had never made a long documentary. She came to the ABC with some very interesting material about a family here in Sydney who were planning to adopt a little girl from Ethiopia. Belinda had some footage that had been shot in Ethiopia; it was very wild and shaky, but it was extremely touching. There were two children who were going to be left behind, not brought to Australia, and so we said to go for it. She followed the story through for a whole year: first the bringing of two children from Ethiopia and then going back to get the third one. It's amazing stuff and an incredibly touching film—*Little Brother, Little Sister* (1998). For me the 'touching' aspect is really important.

The fifth principle from my checklist was: is there food for thought? That is, apart from the microcosmic interest of delving into people's lives, is there 'larger food' for thought? Well, in the case of the Ethiopian film we delved into racism to some extent, and into the merits of adopting kids so far from their home and culture. In the case of the film about my sister there is the issue of the older woman who is alone, when in our society it is so much easier for an older man to find somebody—there's food for thought there, too.

Unfortunately I cannot remember the sixth principle, but I'm sure it was a good one. Yes I can, it is the sense of the personal, of authorship. Anyway these principles served me very well at the ABC, and they have gone on to serve as criteria in my own work, although I am constantly forgetting to apply them. I also put them in a farewell letter to our racers, asking them to keep these principles in mind when they are stuck and don't know what story to do.

Could you briefly talk about your own observations on the economies of film? You've talked about the NFB and the freedom experienced there. I know it was the same at Film Australia, and when I started my career in film at the ABC there was a similar sort of freedom. Not much seemed to have been at stake in taking out a few thousand feet of film and shooting material which may have to be thrown away because it just didn't work. Now there's an economic rationalism about the process, one doesn't have that freedom any more. I guess what I'm asking is whether you are forced to apply these principles because of a lack of freedom to paddle about and explore your own ways of working?

I think the paddling about still exists, but it's more constrained. Yet you can actually make up for the economics or create new economies by working smaller.

Smaller in terms of compact and cheaper technology and therefore smaller units of people?

Cheaper technology, yes. In fact there's been a trade-off: where one area is squeezed, another area has opened up. The film I'm making on the violin is very economical, for instance. But beyond the economics I think these sorts of film have to be made in a culture which is really committed to you; the films cannot be solely ratings and profit driven. The culture of commitment is usually fine in the case of the ABC's work with the independents, because people such as Tom Zubrycki or Nick Torrens share the same ethic. They are not really profit driven in any major way. They live their subjects—as, for example, with Tom and *Billal* (1997), or with Nick, who has come back from Hong Kong where he made *It's Glorious To Be Rich* (1998), a documentary about an engaging Chinese businessman called Vincent. For Nick, Vincent becomes a good friend of his and you feel Nick has lived this whole experience for a year. That's the ABC culture from the outside, but we have to preserve that inside as well.

What is happening now with the whole out-sourcing venture is the acceptance of the idea that there is a commercial culture out there which can very quickly and efficiently turn things out for us better than we can do ourselves. I don't think that it always can. I don't want to quote any examples, but there are cases around right now of shows being made in this out-sourced way and which are truly cheap and nasty. They may not even be cheap but, more importantly, the work doesn't have the fundamental philosophy of the exploration of life and of finding truth, a core of truth as does our work at its best.

So the fundamental philosophy is the casualty of rational economics?

I think the internal ABC culture may be the biggest casualty. This present government is pushing us towards out-sourcing and to more product-driven work which is misguided and very depressing. But things turn around. Australians know they need the ABC as a sort of experimenter, as a sort of conscience. They know we have to do this work ourselves to keep in the game, to put our thoughts into action. We can't order up this conscience business like pizza. Young Australia is not surprised by *Race Around the World*, or by the trouble the ABC takes to get it right. They are not surprised that the process is the product. They expect all this from us. As for the rest, I think they'd know what I'm on about.

[PART VI]

THE MAKINGS
OF . . .

i n Jean-Luc Godard's *Breathless* (1959), a long, winding tracking shot of the lead character ambling his way around the Inter-Américana Travel Agency was executed by having his cameraman, Raoul Coutard, pushed around in a wheelchair. The pair repeated the trick in *Une femme marée* (1964), apparently learned from American cinematographer James Wong Howe, who had himself pushed around on skates for the final fight sequence of Robert Rossen's *Body and Soul* (1947). Italian director Mario Bava, in his years as a cameraman and special-effects person, succeeded in taking a technically impossible, full-panoramic shot of the inside dome of St Peter's Basilica in Rome. Bava revealed that he simply took four separate photos, glued them together inside a plastic model of the dome, and photographed that—and this for a government-subsidised documentary, *Il viaggio del Goethe a Roma* (1945).

The makers of any film, whether a skid-row production or a mega-blockbuster, would have a tale of this sort to tell, because no matter the amount of planning, an uncertainty principle always operates in film-making. The pieces collected here are meant to capture the everyday, see-saw world of film-making: how film-makers see a film and, in particular, how they get it made.

The productions of *Kiss or Kill* and *Babe* receive extensive treatment because neither could be more different yet both had set forth on uncharted waters. Bill Bennett and Chris Noonan verify that when problems arise, so too can inventiveness. In these instances accidents are never truly accidents.

Each piece may deal with methods employed for a specific film, but their value as documents rests on the understanding that very practical, hands-on, day-to-day considerations—oft times unforeseen—underlie the conception of any film.

makin' bacon: *babe*

chris noonan

babe has been a seven-year journey for me, from my first day of involvement to the finish of the film. A lot happens in seven years, so I'll set out by first looking at the broad scheme of things.

THE SCREENPLAY

My involvement started in 1988 when George Miller gave me a copy of the book *The Sheep Pig* by Dick King-Smith.[1] I had been looking at a number of feature film projects and kept rejecting them because somehow they didn't seem to have an edge. I loved the story of *The Sheep Pig* but thought that it was almost impossible to make as a film. That only encouraged me. In my experience, when you're faced with the challenge of achieving something on film that you have no idea of how to produce, it forces you to become more inventive, to figure things out. You can't rely on the usual solutions; you're forced to be inventive with film language in order to express the story, and so it becomes a more interesting experience for the viewer as well. I said 'yes' to George and we set about writing the story together.

The first part of the writing process lasted about two-and-a-half months. Every day for about half the day we would get together, pull apart the story and talk through how we might structure the story as a film. As time went by, that process got very detailed and we ended up pretty well talking our way through a whole film scene by scene. We hadn't written the dialogue, but by the end of two-and-a-half months we had a fairly good plan in notes about how the script might be tackled.

At that point I went away and wrote a first draft. I brought the first draft back after about six weeks and together we pulled that apart. Well, I have to say that George led the pulling apart, but together we sort of dismembered it and discussed where it went right and where it went wrong. Then I went away and wrote another draft. That went on for about five or six drafts, the whole process taking about eleven months of writing, destruction, reconstruction, destruction, reconstruction, while all the time the structure of the story was advancing.

As the finance for the film was not yet in place, we were very aware that we were producing a script that wasn't just a blueprint for the making of a film, but also a document that was going to be instrumental in getting funding. Besides being a description of a film, it was also a sales pitch.

When we were writing, we wrote what we wanted to see on screen without consideration for what we thought was possible in terms of special effects of the time. That decision liberated us; enabled us to freely write out of our imaginations rather than restricting ourselves to what we knew was possible. The bulk of that writing took just under a year and towards the end of that time we started on the next stage.

THE DEVELOPMENT

As far as we were aware, no one had made a film as complex as this with animals; no one had tried to do something that required such precision of acting from such a large number of animals and from such a large number of species of animals. I read recently that someone once said the reason so many animal films are about journeys and rescues is because there are two easy commands to teach an animal, one is 'come' and the other is 'fetch'. With those two commands you can quite easily structure a story about a lost animal that decides to try to find its owner and who has adventures along the way that involve rescuing other animals. But it's very difficult to do an animal story that is more psychologically complex than that, and we knew we were trying to do something that was a lot more complex.

I had to meet some pigs as one of my first areas of research for *Babe*. The closest piggery was at the Hawkesbury Agricultural College where students are taught how to raise animals. I remember two things about the first meeting with the man in charge. One was the affectionate way in which he referred to pigs. He told me they are very intelligent creatures: 'We call them horizontal humans—they're pink and they're clever.' The other thing I remember was his response to my query about the natural lifespan of a pig. He scratched his head and said, 'Search me'. He had been working with pigs all his life but had never known one to live long enough to die naturally.

We didn't know where we were going to shoot this film. We thought perhaps we would shoot it in the UK because the original story is set there; it is also the centre of sheepdog trials. Now one of the problems with pigs is that because they're farmed for meat, they've been bred over the centuries to grow fast, to put on as much fat as quickly as possible. This wasn't good for shooting because we faced a long shoot and wanted our pigs to look the same for as long as possible. But we had read some stories about programs in the UK where they were breeding pigs to stay small as part of experimental research to produce hearts for human transplants. When we read this story we thought this could be the answer to our prayers. So I went over to the UK to begin investigating these stories about pig-breeding programs, and also to start casting around for animal trainers.

We began in the UK a program to breed and train these small-type pigs. They were quite ugly, actually, and all of them had strange markings and somehow looked a little bit out of proportion, and that was part of the reason why the idea didn't go very far. But we went ahead with the program with the thought that it might be useful to us in any case. And I also went on a number of expeditions to see all sorts of different breeds of animals because at this stage we had to start casting the breeds of animals we were to use and to decide how old they were going to be.

The other obvious area of development was the technology. We had taken some advice about which combination of technologies we might use to achieve the animal dialogue in this film and it was a much wider range than the two technologies we ended up using. At one point we had thought about shooting the film in high definition television (HDTV) because part of the problem with special effects, apart from the cost, is getting from film into a computer and then out of a computer back on to film at a very high level of resolution. There were some experimental films at that time that had been entirely made in HDTV, and we thought that if we could do that then we would avoid the two steps from film to data and from data to film. There was a little investigation but the idea was finally dismissed.

At that point I went on a tour of the centres of digital animation— that is, computer graphics animation of live-action images (CGI)—and of animatronics, which are essentially very sophisticated mechanised puppets. We investigated the technologies in Australia, the US, Japan and the UK. When we went to Industrial Light & Magic (ILM) in San Francisco, they said, 'We can do everything, we are your one-stop shop and we'll give you a competitive price!' To all the problems we put to them, they would say, 'Oh, we can solve that!' We became very excited, but still kept investigating other avenues; we visited Jim Henson's Creature Shop in the UK for the animatronics, as well as many other organisations that were specialising in different sorts of effects.

One meeting was with a man in San Francisco called Doug Mobley who ran a company called Gilderfluke. Gilderfluke make control mechanisms for animatronic theme-park exhibits. We didn't quite know what that meant, so we visited his workshop, which was a little garage in San Francisco. We were taken into a room where there was a huge puppet donkey. The room had a very low ceiling and the ears of the donkey were touching the ceiling. Doug Mobley went into his back room saying, 'Hang on a minute,' then pressed a few buttons and the donkey jumped into life. It had a guitar in its two front hoofs and started singing a country-and-western song. But Doug had a bit of trouble turning the donkey off. As it turned out, his control systems were a little too imprecise for our purposes.

We began to find that nobody could really answer our questions. No one had really brought computer animation or animatronics to the level that we needed. So what we tried to do at this stage was to entice some of the these companies to join us in the development of the techniques. Rhythm & Hues, a company in Los Angeles that ended up doing the CGI for the film, agreed to do a test. I went out and shot footage for a test (a conversation between a dog and a pig) and they then offered to subsidise the development of techniques that might solve the problem of animating the dialogue. At the same time Jim Henson's agreed to build a test pig, a pig head anyway. We used the test to try to get as close as possible to our ideal Babe character—at least to work out what the ideal size of the pig should be, what the ideal look of our Babe should be.

In the process of developing the model, Henson's solved a huge number of problems that they would have to encounter eventually when they got the job. The critical thing about animatronics for this film was that it wasn't only about getting a good likeness of the creature that the animatronic is going to stand in for: half of the battle was in making the thing move in a way that seemed naturalistic (if pigs could speak).

We didn't want to have live performances on-set of the animatronic for each bit of dialogue. That would have meant getting the actor to provide the voice of the animal to come in afterwards and post-sync the dialogue to a *fait accompli* piece of performance of the pig. Instead we wanted to first record the voices of the animal characters so we could get the timings right and then record performances of the animatronic. Once we'd recorded a performance of movement of the animal speaking which was in sync and had the right facial expression, we would then be able to play it back on the set. So work was done by Henson's on a performance recording system.

At around this time I was also meeting a large number of animal trainers in the UK, the US and Australia. In the UK I misused my then position as Chairman of the Australian Film Commission (AFC) by having animal trainers come into London to meet me in the AFC's office. Many of them would bring dogs and some very funny scenes eventuated there. Typically, the trainers would screen videos of the films they had worked on, their favourite performances of an animal they had controlled, and then they would put a dog through its paces, 'Pick up that book and take it over to the rubbish bin and drop it'. That sort of thing. In one case a woman called Anne Head, a very famous animal trainer, trained me in controlling the dog she'd brought in. I was getting the dog to pick things up and move them across the room.

We met Karl Lewis Miller, who turned out to be the key to unlocking the secret of how to get animals to do what we wanted them to do, on the recommendation of Dean Semler. Karl had been one of a number of animal trainers to have worked on *Dances With Wolves* (1990), which Dean had shot. Dean said, 'The man is a genius. He can do anything—you must meet him.' Actually, Karl makes a very brief appearance in *Babe* when the pups are being sold. He is the pup-buyer whose face is licked when he takes three pups. And yes, Karl Miller is indeed a genius. One thing set Karl apart from the other animal trainers. I would meet with trainers and say, 'Well, we're making a film based on a book about a pig who wants to be a sheepdog. There's dialogue between the animals; all the animals have very complicated roles and we want *acting* from them.' Most of the trainers would reply, 'Yeah sure, no problem. Yep, we can do that, it's all okay.' When Karl was told what we had to do he just said, 'You're joking!' and shook his head. Immediately that set him apart and made me think this guy has his head screwed on straight. I trusted him immediately, more than I could the others.

All through this time I was also recruiting and talking to other principal crew members. It was a very similar process to any other film so I won't go into it.

PRE PRE-PRODUCTION

I had started work on the storyboards by this time. If any film required storyboarding this one did. It was intricately complex in the way it all had to be put together. To create the illusion of a scene happening, different technologies had to be combined in such a way so that it was an effortless experience for an audience, so that viewers weren't continually tempted to 'pick the technique': 'Puppet', 'Animation', 'Puppet', 'Animation'. That was what I feared most, and the greatest challenge as a director was to figure out ways of concealing the joins, of concealing the methodology of how a scene was constructed. There are techno-freaks in this world who love nothing better than to pull things apart in this way and if viewers were pulling things apart then they weren't surrendering themselves to the emotional content of the story.

The other reason storyboarding was important was because I was making my first feature and I wanted it to be a cinematic marvel. It didn't just have to be something where people said, 'Wow, they really did well with the technology in that film', or 'Didn't the animals act well?' Having co-written the script I knew that the core of this film was its story, and the emotional path of the story is what I wanted the audience to experience. I didn't want people spell-bound by technology, I wanted them to surrender to the story as if all the animals were human characters. So I hooked up with a storyboard artist called Peter Pound, a Sydney-based artist who is a sublime and creative artist to work with, and who draws his storyboards in a comic-strip sort of way.

Storyboard artists have all sort of styles, and most put in all the texture of a scene and try to get the whole atmosphere of a shot. But Peter doesn't try to do that; neither did I want him to. He doesn't set himself up as the art department and the designer; instead he goes for the essential piece of expression in each shot, the essential element that the audience has to get, which could be in the face of the pig or the face of a human or a central action that the shot has to convey. So we were always working on distilling each scene: what a drawing had to convey was the core of a shot. There might be other ingredients, but we were always distilling what the scene had to do and Peter was always very clear-headed on what a particular storyboard frame had to convey. Obviously some of those frames were comic-strippy and exaggerated, but when it came to shooting a scene everyone looking at the boards would have understood immediately the central action, mood or feeling which had to come from that frame. It was a great shorthand form of communication.

The storyboarding was incredibly important because of the complexity of *Babe*. It's not the type of film where you can block a scene with a group of animals and then say, 'Well, let's try it', get them to see how it goes, and then take their suggestions on how to improve it. It was something that had to be meticulously planned because all the actions had to be imposed on the animals, and all the animals had to be tricked into performing, into exhibiting the behaviour required for a scene.

Animal trainers pored over these storyboards and would say, 'How in hell are we going to get the duck to do that?' And they would start discussing among themselves what strategies they might use, and it would come down to complexities like, 'Well, if you are doing that to trick the duck to do that, how the hell am I going to get the pig that's standing next to it to do this?' There was territorial warfare between different trainers responsible for different animals. Trying to figure out just how to approach a particular shot was an extraordinary art: the more species of animals you have at any one time in the frame, the more complex it becomes. And the more species of animals you have in the shot the fewer places there are for trainers to hide from the camera. We had to design into the boards hiding places for the trainers, so that when the art department came to design the set they could integrate little hidey-holes for trainers.

But a single storyboarding pass of the whole film wasn't enough. As the technologies developed, new information and ideas kept coming in about how we could achieve technologically the magic of animal dialogue. As the scheme changed, the boards had to be re-drawn to accommodate it. And as more people came on to the film, more and more problems emerged and those problems then had to be incorporated into new versions of the boards. It was very much like a process of re-writing the script. Even though the content of the scenes didn't change much, the approach to the scenes changed radically throughout the whole period leading up to and during pre-production. In this case I'm talking in terms of years.

In discussing the film's style with George during our script sessions, the phrase 'a storybook world' emerged. We felt very strongly that the film should have a high style. I had looked at every animal film made in the last fifty years and one thing that distinguishes them from *Babe* is that they look terrible, really. Most looked like a cross between a wildlife documentary and a half-hearted attempt at drama. We were very deter-mined this film would go right out on its own in terms of filmic style. I looked at many *noir* films because we decided that the phrase 'storybook world' was going to take the film into a very distinctive stylistic realm which would invite the audience to enter a world that was not natural-istic—the animals speak, after all. A world where every ingredient could be exaggerated a little bit, or quite a lot, in order to keep a level of stimulation going, to make the film interesting, and to give the viewer a feeling of cinematic experience and not just a series of animal tricks.

So a film language had to be developed that incorporated this 'storybook world'. One key to achieving it was in the early storyboarding, where I came up with the idea of how to first show the Hoggetts in their farmhouse. Our script said something like, 'Mr Hoggett is working on a doll's house, which will be a gift for his grandchild'. So I decided to try a cinematic trick: the audience is invited to think they are in the Hoggett's house and then the illusion is immediately blown when Hoggett's huge hand comes into shot—you are, in fact, inside the doll's house. That conceit became an icon which we kept referring to throughout the storyboarding of just what 'storybook world' meant in terms of the way shots unfolded, where we could bring in the unexpected, where we could provide a little shock or surprise for the audience. We would always go for the unexpected so that the 'storybook world' approach, the exaggeration, could seep through everything, including the design of the sets and the cinematography. It had to come out of every pore of the movie. It would even end up affecting the discussions we had with Universal about the the animals' accents.

Casting presented two very different challenges: one, the human casting and, the other, the casting of animal voices. We decided very early on that we wanted to cast only the very best people we could possibly find for the roles; their names were unimportant. In the case of the animal voices we didn't want well-known actors, at least not international stars, because although Universal were making suggestions in that direction, the animals were the lead characters in this film and we didn't want them sharing their roles with famous actors. We didn't want the audience to be thinking of Woody Allen when they saw a duck, for example. We cast in the US, the UK and in Australia with the aim of finding the perfect voice for each of the animal roles.

I wanted each animal to have a very vivid character that would impress itself on the audience. The animal casting was an incredibly exhausting process, taking months and months and months. We had a brilliant casting person in Los Angeles, who was working at Universal at that stage, who found a lot of our American cast. Liz Mullinar was working here and did a fabulous job with the Australians. Our London casting efforts were actually a little disappointing; in our first run-through with UK actors we just didn't find anyone who fitted the roles.

PRE-PRODUCTION

When we started our scheduling we also began searching for locations in Australia and then in New Zealand. We looked around Victoria, near Melbourne, and in Tasmania. We wanted something verdant and English-looking. We even looked around San Francisco at one stage at Universal's urging. Finally, we ended up with this little perfect plot of land at Robertson in the Southern Highlands of New South Wales. It was actually two very perfect plots of land. Every image in the film was shot within a thirty-kilometre radius of Robertson. All the major locations, the farmhouse and barn location, the sheep fields, and the location for the final sheepdog trials with the grandstand, were actually

Farmer Hoggett (James Cromwell) and pig, *Babe*

within a one-and-a-half-kilometre radius of Robertson. Just a tiny little pocket of ex-rainforest that had been cleared a century ago. Those weird little trees that look like plug-in trees from a children's toy set are in fact stunted regrowth from the rainforest.

So we were going through all the normal planning, the design, the wardrobe decisions, the final casting decisions and so on. But a few were unique to the production. We had to conduct some experiments with animal cosmetics. We knew by now that our pig was going to be played by a lot of pigs. As it turned out, forty-eight pigs played Babe. Pigs, like humans, have individual differences, so we needed to give the pig a distinctive feature: that way as soon as you saw the pig you'd know it was obviously Babe. The pig was also going to be played by an animatronic and so it was important that as soon as you saw the animatronic, it too had to have the same distinguishing feature. We started experimenting and playing around with a variety of distinctive facial marks on a number of the pigs (much to their disgust) but couldn't find anything that somehow expressed 'Babe'. Then George Miller came up with the idea that instead of a facial mark, maybe Babe should have a black tuft of hair coming out of the top of his head. So we got our make-up person, who is now destined to be a specialist in animal as well as human make-up, to fashion a variety of wigs, which we played around with on a plastic model pig's head. Finally we ended up with a model for a pig-wig that each of our pigs would have to wear. Little did we know that they would find the wigs very tasty—we couldn't leave the pigs alone in a pen for any length of time without them pulling the wigs off each other's head and chewing them up. Pigs will eat anything.

In the script, half the duck's feathers are missing. There is a scene we deleted from the script where the duck is pulling feathers out of itself to make it look less attractive. Our animal trainers couldn't figure out a way of shooting it. The only way you can make a duck look ragged is to actually pull its feathers out. We decided against that because although it's possible, the application of a wig to a pig got very small complaints compared to a duck getting its feathers pulled out. In the end the duck had a very subtle piece of make-up. Every one of the ducks (I think about twenty-five ducks played Ferdinand) had bags applied under their eyes. It's very subtle but it looks like Ferdinand is a bit worried, like he hadn't any sleep the night before.

The only other major piece of animal cosmetics to be developed was for the two principal dog characters. We wanted the two dogs to be distinctively different from one another so we worked up a scheme of dyeing the dog's fur, particularly Rex's fur. Rex has a black face and Fly has a blaze of white down the centre. We also had to have back-ups for each of those dogs in case anything happened to them. As it turned out Fly was played almost 100 per cent of the time by this one dog called Jessie, a most brilliant actress of a dog, who never took a day off.

There were more problems with Rex in that the dog we really loved for Rex—the dog who seemed to perfectly express Rex's character—decided he didn't like being an actor after about a week of shooting. He became very timid, his character changed completely, and the understudy Rex had to be brought in and dyed up to look right. The understudy turned out to be great and carried Rex through to the end.

There are two scenes with Rex and Fly where it's not the Rex and Fly we know and love. One is the scene where they round up sheep. They're both stand-in dogs because our starring dogs just didn't know anything at all about sheep herding. They were trained to go to a mark, stop and look intelligent, and waggle their heads a little bit for the dialogue. But real sheepdogs are very highly trained and it would have been impossible to train a dog to herd sheep from scratch as well as those two ring-ins were able to do. The other scene where it's not *our* Rex and Fly is the dog fight. We didn't want to make our two star dogs fight each other because it might ruin their cooperation in so many other scenes. It just so happened that among the menagerie were two dogs who loathed each other, and we figured we weren't going to see them in close-up anyway. They were both male and whenever one of these dogs was led past the cage of the other, they'd face up to each other and growl menacingly. Karl Miller, in one of his many acts of genius, said, 'Ah hah, I've got a place for you two'. So they became the fight dogs.

We had terrible trouble trying to get the shot at the beginning of the round-up sequence where the camera tilts up, the two dogs race towards the sheep, go together for a little while, and then part and go around to the back of the sheep. The problem was that one dog knew it had to go to the right, the other knew it had to go to the left, but trying to get them to go together for a while was almost impossible. One would scoot left and one would scoot right, and as we tilted the camera up we would be left with nothing in frame until we got to the sheep. The problem was solved in an incredibly simple manner by Karl. He said, 'We'll put the one that's going right on the left and the one that's going left on the right.' When you watch that shot you can see the dogs confused and battling each other, trying to get to their side. Finally they manage it and it becomes a perfect shot.

The process of pre-recording the animal dialogue started early and went on for quite a while. The initial workshopping and recording happened in a studio in Neutral Bay with a mixed group of actors from the UK, the US and Australia. Many specifics had to be worked out, for example figuring out how to do sheep-speak, figuring out how much 'Baa' to put into a voice or when that 'Baa' effect got in the way of actually understanding the dialogue.

We also bred up a trial group of pigs so that we could test the pig-training methods and find out how fast they were going to grow. Karl Miller came over from Los Angeles, where he is based, and we started a trial group of about twelve pigs, which were initially housed in Kennedy Miller's building, in a room that hasn't been occupied since! It was very scientifically based: Karl had to work out the right amount of feed to give them in a day; they had to be measured daily to determine how fast they grew per portion of feed, and we had to work on the best training mechanisms for a pig. Karl Miller had trained pigs before for a film that had not happened. In fact, he had trained pigs twice for the same film that had not happened. We made good use of Karl's experience.

When the pigs got a bit too big for their little room in Orwell Street, Kings Cross, we moved them to one of the pavilions in the Sydney Showground, which became our training centre until we moved the whole works down to our location.

We decided to make the central property we used for the farm and the barn the animal headquarters of our shoot. The site for the farm and the barn is actually a valley. There was nothing in the valley, so the house and barn, all the fencing, the pond—everything that you see in the film was designed, built and put into that valley. We built three huge animal sheds just out of sight of the farmhouse set. By arrangement with the local council they had to have a reticulated animal sewage system built into them for the sake of the environment in the area. We also had to build human reticulated sewage systems because we knew that the crew would be large. It was quite a major development of this unsuspecting farmer's property.

PRODUCTION

We started the shoot at the end of January 1994. It was a five-month shoot, five days a week. We finished it in June of that year. The crew grew and shrank from time to time, but it was a very big crew, much bigger than any other crew I've worked with. If you combine the film crew with the animal trainers, a minimum of ninety people at any one time, and the animatronics team, it was an incredibly large inundation of people to this little area. Robertson is a town with a population of about 270, and our crew exceeded 300. They were accommodated in Bowral, which became the administrative centre of the film. We took up every piece of rental accommodation in the area and in many of the surrounding towns. The manager of the Bowral Hotel said it was worth $20 000 a week for him to have us around.

We set up an additional unit which was led by Daphne Paris, and it was as well-equipped with people and equipment as many first units. This was instigated because it became apparent after the first week of shooting that the schedule was not going to work without expanding our shooting capability. There is very little way of expanding the number of shots in a day when working with animals—you can't tell them to work faster, and unless you take the attitude that near enough is good enough, that if the pigs sort of looked in the sort-of-right direction it would have to do, then there was no other way we could have achieved the film in the planned time.

Our first assistant director Philip Hearnshaw had estimated the correct number of set-ups we would get in a day from the very beginning, but that schedule was thrown out for political reasons. The shooting schedule we were stuck with was much tighter, so we started an additional unit to handle a lot of material with the animals. By the end of it, in order to keep the additional unit supplied with work, they tackled and did a fabulous job with a small number of scenes with humans. Their material is stylistically invisible within the film; there's nothing that distinguishes it from the first-unit material.

We also set up a special effects unit on location to cope with some of the more technically demanding shots, particularly for a number of dream sequences which were never completed. A group of people from Rhythm & Hues, who did most of the CGI work, had visited the set a week prior to the beginning of the shoot to set up a way of shooting all the animal dialogue material that later had to be CGI animated. There was a process, a pattern, that had to be followed through, but there were other shots that were more complex, shots that involved motion control cameras which we decided should be assigned to a special effects unit.

The weather was incredibly kind to us for a film that required 70 per cent exterior shooting. We had unbelievable luck, even for the final sheepdog trial sequence—a sequence full of animals—which was all written and storyboarded with cloudy skies. The sequence took weeks to shoot, yet we had cloudy skies every day we went out to shoot scenes for that sequence.

The interior sets were built in various potato sheds and other farm buildings in the immediate area surrounding our farm set so that we had convenient wet weather cover, but we actually didn't have a lot of rain. The reason we went to Robertson was that it looked so green—it has one of the highest rainfalls in New South Wales. But the only really inconvenient weather we had was a period of dry weather at the beginning where the hills started to brown off a little and so we painted the hillsides green for a couple of days of shooting. They recovered once it started raining.

A few things I should mention about the animal action. Very often with stunts or animal action, the stunt determines or dictates a lot of how a scene is to be shot, what angles are to be used and what it will look like. In this case, the animal action had to be completely subservient to the style of the film, to its filmic language. The cinematic qualities of the film were paramount and that created more challenges for the animal trainers than would otherwise have been the case, or more than they were used to. They are more accustomed to people saying, 'Well, this horse is a bit difficult, so if the shot is good enough, then please let's not do it again'. *Babe*'s trainers were constantly being asked to do things again and consistently agreeing, even suggesting re-takes when I thought I'd got it as good as possible.

All the animation happened after the event—we had to film the animals first. So to get a shot of a pig, say, looking very happy and saying, 'So what's happening?' and then getting a disappointing answer, changing its attitude and walking away dejectedly, I would have to film the animal with exactly the right timing, exactly the right body language, and with its head in exactly the right angle and attitude to deliver the line of dialogue before it was a usable shot for computer graphics. The less you manipulate in a shot in this circumstance the more believable the computer graphic result. Precision in animal performance, particularly if involving a very specific line delivered with very specific timing, required a consistency of body language and attitude from the animal expressing the line. It wasn't just process A to B to C to D and then exit; it was one of A to B excitedly, B to C disappointedly, and C to D dejectedly, which added a huge layer of complication and artistry to the process of working with animals. In the end, we shot fifty-four hours of material for a ninety-minute film, which isn't a huge ratio, but Kodak was happy.

POST-PRODUCTION

We cut the film on Avid and I am now a complete Avid freak. Another key to perfecting the animal performances, and therefore the film, lay in the fact that we shot many takes of any one shot, and so had a lot of alternatives to work with. Of those alternatives, some of them were grossly different from each other and many we had to throw away, but a lot of them were subtly different from one another. Of these, Avid allowed us to try a huge range of alternatives in the cutting of a scene—not just alternate takes—it allowed us to easily compare coming into a shot four frames later, three frames later, two frames later, for instance. Questions like, 'How would that affect the shot? Would the dialogue sit better on the animals' attitudes three frames earlier or four frames later?' were easily answered. For an anal-retentive person Avid allows an extraordinary degree of thoroughness and of getting a cut as right as it can be, and that was certainly what we were aiming for. Had we cut the film on sprockets we would have needed either twice the time or half the fastidiousness that we brought to it.

There were two editors on the film. Initially, Marcus D'Arcy was to be the editor of the film *in toto*, but after a week of shooting when it became apparent how complex handling the CGI material was going to be, we decided to bring in a second editor. That second editor was Jay Friedkin, Marcus's choice, and their relationship sort of went through ups and downs during the whole process. It's difficult to share such a pivotal role with somebody else, where neither of them specialised in one area or another. They truly shared the job and finished it as great friends.

Computer graphics are really expensive. We timed our shots on a seven-second basis. A seven-second shot of an animal talking was costing us between US$20 000 and US$50 000 each, and if we went four frames above seven seconds the cost doubled. We had to be very careful with what we sent to Rhythm & Hues to animate. We didn't want to send them shots that were going to be deleted. We would only dispatch shots after a scene had been fine-cut and, at least theoretically, locked off. We'd make a duplicate negative, send them the original negative, and they would scan the original neg, convert it into data and then would work on that data within their computers. The original negative had the dialogue synced to the footage, with extensive notes and with a cut on video of the whole scene in which the shot appears. The CGI work involved an average of eight weeks per shot.

I'll give you a very broad, schematic description of what that work entailed, but it only relates to about 10 per cent of the shots because most had become more complicated than the theory. In theory what would happen was that they would build three-dimensional models of each of the animals' heads inside their computer, wire-frame diagrams of the animals' heads with working parts like a tongue, jaws, a nose, the eyes—all the parts that had parameters of movement were built into a 3D computer model. They would animate the 3D model to speak the dialogue and then they would get the shot we had supplied and fix the angle and position of the head of the 3D model to the position of the real animal's head throughout the shot. They would then take the textures from the animal in the original shot, frame by frame, and clad their 3D computer model with those textures. The hardest part of all was in deciding what parts of the 3D animated head we wanted to use. We only wanted to use the minimum amount of the fake head created in the computer, so we had to work out which parts of the original shot betrayed the fact that the animal wasn't speaking and only cover those parts. Only the parts that actually required the 3D model were then seamlessly integrated back into the original shot.

My understanding of special effects extends to matte shots and of how hard it is to get invisible matte lines. To this day I still do not understand how they integrate the two so seamlessly without join lines. All I know is that a great deal of software had to be developed for different challenges that arose through the whole process. One of the trickiest things that wasn't solved until the very end was a seemingly very simple thing—dog whiskers. Dogs' whiskers are like little filaments—even the tiniest movement of the head catches the light. If you are watching a shot of a dog and it moves its head almost infinitesimally, you can detect movement by watching reflections from its whiskers. When you make a dog talk, it's of course talking with that part of its face that moves the whiskers. While we could ignore the whiskers in many of the dog shots because they didn't catch the light, in those shots where they caught the light Rhythm & Hues did weeks of work developing a little program that could deal with those reflections.

Once they had produced a draft of a shot, they would transmit the draft to us over the Internet. We had a little low-end Macintosh sitting in the corner of the cutting room and Rhythm & Hues would send shots which would download into our computer overnight. Avid is Mac-based, and so in the morning we would bring the shots over to the Avid, and within five minutes they were cut into the scene and we were able to get an idea of how well the animated shots worked *in situ*. We could phone Rhythm & Hues and say, 'Not good enough', explain why, and they'd start on another draft of the shot and the whole thing would go on again. That is, until close to the very end of the process when they pleaded with us to accept something that they knew wasn't perfect but would take them too long to make right, 'Please, just one time, accept it'. We did make a few little compromises at the end.

Music was a tremendously important part of this film. We didn't have a lot of money for music, so we decided to audition some Australian composers. It was an interesting process: five composers agreed to provide scores of two pieces of music for two parts of the film. Nigel Westlake delivered the most brilliant renditions. We waited for the others to send in their contributions, but Nigel really answered the call. Somehow he had summed up the spirit of the film, which is a very delicate beast. This isn't some sort of action film where as long as the music is exciting it's working. There is a very wry sense of humour throughout; even when it is sad there's a little twist to it, and Nigel managed to tap into the film's sensibility.

Music is also tremendously important because 70 per cent of the time animals are providing the basic performance. The pig isn't projecting sadness, the pig isn't projecting happiness, the pig is just being a pig and doing things in the right order. Unlike a human who can make you cry by just projecting a certain feeling, the pig isn't projecting anything at all and it's *we* who are making the pig project something. The music was essential to focus want we wanted an audience to read in an animal's behaviour.

TEST SCREENING

We had one test screening in Los Angeles, which was imposed on us by Universal. They recruited an audience of adults and children. Everyone filled in cards, but a group of them was asked to stay after the screening to discuss various issues. They call it a focus group. Two things came out of the group that are worth relating. There was a little flurry of protest about the dog fight. One parent said she felt that because Rex never verbally apologised to Fly for attacking her, it was a case of unresolved spousal abuse and she urged us to put in some dialogue from Rex that sort of said, 'I'm sorry, I shouldn't really have done that. It was an inappropriate way to behave.' We liked that line quite a lot. We tried it out, but it just didn't work.

The other thing that happened at that stage was Universal urging us to title the film 'Babe, The Gallant Pig'.[2] We fought them for all we were worth because we didn't believe the film was about gallantry at all. Anyway, at that discussion everyone was packing up to go and someone said, 'Oh, just one more thing. Why are you calling this film 'Gallant Pig'? What does that word mean anyway? If I had known it was going to be called "Babe, The Gallant Pig" I wouldn't have come.' And then other people in the audience said, 'Yeah, that's a real old-fashioned title. You don't want it.' Those comments enabled us to get the title returned to *Babe*, which is what we'd put on the title page of the first draft of the script years before.

QUESTION AND ANSWER SESSION CHAIRED BY GRAHAM THORBURN

You made mention earlier of how the 'storybook world' affected discussions with Universal on the issue of accents.

Chris Noonan: Initially, Universal said, 'Set it in Utah, you can make this work in an American setting.' We were very reluctant to do that and we developed our justifications about a 'storybook world' not being anywhere in particular, that it borrows heavily from lots of cultures and that the accents at most should be neutralised or at least shouldn't be made to fit into an American context. 'Where are the sheepdog trials in Utah?' we said. They weren't very impressed. We did Americanise the accents, almost entirely with the same cast, but it didn't happen until quite late in the cut. I think about two or three of the minor cast members were revoiced with other actors because they couldn't neutralise their original accent without going heavily into an Australian accent, but all of the others revoiced their own voices. In the end, I look on this change positively, because revoicing neutralised where exactly the 'storybook world' was located.

In the seven-year metamorphosis of book to screen we only get a fair picture of the eleven months from the time you started in 1988. Could you lead us through each year of the metamorphosis until you get to the shooting? The second question is whether Universal was the first studio you went to or was there a whole other drama involved in getting funding for the film?

I'll start with your last question. The producers approached a number of the major studios. It was going well with Warner Brothers until it reached the head of the studio. One of his executives recommended it to him and he took the script home, read it, called his executive and said, 'I don't get it'. George Miller approached Universal through Tom Pollock,[3] who had been involved in *Lorenzo's Oil* (1992). They have quite a good relationship. Other executives helped the process along as well, but it was really Tom's enthusiasm for the story that started the ball rolling within Universal.

It's almost impossible for me to give a year-by-year breakdown of what I was doing because so many ingredients happened simultaneously. We were working on so many fronts at the same time. Even in the first year while writing the script, I was working to find animal trainers, people who could do computer graphics, and looking for general specialists in special effects. I was working on all those things and they each moved along steadily—one would become the focus of my attention for a moment, then went away and would return again at a later date. There was a period in 1989 when I went off to make another film at the ABC called *Police State*, a tele-movie. Kennedy Miller were off approaching the studios so I took the opportunity to shoot something else and came back as soon as it was over. *Police State* took less than six months to complete, but it was the only time I had away from the project through those seven years.

The use of 'Jingle Bells' in the film has a very dramatic impact. I understand from an interview you did on radio that it was completely unintentional. Could you relay that story to us? And was there anything else in the film that was never in the script but turned up in the film as result of animal behaviour giving you special moments?

The shot where the pig falls off the ramp. There were lots of tiny little moments, which are total bonus moments, but that's the only one I can think of.

We actually had quite a few troublesome pigs, but one really troublesome pig stood out. This pig had a very bad habit that kept ruining our shots. Whenever the pig hit its mark, it had this instinct or impulse to lift its head in the air and make a crazy chewing motion that was endlessly frustrating to us. It was particularly frustrating on the day we had to shoot the pig walking into shot after the farmer leads Ma, the old sheep, off at the back of the cart on Christmas Eve. When the pig got to its mark, it was supposed to look towards the cart and then look back, but instead it got to its mark, lifted its head and started doing this crazy chewing movement. It was only in the cutting room that George came up with the idea of the pig singing, and we played around with that idea until we hit on the notion of the pig singing 'Jingle Bells'. So the tune was integrated quite a long way back and quite a long way forward from that point in the editing stage, and it became the thematic line through that section of the film. I know it's one of people's favourite moments in the film because it comes out of left field and it's so wacky and unexpected.

Did you have a strategy for keeping the big picture in mind while paying such incredible attention to detail?

I don't know if I had a strategy for it. Part of what kept me on the straight and narrow was having thought through everything so completely and thoroughly over such a long period of time. Having boarded it meticulously was a critical thing—the key, really, that always brought me back to a scheme or the aim, at least in theory, of the big picture. Because I had spent so much time on it, I really knew the story back-to-front. I had co-written the script, had been through the whole process of boarding it, worked out how to shoot it all, so I really knew the themes I wanted to raise or touch on in any particular part of the film. So when something came out of left field very often I was able to say whether it was relevant or not. That was particularly so when working with human actors because they do come up with ideas, much more than animals do.

How much of the soundtrack were you able to do in Australia in relation to getting it eventually to digital sound (DTS)? At what stage did the mice come in—before, during or after the shoot?

A huge amount of our location sound was unusable because it had 'Come, stay, come on, stay, come on' all the way through it. We had probably the best sound recordist working in Australia on this film, but there just isn't a filter that will cut all of that out. So much of the soundtrack is a created soundtrack by a most extraordinary group of dubbing editors. And the foley for this film is a marvel. You wouldn't believe the things that are in the foley. There are about five sounds combined to make one duck footfall on a wooden floor, and that has to be done for every footfall, and there's a whole other recipe concocted for the duck's footfall on carpet, and then there's the pig and so on. There's very little pure sync in this film. To me the soundtrack is a complete marvel because it's very sweet and yet it is completely concocted.

The soundtrack was entirely done in Australia, including the digital mix, which was done at Soundfirm. The only part of the process that was done overseas was the mastering of the digital sound (DTS) CD. For those who don't know, the film was released with a digital soundtrack, but not all cinemas are equipped to play it, and the particular system we used is the one favoured by Universal, which is called DTS.

It's one of a number of digital systems, but DTS is characterised by the fact that the print of the film arrives at the cinema with a CD. Encoded on the side of the film is a time-code track and the time-code keeps the CD player running at the right speed and so you are actually hearing a six-track CD in the cinema. I haven't watched the film that many times with its Dolby stereo track and there are quite a few surprises in it, but I've heard it quite often with its DTS soundtrack, which I really love because of its clarity and its ability at times to give you very loud volumes without going haywire. You have a much greater range of sound response when working with a digital track. It's a great system.

The mice were written into the script, but they weren't written for the number of appearances they finally make. What was written in the script were their singing appearances—the 'Blue Moon' and the 'Toreador' songs. The idea of the mice appearing in the title cards didn't arise until the test screening in Los Angeles, which was the first time we had seen the film in a large theatre full of a mixed group of people. We noticed everyone sitting there attentively but whenever the 'chapter heading' title cards came up, the parents would all go into huddles with their children explaining what the words meant. We thought we had to somehow make these cards accessible to non-readers, because Universal was marketing the film as a children's film. Even though we disagreed with that to some degree, we none the less had to make it accessible to children. It was actually producer Bill Miller's idea that the mice should voice the title cards, and so we banded together a new little group of mice voices to do just that.

Why didn't the mice appear with the first card?

To keep the audience guessing. You'll notice their appearances vary quite a bit. All the way through the film we've tried to create surprises and I was anxious to make that approach inform every decision. If we had the mice appear at a bottom corner of the frame every time, then after the first three the audience would say, 'Oh, here are the mice again'. The idea was to maintain stimulation.

Can you talk a little more about why you had the title cards, why you sectioned the film?

We were attracted to the idea of chapters because of the film's 'storybook world', but the main reason is a structural one. When we first screened it to friends the only negative comment we got was that it took a long time for this story about a pig who wants to be a sheepdog to get going. People were sort of impatient. Now an audience going to the cinema would probably have heard already that it's a film about a pig that becomes a sheepdog, and yet it's not until beyond a third of the way through that the pig actually starts looking like it might become a sheepdog. We decided on the chapter cards as a way of saying to the audience, 'Now this bit isn't about a pig becoming a sheepdog, this bit is about X'. 'And this bit is not yet about a pig becoming a sheepdog, this bit is about Y', and so on. That was the reason for the cards. Universal actually fought us all the way on the title cards; they really didn't want us to use them and felt the cards segmented the film too much, but I really believe in them. I think they actually solved a problem in a witty way without the cards looking like a solution to a problem. I think they're good.

How many extras did you use at the end of the film and did they all have to be paid for?

They all had to be paid for except for my wife. I think our biggest extras day was 550, and I believe we used almost the whole population of the Southern Highlands on one day or another. We had the best time with that group of extras. It was very different from working with a group of Sydney extras. The level of enthusiasm was just huge and I think that is borne out in the end scenes where they're really going wild. I think you'd be hard pressed to get that level of performance out of a group of experienced city extras.

Can you talk about working with the animatronic puppets? What percentage of the animals we see on screen are puppets? How did you go about marrying those puppets with the live animals? And how happy are you with the results—did they vary between animals?

We started off with the idea that we would use computer graphics to achieve the dialogue. When we found out about the cost we started looking for another solution and that's how we ended up with the joint solution. Broadly, animatronics was the only other solution we could find to give the animals dialogue. We looked at all the other films that had used animatronics and none of them had done it terribly well. Also animatronics has a history of failure in big Hollywood films. There's a long history of animatronics being developed and then never used, or of the footage being tossed out and other solutions found at great expense.

Animatronics is not a cheap thing to do in itself. In the storyboarding of the film I worked off the theory that we would use animatronics for static close-ups and CGI for anything else that required dialogue. The reason is because no one has yet made an animatronic animal that looks believable when it's doing gross body movement. It's almost impossible to give an animatronic a gross body movement that looks naturalistically like a real animal moving. However, we had a group of animatronics people who were determined to prove me wrong and they did some amazing development. For example, they developed muscles for dog legs that moved in the same way muscles move when a dog transfers its weight on to its front legs. There are some extraordinary subtleties in those animatronics. It allowed me to break the rules, and so I developed a secondary rule which was, 'Try to break the rules', because I felt that if we had a sort of tick-tock arrangement where a certain category of shot was always an animatronic, a certain category of shot was always a computer graphic, then it was inviting the more technologically minded members of an audience to pick at the film: 'Puppet', 'Animation', 'Puppet', 'Animation'. Part of the success of the strategy for achieving seamless integration relied on breaking the rule. In many ways, I think most of the animatronics were incredibly successful; a film-literate group may be able to pick up some of the animatronics.

The sheep were largely achieved through the animatronics, although there are some shots where, for instance, an animatronic sheep is in the foreground delivering a line and there's a moving CGI sheep in the background that comes up and then delivers a line—that is, a computer graphic animated sheep B coming up behind an animatronic sheep A. Where animatronics didn't work for us were with the dogs. There were maybe only one or two dialogue shots with an animatronic dog. I think the reason they didn't work is because we know dogs so well. You look into a dog's face and you can read incredible subtleties of response, even a minute's hesitation. We are so very attuned to reading dogs' faces that as soon as you put an inanimate dog in front of the camera, no matter how brilliantly you've made its eyes or mouth to mimic a real dog's, after a certain time on-screen you can pick it as an inanimate object. In the end we largely tossed the footage of the animatronic dogs out and re-shot a number of scenes for dialogue with the real dogs. These were usually rule-breaking scenes where we had straight dialogue—close-up, close-up, close-up, then cut in dialogue—and we were using CGI. Because they were some of the last CGIs done, I believe they are some of the best CGI in the movie. The scene with Rex telling off Fly because she insulted the great 'Ba-hoo' by inviting the pig to round up the sheep is just brilliant animation for the dialogue.

Did the resolution on Avid allow you to pick up the animatronic problem? That's one of my reservations about Avid.

The resolution is a problem because with Avid you are watching a film at less than 35 mm film resolution, but we could still pick it. We were at something like a second-grade resolution on the Avid, which is still pretty good resolution. And in finishing we post-conformed the film before we locked off any scenes, which meant we ordered up a work print for a scene, conformed that scene on film and then put it up on a screen before we said, 'Okay, that scene is locked off'. Occasionally we made some adjustments just because watching something on a television screen is very different to watching it on a big screen.

I have two questions. You said you had been working on Babe *for seven years from start to finish. What kept you going because so many other people have an idea, a script, a storyboard, but they stumble at the first block? What kind of beliefs do you think helped you?*

Why don't I answer that now and you can ask a second one as a kind of a special dispensation. It was really just a love for the story, a love of its humour, and a belief that it would be the sort of film I would want to go to see. I loved the story so much that I really developed an obsessional relationship with it. People around me were saying, 'He's making a film about a pig?' and I think they thought I had entered some other realm. But I should say that I am really proud of the script George and I wrote. It is a script I can actually go back to and read and I can still get emotionally caught up in the story. I think it's pretty amazing that we wrote a script so compelling that even I, who knows everything that's coming, can still be moved by it. So it wasn't that hard to stay in there. The darkest moments came after we had been working on it for a few years and had no guarantee that we would get any funding. Kennedy Miller were putting all this money in and didn't know whether we were ever going to shoot anything. That was the hardest time, three years in, where we began to think, 'Are we ever going to get a camera out and start filming?'

My second one is that I found myself kind of beautifully sombre at certain moments and then I noticed around me that some people were chuckling. Either I am weird or . . .

You're weird!

All right, thanks. But the question is, how much of the humour did you intend and how much just opened itself to you?

The humour grew as the film progressed. One of the greatest experiences for me was watching the film for the first time with a paying audience in Los Angeles when it was released there in August 1996. What surprised me was exactly what you are saying, that during a sombre or sad scene, up to three-quarters of the way through, I'd hear a little giggle somewhere off in the audience. I've assumed, I don't know if I am right, that there is a sense of delight in suddenly realising that an animal is talking, that you are involved in an animal's life and it's really talking!

You do get these out-of-context giggles and it gives me great delight to hear them.

Is that why you chose live action over animation?

Live action was the obvious way to go. We believed that if we made *Babe* as an animated film, it would have declared itself a children's film. I don't think animation deserves that reputation and I am sure there are possibilities for animation beyond being something suitable for children. But to get an adult audience to go to an animated film about a talking pig who wants to be a sheepdog would have been even harder than getting adults to come to a live-action film with the same theme. One of the great challenges in marketing this film was getting adults to it. There are a lot of dark themes—both George and I delight in the dark side of things—and I think it's a very complex film and rewarding for an adult audience. We were certainly writing for an adult audience and the actors were performing for an adult audience. In Australia, somehow or other, the distributors really got the adult audience, while in the US they got a limited adult audience. It never fully crossed over into the adult market in the US.

Why do you think that was the case?

I think it was a limited vision on the part of Universal, frankly. They saw it as a children's film. We said it had bigger possibilities and they said, 'Yes, we agree, it's got bigger possibilities, but you have to go for the children's market first'. After the first three weeks I was faxing their marketing people, saying, 'Now's the time, you've got to broaden it. Use all these quotes from the reviews that say it's hip and witty and sophisticated, and stop using "beautiful family fare" in the ads.' But they still tended to plug the 'wholesome family entertainment' line, which is a real turn-off for a sophisticated adult audience without kids.

It was interesting that The New Yorker *and* The Atlantic Monthly *were saying* Babe *is not specifically a children's movie, that it's a sophisticated movie, while the ads nevertheless kept plugging it as a children's movie.*

Yes. I really don't know whether the film had greater potential in the US. It might be just my fantasy, it might be the film-maker in me saying I was robbed of all this audience. But I have an instinct from seeing it work here and in the UK, where it was handled a bit differently, that it was slightly mishandled in the US.

I am interested in the question of collaboration. You sometimes refer to 'we' and sometimes to 'I', and it is a very interesting break-up. Apart from the technical areas, where obviously there's much collaboration, can you talk a little about the creative side of collaboration?

Okay, I'll start at the writing. But it's a difficult subject to talk about because it's difficult to pin down something that's amorphous and moving all the time. In the writing of this script I basically did most of the pen-to-paper work, but George made a huge input into the story structure and with individual ideas. So even on the point of the actual act of writing being just one ingredient in the process, it seems appropriate to acknowledge the script as a piece of co-writing. It is very difficult when you are the person writing, when you're the one having to commit words to paper, and then continually having what you write pulled apart by either one person or more. But I believe we both respected each other's judgements and instincts at that time, and I believe that George's instincts are very fine as a film-maker. It was a wonderful opportunity to share that process and to match my instincts with his. That went on through the production process and through every part of the making. It wasn't just George and me either; there were other people involved, an increasing number as time went by. I am a great believer in the collaborative process as a way of solving problems and creating something that involves every participant in the process. The relationship between George and me, in some ways, was like a marriage—this was a seven-year project and plenty of marriages do not last seven years. We went through a process where we challenged each other constantly, where we were at each other's throats a fair bit of the time, where we were fighting rear-guard actions against each other's opinions and still, at the end of it, we came out with a film that doesn't speak of conflict. It speaks with one voice. It's a good film that I am proud of, and we are still talking to one another. What more can I ask for?

Why do you think Disney were not interested?

It beats me why Disney were not interested. I actually found myself on a plane with Roy Disney when I was coming back from a promotional tour of Europe, and I introduced myself to him. He said, 'Why didn't we make that picture?' I wondered as well. But in a way I do understand why they didn't. I think the main reason was that it is a very dangerous film. It's a film with an off-the-wall sensibility, a very wacky idea, and in practical terms it is full of exteriors, animals and special effects—all of which have been proven, in recent times particularly, to throw budgets out the window. They tend to become uncontrollable ingredients and when they go out of control, particularly special effects, they can go out of control in a very spectacular fashion. So I can understand from a business point of view, from a sensible point of view, why they didn't do it.

You talked about how the animals could change emotions from one location to the next. Can you touch on how the animal trainers actually went about it?

There's a question! Generally, animals are motivated by food. Basically, what you are watching in this film is a whole lot of actors looking for their meal. Many animal trainers, if they want a pig to walk from one side of a room to another, will just get out of shot with some food and say, 'Here it is', and then the animal will think, 'There it is', and make a bee-line for it. But Karl Miller's trick, and it's his signature, is he will show the animal through training that once it has walked over and stood on a mark successfully, it may take its reward when told to do so by a signifying sound. In the case of the pigs, the sound was a party clicker, in the case of the ducks it was an electronic beeper, in the case of the dogs it was a human voice. Always when they successfully complete a task, they will hear the sound, their signal to take a reward. But the reward will not be placed just out of shot, it will be somewhere else entirely. What Karl does is take the food away from where the animal is going so that it is not running to its food, it is completing a task that it knows it needs to complete before it can get its food. The beauty of this method is that you can invest the task with all sorts of complexities depending on the intelligence of the animal. You can train the pig, for instance, that just going to a mark will not get him food; going to the mark and looking over in a particular direction quite calmly for about four seconds will get him food. It is a water-dripping, brainwashing, repetitive and patient process of training the animals from a very young age. First they learn that performing a task will get them a reward and then they have to learn each task to be performed before they actually get a reward, which allows you to extend the task a little bit further each time. That's the broad principle at work.

The reason each animal is given a different sound cue for its reward is because very often you have more than one animal performing on set at the one time. Each sound is totally distinctive, so if you have a duck and a pig in the same frame doing their thing, the duck won't think it has done its task when it hears the party clicker. It will ignore the party clicker; the duck wants to hear the beeper. It makes for a very noisy set, but at least the animals understand what's going on.

Did you ever realise what Babe *would do to the food industry, particularly in the US?*

To tell you the truth I don't know what it has done to the food industry in the US. I don't know whether the story is hype or whether it's real.

Is the McDonald's story the one you are referring to?

No, you tell me that one.

Because the sale of pork went down in the US, McDonald's spent a huge amount of money promoting their beef hamburgers.

It may be true, but as with everything in the hype-industry of Hollywood I find it very difficult to sort the truth from the hype. Two days after the film was released in the US, people were saying, 'It's a hit, you got a hit!' But people are so effusive and overly enthusiastic about everything that I didn't trust this at all. I had no idea of how the film was going and I was asking people, 'Just how successful is it? What's really happening?'

I didn't really expect it to have an effect on the food industry because *Babe* doesn't take a stand on vegetarianism; its theme is not whether you should eat meat or not. But I guess I would prefer to be blamed for turning people off meat than I would for copy-cat serial murders.

Quite often Australians get movies down here to shoot but both the special effects and post-production go overseas. What do you think we can do to help keep it here?

I think this film helps to a degree—the fact that virtually all the creative input is from Australia and that it's one of a long line of films that have made money elsewhere in the world. As this continues to happen, Hollywood studio executives, who I guess are the people who start getting worried if you say you want to do your post-production and special effects in Australia, are more likely to listen because there will be more successful precedents.

We decided to go overseas for our computer graphic special effects not because we didn't believe there was talent here, but because it was unproven talent and the studio would not agree to us going to an Australian company for the special effects. I'm pleased we went where we did because I think we ended up with some extremely experienced people who were very brilliant. I am very happy with the computer graphic work. We decided to split the animatronics between an English company and an Australian one. The English company, Henson's Creature Shop, have extraordinary resources and years and years of experience with this sort of thing, while the Australian company, John Cox & Robotechnology, have shown great brilliance in their pitch to us, and I am very happy about that outcome as well. In fact, the sheep by Robotechnology are some of the best animatronics in *Babe*. With the exception of a couple of shots, the animatronic sheep are relied on exclusively, and I really love the way the animatronic sheep have worked out.

To be fair though, Fred Schepisi, Gillian Armstrong, Peter Weir and others all post-produce here. If you look at the numbers, I think the reality with Australian directors working in Hollywood is that they basically get their post-production out of Hollywood to here.

Very often, yes.

In pre-production rehearsals for characterisations, especially with the actors doing the animal voices, how did you develop the characters to get them finely tuned?

We had a voice workshop where we played around with many approaches for each of the different animals. One thing I would like to say about the casting is that in my mind I had a notion of the character for each of the animals, so when I was casting a voice I would sit there with my eyes closed, listening to the actor. Even when I was talking to the actor I was imagining the animal the actor was being casted for and then working on the voice from there.

There were a number of people whom I thought were real candidates for parts. I won't say people, I'll say voices. I'll deal with it out there in the ether because that's what I wanted, a 'voice' for a sheep, say. When I heard the recording I thought, 'This is fabulous, this is just what I want'. Then when I got footage of a sheep of the right breed and look, and played the voice while watching this animal, the voice just didn't work, it fell apart. There had to be something about a voice that not only captured the character, but also had to seem natural coming out of the mouth of an animal with its own physiological qualities. Part of the aim of the rehearsal and workshop process was to find ways of producing a voice that seemed more and more natural coming out of the mouth of a particular breed and type of animal. We used many images of the animals and the actors played around with them a lot. It was a really nice group effort with different actors advising other actors and suggesting differences in approach. Again, it was an amorphous process. It's hard to say that we approached the rehearsals from a particular point of view or with a particular program. There wasn't one. It was a matter of sitting down with footage of the animals and with a group of actors and trying different approaches to the voices.

You mentioned a couple of times that you fought Universal all the way on things like the title cards. Could you comment on your relationship with Universal, whether you felt at an advantage or disadvantage as a non-American production company working with an American studio?

We were at a huge advantage working as a non-American production company, particularly shooting it in Australia. During the shoot not one Universal executive visited the set. I am sure quite a few of them would have liked to come out here for the holiday, but Doug Mitchell [producer for Kennedy Miller], who was basically in charge of dealing with Universal, successfully deflected their attempts. I don't quite know how he did it, but I was very grateful he did. Their interferences with us very rarely amounted to anything more than an annoyance, and there were no major changes to the film.

One of the most annoying things, which amounted to nothing much at all, was that the contract between Kennedy Miller and Universal had Kennedy Miller agreeing to guarantee that the film would get a G rating. Now in the US a G rating is really quite hard to come by, and this required us, for example, to eliminate all uses of the word 'hell'. There was a line at the beginning when Mr Hoggett goes to the fair and the guy at the 'Guess the Weight' competition says to Hoggett, 'How the hell are those sheep of yours?' Not any more he doesn't, that was not allowed. 'How're those sheep of yours?' is what he says now. When Babe first meets Ma, she says, 'Damn wolf, never leave nobody alone'. 'Damn' is an instant no-no. Instant PG rating. These things are completely context irrelevant, it's just the use of the word. It's like they have an electronic scanner and if an offending word is there, 'meep!', the lights go on and it has to go. There was a lot of that sort of thing which we took note of and it influenced details around the edges, but nothing that really changed the film. We were very lucky. If you've read any of the books about people dealing with the studio system you'll know that we got out of it very, very lightly. I think that was due to George's relationship with Tom Pollock and the fact that Tom wanted to keep George in his good books, and vice versa.

The lighting of the film really enhances the 'storybook' feel. Did you do a lot of tests on film stocks with the director of photography to achieve the look?

Yes, we did a lot of tests, and I'm glad you raised it. One of the reasons we were attracted to a *noirish*, high-contrast lighting approach wasn't just to do with the style and visual language of the film, it had to do with the fact that this film was going to be very testing on the audience's perception of whether Babe had just been swapped for an animatronic, then swapped back to a pig and then swapped again for an animatronic during the cut of a scene. When we shot tests of our first animatronic pig, we discovered that the more contrasty the lighting, the less honest it was to the textures and surface reality of the animatronic. We found that with a more dramatic approach to the lighting we got away with more—the sleight of hand was less obvious.

We did do a lot of testing of lighting schemes, colour in particular. The film basically has a gold colour wash to it. We experimented with a range of colours to decide on a focal colour—a colour that would pervade everything. The film keeps going back to gold and testing determined just how far we wanted to go into a yellow look.

Are the cloudscapes mattes or are they real?

They are real.

Is the farmhouse real?

The house is a real set. It's very small and that's what gives it its cuteness. The interior sets would never fit inside the house set. The house set is a shell built in that little valley. We only shot one scene in the interior of the exterior house set, that is, the scene when Mrs Hoggett is washing up and the pig is rounding up the chooks outside the window. I wanted to bring the camera in from the window to see our characters, but as she passes the plate across the camera we've cut to a reverse shot which is an interior set, not the interior of our exterior set.

Could you roughly break down the techniques used for each of the principal characters? For example, were the dogs mostly computer in terms of the mouths? What was the duck and so on?

All the characters are mixed up. There's the very broad rule that static close-ups are going to be animatronic, but we consciously broke that rule time and time again, partly to keep everyone guessing. Animatronics were built for each of the characters—the duck, the dogs, the pig, the sheep—and we tried to use the animatronics as much as possible because it made good economic sense. When you are paying US$25 000 to US$50 000 for a CGI shot, the more animatronics you use the more cost-effective they are. They cost a lot to build, but once you've got the animatronics built then every use of them is cost effective. In the case of the duck, it is really a combination of animatronics and CGI. Animatronics generally didn't work with the dogs.

What about puppetry?

Animatronics is puppetry. The only real non-animatronic puppets, meaning manually operated or computer-manipulated puppets, are the mice. When the mice are singing 'Blue Moon' and 'Toreador' the puppeteers are buried underground, lying on their backs and looking at TV monitors so they can see the effect of what they are doing.

There was no real rule and it was only with the dogs that we came unstuck. The rest of the animatronics worked pretty successfully.

How do you think the film would be now had you decided to go with high definition television (HDTV)? Also, did you consider Super 35? And how might the film be had you gone to Industrial Light & Magic (ILM)?

That's very hard to know—when you take the turn-off and go down a particular road there's no knowing what would have happened if we had taken another road. I believe we made the right decision not to shoot with HDTV, because I think we would never have got the glowing warmth of the film. There is a sort of 'coolness' to HDTV which I think is somehow inherent to the medium as it exists at the moment.

ILM gave us a quote which was very competitive with all of the smaller companies. Because ILM have such a good reputation, we were very tempted to go with them, but a little way down the track they suddenly changed their quote and said, 'Oops, we've made a mistake'. It was a much higher figure than the original quote. Only later did someone suggest that it was changed because they had just been offered *Casper* (1995). The gossip was that they decided not to do *Babe* because it is a film where the special effects are never noticed, whereas with a film like *Casper* everyone is going to go, 'Ooh, ah, look at that transparent ghost!' *Babe* is the worst sort of film for special effects people to work on because they've done a bad job if you can see that they had been at work. So it was less attractive to ILM. It's very hard to know how it would have turned out, other than it would have been more expensive.

We did consider Super 35 for awhile. I can't remember exactly what counted against it, but it was the combination of greater image area to scan being a slight problem for CGI and that inevitably Super 35 was going to mean another generation to the final prints. The combination of those two is I think what finally turned us away from it.

Did the Celtic jig that Mr Hoggett does to cheer up Babe spring from the British roots of the story, or was it borne of the resurgent interest in Celtic culture?

I liked the idea of it having a Celtic flavour. Annouchka De Jong, the choreographer we hired to help formulate the dance, is classically ballet trained, but she actually came up with a dance that I think is called the *tarantella*,[4] which is not Celtic at all. She drew on all sorts of different sources.

James Cromwell, who plays Mr Hoggett, figured it somehow had to believable to his character even though he was jumping right out of character by doing it. Being a traditional sort of farmer we felt the dance had to come from some recognisable, rural tradition, and so it seemed to ring true to us that basically the dance be an Irish jig.

Is there going to be a sequel to Babe? *Have you been inundated with offers to direct special effects movies? Would you direct a special effects movie with this amount of detail? And if not, are you desperate to get out there with live action and no animals?*

I did dream of the classic story of the three people trapped in the lift for ninety minutes while I was making this film. Universal have said they are interested in a sequel; I've said I am not interested in doing it.

In answer to the special effects question, I didn't approach this movie because I wanted to make an animal movie or because I wanted to make a special effects movie. I made it because I fell in love with the story and wanted to tell that story. It's par for the course that in order to make the movie I had to learn a lot about animals and special effects. It's the case with most movies. Let's say you agree to make an action movie, it would probably involve you being patient enough to gather all the little bits and pieces you require to shoot a particular action sequence, and perhaps learning how to successfully achieve various stunts. Every film creates its own set of challenges. I regard special effects not as a passion or special interest, but as part of the vocabulary available to us as film-makers and, where necessary, a vocabulary which we develop to say what we have to say. I am very pleased I now know a lot about special effects, but that doesn't mean I want to run out and do another special effects movie. And my special effects knowledge will probably be out of date in a few minutes.

What are you wanting to do?

It isn't top secret because it doesn't exist yet. I've been offered many projects. The majority of them are from the US and the majority of them I have dismissed outright, including the first two I was submitted which were two camel movies. I predict camels are going to be big. You heard it here first. But most of them are pretty empty when you finish the read. Many scripts that develop within the studio system seem to be characterised by very fine craft in terms of story structure, at least conventional fine craft, but are not about much in the end. That's frustrating and it might be that I write my next movie rather than find a script that has been already written. But I haven't made the decision yet, I am sort of basking for a little while more.

my instinction:
kiss or kill?

bill bennett

Kiss or Kill represents an extensive lineage of my arriving at a style. Before I sat down to write the final draft I was given some advice very early on by Pierre Rissient. Rissient comes to Australia regularly at the behest of the Australian Film Commission (AFC) to guide film into selection at Cannes, and he had been tracking the development of this film for many years. I had actually given up, believing that I couldn't do this story. He said, 'Stop thinking! Your problem is you're thinking too much.' So I decided to give the script one last shot and sat down and wrote the last draft in three weeks. I started at page one and didn't know how or where it was going to end up. I was determined just to do what Pierre had said to do.

The final script of *Kiss or Kill* represented a sixty-page, scene-by-scene breakdown. With the exception of one scene there was no dialogue written, but there was indirect dialogue because sixty pages can be quite detailed. With that document I was then able to raise the money, $2.6 million, in three to four weeks. Gary Hamilton of Beyond came on straightaway; he had been associated with this thing over a long period of time. The most elusive piece was securing Australian theatrical distribution for which I needed Film Finance Corporation (FFC) money. We had the South Australian Film Corporation (SAFC), Newvision with a terrific pay-television deal, and Beyond, but we couldn't get an Australian distributor. My partner and co-producer, Jennifer Cluff, and I were going to reduce the budget, do the film without fees, put in some of our own money, and not go with any FFC money at all. But when Frank Cox at Newvision came in with a distribution deal, Catriona

Hughes and the FFC were very keen for us to do it through them. I must acknowledge I had very supportive distributors in Newvision and Beyond Films, who encouraged me to make something unconventional. So the whole thing fell into place very quickly and I was able to cast it and go into rehearsal.

CASTING AND REHEARSAL

Being on location for rehearsal was incredibly important for this film. The first part of the rehearsal period involved very detailed character work, and then we broke down the film scene by scene. By the time we came to shoot the actors knew pretty much what was required for each scene, what their intentions and their actions were. But we didn't talk about dialogue at all during the rehearsal period. Towards the end of the rehearsal period we went through the physicality of the characters, then we locked the dialogue down once we had done a couple of block-throughs on the day of shooting. Because I had attempted to write this thing so many times before, I always had in my mind how the scenes were to play—and I guess I regarded that fact as a back-up—but I really wanted to see what the actors would come up with, then kind of mould or sculpt the performance according to what the scene required. I took the attitude that it was crazy to go into this film and straitjacket people. I had some very clever people working on this film and I wanted to see what they would bring to it.

I didn't necessarily accommodate the style to a type of actor, but I did cast actors who are very confident and who would be able to take the style on board. Matt Day, Frances O'Connor and I sat down in a coffee-shop for a chat, and twenty minutes later I offered them the parts. I cannot cast by a traditional method because I don't understand how directors make decisions based on reads in auditions. It has often been my experience that actors who do a good read aren't necessarily going to be the best actors for a part. I think the technique of getting to a performance is a result of an extraordinary amount of work over a long period of time. For actors to come in—often they only get a scene or a couple of pages—and pull something out of the bag is trite and without context. It would be like giving Dean Semler a box of redheads [flexible 800-watt lamps, usually painted red] and twenty minutes to light a room without telling him what the scene is about. It is exactly the same thing; most people don't understand that arriving at a performance is equally as technical a skill as lighting.

What I try to do is look at their previous work and then talk to them. Often I don't even talk about the film. I try to determine whether they are smart and what their world view is. It is such an ethereal thing.

[BILL BENNETT, JENNIFER CLUFF AND NEWVISION FILMS]

Al (Matt Day), Detective Crean (Andrew Gilbert) and Nikki (Frances O'Connor), *Kiss or Kill*

It's trickier for people who don't have a body of work to show. On *Two If By Sea* (1996), a film I did in the US, I cast Sandra Bullock in the same way as Matt and Frances: we just sat down and had a chat. But I also had to go to Toronto to cast about fifteen critical speaking parts with Canadian actors. I went into a place where I didn't know the people at all and didn't know the agents. I can often tell a lot about an actor by the agency representing them in Australia, or I can look at their CVs and look at their credits and know what theatre they have done. But in Toronto the people had credits that I didn't know of, so I had nothing, no information at all, other than what the casting agent could give me, which was usually a quick sketch before the person came in. I had two days to see about a hundred people which meant I had about five minutes per person in a totally foreign city. I couldn't give them a script to read because that's not the way I can judge their suitability, so I decided to ask each person what their favourite colour is. What this did was to totally put them on the back foot because they were not expecting it. It was a process that allowed me to follow a line of conversation and get to the essence of the person in a very short span of time. And it worked! Within the five minutes I was able to get the most heart-felt, personal things from people, often from the ones I ended up casting. It turned out to be a very accurate way of doing the casting.

When writing *Kiss or Kill* I didn't have anybody in mind for any of the roles except Andrew Gilbert for the part of Chris Haywood's sidekick. I wrote that part specifically with Andrew in mind and I would have put the shoot back if there had been a problem with his availability. He was the only person I knew who could really pull off what I call the 'bacon scene'.

Every major role for me has a bottleneck through which the actor has to pass. I try to determine what that bottleneck is and then look for that in the rehearsal. In *Mortgage* (1989), for instance, the bottleneck for the lead, played by Brian Vriends, was the character's ability to create rage instantaneously. Many actors can do a part, but very few can actually get through a moment in a film that is like the narrowest point in a bottle. An actor who passes through the bottleneck is what I look for.

Working on the physicality or movements of the characters happens near the end of the rehearsal process because by that stage I feel the actors know their characters so well they can then make physical choices. Some actors like to make physical choices early on in the process and that helps them. It is really up to them, but certainly when I structure the rehearsal process I factor the physicality in towards the end. It was interesting watching Andrew Gilbert work. Near the end of *Kiss or Kill* there is a body lying on the road. Andrew leans over and touches the head, walks off and says, 'We've got a dead one'. The way he walks is so perfect for a cop: at that point he is a cop. He had absorbed the character information to such a great extent that he was probably totally unaware of it.

I have refined it over the years, but the rehearsal process with *Kiss or Kill* was really a culmination of taking very smart actors and getting them to the point where they understood their characters so well that if we decided to deviate from the script they would still know their characters and know what their dynamic is. The characters would still ring true. What I try to do as a director is to create an environment where the actors can get very close to the character, and that's really what the rehearsal process is about: a way of getting the actors to the point where they live and breathe their characters.

IMPROVISATION

Improvisation is a word that can carry a multitude of meanings. For different directors it means different things and certainly it means differ-ent things for different actors. I think most people have the impression that improvisation means turning up on the day and making up the action and dialogue as you go along. But, in fact, you could not make a film like *Kiss or Kill* in twenty-six shooting days without the shoot being incredibly disciplined and with everybody knowing exactly what they are doing. You would get into an almighty mess.

First, I encouraged everybody to approach the film as if we were doing a documentary. The production didn't have a continuity person and even though there was a freedom allowed for both the actors and the camera, what I discovered in the cutting room was a strong sense of discipline in everybody involved. I don't know whether this came about because there was no continuity person, but it was certainly interesting seeing that happen without the guidance of someone ducking in to check on continuity.

Second, despite the fact that almost all the scenes in the film are improvised, there is nevertheless a highly defined story outline, including suggested dialogue that the actors and the crew are following. I brought all the actors out on to location, which was Ceduna on the eastern side of the Great Australian Bight, and for two weeks we went through the scene-by-scene breakdown and did very comprehensive character break-downs so that the actors could have a very keen understanding of who the characters were. Then I talked them through the dramatics on both a macro and micro level. On the macro level, explaining the dramatic structure of how everything fits together, how it all works, and why it has the structure that it has. Then, at the micro level, working out the action in each particular scene.

I regard improvisation as largely a process of creating the right rhythm within a scene and then making sure the scene's rhythm works with the overall rhythm of the film. The scenes as finally chosen have to be pretty much accurate according to the film's structure. While writing the film I went back to something else Pierre had said to me, which was to 'write action'. I interpreted that to mean characters 'doing' rather than 'saying'. In many ways I regard the action as something like music and that the narrative would work almost irrespective of the dialogue. If you like, the dialogue merely joined the dots. To step back a moment, for one particular scene in *Backlash* (1986) I remember sitting down and singing the scene to the actors, not worrying about the dialogue, just singing the scene so they could work out the rhythmic beats of their actions. For me *Backlash* is a film that works with the 'music' of the performances. I wrote scenes with music in mind and so whatever information the characters impart is sometimes incidental to the 'music' of a scene.

Improvisation for an actor can be a terrifying process, but part of the process involves an actor totally accepting on faith that I will keep the safety net down. At no point in the rehearsal process do I allow the actors to actually enact a scene off the top of their heads. I should also mention that actors taking a proprietory interest in their character can in many ways be a potentially dangerous by-product of improvisation. Because I give them so much freedom, in a sense they begin to feel as though they can determine what their characters can say or do. This happened on *Backlash*, where the actors wanted to try to take over the circus and I didn't really have the experience to be able to control it as I do now. This time I warned the actors to be aware of what might happen and that they would probably not even know it's happening. It's a tricky thing for an actor to come to terms with because on the one hand you require actors to give so much, but on the other you are telling them to get back in their corner.

My feeling is that the actors do not have the knowledge to be able to spontaneously come out with appropriate dialogue until the end of the rehearsal process. They don't understand who the characters are, where they fit into the whole, or what their interaction or dynamic is within any given scene. So getting up and actually saying words is nonsense because one is operating on insufficient information. Actors are quite confronted by this at first, because they think a rehearsal process for an improvised film is about acting spontaneously. But that is not the way it works for me. There is certainly room for negotiation and for accommodating all sorts of intangibles that emerge spontaneously while on the set, but not in rehearsal.

I guess this is where I differ from, say, Mike Leigh in the use of improvisation. I haven't actually spoken to him, but from what I understand, Leigh tends to use the rehearsal process to lock down the dialogue and then goes into the filming in a more traditional way. I don't lock down any dialogue at the rehearsal stage. What I try to do instead is to create an environment on the set where the actors will feed off the locations, from my input and from the blocking through of the action. For example, in *Kiss or Kill* Max Cullen plays a support role as Stan who runs a motel, and there is a funny piece of business where he is standing at the registry desk holding a big knife and Matt Day comes in and says, 'Gee, that's a nice big knife you've got there'. Max, in a very laconic manner, replies, 'Yeah, and it's a nice big orange to go with it'. Max came up with that line and just threw it in; it wasn't preconceived yet it was true to his character. Then later on Stan's body is found in his motel bed with his throat cut and the camera pans up to a picture of very tacky sea-side scene and then there's an immediate cut to a real sea-side. Again, that wasn't carefully scripted or planned: on the day of shooting that scene I noticed the art department had put the picture of the sea-scape on the wall and thought it would make a nice little segue.

The beauty of writing a fully fledged script is that you are able to play with what is underneath the dialogue, but the process of improvisation almost works against that. The nature of improvisation has actors listening, thinking, and then responding, and so what we are watching on screen are the cogs turning over. We often notice an improvisation because we can see the process of actors responding to words, but they don't often respond to what is underneath the words. To give another example, *A Street to Die* (1985) was scripted, but there is one scene that was totally improvised. On one particular morning I arrived on set and thought the film needed a scene that would work on a sub-textual level. It's the scene where Chris Haywood's character, who is dying of cancer, is fixing the fridge because he wants to make sure things are in order for his family after he's gone, and it's scene of domestic conflict with his wife who doesn't want him to fix the fridge. One of the things I often feel lacking in an improvised scene is a subject, so what we did was to use symbolism to draw out the subject. This man is dying of cancer and, ironically, his fixing of the fridge represents his breakdown. The woman doesn't want him to die; she doesn't mind if the fridge breaks down because she doesn't want things to change, she wants things within the family to stay exactly as they are, which means that her husband lives.

Because that scene was done in one take I had absolutely no control over its pacing, no control over repetition or stumbles, which are dead give-aways of improvisation. I just talked the actors through the actions prior to shooting the scene, I didn't talk in terms of sub-text or symbolism. That day I figured out that a very simple way of having some kind of sub-text happening is to give the actors a very specific action in a scene—like Chris's fixing of the fridge or having Max about to peel an orange with his knife—and if the actors are truly inside their characters then they will act accordingly.

The best drama works when the action not only works within a scene, but works consistently with the through-line of the film. Scenes become messy when the actor or dramatist confuses the action within a scene or between scenes. *Two If By Sea* wasn't successful, but I'm very fond of the film—I think there are some lovely moments in the film. It becomes very dangerous if you try to mix your styles too much, which I guess is really what happened with *Two If By Sea*. When making *Kiss or Kill* I was very conscious of the fact that the style had to be totally consistent. The overall structure of *Kiss or Kill* relies on rhythms and actions being followed through. So what I am saying is that improvisation—despite it being perceived as an arbitrary process—involves trusting that you are going to be fed by what is around you and being disciplined about it.

CAMERA STYLE

Pierre's words rang in my ears and so, once I worked out the intellectual framework, I decided to go out on this shoot and do the film instinctively.

But not only me, it also required everybody working with me to do exactly the same thing, particularly the actors, but so too Malcolm McCulloch—the director of photography—with his camera and lighting. I wanted something that came from the emotional core of each of the people I was working with, and I was determined at the very start that the technical processes of this film would serve the actors and their performance. This film wouldn't have worked if it was cerebral, it had to be visceral, which meant resolutely refusing to do much technical preparation—such as storyboarding—prior to the start of the shoot or on each day of shooting, whereas in previous films I had worked things out very carefully beforehand. I even stopped looking at the rushes at one point, obviously deliberately taking a risk and jumping into the deep end.

With this I was going to be led by what happened on the day, but still keep it within the framework that had been established right at the start. What it meant was that the actors would come on the location, we'd physically walk through what looked right, stick a viewfinder on it, and then shoot. The thing with this type of style is that you pretty much shoot down a primary axis. On conventional drama or with a conventional style, you are looking at a scene being blocked through by the actors and then you would think about doing, for example, reverse shots or wide-angle shifts to justify a cut. What I was doing with *Kiss or Kill* was to find a favoured angle for a scene, but not looking to justify a cut; I was looking for increments. Having looked at the block-through and found the primary angle, I'd work just slightly skew of that angle, or I'd choreograph the camera movement a couple of beats forward or back, or I'd change the lens size a couple of millimetres. I was looking for incremental things knowing the 'live' camera, or hand-held camera, would allow for the cuts.

Conventionally a director would choreograph an actor's movements and then coordinate the camera movement—you move the camera consistent with the action so that you have some idea of cutting for continuity. That's always a constant. But for *Kiss or Kill* we purposely did a-rhythmic choreography regarding the 'beats' as to when you move the camera so that we could have back-cutting, which adds an extra bit of tension or drama to a scene.

CUTTING STYLE

The story of *Kiss or Kill* is very simple: the Frances O'Connor and Matt Day characters—Nikki and Al—are two hustlers and they're conning a fellow she has met at a bar. Nikki goes off to a hotel room with the guy, but he ends up dying accidentally and so Matt and Frances decide to split. But as they head off into the desert, other people start to die in their path and they each think the other one is the killer. That's the basic story. Now the scene at the bar in many ways encapsulates the whole cutting style of the film. It is the second scene up and it was my intention at that stage in the film to let the audience know that the cutting style wasn't a mistake. It's meant to have the audience witness a lot of jump-cuts and get them used to the fact that it's setting the tone for the remainder of the film. That's why the camera holds on Frances for quite a length of time and for quite a number of cuts, and why we withhold information about who she is actually talking to.

The editing style wasn't invented in the cutting room; it was something I had very consciously decided to do at script stage. It occurred to me that the two main characters had such fractured lives that the film really required a very bold cutting style—one intellectually appropriate to their 'fracturedness'. I love the scene at the bar so much because at one moment Frances has a cigarette in her mouth, but in the next she doesn't; one minute the fellow she's talking to is there, in the next he is somewhere else. A purist would look at that scene and think it is a god-awful mess. It's probably difficult to watch that scene in isolation because one doesn't have the emotional through-line to understand how it's working for the whole film.

On a purely practical level it looks like there are a lot of shots in the bar scene. In fact, discounting three wide-shots, I think there are only another three shots covering the dialogue section. What is actually happening is that the camera is alive, it is hand-held, which makes the images very dynamic; the frame size is seemingly changing within one take and so it allows one to cut forward or back using the one take. Moreover, one decision taken as we approached the start of shooting was to print at a much higher ratio than would normally occur. Given that we were cutting in and out all over the place, we knew that even with NG [no good] takes there would be a beat that could perhaps be used and so when it looks like there is a lot of coverage, in fact there's very little. But, of course, the great skill of Malcolm McCulloch was in making the camera look like it was continually hand-held and that the images are constantly changing, thus making the cuts quite dynamic in their rhythm. Consequently, there's the illusion of quite extensive coverage.

About a month before I went into production I called the editor, Henry Dangar, to let him know I was going to do *Kiss or Kill*. We talked briefly about the way I intended to shoot the film and have it edited, and after the phone call I sent Henry a videotape of a car commercial I had done, which was along the style I wanted for the film. It was a commercial I had committed to doing some time ago and, to be honest, didn't think was ever going to happen. I finally got confirmed on it when I was in pre-production for *Kiss or Kill*, which annoyed the hell out of the people I was working with. It just so happened it was a commercial that lent itself to the style I wanted for the film, so I experimented to see whether or not the style was going to work for the film. I learned a lot from the commercial because I knew one could not cut a film like this with a traditional camera approach. If the cutting style was to work then it meant figuring out how the camera was to work. It didn't make you want to run out and buy a car, but the commercial did give me the confidence to go into the shoot knowing that what we were to do with the camera would enable the picture to be cut in a 'jagged' style.

To give an example, there are moments of back-cutting in the commercial where the action is choreographed in a couple of beats different to the way you would normally choreograph. Usually when setting up a scene the director is trying to get everything the same way each time—that is, to have continuity—so that everything will cut together imperceptibly. With this style, however, the idea is to make everything a-rhythmic or dysfunctional, according to the 'beats' that are required for any particular scene. There's a moment in the commercial when the actor is delivering a line and he is coming around a corner, and then we cut to a wider shot and he's delivering the next line but he's further back from the corner. You can usually justify a jump-cut if the action is happening in a forward direction; in other words, it makes sense if the person is delivering a line and he's coming around a corner and then you jump-cut and he is now around the corner walking towards you. But the jump-cut becomes much more interesting if he is coming around a corner and the next time you cut he's continuing along in his conversation yet physically further back. Now in *Kiss or Kill*, there is an early scene where Frances O'Connor has seen a tape of a guy who is a paedophile, and she goes into the kitchen, pulls open a drawer, picks up a phone book and dials his number. In the film she does it three times, and in simplistic terms it's to emphasise the point that she is feeling angry. Once we determined the action and blocked it through, we did three takes, each take with a slightly larger lens size than the one before. We just took those simple actions of pulling at a drawer, getting a phone book out, slamming it down on the table, and lifting up the handpiece on the phone. Then in the cutting room started the process of her doing it again and again, always a few 'beats' back, before she actually speaks into the phone. That's what I was really trying for with *Kiss or Kill*.

Perhaps the one exception to this cutting approach is the 'bacon scene' because it was scripted very tightly and was more conventionally shot. I finished the final draft after three weeks and then looked at the script and thought there was a major set piece missing, a scene that underscored the emotional core of the story even if it didn't move the story along. So I went back and wrote the 'bacon scene' in ten minutes, pretty much word for word as it's seen on screen.

Because the scene was shot more conventionally, it became for Henry the hardest scene to make work—we were looking to get the rhythms and the little nuances of it somewhat consistent with the rest of the film. We were cutting the 'bacon scene' right up until we locked off, and the 'beat' right at the end when Andrew Gilbert pops the bacon in his mouth, we just couldn't get right. We recut and recut and recut. For me the best scenes are the ones that work 'musically', and if the 'music' isn't right then the scene isn't playing right. In the editing it came down to using frames just to get the rhythms right—it was truly artful but it meant cutting the scene more conventionally. In fact, the rhythm of the 'bacon scene' is largely taken from the rhythm of the actors because their sense of comic timing allowed for pauses. Andrew and Chris produced the rhythm and Henry only enhanced it a little; whereas in all the other scenes Henry's editing goes a long way in expressing the emotional content of the scenes.

From watching *Kiss or Kill* one would think that it was a free-for-all, that all the rules went out the window and we just cobbled it all together in the editing room. That's in fact very far from the case. Basic principles of continuity had to be adhered to, otherwise scenes wouldn't make sense when strung together. So we had to be very careful with the 'bacon scene' because if the cutting style was not appropriate to the emotion of the moment then it would have become gimmicky. The cutting style of *Kiss or Kill* is a very delicate thing—back-cutting, for instance, would have been totally inappropriate in the 'bacon scene', we just would not have got away with it. It would have been style for style's sake.

SOUND DESIGN

Those who have seen *Kiss or Kill* have probably noticed there is no music. And with the exception of maybe two scenes, the movie is post-synced. We just threw everything out. Our recordist, Tovio Lember, went back out into the desert and re-recorded a whole lot of stuff and recorded some new stuff and then Wayne Pashley and his crew built the sound up from there.

We totally reconstructed the sound from nothing, and we had absolute control over all aspects of the sound. It meant we could use sound like music, and not only could we create tension through the use of very specific effects and atmospheres, we could also create tension through the use of silence. That's one of the reasons I decided to post-sync. Also, because the whole film is pretty much hand-held, it meant we had to use a camera that wasn't blimped [soundproofed] terribly well. There was a lot of camera noise, especially in interiors and, although we could filter out camera noise, we decided to throw out all the dialogue and re-record it.

Not to have music was a decision I made in post-production. I had actually hired a composer right from the start and was going to have Aboriginal rock music throughout the film. I brought on Christine Woodruff and we had lined up a whole lot of bands, and the composer had already started working by that stage. The idea not to have music started to emerge when we were out on location doing an interior scene at one of the diners—the scene where Nikki and Al hear the radio report. We had put the slate [board identifying scene photographed] on but then realised there was a road train going by in the background and so we had to wait before we could start the scene. While watching the rushes of that scene I was listening to the sound of the road train go by before the dialogue started and thought there was nothing that defined this place more accurately than that sound. I started to wonder how that sound could be interpreted in music and couldn't come up with anything.

We stayed at a roadhouse in Ceduna and there are road trains that come in at 3.00 a.m. and have to do big U-turns to line up at the diesel pumps. Ceduna is the half-way spot between Melbourne and Perth and there must be about a hundred of these road trains which go through every night. It felt like it was the heartbeat of this place. That's when I started to think about not having music at all and just going with sound, which could have been a problem because obviously a music soundtrack is a very important commercial aspect to film-making. I told Christine and the composer what I was thinking as soon as I got back, but waited on making a decision until I had seen a first cut. When I had a look at the first cut I thought there was nothing music could do that we couldn't do just as effectively with sound.

That's when I also made the decision to post-sync. (I always wanted to totally post-sync a picture anyway, but I have to say that post-syncing *Kiss or Kill* was without doubt the most painful thing I've ever done as a director and I think the actors would have to agree.) It became apparent that we could go with a 'jagged' visual style more effectively if there was a continuum of audio. In other words, the eye would allow you to make the jump as long as the sound was continuous. It was a tricky decision to make. I knew the cutting style was going to work and I knew the visual style was going to work, but having made that decision I was terrified *Kiss or Kill* was going to look like a cheap spaghetti western. I'm not being disrespectful here, but I was concerned that the film was going to look fake and that people would know it was dubbed. To be honest it was something we were most scared of because we weren't sure how the audience was going to respond. If an audience laughed then we would have lost it totally. We all worked very hard to get the film to a point where we felt the dubbing was imperceptible.

SPHERES OF INFLUENCE

Generally, I think I started working in this way because I've come through documentaries. I love documentaries, but I do not regard myself as a particularly good documentary-maker because I want to control things—and, really, the best documentarians don't. I was a kind of frustrated documentary-maker, but when I got to drama I was frustrated because I really missed the excitement and the unpredictability of documentary.

I came to do my second feature, *Backlash*, because I had originally raised money to make a documentary on a black tracker, Jimmy James. The BBC and the ABC had come in with pre-sales, I had the money sitting in the bank, I'd done all the research, but each morning I would get out of bed and just couldn't bring myself to make the documentary. There was something holding me back and I couldn't figure out what it was; all I knew was that I really didn't want to make this documentary. But I had the idea for *Backlash* and so I asked both the ABC and BBC if they would mind if I made it into a feature film. Of course they said no because it was their documentary divisions that had put up the pre-sales. The BBC pulled out and so did the ABC. I had raised the money based on the pre-sales, suddenly I had the money sitting in the bank, but no pre-sales and I had to make a film. I went to all the investors and told them the idea for the feature, and when I found a distributor to match the pre-sales that had fallen through, which made the investors happy, I then went out and made *Backlash* using documentary techniques and improvisation. Originally *Backlash* was just going to involve getting into a car and driving out on location with a small cast and crew; it was going to be as free flowing as that, although the shoot did become a bit more formalised. The whole idea was to get the actors and create characters as if they were 'real' people in a documentary, and as a dramatist I would put them into situations where they would act accordingly with whatever presented itself. I suppose I was trying to fuse the two forms.

When I finished the script of *Kiss or Kill*, Malcolm wanted me to look at other films for technical reasons. I had looked at *Paris, Texas* (1984) for lighting style, and it had occurred to me that it is one of the few road movies that actually points the camera out the front window. It may sound like such an obvious thing, but most road movies look out the back window. It's easier that way and very rarely do you see a road movie looking through the front windscreen. *Paris, Texas* is one of the few exceptions and I was really intrigued by it. I had been thwarted from doing that on *Spider & Rose* (1994) because of the nature of the shoot. With this film, there's a shot where Frances has her hand out of the side window and she's playing with the air. Now we've seen this type of shot before, but invariably it's looking behind. I really wanted that shot looking ahead because it is what the film is about.

It occurred to me when looking over the script that *Kiss or Kill* was missing that kind of thing on a more elaborate scale—what I call a 'nonsense' scene which doesn't in any way further the narrative yet absolutely encapsulates what the film is saying. In this regard, another film I looked at was *Breathless* (1959), the Jean-Luc Godard film; anybody going into a film with a style like *Kiss or Kill*'s has to look at *Breathless*. In *Breathless* there is a scene where Jean Seberg goes to the airport and interviews the novelist, played by Jean-Pierre Melville, who talks about the male perspective on sex and love. Again, it's a scene that doesn't further the story. You could actually take that scene out of the movie and the movie would still stand, and yet that scene absolutely underpins what *Breathless* is about. That's really what the 'bacon scene' is meant to do in *Kiss or Kill*.

THE PROBLEM OF GENRE

My favourite road movies aren't really road movies; the term 'road movie' brings with it certain preconceptions. There is no doubt that Frances and Matt are in a car and that they travel from point A to point B, but I regard *Apocalypse Now* (1979) and *The Wizard of Oz* (1939) as being road movies. It's a term that just seems to be part of a pigeon-holing process, but I think 'road movie' actually has a much broader application than we give credence to.

Kiss or Kill was hugely successful in the marketplace at Cannes in 1997, one of the most successful Australian films in terms of sales even though it wasn't in the official competition. It was sold to every territory in the world other than Benelux, Scandinavia, and a couple of South American territories. We got our budget back within three days of the first screening in Cannes, so it is one of the few films that have gone into real profit. What was interesting is that it was picked up by very prestigious distributors in the various territories, and picked up for theatrical release. It wasn't perceived as a schlock, B-grade, exploitation film that would go out on video. In fact, the genre aspect works against it because nobody really wants to pick up a film that has been made already, particularly in the specialised market.

Because I have spent quite a bit of time in film markets as both a producer and director, I've come to understand that what people are looking for is something totally different, and so going into the film I was very aware that positioning *Kiss or Kill* as a genre film—a road movie—could work against it. What has worked, and countered the genre aspect, I think, is the style of the film. If the film had been done in a more conventional style then it wouldn't have sold, particularly not in North America because they are very familiar with genre pictures. Nowadays genre films don't work unless they are big American pictures with big stars. They are always done better with more money and with identifiable actors out of Hollywood.

Talking as a producer, going into this film as a genre piece alone would have been a disadvantage. It had to be approached in a totally original, fresh way, and as a director I wanted to do something that was really unsafe, just for my own satisfaction. But if it was just style, then I am sure *Kiss or Kill* wouldn't have sold. And if it was just substance and not done in a stylish way, it probably wouldn't have sold as well either. But *Kiss or Kill* is sufficiently different in style to have made people excited.

FROM *TWO IF BY SEA* TO *KISS OR KILL*

I'd been courted by American companies, particularly after *Backlash*, but I never took up the option until *Two If By Sea*. I guess I was always very suspicious of the whole Hollywood thing. Working on *Two If By Sea* confirmed my suspicions.

Overall I feel burned by the experience of working in Hollywood. I learned a huge amount about the politics of the studio system and where a director fits within the whole scheme of things. When you work in Hollywood a film is finally a product, particularly if you work with a big star.

I was originally hired for *Two If By Sea* by Don Simpson and Jerry Bruckheimer—they were going to be the producers. They hired me on the basis of *Spider & Rose*. At that stage *Two If By Sea* was going to go out through Hollywood Pictures, they had a deal there and I signed on the understanding that they were going to be the producers. But then the budget started creeping up: originally it was about US$12.5 million and then it went up to about US$14.8 million, and so Hollywood Pictures baulked and put it into turn-around. Now because Simpson–Bruckheimer had an exclusive deal with Hollywood Pictures, they couldn't move across to another company as producers. The film then got picked up by Morgan Creek through Warner Brothers and I was working with producers I didn't know. I started to get concerned when they seemed not to be really interested. Simpson–Bruckheimer, irrespective of the kind of films they make, are extraordinarily professional and have the clout to be able to guide a director through the system. Whereas the Morgan Creek people operated as a little enclave within Warner Brothers and so I had four producers on the film, but only one of them had actually ever produced a film before.

The original script of *Two If By Sea* was a real Dennis Leary script—dark, edgy, a very independent-type film—and I have to say that Dennis was extremely good on the film, both as an actor and in the sense that he was prepared to let go of the script. What changed the script was the casting of Sandra Bullock, not her personally, but because when I originally cast her she wasn't a star. She was a really interesting actor who just happened to do the action movie *Speed* (1994). Instinctively, I thought she was right for the part, but in-between casting her and getting to final cut, *While You Were Sleeping* (1996) and *The Net* (1996) had come out and she was suddenly a big star. At that point the producers started rubbing their hands together with glee because Sandra's price had risen since they had hired her. They had international rights to the film and because Sandra Bullock movies had sold well overseas, they were phoning up their distributors to figure out how much they could sell it for in foreign territories. Not only that, she now had a persona out there, a sort of cute girl-next-door persona which was at variance to the character in the original script—a swearing, profane, small-time criminal—so Sandra's minders had become concerned that this was going to be inconsistent with the image that made her successful. And then the studio was concerned that *Two If By Sea* was not going to be like *While You Were Sleeping*, which is schmaltzy and sentimental, so enormous pressure came to bear on me to change it around. I think that is really where the problems started.

Part of my doing *Kiss or Kill* was as a reaction to having done *Two If By Sea* in Hollywood, where I was totally moribund and couldn't step outside of decisions that were made six months earlier. I had total control over every aspect of *Kiss or Kill*, which I didn't have on *Two If By Sea*. On *Kiss or Kill* I really wanted to be able to wake up in the morning, drive out to location and do what felt right. I wanted to take a very small crew on location, just twelve or fifteen people—we ended up with a crew of about forty, which is a shame in a sense. In simple terms, the problem is in finding the balance between needing the spontaneity and flexibility of documentary and needing the hierarchical structure of a conventional feature film.

I must admit I have had enormous fun on *Kiss or Kill*. It's been so liberating to make a film and not be tied to the conventions of cinema and, really, one of the purposes of doing the film was for me to rediscover the joy of cinema. I don't think I can take the style of *Kiss or Kill* and necessarily place it on top of another film and be absolutely sure it will work. But, having said that, I've learned so much about the craft and there are things now that I would like to push further. You look back on the stuff you have done for years, the stuff that's worked and the stuff that hasn't, and try to figure out what you have done right and what you've done wrong. I am still going through that kind of evaluation at the moment—that's part of the joy.

[PART VII]
DEAR DIARY

jean Cocteau opened his *Diary of a Film*[1] with the words: 'I have decided to write a diary of *La Belle et la Bête* as the work of the film progresses. After a year of preparations and difficulties, the moment had come to grapple with a dream.' Journals and diaries are fascinating because, made up of fragments, they can be read as if they are daily counterparts to the nightly sequences of visions and sensations passing through a sleeper's mind. After all, how many of us have felt, if not actually carried through, the impulse to commit a dream to paper?

The dreamers in this case are Richard Lowenstein and Scott Hicks. Lowenstein's begins at the completion of *Strikebound* and ends at the commencement of shooting *Dogs in Space*; Hicks's diary opens with *Shine*'s entry into the Sundance Film Festival, and tails off at the Golden Globe Awards. Like most diaries, theirs are records of events and notable personages encountered along their journeys, of opportunities won and lost; they are at times reflective, lucid, and impart little gems of wisdom. Though often at their best when brimming with impressionable bits and pieces, they are sometimes mundane like the weather, sometimes dramatic like the quick mutation of hopes into doubts and fears, or vice versa. And if hastily written their commentaries are perhaps imprecise, contradictory and certainly unguarded.

The diary entries appear complete in themselves, and yet, like dreams, they form a fragment of a fragment of a fragment. The whole picture is always deferred, or suspended, as though existing in another time and place. How apt that Lowenstein ends his dairy with 'To be continued'. Or, to quote Cocteau's entry for Friday, 11 January 1946: 'Have finished.

In other words, I'm beginning.' Thus if a film diary bears witness to all that the finished film did not or could not reveal, in having reserved their words for the extreme ends of a film's life, both Lowenstein and Hicks suggest that the core of a film-maker's life is always a work-in-progress.

telexes in space:
a tale of two films

richard lowenstein

OCTOBER 1983

At the age of twenty-four and after a period of two years of trauma, disillusionment and conflict, I completed my first feature film, *Strikebound* [released 1984].

During the final weeks of *Strikebound*, the entire production was fraught with 'schisms'. I had fallen out with both of the co-producers. The sound editor wasn't talking to the picture editor, both of whom weren't talking to the producers. The two producers weren't talking to each other; I wasn't talking to either producer. I was fighting with my mother—the film is based on her research—over the final cut of the film. My father wasn't talking to me because I wasn't talking to my mother.

I was also $35 000 out of pocket due to my insistence on a Dolby stereo soundtrack. I had resigned myself to a lifetime of music videos.

The Australian film industry seemed to be going downhill and getting worse. The praise-filled Oz film renaissance—the heydays of *The Devil's Playground* (1976), *'Breaker' Morant* (1980), *Sunday Too Far Away* (1975) and *Picnic at Hanging Rock* (1975) and so on—was beginning to wane.

To understand why this was so, you first of all have to understand the 150/50 10BA Tax Incentive Scheme for investors in the Australian film industry. Introduced in 1978 as a way of encouraging our then fledgling industry, the scheme was very simple. If you were in the 60 per cent tax bracket (then over $50 000 per annum) and sixty cents out of every dollar earned is taken in tax, then you were able to claim

150 per cent on any investment in an Australian feature film as a tax deduction on your gross income, on top of which the first 50 per cent of your investment returned in earnings would be tax-free.

The original quote by the government as to the cost in lost tax revenue was a few million dollars. When the final tally came in from the first year of tax incentives the cost was found to be close to $200 million. Productions began to be geared to fit in with the financial year, with the majority of films being financed in the last few weeks of June, the deadline for funding being 30 June. An offer document became necessary—a glossy prospectus that was registered with the tax department and which gave a rundown of the film: stills, graphics, synopsis, CVs, etc. This would sit on the desks of various accountants and lawyer-investors, hoping vainly to attract money.

What the 10BA Tax Incentive Scheme had created was a sharp upturn in the quantity of Australian feature films produced, along with a corresponding downturn in the quality. For a country with a population of fifteen million (a trifle more than the city of London), we were averaging thirty to thirty-five feature films a year. Few of them were watchable. Internationally, most of them were being dismissed. The annual AFI (Australian Film Institute) Award screenings became a dreadful ordeal to sit through, which was followed by a correspondingly embarrassing lack of votes—to vote you have to sit through all the films—at the end of it all.

Above-the-line budgets sky-rocketed: executive production and production fees of $500 000 or $1 million on mere $2 to $3 million budgets were not unheard of. The average budget was $2 to $3 million. Ten million dollars was a big budget. One million was low budget.

With the just-completed film under my belt, I proceed to go about the formidable task of submitting it for selection in the 1984 Cannes Film Festival.

Cannes is basically a zoo. A place where all the film-makers, actors and actresses, journalists, buyers, sellers and other animals in the film world can come and congregate, vying for mainstream attention. Unless a film has been accepted in one of the official sections of the Festival—that is, in Competition, La Quinzaine des Realisateurs (Directors' Fortnight), La Semaine de la Critique (Critics' Week) or Un Certain Regard—where publicity and distribution are usually assured, then it is placed in Hors Concours (the marketplace), to be swallowed up alongside hundreds of other films.

To get an Australian film even considered for one of these official categories seemed to involve a very mystical and obscure process. It is not enough to just fill in an application form and send it off, hoping for acceptance. In fact, upon approaching the AFC (Australian Film

Commission) in February of 1984, I was told that not only did they not have any registration forms, but they didn't even have an address to send the film to. No one could tell me how one got a film even viewed for recommendation or who I had to sleep with in order to get in one of the official categories. Three weeks later I received the registration papers for the Festival. I noticed a stamp on the forms indicating that the AFC had received them from the Festival organisers almost three months before.

It was becoming obvious that we were going to be cutting it a bit fine as far as deadlines were concerned. After a few more frantic phone calls to the AFC, I was informed that to be selected for competition one had to be recommended by a certain French 'spotter' with an overblown ego and a bigoted sense of cinema, whose yearly trip over here in order to lord it over the monkeys was generously paid for by those self-same monkeys. If I had made my film in any other nation of the world, a print could've been sent direct to the head office in Paris for submission to all categories. Not the Australians. The AFC and the lone French 'spotter' prefer to keep the whole thing under tight controls and anyone who dares to rock the boat by sending their film direct to Paris (see *Proof* (1992) and *Muriel's Wedding* (1994)) causes an arrogant French tirade to the tune of 'Your country will never get another film in Competition again!' Obviously I hadn't been taking the right people out to lunch.

It turns out that the Australians and the lone Frenchman had already decided on the glossy production they were going to push for selection that year (little did they know the French audiences would hate it), and didn't want a 'small' film from Melbourne cramping their style. Consequently, *Strikebound* was never screened for selection in the Competition, Directors' Fortnight or Un Certain Regard sections of the Cannes Film Festival. But due to the tireless persistence of Mike Lynskey (then of the AFC Marketing Branch), along with some help from the upper echelons, we received a small travel grant enabling us to book some cargo space on the next Garuda flight to Cannes.

APRIL 1984

Two weeks before the 1984 Cannes Film Festival, I get a phone call from a strange character by the name of Gary Grant, from a rock-and-roll management and publishing company called MMA Management. An Australian band called INXS had seen and loved one of my music videos for a Melbourne band called Hunters & Collectors and were wondering if I would do one for them.

I begin to say that I'd never heard any of their records, hadn't liked what I'd seen and since I was leaving for Cannes in four days, we wouldn't have the time for pre-production let alone shooting and editing. He butts in with, 'But we're ready now! Just grab your camera and catch the next plane for Queensland and you can finish the rest in London after Cannes.' It is this sort of naivety that you just can't contend with. And so three, pale, skinny, little figures in black from the drizzle and rain of Melbourne end up coming face-to-face, under the Queensland sun, with six bronzed males and their girlfriends sitting around a pool wearing Ray-bans, Hawaiian shirts and board shorts. The most effusive of the males stood up and lopped over, shaking our hands with an eager puppy-dog gleam in his eye and a smile to die for . . . 'Hi, I'm Michael.'

MAY 1984

Cannes Film Festival, France. Having been relegated to the 'meat market' along with twenty-five or so other Australian films, I arrived in Cannes. It was to be the beginning of an odyssey which would occupy five months of my time. The *Strikebound* producers had arranged a New York agent called Affinity Enterprises (Joy Pereths) for the sale of the film world-wide. This turned out to be one of our major mistakes. Affinity were more interested in a film that was going to throw them into the limelight rather than something they were going to have to put some effort into—a rather common affliction, so it seems.

In Cannes the AFC make up for their lack of presence at every other important film festival in the world by sending all their personnel and money to this one. It is the place where the journalists started asking me that gut-wrenching question, 'Why isn't your film in Competition?' while the French national daily *Le Matin* printed: 'This film is better than many in the official Competition selection.' My standard response became 'Don't ask!'

Strikebound was picked up—mainly by the British, French and Italians—as an unofficial festival success, and invited to every other major film festival in the world (including official selection in the Critics' Week at the Venice Film Festival). It makes it hard to complain to any great degree, yet one can't help wondering how, not only *Strikebound*, but some of the other more worthwhile Australian films being shown, would've fared given a more even-handed and less mainstream treatment.

By coincidence INXS are playing in Nice (just a few miles from Cannes). I rustle a few Australians together, along with the odd Pom, the French publicist and her fourteen-year-old daughter. Michael ends up fixating on the daughter and we end up spending the entire night focusing all our attention on her. We both leave her mother's place at six in the morning, swearing that we'd be back to take her to school

[RICHARD LOWENSTEIN]

Director Richard Lowenstein with leading actors Michael Hutchence and Saskia Post, *Dogs in Space*

and beat up those boys that'd been hassling her for sex at such a tender age . . .

The publicist drives us back to the Croisette where I get Michael to tag along to a meeting with Joan Long, a prominent, matronly and respectable Australian film producer. While moaning artistically and collapsing into our $10 orange juices, I explained the plot of my political thriller. The response was minimal. I am suddenly hit by a bolt of lightning. I sit up and say, 'And of course there's the film that me and Michael are doing!' Michael looks up in a vague stupor and says, 'Yeah!' I say, 'Yeah, it's all about this young girl who comes into a household full of hippies and punks and other assorted weirdos in the late seventies . . .' 'That's right, and then there's . . .'

Michael and I ad-lib the story-line, which wasn't bad since we hadn't discussed it at all up to that moment. The producer is delighted. We promise to get in touch with her as soon as we got back to Australia. We never did . . .

I left a rather bedraggled Michael on the sidewalk lying in the sun waiting for his tour bus to pick him up, something I wasn't sure they would know how to do since they didn't have the slightest inkling where we were. As I was leaving, David Stratton (prominent Australian film critic) walked by, dropping a coin into Michael's out-stretched palm.

Michael opened his eyes, looked up bleary-eyed, smiled and said thanks.
A few weeks earlier an INXS song had been number one in France. I
guess Michael was beginning to understand how long it can take for the
royalties to come through.

JUNE–SEPTEMBER 1984

A few weeks in London. We finish the 'Burn For You' clip for INXS
and get talked into doing another one, 'Dancing on the Jetty'. I travel
to Pia Film Festival in Japan, Karlovy Vary Film Festival in Czecho-
slovakia, Edinburgh, Venice and finally New York.

Strikebound gets released in Australia and does moderately well, getting
good reviews and earning its advertising and prints budget back. The
release of Strikebound is through Ronin Films, an independent distributor
(who are later to achieve success with the release of Strictly Ballroom (1992)
and Shine (1996)) specialising in mainly art-house releases. The release
coordinator and publicist for the Strikebound release was one Glenys Rowe.

I had met Glenys at the Oberhausen Short Film Festival in Germany in
the spring of 1980. My graduate film from the Swinburne Film and Television
School, Evictions (1979), had been invited and I tagged along for the ride.
She was handling the Australian contingent of short films as a travelling
representative for the AFC. With her was Tony Kirkhope from The Other
Cinema, who later went on to distribute Strikebound non-theatrically in the
UK and later still to set up the Metro Cinema in the West End.

So impressed was I with the efficiency, organisation and openness of
the Strikebound release, especially after the extreme disorganisation, lies,
back-stabbing and power games that took place during the production
stage of the film, that I immediately put Glenys on the top of my list
for future producers.

OCTOBER 1984

The New York Film Festival. Not a bad turn-out, considering mine is
the only film that has been scheduled to screen on a Jewish holiday
when the whole of New York has closed up shop and the streets are
deserted. With a name like Lowenstein I consider it ironic justice. Either
that or the festival programmer's got an absurd sense of humour.

NOVEMBER–DECEMBER 1984

I begin to develop an idea that has been going through my head for a
number of years, following up on the ideas Michael and I were tossing

around over our breakfast in Cannes. It is a chronicle of the same events that took place in a student house I was living in, with a group of mismatched people in the late 1970s. I get enthusiastic reactions from people I show the treatment to. The characters stand out on the page, and I start to get pangs of nostalgia.

One of the central story-lines is of a young girl who appears one morning on the doorstep of a large student house in Richmond. Set in the late 1970s, the girl becomes intertwined with the variety of different subcultures, peer groups and distinctive characters that were unique to the era.

I ask Glenys if she would be interested in producing a film. She said she would, except she didn't know anything about it. I tell her there is nothing to know as long as one is methodical, organised and has a willingness to learn. She has been offered a low-budget feminist feature that the AFC are funding. I assure her that the funding will fall through. She also hopes to be pregnant by the time the film goes ahead. All I can do is offer her childcare on set. I don't mention what I am working on and let the thought stew in her mind for a while.

FEBRUARY 1985

First draft of the script. It is basically a stream of episodes of various humorous and dramatic intensities strung together in a vague sort of manner. I don't even know if an audience would want to see a film like this. Does it say anything to anyone or is it just a self-indulgent, personal, nostalgia trip? It's hard to tell.

I have an appointment with Greg Tepper of Film Victoria (the major funding body on *Strikebound*) about my political thriller script. Just out of interest, I gave him a copy of the *Dogs* script along with the thriller treatment. The reception to the thriller was rather cool, yet the *Dogs* script got a great reception. Greg has given the script to John Kearney, the financial adviser at Film Victoria, and word is that he loves it too. There is no accounting for taste . . .

Glenys is worried about coming to Melbourne. I send her the first draft of the script, then ring her to see what she thinks. Very vague. Doesn't sound like she's read it. She feels committed to the low-budget feminist feature and doesn't think she can handle both. I get a letter saying she's read it and laughed all the way through. Madly enthusiastic! She begins to do a budget. The plan is to submit it to the Creative Development Board of the AFC for Low-Budget Feature Funding. They will consider it as long as the budget is less than $300 000.

Two weeks later she rings up, distraught and a nervous wreck. She says she can't do it. The feminist film, the pressure, it's all too much.

I act casual about it, telling her she can think about it for a week or so. In actual fact, I panic! Everything drops away and I don't know which way to turn. I had pinned all my hopes on her, although I feel sure the feminist film is gonna collapse.

In the meantime, I show the script to Timothy White, co-producer of *Strikebound* (the better one), more for feedback than anything else. He rejects it, finding all the characters, especially Sam (the character Michael would be playing), thoroughly unlikeable. It had never struck me before that characters in a film had to be likeable. How limiting! I'd always found Sam appealing in a cute, selfish sort of way. Maybe that says something about myself. After all he was only twenty-one. There must've been some reason why girls would throw themselves at him. Maybe things had changed in the last few years.

Glenys rings back hoping I didn't take her 'nervous breakdown' seriously and maybe we shouldn't take the film to the AFC in case we get rejected, and when can we get together to go over the script. I can't keep up!

APRIL 1985

I am sitting at home at two in the morning re-writing the script in front of the television. Keith Moon and David Essex are on the screen in a film called *Stardust* (1975). The phone rings. Keith's banging away on a whole lot of drums and acting loony. I pick it up and the satellites begin to make funny noises in among the ISD hiss. 'Is that Richard?' 'Yesss?' 'This is Peter Townshend . . .' Keith's still banging away. 'I've just seen your film *Strikebound* and was very impressed . . .'

Pete's got a film that he wants doing, but he won't send me the script because he needs to explain it in person, and he's just seen *Strikebound* and *Purple Rain* (1984) together in one sitting and what he needs is a combination of the two. He'll fly me to London, we'll talk about the script, then we'll both catch the Concorde to New York to sell it to the record company executives. The film is to be called *White City* (1986). On the telly it's getting to the bit where David's taking lots of drugs.

On my way to England I stop off in Sydney to talk with Glenys. We go to meet the 'lions in their den' and arrive at the offices of MMA to see Chris Murphy and Gary Grant on their home turf. It is an enlightening experience. They bluster and bullshit and carry on about how many millions they could've raised for us at the snap of a finger if only we'd come and asked them in the first place. We smile and nod knowingly. All we want from them is a letter saying that Michael is interested in doing the film. They suggest having INXS as the main band in the film. I shudder. They ask me what I am doing wasting my time with Pete Townshend. I smile and pat them on the head. It is something they'll probably never understand. Glenys is in a state of catatonic shock. Compared to the emancipation of women in the film industry, the music industry is in the dark ages. These people seem to have no comprehension of music. Thankfully, the band members probably have more sense than their management.

I arrive in England the day the miners' strike collapses, a fact commented on by Paul, Pete's driver and right-hand man, who has picked me up from the airport. He seems to think that it's a sign, seeing that I'd made *Strikebound* an' all. He'd seen *Strikebound* with Pete and liked it, even though he thinks 'Scargill should be put in jail' and that 'the miners are a bunch of thugs'. I notice he has all the tabloid papers with Samantha Fox on page three stuffed next to his seat in the car.

I get to meet Walter Donohue—producer, talent scout, patron of the arts and general pie-fingerer—and Colin Callender—executive producer, moneyman and diplomat. I give them the *Dogs* script to read and try to hit them for a million dollars.

After a while of getting over the jet lag, we go and meet Pete (maybe he's got a million dollars?). He seems likeable enough, with the same nervous habits that I have. The *White City* script needs a lot more work than I had hoped, but its redeeming qualities make it worth persevering with. I agree to do it on the condition that I rewrite it, use my own DOP, editor and animator, and as long as it doesn't interfere with the production of *Dogs*. He agrees and I get closeted in a hotel room with an electric typewriter. My agent starts hassling. Film Victoria sends a telex.

Back in Oz, Glenys assures me that there is nothing I can do until the money's raised by the end of June. She is trying to raise money independently, hustling investors, seeing brokers, underwriters, lawyers, and so on. It is lonely work, especially when you haven't done it before, but she suggests that I do the *White City* job.

Just when Pete and me are about to fly to New York on the Concorde, we hear that all the record executives are in Hawaii on their annual conference. I suggest flying there instead, but no one is amused—I always miss out on all the fun. Pete begins to involve me in the process of recording the music for the *White City* album and film. Chris Thomas (his producer) is in Australia producing the new INXS album 'Listen Like Thieves'. Pete is remarkably open to ideas. I get brass and backing singers, everything that a film-maker wants.

Pete complains to me about having to book studio time in London for MMA in order to mix the INXS album. Apparently, every studio he speaks to is owed money by them and won't take the booking. I fly home to finish the script while the Pommy crowd figures out how to make films.

MAY 1985

Glenys is having self-doubts about her ability to produce a film. She says that 'The Industry' seems very resistant to her doing it independently. I tell her it's because they're scared she'll find out how easy it is and that all she needs is a powerful sense of organisation coupled with some strong aesthetics.

I finish the *White City* script. I have tried to simplify it, make it more realistic, visual, and less melodramatic. I find it hard to write a screenplay set in a working-class area of London among unemployment and racial strife when I know very little of the life, the language, the customs and the social conditions of the society. Pete's answer is that since all the streets of *White City* are named after colonies of the British Empire, who better to make the film than an Australian . . . I don't see the logic to it myself.

JUNE 1985

We are in the middle of shooting *White City*. All my worst fears are coming true. The catering is atrocious (an English problem it seems). The crew is very much working to rules. The art department is a joke. The first AD has never done the job before and it shows. Andrew de Groot likes his gaffer and his camera-operator but the grip makes Alf Garnett look like a human rights campaigner. The whole thing is only just saved by a few of the younger assistants and crew members who give the enthusiasm and energy something like this deserves.

It is interesting, though, that a lot of these crew members seem to be a product of unwritten rules and a rigidity that do not exist in the Australian industry. Most of them had never been invited to a rushes screening before, the British tradition being that only the producer, director, DOP and camera-operator get to see them. Limited involvement is understandable given that the crew never gets to see the fruits of their labour. The rushes screening is a traditional booze-up time for Australian crews and after a couple of weeks of me personally asking everyone to attend, the atmosphere begins to get a bit more productive.

The same old production bullshit happens in the UK just the same as anywhere else. It's good to see that the Pommies don't know anything more about the actual processes of film-making than we do.

After many trials and tribulations we finish the *White City* shoot.

The high point of it all for me was the morning the runner forgot to pick up both me and Andrew and we had to catch the Tube to the location. We both arrived an hour late, but no one seemed to notice. It reminded us of how important we were.

Lynn-Maree Milburn does an amazing job on the pixelation and time-lapse sections of the film, the cost of which the line producer thinks should come out of my fee. After I threatened to burn the negative, they finally see reason. After a very weird wrap-party on the roof of a London department store, complete with pink flamingos (real ones), I go to Japan for three weeks with Lynn-Maree and my father.

I stop in Sydney the day I get back to have a meeting with Glenys about *Dogs* and the shooting of the 'What You Need' clip for INXS that is to happen in the next few days. I have asked her to produce the clip, but we ended up shooting in Melbourne so I did it myself.

The future for *Dogs* seems pretty grim. Now that the 30 June deadline has passed it is unlikely that we'll have another chance at raising the money in Australia before June next year. INXS are touring Australia and Europe until 8 January, which will be the only time Michael has available to shoot the film in the next twelve months. It becomes obvious that if we can't raise the money for the January shooting date then the project will have to be dropped.

We shoot the INXS 'What You Need' video. The management's idea is to have the band playing in a room with models walking in one door and out the other. Lynn-Maree suggests shooting the entire thing on a still camera with a motor-drive and animating it all back to sync-action. This enables her to animate and edit together the one-and-a-half-thousand photographs while I'm in England editing the Pete Townshend film. We drop the girls, we drop the room, we drop the big 'INXS' sign on the wall. We go with the stills. The manager comes on set and asks, 'Where's the big INXS on the wall?' We smile and say, 'Later . . .'

SEPTEMBER 1985

I finish editing *White City* at 7 a.m. on the same day I'm due to leave London at noon.

Our first meeting with the Burrowes Film Group is the day after I get back. The only way we can make them understand who Michael Hutchence is, is to take them the most recent copy of *Rolling Stone* magazine with his picture on the cover. His band, INXS, were the only Australian band to appear on the international transmission of *Live Aid*; their 1984 album 'The Swing' had sold more than half a million copies world-wide; their present album to date, *Listen Like Thieves* over half a million copies—even then they only slightly comprehend. Geoff

Burrowes is telling us that they have hit upon a formula for success and until that formula fails they will continue to travel in the same direction. I think to myself that 'we should all hang on cos it's gonna be a bumpy ride'. They have three films in various stages of production at the moment, all with budgets of between $5 and $10 million and they all smell of disaster. The ones I know anything about (*Running From the Guns* (1987), *Backstage* (1988)) sound embarrassingly dreadful, and another three are on the drawing board. One of them, *Backstage*, is even based on the music industry: a nightclub singer (played by Laura Branigan) falls in love with the music critic who pans her show . . . Have you ever had the experience of trying to explain a project to someone who is on a totally different wavelength?

When I mentioned that *Dogs* would be the *Easy Rider* (1969) of the 1980s, Geoff Burrowes seemed to think *Easy Rider* was a rock'n'roll magazine. Mention of *Animal House* (1978), *Purple Rain*, Prince and Madonna are just water off a duck's back. Due to the conservatism of some of their investors, they suggest the title 'Future Tense'. This is about par for the course for them as it is a nice, meaningless title that's going straight to the video shelf.

A couple of days after this meeting, we finish the on-line editing of the INXS music video 'What You Need'. The finished product surpasses everyone's expectations. Lynn-Maree has done a fantastic job. The band is ecstatic. Chris Murphy's (INXS's and Michael Hutchence's manager) comment is, 'My daughter will really like it—she likes colouring-in'. Sometimes Lynn-Maree and I wonder why we bother. The clip goes into high rotation on MTV as soon as they see it. The song goes to number four on the US charts.

MID-SEPTEMBER 1985

A few days later I fly back to London for the *White City* sound mix. I am not very happy with the film as both the shooting and the editing were completed under a great deal of stress and bad management. I take over cutting the film myself between the hours of two in the 'arvo' to four in the morning everyday. A further week in UK and then I'm finally back in Australia—for good!

Hopefully, now, we can finally get *Dogs* off the ground . . .

OCTOBER 1985

Glenys tells me the story of the round-table discussion she had with the Burrowes boys while I was away. They opened with the line, 'We could screw you any time we want to . . . We could screw you on the table, right now . . .' Very 1980s . . . I take the fact that Glenys—a feminist who still holds 'the movement' dear to her heart—wanting to persevere with these guys as executive producers means she's very dedicated to the project.

I settle down to write a shorter version of the script and start casting, crewing and doing pre-production despite no available funds. The small amount of money left over from a Film Victoria script-development grant has long ago been used up, and getting any money from the exec-producers, even though they have agreed to fund us, is like getting blood from a stone.

Glenys and I go back to the original house where *Dogs in Space* is set and knock on the door. A very talkative American lady is at home. We slowly get around to the idea of shooting a film in her house which she doesn't seem totally adverse to. This would be great for me since the script is very descriptively written with this particular house in mind. We let her dwell on the idea and to tell the rest of the family. Still no word on the financing of the film.

NOVEMBER 1985

The plan at the moment is to raise the money through the Burrowes Film Group for an official budget of $3 million, roughly ten times what we first approached the AFC for. But it's a 'Catch 22' situation. It seems to cost nearly as much money to raise the money as it costs to make the film. Perhaps that's what's wrong with the film industry in this country—so much money is being made before the actual film is released that no one actually cares about the quality of the film they're making.

We intend shooting the film in late January as this is the only time Michael Hutchence is available for the next twelve months in between tours of Europe and America. INXS have recently played to 30 000 people in Argentina before coming home to play for 10 000 at a 'Rocking the Royals' concert in Melbourne, with Charles and Di in the audience.

We set up a meeting between Chris Murphy, Geoff Burrowes and Dennis Wright (executive producer) for the day of the royal concert, while I do a screen test with Michael opposite Jo Kennedy, whom we have tentatively cast in the role of Anna. Chris doesn't turn up to the meeting. Michael turns in a rushed performance in half an hour between interviews. Jo Kennedy is great, although not quite right for the part. She doesn't seem to glow; Anna needs to glow.

At the Charles and Di concert, one of the 'lions' was heard proclaiming at the top of his voice that this band are gonna be the hottest thing in Australia and how he'd just signed the singer for a film. Nothing makes me sick . . .

Dennis Wright, Glenys and I have a breakfast meeting with Chris Murphy the morning after the concert. It's just like Los Angeles. The bullshit is flying back and forth across the table so fast that Glenys and I just smile at each other. It seems more of an exercise in who can out-hype the other with how big they are in America than a serious discussion about where and when Michael is going to be available. We finally resolve to make it all legal and get our lawyers to contact theirs and see what we can sort out. The coffee gives me a stomachache and I feel that ol' LA 'let's do lunch' buzz getting to me again.

MID-DECEMBER 1985

Glenys takes the actress we've tentatively cast to play Stacey (Caroline Lee) to meet one of the EPs at Burrowes Film Group. Caroline is asked to lift her skirt so he can see her legs. Glenys relates the story to me through gritted teeth and I can only deduce that Glenys must really, really like the script since she's still continuing with the project.

20 DECEMBER 1985

We are supposed to be shooting in five weeks. The exec-producers inform Glenys that 'the money is now all in place' and that they can't get a reply out of Chris Murphy as regards the contract with Michael. It is seen to be our fault. They claim they can't get him to answer their calls or find out where he is. It has all been left to the last minute.

I ring Chris in London and I'm speaking to him within five minutes. He is naturally offended at the tone of Dennis's telex and has been refusing to speak with him. He admonishes me for 'getting jerks to deal with him', and tells me if he's gonna deal with jerks he 'may as well deal with some American jerk who at least would know something about the music industry'. I tell him 'it's better the jerk you know than the jerk you don't know'. He didn't sound too impressed, but after half an hour of being yelled at from London I finally patch things together again.

It is becoming obvious that whenever the so-called executive producers have to tackle something that has been set up by us—as in the Michael case—they fuck it up. Sometimes it seems irredeemable until either Glenys or I tack it back together again with tactful words. Let's hope they are better at raising the money.

That night Gary Foley, an Aboriginal activist actor who is playing a role based on himself in the film, rings me up at midnight saying he refuses to do the film unless the real 'Stacey' (his rock-climbing ex-girlfriend from the era) talks to him. He then hangs up. The following day he rings up sheepishly to apologise for being drunk after the Aboriginal Arts Board party.

21 DECEMBER 1985

Since it is obviously important to Gary and as it would be virtually impossible to replace him, I go off in search of the real 'Stacey', the ex-girlfriend.

I discover her dressed in a Muslim veil directing a rock-climbing film on a grant from the AFC. She is married to a Moroccan Muslim guy whom she met overseas and has brought both him and his mother back to Australia to live together. From being a staunch feminist in the late 1970s, she is now a firm believer in the Muslim faith and diligently wears her veil whenever she is to be seen in public.

Timothy White (producer) has been brought on as a 1st AD and to schedule the film. We bring the shooting date three days forward so as to avoid shooting on a public holiday where everybody gets paid double.

22 DECEMBER 1985

Dean Gawen, the sound recordist, resigns from the film due to the schedule being brought forward three days. He says it clashes with his baby being born, which is due the day before the old shoot date. The shift in dates 'has ruined everything' because he 'won't be able to be at the birth'. I never knew babies could be so reliable, and I put the incident down to pre-parental tension. I'm not unduly worried as resigning is a pretty common threat from him.

23 DECEMBER 1985

The real 'Sam' does an interview for *TV Week* announcing proudly that he is the real character around whom the script is based. He read the script one night at my place and seemed to enjoy it, rolling around on the floor and laughing at all the funny bits. He did ask me to consider changing his name in the script to avoid publicity, and so his mother wouldn't be embarrassed at the scene where she arrives with his dinner and cleans his room. I take the full page of the 'Sam Tells All!' article in *TV Week* to mean he now wants all the publicity he can get.

Pre-production money is still only coming through in a very small trickle from the Burrowes Film Group. Even though the 'Burrowes boys' have told us on the one hand they have raised the money, on the other they are acting as if they don't really believe it themselves.

Everything can only be planned for a few days in advance. Contracts cannot be signed, crew cannot be finalised, people are working on the hope that the film may one day go ahead, and yet we are scheduled to shoot in five weeks. Some of the best technicians, continuity, grips and assistant directors are slipping out of our grasp because we are unable to say we are definitely going ahead.

28 DECEMBER 1985

The American owners of the Berry Street house are becoming restless. Me, Andrew de Groot (the director of photographer) and Jody Borland (the art director) spend four hours of incessant chatter there, trying to calm them down. We showed them our video clips, all through which they talked non-stop. They are very nice, seem keen, but are still hesitant about having a film crew destroy their house. The mother of the family engages us all in seemingly endless conversation. We will need to pay someone to talk with her full-time if we're ever gonna be able to use the house to shoot the film.

29 DECEMBER 1985

They demand $20 000 for the use of the house. Was it to do with the way I dressed the day before? I wish I hadn't been so nice to them. They've heard that people get $100 000 in the US—so much for low-budget independent cinema! We consider hiring some PLO terrorists to get them out.

There are four weeks to go before we start shooting. Every Tom, Dick and Harry is ringing up the papers claiming that they are working on the film. *Dogs* would have to be the most talked about film in Australia at the moment. Let's hope we can keep the momentum going until it opens in the cinemas.

Later that day, Gary Grant (a nice INXS manager) rings Glenys to inform her that they have scheduled an INXS concert, for Michael, in Vancouver, Canada, on 20 February, two weeks into our scheduled shooting dates. On the one hand, it is catastrophic since everything—cast, crew, house, etc.—has been lined up for an early February start. On the other hand, it gives us an extra two weeks to raise the money given that it seems the Burrowes boys were stretching the facts when they previously said they'd raised it.

Our fingers are crossed. Even though there is now an increased element of uncertainty, everyone is still confident. We seem to be past the point of no return.

Jill Bilcock (the editor) mentions the problem to Fred Schepisi (esteemed Australian director) since he is in town, back from finishing *Plenty* (1985) in the US. Fred tells me the trick is to spend as much of the executive producer's money as fast as you can, then the only hope they have of getting it back is to raise the rest of the budget and put the film into production. We're taking his advice and spending money as fast as we can get our hands on it. The trouble is we are having trouble getting our hands on it. We are in limbo.

8 JANUARY 1986

This is it. It has finally happened. The Burrowes boys have finally summoned Glenys and me into a meeting and told us they can't raise the money in time. We are both in shock. They are still using the 'waiting for government clarification' line with regard to whether a film underwritten before the last federal budget (in which the 10BA tax laws were reduced from a 133 per cent deduction on an investment to a 120 per cent one) would be eligible for the 133 per cent rate. They have been using this excuse for the last six months, in which time they have raised money for three other films. They suggest a July shoot date, wanting us to confirm that on the spot. We leave the meeting not committing ourselves either way, letting them sweat it out. There is no way I would delay the film another six months, and if I did it wouldn't be with those bastards.

Outside, Glenys bursts into tears. I just laugh and say we always knew they were arseholes, we just didn't know how big. It is obvious that they could fund us if they really wanted to push it, but they have over-committed themselves and are only willing to push for *Backstage*, the Laura Branigan movie with a budget of $9 million, three times the cost of ours. It is quite ironic that we have been pushed out not by their normal fare of horse pics and Oz legends (*The Man From Snowy River* (1982) and *ANZACS* (1985)), with their guaranteed local box-office, but by a blatant, misguided and way-off-the-mark attempt to capture the youth/music video market—and to be made by people who have no idea about the market they're aiming the film at. They obviously underestimate the audience's ability to detect crap when they see it.

Within half an hour of walking out of the Burrowes Film Group offices, we are sitting in front of Fred Schepisi, Peter Beilby and Robert Le Tet of Entertainment Media with our dilemma. We are desperate. We cannot delay because of Michael Hutchence, and even if we did I wouldn't do it with the Burrowes on principal. They seem interested and need twenty-four hours to consider the ramifications and to read the script. We ask Schepisi's mob to keep our approach to them secret as we are owed redundancy cheques from the Burrowes boys and we don't want to get too nasty until they are cashed.

I get back to the office to find a wrap party happening. An ex-member of Boys Next Door and Birthday Party rings up to tell us that he wants $3000 for thirty seconds of 'Shivers' (one of the major songs in the film). His timing couldn't have been worse. We laugh at him and drink more champers. I ring Walter in England and wake him up. It is 8 a.m. in London. I ask him if anyone wants a diary of a film that was never made? 'An interesting question . . .' Then he tells me that the Pete Townshend *White City* film got described in *Time Out* as 'the most intelligent long-form video yet made'. Then it went on to say that 'that wasn't saying much'. That's life.

I think Walter's cracking up. He has sent me a telex in which he writes his own reply from me back to him, and then instead of sending it on the machine he puts it in an envelope and posts it. Very strange . . .

9 JANUARY 1986

Today we officially announced the film's collapse. As soon as we got our redundancy pay cheques, everyone rushed up to the bank and got them cleared before the Burrowes boys changed their minds. Glenys is very down and fatalistic. It has been left up to me to keep everyone's morale up. That's quite easy as I feel confident we'll get the money from somewhere else and, even if we don't, I'm looking forward to not making the film. I need the rest.

We begin to ring around in search of more money. We ring up Matt Carroll from Roadshow, Coote and Carroll, Alan Finney from Roadshow, Terry Hayes from Kennedy Miller. We still haven't heard from Filmhouse (Fred Schepisi's company). Everyone expresses doubt without a big pre-sale. Glenys is booked in to see Terry Hayes in Sydney on Monday.

I ring an agent in America who's been pestering me for a number of months, Melinda Jason from The Client's Agency. She suggests I fly to LA as soon as possible for a number of meetings with companies such as Orion, Lorimar, New World, etc.

Filmhouse finally ring back and offer to take us on, although they can't guarantee anything. I suggest that if I can get some interest from the Yanks, then Filmhouse can float us. They seem to agree. We drop off script and budget to them and arrange an 11.30 a.m. meeting with them for tomorrow. I get drunk with Fred Schepisi and he shows me his word processor, the one he 'wrote' *Plenty* on. I look on in awe, but I still think mine's better. I have to wait to hear from Melinda Jason about the US meetings.

Walter rings from London at 2.30 a.m. and tells me Bill Gavin will be in LA at the same time I'm there and the Hill-Samuel group has offered us A$400 000 towards the budget. Glenys leaves a message on my machine saying that she is confident and enthusiastic again and she thinks Kennedy Miller might be interested. I can see it now . . . 'Mad Sam III'.

10 JANUARY 1986

We go to an 11 a.m. meeting with Fred Schepisi, Robert Le Tet and Peter Beilby. Fred has read the script and is enthused, although he only says so when I'm out of the room. I ring Melinda Jason in LA again and get to speak to her. She has discussed it with her partner and they think it might be advisable for them to read the final draft of the script before they set up any meetings. They've already read the first draft and are worried whether the Americans will go for it. The chances of a major investment or a US pre-sale for 50 per cent of the budget are extremely slim. This is very depressing.

I am extremely depressed and Glenys is confident, although I know she's very worried underneath. Tim White and I attempt a script conference which degenerates when the wrap party starts, held in order to drink and eat the remains of the Burrowes Film Group petty cash float.

Glenys prises a very non-committal letter out of John Kearney, saying that Burrowes Film Group would buy out of *Dogs* as long as no other production company is involved. Peter Beilby rings up to complain about it and I tell him that whoever takes over the project will have to come clean and approach the 'cowboys' themselves.

The wrap party ends up with the hard-core crew members, including Jody, Andrew, Karen Ansel (wardrobe), Lynn-Maree (wardrobe), Troy Davies (make-up), George Huxley (assistant make-up) and me. I take a photo for the diary. We all end up extremely drunk at a Japanese restaurant in Collins Plaza, after which we all crowd into the glass lift there and go up and down a few times.

11 JANUARY 1986

Tension, waiting and boredom. Can't work on the script. I'm almost hoping the film will collapse so I can just sleep forever.

13 JANUARY 1986

Glenys has a meeting with Kennedy Miller, makers of the *Mad Max* films. She rings at 1 p.m. after a two-hour meeting. They say there is a 10 per cent chance of raising the money, but haven't read the script. Jill had rung Fred Schepisi over the weekend and he'd said there was a 50 per cent chance. We go with Fred. Ten a.m. meeting with Fred's boys tomorrow. May have to fly to LA tomorrow at 4 p.m. I speak to Chris Murphy in Paris and assure him that everything is all right. (Ha! Ha!) He says Michael could have another week at the end of the shoot. I kiss his boots and assure him he'll go to heaven. Walter rings me to get his name on the door when INXS play the Marquee Club in London. The phone call would've cost more than the ticket. These anglophile Americans are crazy . . .

Dolly, the local glossy magazine for sixteen-year-old girls, prints a full-page photo of me looking over the top of my sunglasses. A reader sends a letter into the production office. She loves me apparently . . . It gets pinned up on the noticeboard and everyone makes fun of me.

14 JANUARY 1986

Ten a.m. meeting with Fred and the boys. It is very optimistic and exciting. We have four working days to raise $2.25 million. The shoot can only go back one week at the most. They draw up a letter of agreement for the next week or so. Fred tries to ring contacts in the US—we need a pre-sale worth US$700 000. Methinks fat chance!

We get back to the office and I finally get to ring Melinda Jason in LA. She has read the script and believes, 'It is the vilest thing I've ever read, with no redeeming values.' Is she trying to tell me the LA trip is off? I offer the suggestion that there may be cultural differences between the late 1970s in the US and the same era in Australia. 'No,' she says, 'nothing happens for the first eighty pages.' (The script is only 100 pages long.) 'It is depressing. Just a lot of junkies lying around getting bored.' She then goes into her normal routine of 'Hey, Richard, you are a very talented director of international potential . . . We can get you *Witness* (1985) . . . We can get you *The Killing Fields* (1984).' It seems a shame to break it to her that those films have already been made. I hope the news doesn't come as too great a shock when she finds out. I sign off quickly and politely and cancel my ticket to LA.

Walter's posted telexes arrive:

CANFILMSREALLYBETHISDIFFICULTTOMAKE?

IMAGINARY TELEX 1 ATT: RICK FROM: WALT

THERE'S BEEN AN AIR OF DESPONDENCY HERE RECENTLY. I THEN SUDDENLY REALISED IT WAS BECAUSE THE AUSSIE TELEXES HAD STOPPED ARRIVING. SO THE ONLY SOLUTION WOULD BE TO START SENDING THEM AGAIN.

I SPOKE TO VINCENT WARD (NZ DIR: 'VIGIL') LAST NIGHT. I'VE ALWAYS THOUGHT NEW ZEALAND WAS A BIG ISLAND ON THE TOP OF AUS-TRALIA. ACCORDING TO HIM, IT IS TWO ISLANDS LYING TO THE SIDE OF AUSTRALIA. WELL, I GUESS YOU LEARN SOMETHING NEW EVERY DAY.

YOU KNOW, IT HAS SUDDENLY OCCURRED TO ME THAT IF THIS TELEX IS IMAGINARY HOW AM I GOING TO GET A RESPONSE . . . ?

SEE YA. ME

IMAGINARY TELEX 2 ATT: WD FROM: RICHARD (I'M FEELING) LOWE ETC (AT THE MOMENT)

GIDDAY. THOSE BASTARDS THINK THEY'VE BEATEN ME BUT I'LL SHOW 'EM. I'M SITTING HERE IN FRONT OF THE TELE GLUING MY EYEBALLS TO OLD JACK THOMPSON MOVIES, RECHARGING MYSELF, GETTING READY TO START KICKING SHIT. THIS FILM IS GONNA GO INTO PRODUCTION OR MY NAME ISN'T . . .

I'VE JUST REREAD SOME OF THIS AND IT'S ABSOLUTE DRIVEL. I'D BETTER SIGH [SIC] OFF.

WD.

I think he's going mad.

A strange letter arrives from one of the real-life characters who lived in the house and is portrayed in the script. The character of the womanising graphic-designer who lives upstairs, called Grant in the script.

Dear Richard,

I write from Japan. I should of [sic] seen you before I left Melbourne. I should of [sic] confronted you after you'd chosen not to recognise me when we were in our cars in the city all those months ago.

   Coming up behind a brown VW beetle I didn't know and not recognising the driver's hair—something indicated it might've been you. Staring into your rear-vision mirror I recognised the eyes. Our eyes met intensely through that

mirror and yet after turning the corner and then sitting side by side at the
lights you pretended I wasn't there.

 Sometime later I was in Adelaide where I saw Sam. He told me about
your forthcoming project. I felt vulnerable, possibly because I felt I was in the
process of being 'used'.

 I don't know if you've seeked [sic] out any contact with the others of the
house. I don't really know what you're intending to do. But the incident in
our cars does nothing to instil any trust in you.

 This letter is to you Richard. Don't make it public as it appears you are
to make our lives.

Yours Sincerely,

(Name Deleted)

I replied thus:

Dear (Name Deleted),

Have no fear . . . !! There is no character based on yourself in the screenplay
of 'DOGS IN SPACE', all your dark secrets can remain hidden. Even if there
was, surely you haven't got anything to be embarrassed about . . , ??

See ya,

Richard Lowenstein

16 JANUARY 1986

Melinda Jason has left a message on my machine saying that Fred has
convinced her to send the script to the head of Orion, Hemdale and
New World. Whacko . . .

17 JANUARY 1986

This is the last day of fully paid crew, although we haven't had any cash
float all week. Everyone has agreed to keep working next week in the
hope that the money will come through, although enthusiasm is definitely waning. I ring Melinda Jason in LA and assure her that unless I
get to make this film I have no intention of using her as an agent. About
five hours later, a telex comes through from Hemdale (New Line, the
exec-producers of *The Falcon and the Snowman* (1985) and *Terminator*
(1984), and a little later, *Platoon* (1986) and *Salvador* (1986)) with an
offer of US$500 000.

telexes in space: a tale of two films

19 JANUARY 1986

Location trip out on Ballarat Road to discover that the vista of Melbourne I was depending on—as written in the script—has been destroyed by a freeway and an overpass.

20 JANUARY 1986

Today is D-Day, the day Filmhouse will tell us whether they can deliver the money or not. Glenys is unreasonably optimistic. Maybe it's just protection. I am not so keen. Come 8 a.m. and we arrive at Filmhouse. Fred and Peter's faces are grim. Roadshow has rejected our offer of an Australian pre-sale. Robert is not at the meeting. They won't really know anything until 11 a.m. tomorrow. We inform the crew and go home.

21 JANUARY 1986, 11 A.M.

Still grim faces. Robert is back. The Hemdale pre-sale is not as good as it seems—their reputation seems a bit dodgy. They may not honour it if they deem the film not marketable. There are two options open to us. One is to delay the film for six months and start all over again, the other is to see if the Burrowes will be interested in a co-production and the possibility of re-instating the cash flow, something they would loath to do since the two companies hate each other. I am in favour of going for the co-production, but Glenys wants to dwell on it. She seems to be losing a bit of heart, with a family crisis back in Sydney affecting her. Glenys tells me if the film's delayed she doesn't think she is able to keep working on it. I don't really care since I cannot believe she is considering not going for a co-production. We put the question to the crew. They want to go for the co-production. We go back to tell Robert Le Tet. He arranges a meeting with the Burrowes Film Group for 4 p.m.

Christina, from Macau Light Company, rings up from Sydney and tells me that one of the Sydney actors we had cast has died of a brain haemorrhage in the shower. Another young boy from Melbourne that I had cast in a featured role is found hanging from the ceiling of his rented room in a self-made noose. A Nick Cave record is found in his room and the gutter press accuse Nick of propagating self-destruction and suicide. The number of people who underestimate the young continues to amaze me.

At 7.30 p.m. Robert Le Tet finally comes out of the meeting. We race over to Filmhouse to hear the verdict. The scheme is that the

Burrowes will match Filmhouse dollar for dollar for two weeks of cash flow, giving them all the time needed to raise the money and pre-sales properly. We deliberate for five seconds and then decide to accept. At last we have a reprieve!! We telex MMA with the good news. Maybe now we can get them to send us a contract for Michael.

22 JANUARY 1986

Another bombshell—Michael's contract has arrived. 'Wot a laff!' They want creative control, us to pay for the cost of the album, and the dates they mention are two weeks after the start of the film's shoot, something they knew well in advance. On top of it all they want us to accept it all in twenty-four hours otherwise the deal is off. It stinks!

Another summit meeting. The lack of a contract is threatening the financing. These rock'n'roll tycoons are such jerks. When are they gonna learn that they work for their artists and not vice versa?

Robert Le Tet asks if we can put INXS in the film since his investors would require it. I suggest they could go in at the end, when Sam's band become slick and commercial. I can't tell INXS this. Telexes are drafted and sent. The date changes are my biggest worry. If I know that fucking management, they'd have sneaked in a few last-minute concerts to squeeze the most out of the band before they have their break.

23 JANUARY 1986

Go to Springvale cemetery. I nearly blow it by telling the caretaker that the story is based on a real one. The caretaker goes all funny and begins talking about lawsuits etc. A lot of fast talking gets me out of it. Hopefully?

Glenys comes back from the lawyers all bubbly and optimistic, telling me that we have to change all the names in order to be safe against any defamation suits. I keep casting regardless.

Ollie Olsen, the lead singer and songwriter of an infamous, Melbourne, late-1970s, cult, electro-punk-disco band Whirlywirld, takes over my office in order to coordinate all the little bands. He puts his name on the door and underneath it writes 'Musical Director'. A small price to pay for enthusiasm. At last I have found someone I can trust creatively and who understands the sort of music I'm talking about. The production manager, Lynda House, seems to have fallen for Ollie's friend John Murphy, who looks like an overweight, black-leathered, Gothic-punk Hell's Angel. Good drummer, though. Their current bands, The Slub and Orchestra of Skin and Bone, are playing on Monday and

Lynda wants to go. Hope she doesn't lose control. Waiting for MMA to reply . . .

24 JANUARY 1986

Very little happens today. We have an art department meeting first thing, then we prepare for a fully fledged production meeting. In between these two meetings we get an urgent telex from Chris Murphy stating that due to a conversation he had with me and the dubiousness of our funding situation, he had rescheduled the INXS US tour. It is now impossible to have Michael on 24 February, so unless we can move back to 6 March the whole deal is off. Looks like we have to delay. It's gonna cost at least $50 000. I hate those fuckers! Glenys is downcast and is beginning to get nihilistic thoughts. I am angry and kick a lot of things.

After ringing Peter Beilby at Filmhouse, Glenys is a lot cheerier about getting the extra money. The art and costume departments seem pleased with the extra time. It seems to me that the shooting date's getting further away than closer. Will we ever get to make this film? Our production meeting goes ahead, but before anything constructive is achieved it gets pulled to a halt by Glenys due to her 2 p.m. meeting with the lawyers.

27 JANUARY 1986

About lunchtime I get a frantic phone call from Cannes, France, where Chris Murphy is panicking about the telex we sent him, not giving him any creative control at all, only the right of consultation. He rambles on for about half an hour on how INXS are about to break England, getting rave reviews everywhere.

It seems that due to Lynn-Maree's *tour de force* music video for the INXS 'What You Need' single, it has been put on high rotation on MTV and has shot up forty places in the charts in the US. Consequently, MMA want to jam in as many concerts there as possible before the film starts shooting. The success of Lynn-Maree's film clip, its striking appeal, and the attention placed on the single is working against us. We shouldn't have made it so interesting.

Chris continues to yell at me about having to protect Michael and himself in case we decide to have shots of 'Michael dragging his dick along the floor'. I mention the fact that 'if Michael doesn't want to drag his dick along the floor, he doesn't have to. And, anyway, would it be long enough?' He says Michael is impressionable and would do anything

I told him to. He adds that if the rumours he hears are true, it may very well be long enough.

I finally lose my temper and break in on a pause in his monologue. I yell at him for about five minutes, telling him I would never give over creative control to anyone, and if he wants it he can go get fucked. He is obviously shit-scared of what Michael will do when he's not around. I give him my personal guarantee that I will listen to whatever gripes he has about the finished cut of the film and that he can have right of control over the drug scene. This seems to calm him down somewhat. We finish by coming to some tentative arrangement. I think I should get an associate producer credit on this film!

29 JANUARY 1986

A bout of food poisoning from the new Swan Deli—now deceased—in Clarendon Street has knocked me out for half the day. If it still existed I would warn everyone not to go there! They had a microwave hidden under the counter, so it was probably radiation poisoning. It reminds me of London. They microwave everything due to the cost of keeping things warm. They don't notice it there as the standard of the food must be the lowest in the world. Even Pete Townshend has a food automat and a microwave in his studio. And you'd think he'd be organic—having a guru and everything. Actually there is an Orange People food shop in Sydney with a microwave under the counter . . . Have they no shame?

A few screen tests. No one exciting. Casting doesn't seem to be happening too well. Seems to consist of whoever wanders into the office. Must talk to Glenys . . .

30 JANUARY 1986

Flat tyre. No 'cunts'. Co-producer. My car has a flat tyre!

We get summoned to the EON-FM offices where Robert Le Tet (Entertainment Media) tries to hug Glenys and nearly kills her in the process. He's one big mother. I just shake his hand and pat him on the back. He's my man—$2.7 million, a Filmhouse co-production with Burrowes, and the investors insist that there be no 'cunts' in the film. I tell him that means we'll have to get rid of most of the crew. He's not amused. Maybe a title change? Maybe an associate producer? I say yes to everything except the title change—some things are sacred.

Walter tells me I have to put what I am feeling into the diary: I am feeling down and now I have to make the fucker. Is this what it's like after all this time of never actually believing it would go ahead? It feels so anti-climactic. All the real work lies ahead of us. All of a sudden I feel very tired. I don't even know if people are going to want to see this sort of film. If done properly it should look sort of grungy and that tends to upset a lot of people. (I didn't realise at this point to what extent!)

I'm feeling very tired . . .

Name Deleted's reply arrives:

Dear Richard,

Thanks for your reply, although you've neglected to address why you acted like a snob.

Dogs in Space . . . ? Pre-trained animals who spent their formative years under a leash . . . ? Finding themselves grown, the leash-cord cut, in an infinite domain . . . ?

Regards,

(Name Deleted)

It is all beyond me. To this very day I have no recollection of 'eyes meeting intensely' or 'sitting side by side at the lights you pretended I wasn't there'. I was probably thinking about where the money was gonna come from.

2 FEBRUARY 1986

What if the acting's no good? We haven't even been casting properly. Me having yelled at Glenys about the casting produced a couple of days of serious looking, then it was back to normal. Now all we need is Michael's contract. I don't want to have anything to do with it. The weather is beginning to get fuckin' hot.

7 FEBRUARY 1986

Everything is slowly picking up. Filmhouse call a private meeting—without Glenys, just me. Very suspicious. Turns out to be about another project. They tell me they don't want me agreeing to do it just because they are funding *Dogs*. I say, 'No, no, no', and think, 'That's exactly what I'm doing'. Then I think, 'I have no idea what I want to do next but I don't think this is the one.'

Michael Hamlyn of Midnight Films and *White City* production fame rings me up from Sydney, telling me it is paradise on earth. That's the trouble with these Pommie bastards, they're so easily impressed. He tells me he might be coming down to Melbourne. I go into hiding. Andrew de Groot trembles at the thought.

8–9 FEBRUARY 1986

Camera tests. We try out a few acting-type people, including Briana for the young girl. She seems very good, though we have to be careful with the costume. I make the decision to cast her. No luck with the Nick character, the pale, emaciated, black-clothed, skeletal type. They don't make 'em like that any more, or maybe the speed isn't as good any more.

10 FEBRUARY 1986

Sydney. Casting. PANIC!! Seems like Robert has told Glenys that we will have to cut the budget by $400 000, roughly 20 per cent. I can hear her trembling as she tells me we have to take all the music out of the script. I don't worry greatly as I know there is a bit of fat in the budget. Little do I know frantic producers.

I have lunch with Saskia Post (a possible Anna) in Sydney, and who should walk in but Chris 'Chainsaw Man' Haywood. He tells us about the 'Artists for Antarctica Expo', which turns out to be a giant ruse for him to get to see his girlfriend, who works out there. Typical. I lose Saskia's attention as she is quite impressed with Chris. He eventually drives us to the AFI to see Nique Needles, someone who will be a great asset to the film. We go on to see Gary Foley. Visit Dean's baby and home.

11 FEBRUARY 1986

Another day, another crisis. I arrive to discover Andrew de Groot (director of photography) is beside himself because, unbeknownst to me, Glenys has told him we now have to shoot the film in Super 16 instead of Super 35 Techniscope. He is in the process of signing over his entire fee to boost the camera equipment budget. I assure him that this will not be the case and I wouldn't make the film if it were. We have actually been cut by $200 000, still quite a sizeable amount. A casual investigation of the budget, trimming excess equipment, yelling at Glenys and Lynda, forcing them not to pay an extra full actor's rate if their stomach rumbles, cutting overseas music, renegotiating some package fees and not accommodating actors in luxury apartments saves $100 000 and the film from being cut by twenty minutes instead of only ten. A few minor script cuts here and there, and redoing all the timings cut out three days of shooting and save another $100 000. Bingo!

12 FEBRUARY 1986

Saw the rushes for tests. Wide screen. Wow!! Costume for Briana is a bit disappointing. Might have to reassess against the authenticity of character?

13 FEBRUARY 1986

Fuckin' hot . . .

14 FEBRUARY 1986

Still fuckin' hot. Briana (the young girl) has been accepted into the photography course at Prahran Technical College, an extremely hard course to get into. Unless we can arrange a one-year deferral for her, she won't be able to take the role. Glenys sees the Dean of the College . . . He doesn't seem too receptive. Lynn-Maree seems to like a boy from Adelaide who has been screen-tested for little Mark, so I tell Glenys to cast him. Things are getting desperate. The casting doesn't seem to have been handled very well. There has been a definite lack of initiative in the types of places to look. Casting agencies don't always have the answers. Possibility for 'Nick' found—Ed—though he has a bit of a drug habit. Or is he method acting?

15 FEBRUARY 1986

Big fight with Glenys on the phone about the casting after I see the photos of Dan and still don't think he's right for the part. Girlfriend number two is also no good and I have to recast. Have to go through all the photos again for a 'Stacey' (the rock-climbing girl), a young girl fall-back to replace Briana, and 'Jenny' (the hippy girl who becomes a feminist).

　　Two in the morning . . . the phone rings and some fuckin' American (not Walter) wakes me up wanting to arrange an interview for some fuckin' documentary. I find it hard to decide whether it is some actor trying to convince me of his acting abilities or whether the guy is for real. These Yanks are too much . . . I am surprised I was so polite to him and that I told him to come round tomorrow 'arvo' (Sunday).

16 FEBRUARY 1986

Thank God the bastard didn't come. I'm in no mood for belligerent Yanks. There is a possibility that it was a dream—I'm cracking up. Do shot list.

17 FEBRUARY 1986

I get interviewed on *Rock Arena*, the ABC's late-night music video show. Ollie rings up and laughs. I've decided the best way to chronicle a diary of this film would be to keep a copy of all the messages left on my answering machine. Every major disaster and trivial incident is there. I should release a cassette along with a book.

24 FEBRUARY 1986

First day of rehearsals. Read-through good. Gary has a tantrum over the phone with Glenys—he's making demands, acting like a Hollywood star. Gary arrives at rehearsal perfectly behaved.

25 FEBRUARY 1986

Second day, not so good. Barbara and the feminist?

26–27 FEBRUARY 1986

Third and fourth days good. Improvising. Ed is stoned and thinks we can't tell—that maybe we think he's just method acting.

28 FEBRUARY 1986

Tim McLaughlan's wedding. Tim is the real character being played in the film by Nique Needles, one of the co-writers of the script and original residents of the house. I embarrassingly have to leave the wedding early because Gary Foley insisted on a meeting with me or else the whole deal is off. I arrive back, feeling like a rotten heel for walking out of a friend's wedding, only to find Gary has cancelled.

    We are unable to defer Briana and so she gives up the role in favour of the photography course. I ask her if she knows anyone who would be good for the part, since we have been looking for months and it is now only a week before the shoot starts. She mentions a girl named

Deeana and later rings back with her phone number. I ring Deeana on Sunday night and arrange for her to come in for a screen test on Tuesday.

Allanah Hill takes the part of Anna's girlfriend number two. Allanah is a whirlwind of a character who amuses or offends everybody with her vivid descriptions of her boyfriend's sexual deviations. The fact that her boyfriend works in the art department, in full ear-shot of all her lurid tales, does not seem to stop her. He just shakes his head in perplexity and continues to work.

We rehearse the *Dogs in Space* band and it's pretty horrendous. But then again, it's supposed to be. Ed goes off to score. His future on the film is in doubt. Must talk with him. I am still tossing up whether to use the real Sam's song in the film or Ollie's 'Rooms For The Memory'. Sam is still scheming like in the old days, trying to replace—musically—the people in the film with people from his ailing band Beargarden. I am not impressed. How long does he think he can pull wool over people's eyes? I decide to put a hold on 'Dance With Her' (Sam's song). The arrangements lack inspiration. 'Dogs' and 'Golfcourse' are all right, though.

The production is in a bit of a mess-up at the moment. People can't get used to the fact that it is finally going ahead. A lot of things have been left to the last minute due to the lack of funding. Let's hope the shoot goes better than this. Tim White is proving to be valuable asset in scripting and pre-production.

Telex arrives:

TO: RICHARD LOWENSTEIN FROM: CHRIS MURPHY

THE GOOD NEWS IS THAT 'WHAT YOU NEED' WENT TO 23 WITH A BULLET HERE IN THE BILLBOARD CHARTS. THE PROBLEM IS THAT ATLANTIC RECORDS NOW URGENTLY NEED A VIDEO TO 'LISTEN LIKE THIEVES', WHICH WILL BE THE NEXT SINGLE.

WHEN COULD YOU SHOOT A VIDEO FOR THIS TRACK? PLEASE ADVISE.

BEST REGARDS, CHRIS MURPHY. MMA.

I don't want to think about it at the moment so we quote no less than A$100 000, thinking they'll reject us out of hand. They accept. I say they'll have to wait until after the *Dogs* shoot. They accept that too. Is there no getting rid of these guys? Judas Priest, the gay heavy-metal rock band, want one for US$80 000.

1 MARCH 1986

My birthday. Glenys has a party for me at the office. I don't turn up since I'm stuck in the recording studio with Sam, Ollie, John Murphy, et al. We record all the *Dogs in Space* band backing tracks. Sam, who has been given a chance to record his alternative song for the final ballad, keeps on trying to get me to drive him to St Kilda so he can score. I begin to wonder which is more important to him and whether he has learned anything in the past few years. He persists and I make a final decision about him—while driving him to St Kilda. If I had any doubts previously about the two competing songs for the end, they are cleared up now. The previous day with Ollie had gone well. 'Rooms For The Memory' is fantastic.

2 MARCH 1986

We find a young, emaciated-looking boy called Martii at a Nico concert, who would be ideal for playing little Mark. Things are getting a little last minute . . . The girl Briana recommended, Deeana Bond, finally walks into the rehearsal room, a day late. She is fantastic. The spitting image of the character. There is an uncanny resemblance between her and the real girl the character is based on, and a very similar approach to life. A stand-in had already been learning the young girl's part and has to be put off.

3 MARCH 1986

Michael arrives. Rehearsals okay. Steve Pyke, the English photographer, arrives. A lot of the girls begin to swoon. Maybe it's the heat.

5 MARCH 1986

Telex arrives:

> ATTN: RICHARD LOWENSTEIN FROM: WALTER DONOHUE, THE CALLENDER COMPANY.
>
> HOPE ALL GOES WELL ON THE FIRST DAY'S SHOOTING. WILL PHONE YOU ON THE WEEKEND.
>
> W.
>
> P.S. LOVE FROM ALL THE CALLENDER GIRLS.

6 MARCH 1986

Finally the film starts shooting. I can't believe it!
    To be continued . . .

from sundance to golden globes: how *shine* seduced hollywood

scott hicks

MELBOURNE, OCTOBER 1995

Ernst Goldschmidt (Pandora Cinema, the Paris-based international distribution agent) is suggesting we submit the double-head (a print with separate dialogue) to Sundance (Film Festival, in Utah). It seems so far-fetched to me. But *sex, lies and videotape* (1989) broke out of there and *Pulp Fiction* (1994) too, and both went on to win at Cannes. They can do that, since the festival is a domestic one for them. If we were to get in, it will likely cut us out of Cannes, which likes foreigners to be virgins.

Jane Scott (producer, who pitched *Shine* to Goldschmidt in mid-1994) also has Sundance doubts. We thrash it out and eventually say, 'Why not?' Chances are we won't get in, and we can then focus on Cannes. Meanwhile we can get on with finishing the picture.

MELBOURNE, NOVEMBER 1995

Double-head screening for government investors—FFC, SAFC, FilmVic (Film Finance Corporation, South Australian Film Corporation and Film Victoria). Difficult kind of audience, usually unable to articulate honest responses. But one person, sobbing, serves as a catalyst for others' reactions. An FFC rep floors me, suggesting 'testing' the film in America! I'm flabbergasted. What on earth for? Why let an audience in Orange County decide what works and what doesn't?

[305]

A WEEK LATER

FFC rep is still on about testing. I take him to task on the phone. Does the film work or not? Eventually, rather grudgingly, he admits it does.

MELBOURNE, 16 NOVEMBER

Eleven-thirty p.m. Ernst calls. 'Sundance loves it!' I whoop up and down the hallway of my inner-city apartment. No one to share the moment. Kerry (Heysen, Hicks's wife and *Shine*'s creative consultant) asleep at home (Adelaide). Jane unreachable in the wilds of Rottnest Island. It's about a year since the finance clicked in. What a journey, now this little vindication. Ecstasy followed by panic. How will we ever finish in time to get the print to Utah fully two weeks ahead of delivery schedule? We're still mixing.

ADELAIDE, JANUARY 1996

Jane's indefatigable efforts succeed in choking a print out of the lab, and heaving it onto a flight to Park City (Utah). We're both assailed by doubts but also driven by fear of subjecting ourselves to the tyranny of Cannes selection, still five months away. Plus the thought of joining the queue of sixteen Oz flicks. I wake from a ghastly nightmare where no one turns up to the screening. How could they hear about this unknown Australian picture with nothing to sell it?

SUNDANCE, 20 JANUARY

Kerry, Jan (Sardi, scriptwriter) and I drive through the snow up to Park City. Check into the ski lodge-style hotel. Exhausted and tense.

21 JANUARY

Seven p.m. The Egyptian Theatre. It's snowing and an anxious crowd presses to get in. The cinema's already packed and an eager Jonathan Taplin (Pandora's LA executive) tells me there are between twenty and twenty-five potential buyers in the auditorium. I briefly encounter Tony Safford (from Miramax, the US-based distributor of *Strictly Ballroom* (1992) and *The Piano* (1993)), who smiles inscrutably. He's made no comment since viewing the film privately days ago, so what can that mean?

[ANDREW PIKE, RONIN FILMS]

Scott Hicks and Geoffrey Rush on set of *Shine*

The audience's feeling is palpable in the dark. Our tension becomes excitement. The end credits roll and the applause begins, continuing right through the endless roll-up. The festival director leads us down the side aisle, and as the audience members spot us they begin to stand. On-stage, we look down into the sea of faces, some moved to tears. We move off-stage to be mobbed by well-wishers, agents, producers, attorneys, record company execs—many pressing cards into my hands, pockets, whatever they can reach. A pop star fantasy fulfilled!

22 JANUARY

Barely twelve hours later, the scene is repeated. Word has spread and there's a frenzy to get into the cinema. Back at the hotel there are thirty-five messages on the voice mail. In the three-quarters of an hour it takes to clear them, seventeen more come in. Notes accumulate at the reception desk. Already SWAT teams of agents from CAA, ICM, William Morris et al. (talent agents) are on their way. Over the next two days, 135 messages come to our room.

Six-fifteen p.m. There's an urgent call from Taplin. He has the Fine Line (US-based distributor of *Proof* (1992) and *Once Were Warriors* (1994)) people in his condo. Of all the serious bids, it seems it's down to them and Miramax. The price has hit US$2 million and Miramax are apparently coming back with a bid in writing. Jane's line is constantly busy, so Kerry and I set off for Taplin's, planning to contact her on arrival.

It's tense enough to snap in there. Jonathan Weisgal and Mark Ordesky (from Fine Line) have set up camp, clearly not about to leave without ink on paper. The phone keeps ringing until eventually Weisgal pulls it out of the wall to shut it up.

Jane arrives and we go over the deal choices. At the back of our minds are: Miramax has seen the film a week ago and made no comment; do they actually like it? They have forty-odd films to release this year against Fine Line's half-dozen. How important will it be to them? Will they want to make cuts?

We extract pledges from Fine Line: no cuts, strong P & A (prints and advertising budget), platform release (in three stages). They offer resources for Oscar push, consultation with us all down the line and US$2 million advance for North American rights.

We agonise, and reflect on the Miramax saga: the enticement to LA in 1993 followed by no returned calls for a year and heart-breaking delays. Almost the death of the project. The attempt in London to dislodge Geoffrey Rush (who plays the adult David Helfgott).

At last, 8 p.m., guided by Pandora's Taplin, we opt for Fine Line, excited and in trepidation. A handshake all round and Bollinger seal the deal. We have sold the North American rights for close to half the film's budget ($6 million).

23 JANUARY

We discover Taplin holding court with *Variety* at the condo. It seems an altercation broke out between Harvey Weinstein (co-chairman of Miramax) and Taplin in a restaurant last night and it's about to become legend. (Hicks wasn't there but, according to *GQ* magazine, Weinstein rounded on Taplin, telling him: 'You f—. You tried to f— me.' And got a tad physical before he was escorted by the *maître d'* into the Utah night.)

Mid-morning I go for coffee with Jason Hoffs from a company called DreamWorks (which none of us has heard of). He tells us he works for Steven Spielberg (whom I have heard of) and would like to arrange for a print of *Shine* to be made available for him to view at home as soon as possible. Like this weekend.

Lunch hosted by Ruth Vitale, president of Fine Line, in Robert Redford's restaurant, Zoom Cafe. Back at the hotel, a mountain more calls and messages, including one from Weinstein. We agree to meet the next day. At high noon.

24 JANUARY

Another dawn call from Ernst, who can't get through to Jane. Disney/Buena Vista have offered nearly US$3.5 million for a half-a-dozen foreign territories. At this rate, the film is already into profit! I can't help thinking of the hammering we withstood over Jane's realistic budgeting. Seems remote now.

Noon. Zoom Cafe. Harvey turns out to be every bit larger than life, as anticipated. He harangues Jane and me for close on twenty minutes, swearing he's not through with *Shine* yet. He wants to know what Jane and I want to do next. He offers scripts, future plans. It's alluring, this mix of charm and bullying. I assume the right of reply when he's through.

With Safford at the table, I run through the sorry saga of all our attempts to involve Miramax over two years ago, the delays and heartaches that resulted, the failure to return calls, the lack of response to the advance viewing, even the information we had from an FFC rep at Sundance the night before that Safford reportedly 'didn't like the film'. Harvey stabs a finger at me: 'You're 100 per cent right. A thousand per cent right. You couldn't be more right!' Safford cops his belligerent edge. I like Harvey. He's dangerous and funny.

He makes to order lunch. It's already 1 p.m. and Kerry and I have to leave to catch our LA flight. 'You stay,' barks Harvey. 'You can take the Miramax jet.' Later, he insists on Safford carrying my bag out to the car.

Jane stops in LA and meets Spielberg. 'At last, a great movie,' he tells her.

ADELAIDE, MAY

Cast and crew screenings. I don't like the first trailer cut; it seems too soppy. Pip Karmel (*Shine*'s editor) and I spend a day cutting a harder-edged, shorter trailer. It has to compete with *Independence Day* (1996), *Mission: Impossible* (1996), *Time to Kill* (1996), *Phenomenon* (1996)—block-buster movie trailers. The last thing we want is jeering in the midst of all that.

SYDNEY, JUNE

Ronin Films hold a two-day seminar at Ravesi's to plan the *Shine* release campaign. Numerous exhibitors' reps are there, with publicists from each state, and the video distributor (working a year ahead of release date).

Confirms everything I feel about Andrew Pike and his team: care, commitment, detail, inclusiveness.

Advance screenings for exhibitors have been off-the-scale positive. And they're the hardest to please—these people can smell a pup. They love the cut of the trailer I've done with Pip. It's deliberately tough and unsentimental, with multiplex potential in mind. The shot which looks like Noah Taylor (who plays the teenage David Helfgott) having sex with the piano is picked for the poster.

LOS ANGELES, 12 JUNE

Back to LA with Kerry, courtesy of DreamWorks SKG, to meet the 'S' of SKG.

Three-thirty p.m. Spielberg offers us a housekeeping deal. In exchange for a first look at any project we initiate or control, DreamWorks will cover our overhead expenses. He urges us to check out all the offers before deciding. Only later do I discover that he has never offered this to another director before.

A meeting with Fine Line/New Line marketing. About forty poster roughs are displayed. They can make the film look like anything from 'Pianospotting' to 'Remains of the Piano'. The shot of Geoffrey bouncing, with zinc on his nose, is a favourite.

There's much nervousness about how to sell the film. It has minimum 'marketability' (that is, no stars) with maximum 'playability' (that is, people love it when they see it). Discussions continue . . .

JULY/AUGUST

We hit the road for the film's Oz release: Jan, Jane, Kerry, me and cast. Introducing the film at premiere screenings, doing back-to-back media. We cover the whole of Australia except Darwin and Hobart in a fortnight. And in the middle of this, the AFI nominations are announced—twelve nominations out of fourteen categories.

ADELAIDE, 15 AUGUST

The Australian premiere. For me, a ten-year odyssey concludes. The Fine Line people arrive. The Helfgott family are our guests. The next day, Ronin hires a train to take the journos and film-makers up to the Barossa Valley where a wonderful winery lunch is organised, followed by a recital by David Helfgott, who weaves his magic spell on everyone. Suddenly, they all feel part of it.

how *shine* seduced hollywood

VENICE, 7 SEPTEMBER

Shine closes the festival, one of the key slots. If Cannes is the most important commercial event in the film calendar, Venice is the prime cultural one. The screening is out of competition, by Pandora's choice. Why go into competition to lose to the next bright thing when you made such an impact at Sundance? But when I see those Golden Lions on the stage, I have a pang of regret.

I spend the first five minutes of the screening stumbling about looking for a switch to turn off a light shining on the screen. The audience gives nothing away and I sit there mortified, thinking: 'They hate us.' But at the fade-out, the applause begins and rolls like a gigantic wave down the auditorium. The applause goes for eight minutes; even the *paparazzi* are weeping.

TORONTO, 10 SEPTEMBER

Maybe the second-most important festival in commercial terms. A huge disseminator into the North American market. *Shine* has a gala screening in the middle of the festival. Gigantic cinema, more than 2000 people; it sounds and looks magnificent.

On the way to LA, Kerry and I decided to take the DreamWorks deal. It offers final cut on any project up to US$15 million and is generally more flexible about creative controls than the other offers.

LOS ANGELES, 14 SEPTEMBER

A week of press and studio meetings. Lunch 1.15 p.m. Sharon Stone. Her shout.

NEW ORLEANS, 12 OCTOBER

First leg of the travelling *Shine* roadshow. A small-town feel to the eighth film festival. Great buzz on *Shine*—the only sell-out of the calendar. A day of mixed media: TV chats, a 'phoner' to Denver from the ludicrous white stretch limo, lunch with the local 'big cojones' critic.

CHICAGO, 13 OCTOBER

A different vibe here—much bigger, more 'filmy'. Chris Pula (New Line marketing head) is here. The Music Box is a big theatre, late-rococo chocolate-box style. It's packed, 750 tonight. We wander back for the ending, to a colossal reception and receptive Q & A (about 90 per cent stay back for it). These are 'word of mouth' screenings—designed to sow seeds among the film crowds of each individual market. Spectacular full-page colour ads have appeared in the otherwise black-and-white *LA Times* and *New York Times*. There's a bus-shelter poster campaign: 'New York is about to *Shine*'. A sixty-second ad on America's *60 Minutes* has been booked for $400 000—enough to open a modest pic in Oz.

14 OCTOBER

Press all day in Suite 904, at hourly intervals from 8.15 a.m. to 3 p.m. as Geoffrey and I polish up our double act.

PHILADELPHIA, 15 OCTOBER

Interviews in the morning, after lunch and after check-out. Philadelphia is the fourth-largest market after New York, Los Angeles and Chicago. The film will open Christmas Day on its first 'platform' into ten 'markets' outside of New York, Los Angeles, Toronto and Chicago (200-plus screens).

WASHINGTON, 16 OCTOBER

DC press, the heavyweights, *The Washington Post*, etc.

DENVER, 17 OCTOBER

Yet another stretch limo. Oprah Winfrey has flipped for *Shine* and wants me to direct her in a film she is developing. I need to be reminded of her Academy nomination in *The Color Purple* (1985).

The screening unfurls for 900 at $150 a head. Tony Curtis, looking kind of Liberace-ish, but that voice! Huge auditorium has me nerve-racked.

NEW YORK, 20 OCTOBER

Eight-thirty p.m. Liz Manne (Fine Line publicity) arrives with the limo, plus Lynn Redgrave and John Clarke (her husband), to collect Geoffrey and me for the *Shine* dinner. It's part of the New York release strategy. No glitzy premiere for this cynical town. Rather, a series of screenings for opinion-makers and social glitterati, followed by an intimate dinner for seventy-five or so in a private house or apartment.

These are being organised by society maven and publicist Peggy Siegal— she of the 'Rolodex from heaven'. Tonight's is held at a palazzo-style apartment overlooking the Hudson. A fabulous supper, then an impromptu recital by the Broadway legend Cy Coleman, joined by Betty Buckley.

SAN FRANCISCO, 21 OCTOBER

Arrive 3.30 p.m. Check into Ritz Carlton, and interviews begin: 'How did you get the idea to make this film?' for maybe the 200th time.

ADELAIDE, 24 OCTOBER

After all the regional festival coverage and the 600-strong Toronto media attendance, Fine Line cancels the New York mega-press junket in favour of a mini-junket in LA.

2 NOVEMBER

Presenting the Australian Cinematographers' Society awards tonight. An evening of bonhomie and a viewing of some dazzling work. Evening ends with a surprise presentation of a Gold Award to me for *Shine*, Best South Australian Film.

7 NOVEMBER

Protracted calls with (Alan) Wertheimer (attorney), (Beth) Swofford (agent) and Weisgal (Fine Line). Jane wrestling with Bloomsbury (publisher of screenplay). They want to quote Steven Spielberg on the cover and we tell them they can't. The phone rings, and 'It's Steven Spielberg' on his way home from location on *Jurassic Park II*. He's five days ahead of schedule and casting his next picture to shoot in April and wants some advice! 'Tell me about X (an actor).'

Our personal assistant, Alison Bowman, starts, courtesy of the DreamWorks deal—a huge psychological and practical relief.

MELBOURNE, 15 NOVEMBER

Eight-twenty a.m. flight with Kerry, Scott and Jethro (Hicks's children) for tonight's AFI awards. Kerry panics and buys a jacket for the price of a small car. I feel tense enough to twang. As the evening unfolds and awards tumble our way, I somehow remain tense, with what feels like a rictus of a grin frozen on my face for a smile. As the final major awards approach, my conviction mounts that we will be 'punished', but no. As I try to make my acceptance speech, I am almost utterly undone with emotion. I stumble backstage and watch Jane's gracious acceptance. Nine awards!

ADELAIDE, 17 NOVEMBER

Off to the LA premiere. Fine Line send a stretch to collect the family, which causes a stir in our suburban street!

LOS ANGELES

The room at the Beverly Hills Nikko resembles a conservatory, packed with flowers, gift baskets and Dom Perignon from CAA, Fine Line, Disney/Touchstone, DreamWorks, etc. Open the *LA Times* to find *Shine* is the cover of the 'Calendar' section. Extraordinary coverage with good pix. News that *Shine* has won the audience prize at Fort Lauderdale and Noah is Best Actor! Adds to our Melbourne, Toronto, Aspen, Boston, New Orleans, Denver and other audience prizes. The film has such a life of its own.

18 NOVEMBER

A full day of press/media in and out of the hotel. *NY Times* phoner, *Chicago Tribune, Washington Post, Associated Press, People, Esquire, Orange County Register.*

Dinner at the hotel, alongside the table of the Fine Line publicity crew. Utterly focused and brimming with energy and enthusiasm. Unbelievably hard-working.

An evening Q & A at the UCLA Sneak Preview class with Jan, Armin (Meuller-Stahl, who plays the father), Jane, Noah, Geoffrey and me on the platform. I seize the moment to present Armin with his AFI Award.

19 NOVEMBER

Tonight's the night! The American premiere. First, the Hollywood Foreign Press conference with the cast at the Beverly Hilton. An eclectic group with enormous power. They will be nominating for the Golden Globes in about three weeks.

Back at the hotel, I hear the White House will screen the film over Thanksgiving. In Australia, Michael Jackson has requested a private screening.

Afternoon is a bedlam of international TV. We wrap about 5 p.m. More limos. We arrive at the Academy of Motion Picture Arts and Sciences on Wilshire Boulevard and inch our way along the red carpet from interview to TV interview.

The reaction is enormous and huge applause at the end with a standing ovation. We go down the front to receive it. Jane whispers to me, 'We've done it!' and in some way it feels like it, with this hard-boiled crowd. Barbara Hershey tries to talk to me, but dissolves in tears. We take the limos to legendary Chasen's for the packed party.

20 NOVEMBER

Interviews all morning. After lunch the DreamWorks van takes us to the *Jurassic Park II* set, where we watch Steven direct a couple of set-ups. Very smooth, quiet and fast, he keeps the throttle on the crew. I do a taping of a New York late, late radio program. I come off feeling either a chameleon or a slut, I don't know which.

LONDON, 27 NOVEMBER

A full-on media junket at the Athenaeum with major national and regional media, plus some international. At the end of Lynn Redgrave's show, *Shakespeare for My Father*, she is surprised by *This Is Your Life* and her newest co-star, Geoffrey Rush.

CAPRI, 29 NOVEMBER

Shine opens the film festival. What, no limo? Geoffrey and I drag our bags onto a bus into Naples and then two kilometres through the rain to the hydrofoil. Midnight screening. Lina Wertmüller (Italian director) raves afterwards.

ADELAIDE, 17 DECEMBER

Spend week with New York writer Rafael Yglesias on the script for Warner Brothers' *The Secret History*. A daily fix—or fax—of awards and nomination announcements. Geoffrey wins best actor from New York Film Critics and LA Film Critics circles. This positions him squarely for Oscar nomination. We have also been nominated for Best Film, Best Director, Best Actor by the breakaway group of the Hollywood Foreign Press, calling themselves the Golden Satellites.

19 DECEMBER

One-twenty a.m. Jan Sardi calls. We have five Golden Globe nominations (he's been Internet surfing). I call Jonathan in New York—Fine Line is in a bacchanalian frenzy. All major categories: film, director, screenplay, actor, music. These are often a pointer to Academy nominations: at the very least it guarantees the members will view the film among the 200 or so that vie for their attention. So it's off to LA for the Globes. Unbelievably, a year to the day since Sundance! What a trip.

EPILOGUE

Stage 1: November 22—Christmas. *Shine* grosses $1.2 million on ten screens.

Stage 2: December 25. Goes to 208 screens and, by time of going to press [in *Sydney Morning Herald*, 18 January 1997], has grossed more than US$8.7 million, about $7500 per screen. Currently at number sixteen in *Variety* box-office charts. The soundtrack reached number one on the *Billboard* classical cross-over chart.

Stage 3: By January 31 goes to between 650 and 800 screens nationwide in the US.

POST-EPILOGUE [eds]

By early 1998 Hicks is shooting *Snow Falling in Cedars* in Canada, an adaptation of David Guterson's 1995 novel of same name. Hicks is also reported to have in preparation two other adaptations—Donna Tartt's *The Secret History* (1992) and Jean-Dominque Bauby's *The Diving-Bell and the Butterfly* (1996).

Hicks's diary extracts were faxed daily to Helen Greenwood, features writer for the *Sydney Morning Herald*, and were published on 18 January 1997, the eve of the Golden Globes.

notes

NB: All notes provided by the editors are distinguished from those of the contributors by the notation '[eds]'.

WHAT DO FILM-MAKERS DREAM ABOUT?

1   See '*Irma Vep*: La femme d'Est', Olivier Assayas interviewed by Raffaele Caputo, Rolando Caputo and Clare Stewart, *Metro*, no. 113–114, 1998.
2   The expression is on loan from Arthur Koestler's book *The Ghost in the Machine*, Danube Edition, Hutchison & Co., London, 1979. For the most part Koestler uses the term to describe a principal tactic of biological evolution, but also argues it is a fundamental aspect of cultural evolution.
3   The use of the metaphor of the noon-day sun in this introduction is informed by its use and interpretation by Arthur Koestler, *Darkness at Noon* (Penguin Books, Harmondsworth, 1985 edition); Claude Lévi-Strauss, *The Origin of Table Manners* (Harper-Colophon edition, New York, 1979); and Joseph Campbell, *The Masks of God: Creative Mythology*, (Arkana-Penguin, New York, 1991 edition).
4   Adrian Martin, 'S.O.S.', *Continuum: Film—Matters of Style*, vol. 5, no. 2, 1992.
5   David Bordwell, *Making Meaning: Inference and Rhetoric in the Interpretation of Film*, Harvard University Press, 1989.
6   Jorge Amado, *Doña Flor and Her Two Husbands*, first published in English by Knopf, New York, 1969.
7   Another expression on loan, this time from James Joyce's 'the Hereweareagain Gaieties' in Part III of *Finnegans Wake* (Penguin Books, Harmondsworth, 1992 edition).
8   Tom O'Regan and Albert Moran (eds), *An Australian Film Reader*, Currency Press, Sydney, 1985.
9   François Truffaut, *The Films in My Life*, Da Capo Press, New York, 1978.
10   Michel Ciment, 'For Pleasure', in John Boorman and Walter Donohue (eds), *Projections* 4$\frac{1}{2}$, in association with *Positif*, Faber & Faber, London, 1995.

TABLE TALK

1 Paul Schrader, *Transcendental Style in Film*, Da Capo Press edition, New York, 1972.
2 André Bazin, *What is Cinema?* Volume II, essays selected and translated by Hugh Gray, University of California Press, Berkeley, 1971.
3 Raymond Durgnat, *Eros in the Cinema*, Calder and Boyars, London, 1966.

THE EVER-PRESENT SERPENT [eds]

1 This story was first published in *Life and Letters To-Day* in 1937 and was subsequently reprinted in a collection entitled *A Prospect of the Sea and other stories and prose writing by Dylan Thomas* (edited by Daniel Jones, J. M. Deart & Sons Ltd, London) in 1955. The material in this volume was chosen by Thomas (1914–53) before his death.
2 Both paintings are by John William Waterhouse (1849–1917). *Hylas and the Nymphs* is dated 1896. *Ophelia* is dated 1910, though Waterhouse painted two earlier versions in 1884 and 1889.

TWO OUT OF THREE [eds]

1 Jean-Paul Sartre (1905–80). Original French titles and first publication dates for the works cited: *L'Être et le néant* (*Being and Nothingness*) first appeared in France in 1943, and its first English translation published in 1957; *La Nausée* (*Nausea*) first appeared in 1938 and its English translation published in 1949; while *La Mort dans l'âme* (*Iron in the Soul*) was first published in 1949 and then in English in 1950. The latter, when first published, was part of a trilogy of works titled *Les Chemins de la liberté* (1945–47).
2 Albert Camus (1913–60). Original French titles and first publication dates for the works cited: *L'Étranger* (*The Outsider*) was first published in 1942 and translated into English in 1946; *La Peste* (*The Plague*) appeared in France in 1947 and was published in English in 1948.

THE APOCALYPSE AND THE PIG [eds]

This paper was originally presented at the Sydney Institute's 'The Larry Adler Lecture' for 1996 and was published in the *Sydney Papers*, vol. 8, no. 4, Spring 1996.

1 Gerard Henderson is Executive Director of the Sydney Institute and Editor-in-Chief of the *Sydney Papers*.
2 Carl G. Jung (1875–1961), a psychiatrist, was born in Basel, Switzerland. Jung was a friend and leading collaborator of Sigmund Freud's until 1912 when the publication of Jung's *The Psychology of the Unconscious*, which was critical of Freud's approach, caused a split. He called his theories 'analytical psychology' to distinguish them from Freud's psychoanalysis, and they included exploration of the concepts of 'archetypal images', the 'collective unconscious', and of the psyche as a 'self regulating system'.
3 Joseph Campbell (1904–87) was born in New York. He wrote, contributed to and edited scores of books on mythology and comparative religion. His best-known work is perhaps *The Hero With a Thousand Faces* (1949), though he gained considerable posthumous renown from the 1988 PBS television series and book

The Power of Myth, with Bill Moyers. Apart from his influence on film-makers such as George Lucas, Steven Spielberg and George Miller, Campbell encouraged the writing of, and edited, the book *Divine Horseman: The Living Gods of Haiti* (1953) by American avant-garde film-maker Maya Deren.

4   Miriam Makeba (1932–), a singer born in Johannesburg, South Africa, was exiled because of her political views. She settled in the US where she became internationally known for her 'click' songs. She married Hugh Masekela in 1964. Her singing career in the US ended when she divorced Masekela and married Black Panther activist Stokely Carmichael. Hugh Masekela (1939–), trumpeter and band leader, was born in Johannesburg, South Africa. Masekela was forced to emigrate to the US in 1960 due to a ban on black musicians working in inner-city clubs. Throughout the 1960s and into the 1970s he found considerable critical success in the US for his solo albums. In 1980, with ex-wife Makeba, Masekela headlined the Goin' Home concert in Lesotho, and in 1982 they headlined a similar venture in neighbouring Botswana, where Masekela is now settled. Desmond Tutu (1931–), Archbishop of Cape Town, was born in Klerksdorp, South Africa. A foremost political activist against the apartheid system in South Africa from within the Anglican Church, he received the Nobel Peace Prize in 1984. Athol Fugard (1932–) was born in Middleburg, Cape Province, South Africa. A playwright and theatre director critical of official separatist racial policies, his plays often received government opposition, notably *Blood Knot* (1960) and *Boesman and Lena* (1969). Alan Paton (1903–88), a teacher and novelist, was born in Pietermaritzburg, South Africa. His best-known novel, *Cry, the Beloved Country* (1948), grew out of the racial problems of apartheid. Trevor Huddleston (1913–) is a British Anglican missionary who was ordained in 1937. He held a string of posts: Provincial of the Order, Johannesburg (1949–55), Bishop of Masasi, Tanzania (1960–68), Bishop Suffragen of Stepney until 1978, and finally Bishop of Mauritius and Archbishop of the Indian Ocean. He returned to London after his retirement and became chairman of the Anti-Apartheid Movement.

5   Greg Louganis (1960–) was born in El Cajon, California. Olympic champion in 1984 and 1988, he was also the first diver to ever achieve a score of 700 points for eleven dives at the 1983 World Championships.

6   Nicolas Copernicus (1473–1543) was born in Torun, Poland. Known as the founder of modern astronomy, he completed his four-hundred-page treatise *On the Revolutions of the Celestial Spheres* in 1530, which was met with hostility from the Church when published in 1543.

7   Johannes Kepler (1571–1630) was born in Weil-der-Stadt, Germany. An astronomer who deduced, with the help of data from Tycho Brahe (1546–1601), three fundamental laws showing that planets orbited the sun in ellipses. Isaac Newton (1642–1727) was born in Woolsthorpe, Lincolnshire. A physicist and mathematician, he is perhaps best known for his law of gravitation, which he expounded on in *Mathematical Principles of Natural Philosophy* (published in 1687).

8   Joseph Campbell, *The Inner Reaches of Outer Space: Metaphor as Myth and as Religion*, Alfred Van Der Marck Editions, New York, 1985, p. 18.

TWO INTERVIEWS WITH JANE CAMPION [eds]

The first interview was recorded in Paris on 17 October 1986, and the second in Cannes on 17 May 1989. Both were first published in *Positif* no. 347, January 1990.

1   Claude Lévi-Strauss was born in 1908 in Belgium and educated at the University of Paris in philosophy and law. He taught at the University of São Paolo in Brazil,

worked at the New School for Social Research in New York and the École Pratiques des Hautes Études in Paris. From 1960 he was Professor of Social Anthropology at the Collège de France. His books in English translation include *Structural Anthropology* (1961), *The Raw and the Cooked* (1971) and *From Honey to Ashes* (1972).

2 Precise dates for *Tissues* and *Eden* are unknown but are likely to have been made between 1980 and 1981.

3 Katherine Mansfield (1888–1923) was born Kathleen Mansfield Beauchamp in Wellington, New Zealand. A short-story writer, during her lifetime her collected works included *In a German Pension* (1911), *Prelude* (1918), *Bliss, and Other Stories* (1920). Posthumous works include *Something Childish and Other Stories* (1924), *A Fairy Story* (1932) and *The Collected Stories of Katherine Mansfield* (1945). Her second husband, John Middleton Murry (1889–1957), edited *The Letters of Katherine Mansfield* (1928) and *Katherine Mansfield's Letters to John Middleton Murry: 1913–1922* (1951).

4 Marguerite Duras (1914–96) was born in French Indo-China. A novelist and a film-maker, she became well-known for writing the screenplay of Alain Resnais's *Hiroshima mon amour* (1960). Her autobiographical novel *L'Amant* (*The Lover*, 1984) was brought to the screen by Jean-Jacques Annaud in 1992.

5 Flannery O'Connor (1925–64) was born in Savannah, Georgia. An American short-story writer and novelist, her novels include *Wise Blood* (1952) and *The Violent Bear It Away* (1960). Her short stories are collected in *A Good Man is Hard to Find* (1955).

RED WIGS AND AUTOBIOGRAPHY [eds]

Interview recorded in Venice on 14 September 1990, published in *Positif*, no. 362, April 1991.

1 *Positif* has the poem titled as 'Excalibur', which could be the French title of Tennyson's poem. Unless proven otherwise, there is no such Tennyson poem by that title in English. It is likely Campion was referring to 'Morte D'Arthur', which was inspired by Sir Thomas Malory's *Le Morte D'Arthur* (1469–70). The legendary sword is featured prominently in both works when King Arthur, mortally wounded in the last battle to be fought by the Knights of the Round Table, orders Sir Bedevere to fling Excalibur into the lake.

2 A direct translation from the *Positif* original has the poem as 'Ode to a Red Robin'. Again, there is no such poem by Keats in English, so the poem referred to can only be 'Ode to a Nightingale'.

JANE CAMPION [eds]

Interview recorded in Paris on 23 April 1993, published in *Positif* no. 388, June 1993.

1 Pierre Rissient is a critic, film activist, and distributor who founded the influential ciné-club Cinéma MacMahon in the 1950s. Since 1985 he has acted on the behalf of the Australian Film Commission as a consultant on the programs and procedures of the Cannes Film Festival.

2 Billy MacKinnon (1954–), Scottish producer born in Glasgow, was producer and/or script editor on Campion's *Sweetie* and *The Piano*. While based in Australia,

he also produced Sue Clayton's film *The Last Crop* for Film Australia. MacKinnon returned to Scotland where he produced *Small Faces* (1996) for his brother, the director Gillies MacKinnon.

3   Thomas Hood (1799–1845), a poet and humorist, was born in London. He achieved fame in 1825 when, in collaboration with John Hamilton Reynolds (1796–1852), he published *Odes and Addresses to Great People*. His two best-known comic poems, 'Faithless Nelly Gray' and 'The Ballad of Sally Brown and Ben the Carpenter' appeared in the first series of *Whims and Oddities* (1826). His major serious poem, 'The Song of the Shirt', was published anonymously in *Punch* in 1843.

4   Franz Peter Schubert (1797–1828), Austrian composer. Robert Alexander Schumann (1810–56), German composer, pianist, conductor, critic and teacher.

5   The title in full is *Bad Timing: A Sensual Obsession*.

A VOYAGE OF SELF-DISCOVERY [eds]

Interview recorded in Venice on 11 September 1996, published in *Positif*, no. 430, December 1996.

1   Wojciech Kilar (1932–) was born in Lvov, Poland. He studied at the Katowice State Academy of Music (1950–55), the Cracow State Academy of Music (1955–58), and also in Paris (1959–60) with Nadia Boulanger. A freelance composer, Kilar has written many scores for films and theatre.

LITTLE WOMEN [eds]

1   First published in *Colliers Magazine*, 27 May 1922, then again in 1922 in the short-story collection *Tales of the Jazz Age*.

2   *Matilda* was published in 1988, one of the last prior to Dahl's death in 1990. The book was adapted to the screen in 1996 by Swicord and her husband Nicholas Kazan, and directed by DeVito.

PISTOLS AT DAWN

This article was first published in *Cinema Papers*, no. 95, October 1993.

1   Made in England for Thorn EMI. With the demise of that company, *Link* (along with the rest of its library) passed through the hands of Universal, Alan Bond, Golan and Globus and Jerry Weintraub, before coming to rest (minus some fifteen minutes). I would offer to show each new owner my 'director's cut', but they insisted on seeing the previous owner's cut-down—then they'd cut it down further. My version was shown only once, at the Avoriaz Festival in France, where it won the Jury Prize.

2   *This is Orson Welles*, Orson Welles and Peter Bogdanovich, edited by Jonathan Rosenbaum, HarperCollins, London, 1993.

3   Welles was to direct the omnibus documentary *It's All True* for the Whitney-Rockefeller Committee for Inter-American Affairs, the same group that sponsored Disney's *Three Caballeros* (Norman Ferguson, 1945).

4   With the US entry into World War II, a civilian could not get a plane back to the US. Welles stayed in South America and, against the odds, finished shooting

It's All True. To his death, he was told this film (much of it in Technicolor) had been dumped, unprocessed, in the ocean. After his death, Paramount donated 280 000 feet of uncut negative to the American Film Institute, where it waits for someone to try to piece it together.

5   The enormous fireplace centrepiece of the jigsaw-puzzle scene, for example, was actually from John Ford's *Mary of Scotland* (1936).

6   Even in its present form, *The Magnificent Ambersons* has been a regular on *Sight and Sound's* once-in-a-decade '10 Best' list. In 1972, it rated equal ninth; in 1982, eighth (*Citizen Kane* was the no. 1 film each time). *Ambersons* dropped out of the top ten in 1992, but still has a lot of support and Welles again came out as the most-favoured director of critics. See *Sight and Sound*, December 1992, pp. 18–30.

7   Welles once called Hollywood the best model train set a kid ever got to play with.

8   The first *Magnificent Ambersons* preview was with a Dorothy Lamour musical, *The Fleet's In* (Victor Schertzinger, 1942). No wonder there was 'laffter'.

9   I tried this method in Hollywood during the whittling of *Link*. Borrowing a USC cinema class, I got an entirely different reading of the picture, but when this was shown to the 'experts', it was dismissed with, 'What d'ya expect when you talk to f***king film buffs?'

10   Hitchcock argues in François Truffaut's book *Hitchcock* (Secker & Warburg, London, 1968), among others, that this scene was integral to his concept and he NEVER wavered.

11   The sample is actually NOT representative, but skewed to the demography of the movie audience of predominantly under-25s. The entirely different demographic of the video market (now three times world box office) is therefore in the hands of no more than a handful of people. I've been told, for example, that 'women over fifty think such and such', when I'm aware only one such person attended.

12   I complained about the execution of temporary artwork for the preview of *Cloak & Dagger* (1984), which suggested Dabney Coleman as a pastry chef molesting Henry Thomas in a public lavatory.

13   AVCO, on the other hand, spent the money on final artwork for the *Roadgames* (1981) preview. Though beautifully executed, it apparently suggested an S & M biker movie (the ad actually drew fire in the local paper when we previewed the picture). And in spite of changes to the film (made behind my back), once the money had been spent on the ad, this feedback was never heeded and the picture went out with the ad unchanged.

14   I recall one card emblazoned with the words 'projectionists union #73 are cock suckers'. And this disturbed individual's opinions went into the statistical pot along with the rest.

15   I commend readers to *The Two Ronnies* (Barker and Corbett) sketch where the fellow effusing about a play at intermission is intimidated into hating it by a professional critic.

16   The Director's Guild contract entitled me to two previews. So if I'd left one of 'my' previews, it would have cost them about $10 000 for another (a sort of mistrial by dismissing the jurors).

17   Such was the confidence of the head of their new studio, Irving Thalberg, that it went out unchanged. And brought the house down.

18   At Universal, they said they liked to preview with 'real people'. Las Vegas was one of the 'real' places within range and we met at a private strip at 6 p.m., went by Lear jet and limo to a restaurant overlooking the theatre, where we were notified when they were ready to start. We were thus able to eat, slip in and out of the 'real world' and be back in Hollywood before midnight.

19   For those who don't know, laser disc is a treasure trove of such things and presents

a possible saviour for the director's vision—or any other for that matter. With digital editing, we may yet live to see 'the exec-producer's wife's cut'.
20 There's a laser 'Director's Cut' of *The Fisher King* (Terry Gilliam, 1991).
21 I would argue this procedure is one of the reasons that previews have become the battle-front—though it's possible that without it the front would just move back to the cutting room.
22 With modern computer editing (tape, laser and digital), all cuts can co-exist.
23 He was vindicated, but in this case may have had *his* 'creativity' on the line, since John Ford began only two weeks before shooting. A few years later, Zanuck did the opposite to the Ford-initiated *My Darling Clementine* (1946).
24 William Holden, as a corpse in a morgue, sits up and begins the narration now played over his body in the swimming pool.
25 Frank Capra, *The Name Above the Title*, MacMillan, New York, 1971.
26 His studio boss, Harry Cohn, took this story to heart. Or rather he talked about his own restlessness on screenings, which led someone to ponder an 'entire world wired to Harry Cohn's ass'.
27 In turnaround, 'creatives' are allowed to take the project elsewhere, provided that, IF it is produced, those who funded it are reimbursed for out-of-pocket expenses.
28 At Universal on *Link*, someone proclaimed the 'correct' length for thrillers to be ninety-eight minutes. I pointed out to them that their most successful thriller of recent years, *Psycho II* (1983), ran for 113 minutes. Another expert literally greeted me making a 'scissor' sign with his fingers, saying, 'Great picture but *SNIP, SNIP!*'
29 At Cannon, they added the word 'BADLY' to the threat.
30 James Cameron tells a wonderful 'cobbler's elf' story on one of his early pictures, in which he used to climb through the cutting-room window and work all night. And no one was ever the wiser.

ON THE SLIDE

Thanks to Graham Shirley for providing me with the transcript of his 1980 interview with Reg Baker. 'MBC' refers to the Michael Balcon Collection, a large archive held by the British Film Institute, London.

1 Harry Watt, 'Films in Australia' in William Whitebait, *International Film Annual*, no. 2, John Calder, London, 1958, p. 106.
2 John K, Newnham, 'Mr Balcon's Young Gentlemen', *Film*, Autumn, London, 1946, p. 43.
3 Harry Watt, *Don't Look at the Camera*, Paul Elek, London, 1974, p. 53.
4 Ibid, p. 29.
5 Ibid, p. 92.
6 Unsigned article, 'Film of the Month—*Nine Men*', *Documentary Newsletter*, February 1943, p. 179.
7 National Film Theatre (NFT) program booklet, April–May 1974, p. 49.
8 Watt, 'Films in Australia', p. 106.
9 Harry Watt, 'You Start from Scratch in Australia' in *Penguin Film News*, no. 9, Penguin Books, London, 1949, p. 11.
10 Ibid, p. 10.
11 Ibid, p. 13.
12 Ibid, p. 12.
13 NFT program note, 11 April 1974.
14 Watt, *Penguin Film News*, no. 9, p. 12.

15 Ibid, p. 13.
16 Michael Balcon, *Michael Balcon Presents . . . A Lifetime of Films*, Hutchinson, London, 1969, p. 150.
17 NFT program note, 11 April 1974.
18 Not helped by the revoicing of Daphne Campbell, playing Mary Parsons. Her accent was found 'too Australian', and her lines redubbed by a cut-glass young Englishwoman, to jarring effect.
19 Harry Watt interviewed by BBC television, 8 August 1959.
20 Harry Watt, '*The Overlanders*', *Picture Post,* 18 May 1946, p. 12.
21 Unsigned report, 'Australian Production Scheme', enclosed with M. Balcon to J. Davis, 12 April 1946 (MBC, file G/12).
22 Ibid.
23 Ibid.
24 Harry Watt, 'Why—and how—we made *Eureka Stockade*', Ealing studio publicity handout, undated.
25 Watt, *Penguin Film News*, no. 9, pp. 13–14.
26 Andrew Pike and Ross Cooper, *Australian Film 1900–1977*, Oxford University Press, Melbourne, 1980, p. 267.
27 Watt, studio publicity handout.
28 Watt, *Penguin Film News*, no. 9, p. 14.
29 Balcon to Angus MacPhail, 24 November 1947 (MBC, file G/2).
30 Henry Cornelius to Balcon, 28 November 1947 (MBC file G/2).
31 Balcon to Leslie Norman, 28 November 1947 (MBC file G/2).
32 Norman to Balcon, 16 December 1947 (MBC file G/2).
33 Watt, *Penguin Film News*, pp. 14–15.
34 Watt to Balcon, 11 February 1948 (MBC file G/2).
35 Ibid.
36 Watt, BBC TV, 8 August 1959.
37 Watt, NFT program note, 16 April 1974.
38 Watt to Balcon, 9 March 1948 (MBC file G/2).
39 Watt to Balcon, 10 March 1948 (MBC file G/2).
40 Eric Williams to Balcon, 10 July 1948. (MBC file G/2).
41 Watt to Balcon, 5 August 1948 (MBC file G/2).
42 Ibid.
43 Reginald Baker, interviewed by Graham Shirley, Sydney 6 February 1980.
44 Ken G. Hall, *Australian Film: The Inside Story*, Lansdowne, Melbourne 1977, p. 152.
45 Baker interviewed by Shirley, 6 February 1980.
46 Balcon to Watt, 24 March 1948 (MBC file G/2).
47 *New Chronicle*, 31 January 1949.
48 *Sunday Telegraph*, 23 January 1949.
49 Quoted in Sydney Wynne to Balcon, 26 February 1949 (MBC file G/4).
50 Balcon to Wynne, 28 February 1949 (MBC file G/4).
51 Balcon to Watt, 30 June 1948 (MBC file G/2).
52 Watt to Balcon, 13 July 1948 (MBC file G/2).
53 Balcon to Watt, 27 January 1955 (MBC file H/46)
54 Watt, NFT program note, 23 April 1974.
55 Balcon to Watt, 1 November 1956 (MBC file H/46).
56 Watt, NFT program note, 23 April 1974.
57 Watt to Balcon, 2 May 1958 (MBC file I/29).
58 Watt, NFT program note, 23 April 1974.
59 Ibid.

60 Balcon to Watt, 8 May 1958 (MBC file I/29)
61 Watt, *Penguin Film News*, no. 9, p. 16.
62 L.C. Rudkin to Hal Mason, 9 November 1958 (MBC file I/29).
63 Watt to Balcon. 12 November 1958 (MBC file I/29).
64 Bruce Molloy, 'The View from Outside: Ealing Studio's Australian Features' in *The First Australian History and Film Conference Papers* (1982), p. 278.
65 Balcon to Robert Clark, 6 January 1959 (MBC file I/293a).
66 Watt to Balcon (cable), 26 February 1959 (MBC file I/293a).
67 Balcon to Watt (cable), 26 February 1959 (MBC file I/293a).
68 Jon Cleary to Balcon, 26 February 1959 (MBC file I/293a).
69 Cleary to Balcon, 3 August 1959 (MBC file I/293a).
70 Watt to Balcon, undated (probably July 1959) (MBC file I/293a).
71 71 Watt, NFT program note, 23 April 1974.
72 Bruce Molloy, p. 280.

NOT GOD'S SUNFLOWERS [eds]

1 James Vance Marshall (1887–1964) was actually born in Australia in the New South Wales town of Casino. He was the son of a Presbyterian Minister, and left Australia on a steamer while still in his teenage years. For several years Marshall had worked as a ship's purser, journalist, seaman and dockside worker, and had travelled extensively through Siberia, Japan, China, Canada, the US, England, and most of Central and South America before returning to Australia and settling in Oberon, New South Wales. *The Children* was first published in 1959 by Michael Joseph Ltd, London.
2 Thornton Wilder (1897–1975), an American playwright and novelist, was born in Madison, Wisconsin. *Our Town*, a play set in the New Hampshire town of Grover's Corners and was played without scenery, was the second of his works to have won a Pulitzer Prize. He won his first Pulitzer for the novel *The Bridge of San Luis Rey* (1927), and his third for the play *The Skin of Our Teeth* (1942).
3 Edward Bond (1934–), a British playwright and director, who left school at the age of fourteen. His first play, *The Pope's Wedding*, caused great controversy when performed at the Royal Theatre, London, in 1962. Two of his other plays, *Saved* (1965) and *Early Morning* (1969), were banned in their entirety by the Lord Chamberlain. At the time of *Walkabout*, Bond was working on *Lear* (1971), a re-working of Shakespeare's *King Lear*.
4 Si Litvinoff, producer of *Walkabout*.
5 Max Raab, executive producer of *Walkabout*.
6 Donald Cammell, co-director of *Performance*.
7 f-11 refers to an f-stop number on the lens. An f-stop is a setting on the lens that corresponds to the size of the aperture and is determined by dividing the focal length of the lens by the diameter of the aperture opening. It indicates the amount of light entering the lens.
8 Karlheinz Stockhausen (1928–), composer born in Mödrath, Germany, who has written orchestral, choral and instrumental works.

IN THE MARGINS: DOCUMENTARY

1 Lubitsch was quoted by Jean-Luc Godard in a short piece titled 'Ignored by the Jury', first published in *Arts*, 700, 10 December 1958, and reprinted in *Godard on*

Godard, translated and edited by Jean Narboni and Tom Milne, Secker & Warburg, London, 1972.

DOCUMENTARY: A PERSONAL VIEW

1   For a more detailed description of this work, see *Metro*, no. 107, 1996.
2   'High-ratio' refers to the shooting ratio, that is, the amount of film footage shot compared to the actual footage used in the final product.

THE MAN BEHIND THE PICTURE [eds]

1   The first of the series, twenty-one episodes in all, aired on the ABC from 9 June to 27 October 1997.
2   The festival is also known as Tropfest, a short film festival that was initiated in 1993 at the Tropicana restaurant/café in Kings Cross by actor John Polson. Out of the success of Tropfest has emerged Tropnest, a screenwriting initiative housed at the Fox Studios in Sydney. In recognition of his contribution to the Australian film culture, Polson was a recipient of the AFI Byron Kennedy Award in 1997.
3   *LOUD*, a national festival of youth culture and arts, included short films and documentaries which were broadcast on the ABC and other networks during January 1998.
4   *Race Around the World* is based on a French-Canadian television program called *La Course Tour de Monde*.
5   The title in full is *Sherman's March: A Meditation on the Possibility of Romantic Love in the South During an Era of Nuclear Weapons Proliferation*.
6   *Backyard* (1984). McElwee also co-directed a film with Michel Negroponte in 1979 titled *Space Coast*. Both these films, along with *Sherman's March* and *Time Indefinite*, are all intimate portraits of life in the southern states of America.
7   *The Other Half of the Sky: A China Memoir* (1975).
8   Robert Drew was a photo-journalist for *Life* magazine. He is considered one of the founding fathers of the 'direct cinema' movement in the US. In the 1950s, he formed a partnership with famed cameraman and documentarist Richard Leacock to start the production company Drew Associates, which produced documentaries mainly for distribution on television.
9   Chris Berry, Annette Hamilton and Laleen Jaymanne (eds), *The Filmmaker and the Prositute: Dennis O'Rourke's The Good Woman of Bangkok*, Power Publications, Sydney, 1997.
10 Part of the ABC documentary series *Inside Stories*, which first aired on 30 September 1997.
11 Titled *Uni*, and part of the ABC documentary series *The Big Picture*, which was first broadcast on 20 November 1997.
12 A four-part documentary for the ABC series *The Big Picture*, *Under the Hammer* was based on a 1994 UK series of the same name.
13 The three most famous violin makers: Niccolo Amati (1596–1684), Antonio Stradivari (1644–1737) and Giuseppe Guarneri (1698–1744).
14 *Hotel Sorrento* (1995) directed by Richard Franklin, based on a play by Hannie Rayson.

MAKIN' BACON [eds]

Chris Noonan's paper was presented as a Masterclass session for the Australian Screen Directors Association (ASDA) conference in 1996, held at the Australian Film, Television and Radio School in Sydney and was sponsored by the NSW Film and TV Office. The presentation was then followed by a question-and-answer session chaired by television director Graham Thorburn.

1 *The Sheep Pig* was first published in 1983.
2 If not the film, King-Smith's book was indeed published in the US in 1985 as *Babe, The Gallant Pig*.
3 A US entertainment lawyer.
4 An Italian folk dance believed to have originated in the Southern Italian coastal town of Taranto, and where folklore has it that lively dancing will cure a tarantula's bite.

DEAR DIARY

1 Jean Cocteau, *Diary of a Film* (La Belle et la Bête), edited by Herbert Marshall for the series International Theatre and Film, translated from the French by Ronald Duncan, Dennis Dobson Ltd, London, 1950.

TELEXES IN SPACE [eds]

1 Arthur Scargill (1936–) was born in Leeds, West Yorkshire. A trade unionist, Scargill became president of the National Union of Mineworkers in 1982. His socialist politics provided strong defence for British miners and often brought the union into conflict with the government, most notably during the lengthy miner's strike of 1984–85.

contributors

BILL BENNETT began his career at the ABC in 1972 as a cadet journalist. He came to prominence as a film-maker with *Backlash* and his tele-feature *Malpractice*. He most recent film, *Kiss or Kill*, won the 1997 AFI Award for Best Picture.

BRUCE BERESFORD was born in 1940 in Sydney. He worked at the British Film Institute between 1966 and 1971 before directing his first feature film *The Adventures of Barry McKenzie*. He won the AFI's Best Director award for *Don's Party* and *'Breaker' Morant*, and in 1989 his US film *Driving Miss Daisy* won the Academy Award for Best Picture.

MICHEL CIMENT is Director of the French film magazine *Positif*, Associate Professor in American Studies at the University of Paris 7, and author of a dozen books on cinema.

RICHARD COMBS was editor of the *Monthly Film Bulletin* from 1974 to 1991. He now teaches at the National Film and Television School in London and writes for a variety of publications, including *Film Comment* (US), *The Times Literary Supplement* (UK) and *Metro* (Aust).

JOHN DUIGAN was born in 1949 in England. He arrived in Australia in 1961, and holds a Masters in Philosophy from the University of Melbourne. Duigan is one of Australia's leading writer–directors with such films as *Mouth to Mouth*, *Winter of Our Dreams*, *Far East*, *The Year My Voice Broke*, *Sirens*, as well as the Kennedy-Miller mini-series, *Vietnam*. Other titles include the US-produced *Romero*, *Wide Sargasso Sea*, *The Journey of August King*, *The Leading Man* and *Lawn Dogs*. He is currently working on *Mollie* in the US.

RICHARD FRANKLIN was born in 1948 in Melbourne. After attending Monash University, he undertook film studies at the University of Southern California in Los Angeles. While at USC, Franklin was invited as a guest observer on the set of *Topaz* by his mentor Alfred Hitchcock. He began directing for television upon returning to Australia, and made his feature film debut in 1975 with *The True Story of Eskimo Nell*. He returned to the US in 1982 to direct *Psycho II*, the sequel to Hitchcock's classic. Since his return to Australia in 1994 he has made the films *Hotel Sorrento* and *Brilliant Lies*.

SCOTT HICKS is an Emmy Award-winning director whose work encompasses feature films, television drama and documentary. His first feature film *Sebastian and the Sparrow*, which he also wrote and produced, was awarded the Lucas Prize for Best Film at the Frankfurt Film Festival in 1994. In that same year he was awarded the Emmy for Outstanding Individual Achievement in directing for the series *Submarines: Sharks of Steel*.

PHILIP KEMP is a London-based freelance film historian and critic, author of *Lethal Innocence: The Cinema of Alexander Mackendrick*. He is currently working on a biography of Sir Michael Balcon.

RICHARD LOWENSTEIN was born in 1960 in Melbourne. A graduate of the Swinburne Film & Television School, his feature films include *Strikebound*, *Dogs in Space* and *Say a Little Prayer*. He has also directed shorts, documentaries and music video clips.

GEORGE MILLER was born in 1945 in Brisbane. He is of course best known as the director of the *Mad Max* trilogy. He formed the production company Kennedy Miller with producer Byron Kennedy in 1979. The company went on to produce a string of successful Australian mini-series and feature films: *The Dismissal*, *Vietnam*, *Bodyline*, *Cowra Breakout*, *The Year My Voice Broke*, *Dead Calm* and *Babe*. Miller recently completed *Babe: Pig in the City*.

CHRIS NOONAN wrote and directed television features and mini-series, in particular Kennedy Miller's productions of *Vietnam* and *Cowra Breakout*, before co-writing and directing the highly successful film *Babe*, which picked up an Academy Award for Best Visual Effects. His other credits include the television production *The Police State* and the documentary *Stepping Out*.

MARTIN SCORSESE was born in 1942 in New York City. He studied film at New York University. He directed his first feature film, *Mean Streets*, in 1973. His films since have received many nominations and awards, although he has yet to receive an Oscar for Best Director. He is also a diligent campaigner for film preservation and artists' rights.

TOM ZUBRYCKI is one of Australia's most respected documentary director/ producers. Since the late 1970s he has produced a major body of award-winning films. His feature documentaries include *Waterloo* (1981), *Kemira—Diary of a Strike* (1984), which received an AFI Award for Best Documentary, *Lord of the Bush* (1989), *Amongst Equals* (1990), *Bran Nue Dae* (1991), *Homelands* (1993) and *Billal* (1996). Zubrycki has also worked as a producer on *Exile in Sarajevo* (1997), winner of an International Emmy for Best Documentary, *Dr Jazz* (1998), and *Whities Like Us* (1999). He is currently in production on *The Diplomat*.

index

index

index

index

index